62

ALSO BY BRYAN HOCH

The Baby Bombers

Mission 27

The Bronx Zoom

62

AARON JUDGE,
THE
NEW YORK YANKEES,
AND THE
PURSUIT OF GREATNESS

BRYAN HOCH

ATRIA BOOKS

New York | London | Toronto | Sydney | New Delhi

ATRIA BOOKS

An Imprint of Simon & Schuster, Inc.
1230 Avenue of the Americas
New York, NY 10020

First Atria Books hardcover edition July 2023

ATRIA BOOKS and colophon are trademarks of Simon & Schuster, Inc.

For information about special discounts for bulk purchases, please contact Simon & Schuster Special Sales at 1-866-506-1949 or business@simonandschuster.com.

The Simon & Schuster Speakers Bureau can bring authors to your live event. For more information or to book an event, contact the Simon & Schuster Speakers Bureau at 1-866-248-3049 or visit our website at www.simonspeakers.com.

Interior design by Joy O'Meara

Manufactured in the United States of America

1   3   5   7   9   10   8   6   4   2

Library of Congress Cataloging-in-Publication Data has been applied for.

ISBN 978-1-6680-2795-0
ISBN 978-1-6680-2797-4 (ebook)

For Connie, Penny, and Maddie.
My All-Star team.
Never stop swinging for the fences.

CONTENTS

◆

ROGER MARIS JR.

This record has been a big part of my life. I was almost three years old in 1961 when my father and his teammate Mickey Mantle chased an iconic record held at the time by Babe Ruth, who hit 60 home runs thirty-four years earlier. My dad hit his 61st home run on the season's final day, setting a new single-season home run record that would stand for nearly four decades.

Many resented my father for breaking a mark set by one of the early legends of the game, but my father always maintained that records were made to be broken and that Babe Ruth was still going to be the hero he had always been. He was right.

The record stood largely unchallenged for thirty-seven years, as no one hit more than 52 home runs until the late 1990s. In 1998, Mark McGwire and Sammy Sosa electrified fans with their assault on the record my dad set in 1961. I was in attendance at Busch Stadium in St. Louis to see McGwire tie and break my dad's record. It was the same familiar baseball park where I had spent the summers of 1967 and '68 as a nine- and ten-year-old, watching my father play in two consecutive World Series with the Cardinals before he retired.

McGwire finished the 1998 season with 70 homers, and Sosa with 66. The next year, McGwire hit 65 home runs and Sosa 63. Then in 2001,

Barry Bonds hit 73, and Sosa hit 64. While these were undoubtedly great performances, many suspected that these records were not legitimate. As we learned more about baseball's steroid era, I came to believe that 61 should still be considered the record.

As such, there was a lot of excitement when Giancarlo Stanton of the Miami Marlins hit 59 home runs in 2017; just two short. I've been a big fan of Stanton since he entered the league. That same year, Aaron Judge played his first full season for the Yankees, hitting 52 home runs. When the Yankees traded for Stanton that winter, I had two of my favorite players on the same team. I was looking forward to Giancarlo and Aaron teaming up together, just like Dad and Mick did in the early 1960s.

At the beginning of the 2022 season, I thought that both Judge and Stanton had the ability to break my father's American League single-season home run record, which had stood for sixty-one years. Stanton was injured shortly after being named the All-Star Game MVP, but with Judge off to a great start, I thought he just had to stay healthy and finish strong.

The Yankees invited me to New York on September 20, where I watched Judge hit his 60th home run. The anticipation of Judge tying my father's record created quite a stir, and I followed him for the next eight games, waiting to see if he could match my father's mark. In Toronto, I sat with Aaron's mom, Patty, behind the Yankees dugout, watching her son play for three games. In the seventh inning of the last game in Toronto, Judge hit his 61st home run. The moment the ball left his bat, I knew it was gone. I turned and gave Patty a big congratulatory hug.

I met with Aaron right after the game. We shook hands, hugged, and were immediately surrounded by photographers and media. I told Aaron how my father would have admired him, not just for the way he played but for the way he conducts himself off the field as well. I told him to hit No. 62 in New York at Yankee Stadium, because it would be crazy if he hit it there. Aaron thanked me for the support, and for coming to all these games.

In a press conference that night, I was asked if I'd consider Judge to hold not just the American League record but the real single-season home run record. I said I did and that most people would. It happened on October 4 in Texas, in the second-to-last game of the 2022 season. After Aaron hit No. 62, I tweeted the following:

Congratulations to Aaron Judge and his family on Aaron's historic home run number 62! It has definitely been a baseball season to remember. You are all class and someone who should be revered. For the MAJORITY of the fans, we can now celebrate a new CLEAN HOME RUN KING!!

This book will give you a sensational look through Aaron's historic season as he pursued and ultimately broke my dad's record. The serious baseball fan will find interest in the detailed way the book delves into baseball's history of the single-season home run record, held at separate times by Ruth, Maris, and now Judge.

62 in '22—what an exciting season it was!

Roger Maris Jr.

PREFACE

◆

AARON BOONE

I can't imagine the New York Yankees without Aaron Judge.

From my first day as manager, I've felt that Aaron belongs in pin-stripes, and what we saw him do in 2022 certainly shoots to the top of the list of special things I have experienced in this game. You probably know how special Aaron is, not only to me but to this organization. We're talking about a great player between the lines, and one of the great two-way players in our game.

As much as any home run or great defensive play, I've come to love and appreciate who Aaron is as a person. At his core, he just wants to be a great teammate and win. I think that really does simplify things for him. Being with Aaron for five years and counting now, he's lived that every day that I've known him. It's so awesome getting to manage a player of his caliber, one who cares about his team as much as he does.

When you rewatch the highlights of Aaron's historically incredible season, try to pay attention to how everyone reacted, especially his team-mates. Every step of the way, I think they all got more enjoyment out of it than even Aaron did, and that's because of the consistency of who he is. No matter who walked through our clubhouse, whether it was a rookie getting called up for the first time or a superstar player, Aaron was the same great individual.

But don't be fooled by that. His personality is all very real, but like many of the great ones, he's coming to rip your heart out. He plays this game with an edge and a swagger, which is another thing I love about Aaron Judge. Every now and then, he'll give me a look or say something like, "I've got you today." When he says that, we all know something special is going to happen.

One of the things that I love about this game, and I know Aaron does, too, is that we work really hard to shake hands at the end of the day. A lot goes into that, from the long-term off-season preparation to the short-term decisions on the day of the game. You should never take winning a ball game for granted, because it's not easy. We try to appreciate that every night.

When we look back in twenty, thirty, or forty years, I truly believe that we will be having great conversations about this player, one who will hopefully be in Monument Park and go into the Hall of Fame as a Yankee. I am thrilled that Aaron is continuing his career in New York, where he belongs, leading us to hoist that championship one day.

We really are lucky to have him. I can't think of a better person to be the face of our team moving forward.

Aaron Boone

INTRODUCTION

It was the penultimate day of the regular season, and the sporting world had just witnessed the most incredible individual single-season performance imaginable. With a towering drive to be recalled for all time, the magnificent New York Yankees right fielder stamped his exclamation point upon a monthslong assault of American League pitching, altering the record books while pushing the limits of what seemed achievable by man.

An adoring crowd of all ages cheered wildly as he trotted off the playing field, their crush of humanity surging toward the front row of the seating area. They called the slugger's name, prompting a grin and an appreciative wave. Cries for autographs faded into echoes as the game's most recognizable star bounded from the dugout to the clubhouse, his metal spikes clacking against the concrete runway. He approached a phalanx of news reporters and photographers, each hungrily waiting to document each syllable offered for history.

This was not the scene of Aaron Judge's 62nd home run. That splendid afternoon in September of 1927 belonged to George Herman "Babe" Ruth, a larger-than-life figure who carried more nicknames than most of his fans owned pairs of socks.

He was the Babe, the Bambino, the Sultan of Swat, the Colossus of Clout, and the King of Crash. If you visited McSorley's Old Ale House on East 7th Street in New York City and mentioned the Titan of Terror, the King of Swing, the Big Bam, or Herman the Great, fellow patrons would have nodded. Heck, on the correct night, you had a decent chance of toasting the man in the flesh. Some teammates even referred to Ruth as "Jidge," a distortion of his birth name, just one vowel difference from the superstar who'd patrol his position in the Bronx nearly a century later.

"Sixty! Count 'em, sixty!" Ruth announced that day, having just belted his 60th home run of the season, a two-run shot off Tom Zachary of the Washington Senators. "Let's see some other sonofabitch try to match that!"

Thirty-four years would pass before Roger Maris and Mickey Mantle captivated a generation of baby boomers with their dual pursuit of one of baseball's most hallowed records. It would be sixty-five years before schoolteachers Patty and Wayne Judge filed paperwork with the state of California to adopt a baby boy, one they named Aaron and referred to as their "miracle." In his day, every day, Ruth indisputably commanded the nation's attention with an iron grip. In 1921, Ruth marked his second season in a Yankees uniform by slugging 59 home runs, establishing a record that fans and experts agreed might stand forever. Not so.

No one crushed homers like Ruth, who began his career as a starting pitcher for the Boston Red Sox, then began regularly showcasing his up-percut swing as an outfielder in 1919. The game would never be the same, and Ruth towered over most of his competition in every sense of the phrase. At six foot two and a listed weight of 215 pounds, Ruth's 1927 physique would hardly stand out on a current modern-day roster—in 2022, when the six-foot-seven, 282-pound Judge pounded on the record books, the Yankees' closest body double for Ruth was rookie reliever Greg Weissert (also six foot two and 215 pounds). Yet in Ruth's time, the average major leaguer stood about five foot two and weighed 165 to 175 pounds. Try squeezing into one of the box seats at Boston's Fenway Park or Chicago's Wrigley Field, historic venues that have seen more than a hundred years of ball games apiece, and you'll sense that the world was a smaller place when Ruth was living large.

In January 1920, Ruth's contract was sold to the Yankees in what would be recalled as one of history's great swindles, right up there with

Peter Minuit purchasing Manhattan from the Lenape for sixty guilders (about $1,000 in 2023 dollars). New York paid the then-staggering sum of $100,000 for Ruth, plus a later $300,000 loan that utilized the deed of Fenway Park as collateral. The popular myth is that Harry Frazee, Boston's cash-strapped owner, used the proceeds of the Ruth sale to finance a failed Broadway musical, *No, No, Nanette*. That is inaccurate: *Nanette* did not debut on the Great White Way until 1925, long after Ruth was a Yankee, and the show had been a commercial success. However, Frazee struggled to make ends meet after his 1916 purchase of the ball club and less-than-stellar attendance in 1919, when Boston finished sixth in the eight-team American League.

Much like the Lenape initially believed they were getting the best of their trade, Ruth's sale had not initially seemed ill-advised, at least in Boston circles. Ruth's reckless drinking, womanizing, and gambling were already legendary, and a war of words took place in the newspapers. Ruth had signed a three-year, $30,000 deal before the 1919 season; now that he'd hit 29 homers for Boston, he called it "a bad move" and threatened not to play unless the Red Sox renegotiated. On the day the deal was announced to the press, Frazee said, "While Ruth is undoubtedly the greatest hitter the game has ever seen, he is likewise one of the most selfish and inconsiderate men to ever put on a baseball uniform." Yankees pitcher Bob Shawkey had a different take, gushing: "Gee, I'm glad that guy's not going to hit against me anymore. You take your life in your hands every time you step up against him."

Interestingly, the "Curse of the Bambino" did not enter the lexicon until 1990, when *Boston Globe* columnist Dan Shaughnessy published a book by that title. Shaughnessy's work came a dozen years after the Red Sox blew a 14½ game division lead to the Yankees, prompting a one-game playoff that featured a late three-run homer from light-hitting shortstop Bucky Dent. It reached shelves four years after Mookie Wilson's ground ball trickled through Boston first baseman Bill Buckner's legs, helping the New York Mets pull off a stunning World Series upset. Buckner died in 2019, having spent far too long being tortured by the miscue, an unfortunate blemish on a stellar twenty-two-year career in the majors. Organizational mismanagement by the Red Sox, mainly institutional racism on the part of owner Tom Yawkey in passing on talented Black players like Jackie Robinson and a teenage Willie Mays did far more damage over the decades than Ruth's sale, the deep drive to left field that sealed Dent's new middle name in New England circles, or the creaky Buckner's inability to block Wilson's little roller up along first.

Let's reset the scene now to Yankee Stadium, the afternoon of September 30, 1927. It was a Friday in an already-memorable year that had seen Charles Lindbergh complete his solo flight across the Atlantic Ocean, piloting the *Spirit of St. Louis* from New York's Roosevelt Field to Le Bourget Aerodrome in Paris, France. Lindbergh had been feted in a ticker-tape parade within the month, and now it was Ruth's turn to command the city's attention. His mighty Yanks would be playing in the World Series the following Monday, putting the finishing touches on a dominant 110-win season that earned their lineup the nickname of "Murderers' Row." The visiting Washington Senators would finish in third place with eighty-five wins; long before anyone had considered the concept of a Wild Card, they had effectively bowed out of the pennant race in June. Yankee Stadium was the final stop on the Senators' railroad journey, playing out their last innings before a winter of fishing, golfing, and pheasant hunting.

As Ruth stepped to home plate in the eighth inning, he'd been held to two singles and a walk by Zachary, a fine but not overpowering pitcher from North Carolina farm country who depended upon his changeup and curveball. The score was tied as Mark Koenig danced off third base; the right-handed Zachary offered what Ruth would describe as "a slow screwball," breaking down and in toward the Babe. Ruth swung mightily and produced a drive that did not soar high, traveling on a clothesline toward the right-field seats. Bill Dinneen, that day's home plate umpire, crouched on the foul line and peered carefully in the distance. An eyewitness reported that Ruth's drive rattled in the bleachers about fifteen rows from the top, not fair by more than six inches. Ruth rounded the bases, a joyous smirk spilling across his famous visage as Zachary fired his leather glove to the infield grass, punctuating the moment as Ruth's teammates gleefully rushed from their dugout.

Attendance had been marked at only eight thousand that day; given the Yanks' season-long dominance, a chance to see Ruth swat his 60th wasn't enough to fill the house. Some sixty thousand–plus would pack the four-year-old Bronx ballpark a week later for the World Series, witnessing the completion of New York's four-game sweep of Paul Waner, Pie Traynor, and the Pittsburgh Pirates. The few on hand in the grandstands for Ruth's blast were fervent; in the bleachers and box seats, they stood and cheered, tossing hats and waving handkerchiefs. The ball was retrieved by a man named Joe Forner, whose home address (1937 First Avenue in Manhattan, now a depot for the city's sanitation department) would be published in the next day's newspapers, as was the custom of the time. As Ruth crossed home plate, he lifted his cap high and waved in salute, holding his hand in midair as if to say: "How about it, folks?"

How about it, indeed. Ruth remains the gold standard for baseball royalty, one of the untouchables, nearly a century after swatting his 714th and final home run. In almost every other sport, the greatest athletes played recently enough that we may have watched them in action—Michael Jordan in basketball, Wayne Gretzky in hockey, Tiger Woods in golf. Ruth is an exception. The game has changed markedly since 1927, when balls that bounced into the stands were counted as home runs, but Ruth is believed to have reached the seats on the fly with all 60 clouts in 1927. Some of the typewriter warriors who covered Ruth that summer wondered if he would hit 61 or 62 the following year, but 60 became the nice number that stood for decades—even if it hadn't initially drawn the attention history would have us expect. Fred Lieb, a celebrated sportswriter who covered the 1927 Yankees, said that the scribes hadn't suspected a new record was in the making until "well past Labor Day." Most of the talk around the press box that season concerned Lou Gehrig, who had been on pace to drive in 200 or more runs; Gehrig would finish with 173, a tally that still led the majors.

A member of the National Baseball Hall of Fame and Museum's inaugural 1936 class, Ruth was a figure so grand that his open casket lay in state for two days inside Yankee Stadium's rotunda after he succumbed to cancer in August 1948. Ruth's plump, grinning visage haunted Maris and Mantle throughout their incredible summer of 1961, when newspapers printed day-by-day tallies of how the Yankees sluggers were faring against Ruth's 1927 pace.

It's time to correct another urban legend: despite the widespread notion of an asterisk dotting the record books, perpetuated by the title of Billy Crystal's 2001 meticulously researched film *61**, there is not, and never was, an asterisk placed next to Maris's achievement. However, the concept of one was floated by Commissioner Ford C. Frick in July of that season, when Maris had 35 home runs and stood three weeks ahead of Ruth's clip. Expansion had swelled the regular season schedule from 154 games to 162, and Frick read from a prepared statement to announce that if a player reached 60 homers after his club's 154th game that "there would have to be some distinctive mark in the record books to show that Babe Ruth's record was set under a 154-game schedule and the total of more than 60 was compiled while a 162-game schedule was in effect." Dick Young, an influential columnist for the New York *Daily News*, piped up to suggest that Frick's "distinctive mark" could be an asterisk.

As Crystal's movie makes clear, Frick was no impartial observer. Frick enjoyed an unlikely path from a Colorado-based sportswriter to baseball's third commissioner, behind Kenesaw Mountain Landis and Happy Chandler. Joining the *New York American* in 1922, Frick was a ghostwriter for some of Ruth's newspaper columns and a 1928 book, *Babe Ruth's Own Book of Baseball*. Frick's bond with Ruth was enduring; he claimed to be at Ruth's bedside the day before the slugger died. Frick decreed that Ruth's record must be broken in 154 or fewer games to be considered equal, increasing the pressure on Mantle and Maris.

When injury effectively ended Mantle's pursuit in September, Maris shouldered the crushing load. Once 154 games had passed, so did 162, leaving Maris one final crack at matching Ruth's home run total. An April 22 contest against the Baltimore Orioles had ended in a 5–5 tie and was replayed in its entirety, giving the Yankees a rare 163rd regular season game on October 1, a cool and crisp afternoon in New York. Maris connected in the fourth inning, facing Tracy Stallard of the Red Sox, launching a drive into Yankee Stadium's right-field seats.

Maris's immediate reaction contained little of the theatrics that the

Bambino had exhibited during his 360-foot trot around the same base-path in 1927. The crowd of 23,154, far shy of a sellout, applauded, and Maris's teammates pushed him out of the dugout to accept a curtain call. Maris reluctantly acquiesced. Removing his cap and waving three times, Maris was mercifully permitted to return to the dugout, where he found a seat on the bench. With his head resting against a wall, he let free a deep sigh, bathed with physical and mental exhaustion.

It hadn't been fun, but he'd bested the Babe. No one could ever take that away.

"When I hit 61, I had a feeling of exultation," Maris said. "I also had the feeling that the season was over. I didn't know what I'd have done if the season had gone on a little longer."

Ruth and Maris may have patrolled the same patch of right-field grass a generation apart, but their lives could not have been more different. Ruth craved the spotlight and all of its trappings, dressing in the finest garments of the time and once proclaiming that his salary deserved to be higher than President Herbert Hoover's because, as Ruth said, "I had a better year than he did." Maris was hardworking Midwestern America in the flesh, candid and forthright in dealings with teammates, opponents, and the press. His quotes hardly sizzled, and some reporters labeled him as sullen or worse, preferring the colorful commentary Mantle and other Yankees could provide to distinguish their newspapers from the competition.

Sadly, Maris never seemed to savor his achievement. He was belatedly recognized in Yankee Stadium's Monument Park in 1984, sixteen years after his final big-league at-bat with the St. Louis Cardinals, and only sixteen months before he died at the age of fifty-one from lymphoma. Maris's mark of 61 was surpassed in the big-swinging, performance-enhanced late 1990s and early 2000s, when Mark McGwire, Sammy Sosa, and Barry Bonds each belted 62 or more home runs in various seasons. McGwire and Sosa enthralled the nation with their 1998 home run race, when McGwire hit 70 and Sosa slugged 66, teaming to restore baseball's luster after a strike robbed fans of the 1994 World Series.

Few seemed to ask at the time if McGwire or Sosa were doing it on the level. When Bonds obliterated McGwire's record with 73 homers in

2001, a boatload of baby boomers and hardball purists who suspected performance-enhancing drug use emulated Frick's edict, preferring to view Maris's 61 homers as the legitimate mark. After Bonds hit his 756th home run in 2007, eclipsing Henry Aaron's career record, fashion designer Marc Ecko purchased the baseball at auction for more than $750,000. Taking a cue from the Maris saga, Ecko stamped the ball with an asterisk and offered it to the Baseball Hall of Fame, where it remains on display to this day.

Now there was a third Yankees right fielder in the throes of history. It was October 4, 2022, the penultimate day of baseball's regular season, and Judge stood in right field, black lines of grease streaked under each eye as he pounded a fist into his leather glove and worked on a fresh chaw of Dubble Bubble. One of Judge's superstitions was swapping his gum for a new piece any time he made an out at the plate; his idealized outcome would be still gnawing on a rubbery, flavorless wad at the end of the ninth inning. The Yankees were clinging to a one-run lead in the eighth inning against the Texas Rangers at Globe Life Field in Arlington, a sprawling Lone Star State colossus where the paint still smelled fresh two years after its gates first opened.

The final score of these nine innings mattered little; the Yankees had already punched their ticket into the playoffs, and their best player's performance had helped them survive a late-summer swoon to secure the American League East. The last-place Rangers, also-rans in an American League West dominated by the stacked Houston Astros, had long been playing out the string. As he peered toward the infield, Judge's focus drifted between the opposing hitters and mental calculations, counting the game's remaining outs against the batting order.

He'd already had four trips to home plate, one of the benefits of manager Aaron Boone having batted him in the leadoff spot for the better part of the month. So far, Judge had a single and a run scored; his first three wads of Dubble Bubble had been unceremoniously discarded, still chomping on the piece he'd pulled from its red, yellow, and blue wrapper in the fifth inning. The hit raised his batting average, which helped his fading chances of winning a batting title, watching from afar as the

Minnesota Twins' Luis Arraez continued to fatten his statistics. Judge's ninety-foot dash on a single had provided the margin of victory in a game the Yankees now led, 5–4. Yet the number that mattered most at that moment to Judge's teammates, family members, fans, and the sporting world at large remained unaltered.

Judge had equaled Maris's single-season American League record six days prior against the Blue Jays in Toronto. No. 61 had been witnessed in Rogers Centre's field-level seats by Maris's son Roger Jr., who hugged Judge's mother, Patty, as they celebrated the achievement together. Each at-bat now seemed to carry dump trucks of weight. Tens of thousands of fans stood in unison, a golf-tournament hush falling over the crowd as they angled their smartphones, pressing the record button in hopes of capturing history on tiny, scratch-resistant screens. They waited . . . and waited . . . and waited. Judge had walked to home plate twenty-two times since tying Maris's record, faced eleven different pitchers, traveled some 1,748 miles from Toronto to New York to Arlington, and still carried 61 in the home run column.

"The games started to go a little faster," Judge would say. "Usually, the games kind of drag on; you're locked in on defense and stuff like that. But I can't lie. Those last couple of games, I'd look up, and it's the seventh inning. I'm like, 'Dang, I've only got one more at-bat. We'd better figure this out.'"

If Judge was experiencing frustration, his default setting was to bottle it. However, earlier in the Texas series, he had violently punished a batting helmet for its role in generating a harmless infield pop-out. An outburst like that was not a foreign action for Judge, but he usually waited until he was down the dugout tunnel, out of view from television cameras. This time, he couldn't hold back. On some level, Judge felt that he was beginning to understand the pressure that Maris had experienced sixty-one years prior, though at least most of the fan base seemed to be in his corner. There was no Mantle to share the spotlight; Judge's costars were legends of the past, and this show was all Judge, all the time.

"Dealing with that type of scrutiny and attention and media fanfare, the love-hate, that's tough, besides playing one of the toughest sports in the world," Judge said. "I definitely feel for [Maris]. What he went through at that time, Mantle and Maris, the back-and-forth, it's incredible what he was able to accomplish."

These three Yankees right fielders of different decades, Ruth, Maris, and Judge, black-and-white to Kodachrome to high-definition 4K—with an aw-shucks grin and a shrug of his hulking shoulders, Judge agreed that it was awesome to hear his name spoken in the same sentence as the other two men. But Judge was ready to bid the ghosts farewell; this home run chase needed to end. Game 1 of the doubleheader concluded, and Judge was soon back in the batter's box, again slotted as the leadoff hitter for the nightcap. He blinked twice and took his familiar stance, feet spread apart and bat held stiffly behind his right shoulder, studying Jesús Tinoco, a twenty-seven-year-old right-hander from Venezuela whom teammates affectionately referred to as "Tino."

His adrenaline pulsing, Tinoco pumped a 95 mph fastball high and out of the strike zone, spurring catcher Sam Huff out of his crouch. The next pitch, an 88.6 mph slider, bent over home plate for a called strike; Judge nodded at it. Huff signaled for another slider, then pinned his left knee against the ground, placing his glove between his legs as a target. *Get it low*, the catcher's body language screamed. Tinoco kicked his left leg in the air, reared back, and fired, missing the mark to the game's most dangerous hitter.

Judge barreled the ball, rocketing off his bat at 100.2 mph, data captured by the Statcast systems that had been standard in big-league parks for years. It soared deep to left field, where Texas outfielder Bubba Thompson trotted back toward the wall, a curious witness to history.

Beaming as he jogged around the bases, Judge displayed equal parts elation and exhaustion, pointing through the open roof toward spirits above. Judge stamped his left foot on home plate, where he was received first by outfielder Giancarlo Stanton, then by the rest of his teammates and coaches, who had spilled out of their dugout after the cannon-fire echo of ball hitting bat.

"I was thinking of my wife, my family, my teammates, the fans," Judge said. "The constant support I've gotten through this whole process this whole year, from them especially; that was all running through my head."

Maris Jr. proclaimed, loudly and frequently to anyone who would listen, that he and all correctly thinking baseball fans would consider Judge the "clean home run king." Major League Baseball pointed to the record book, listing Bonds without comment—the placement of asterisks would be left to the individual fan. Judge, a product of California's Bay Area who stayed up past his bedtime to watch Bonds pass McGwire in 2001, said he considered 73 the record. "No matter what people want to say about that era of baseball, for me, they went out there and hit 73 homers and 70 homers," Judge said. "That, to me, is what the record is."

So Judge was, as announcer Michael Kay intoned on the YES Network broadcast, the AL home run king—"Case closed!" Judge's chase for 62 was complete; the hulking he-man with No. 99 across his back having eclipsed Maris, the reluctant star who'd worn No. 9 in the shadows of Ruth and Mantle. Yet there was more to say; Judge's accomplishment highlighted a fantastic contractual walk year, as the league's most valuable player and the franchise's most marketable player since Derek Jeter kept everyone guessing.

Viewed through that lens, 62 meant everything: for Judge's future, the direction of the sport's most storied franchise, and Major League Baseball as a whole. That story was only beginning.

"OK, CAN I GO OUT AND PLAY?"

H eads up!"

The fastball hovered over the heart of home plate, spinning at a comfortable 65 mph, and Aaron Judge's body responded just as he'd trained it for most of the previous twenty-nine years. The ball kissed the barrel of the slugger's wood bat, producing a loud echo throughout the grandstands and dispatching an impressive rocket out toward left-center field, where a gaggle of onlookers peered through a chain-link fence.

One shouted to alert the others of the incoming missile, and the ball came to rest near a row of cabbage palms that lined a quiet two-lane roadway, prompting a foot race to pocket a souvenir. This intimate gathering was burning an hour or two of midweek daylight with free looks at big-league ballplayers dressed in nondescript mesh apparel, moving through the paces of a February 2022 workout behind the shuttered gates of Red McEwen Field, home of the University of South Florida Bulls.

The calendar indicated that Judge, nine years removed from his most recent collegiate at-bat with the Fresno State Bulldogs, should have been taking these hacks some ten miles away. A pristine diamond was waiting for him at George M. Steinbrenner Field, the chilly and formidable battleship of concrete and steel that had served as the Yankees' spring home since Derek Jeter's rookie campaign in 1996.

Yet Judge, arguably the most recognizable player on the present-day New York Yankees roster, bizarrely found himself persona non grata at Steinbrenner Field. A contentious and increasingly ugly Major League Baseball lockout was bleeding on, with owners and players unable to finalize a collective bargaining agreement to open spring camps on time. The owners had voted to lock out all active Major League Baseball Players Association members, effectively confirming the sport's third consecutive spring of tumult.

Judge and his teammates had been in the thick of their preseason preparation on March 12, 2020, when the COVID-19 pandemic halted play and scattered players across the country. There had been orders to shelter in place, but a skeleton crew of ballplayers, including Judge, had voted to continue working out at Steinbrenner Field. Soon after, it became evident that the regular season would not be delayed by only two weeks, as league officials had initially suggested. Initial discussions of health and safety protocols between the players and the league devolved into a money grab, producing distasteful optics during a pre-vaccination period when hospitals were overburdened and even routine trips to the grocery store carried an element of danger for many Americans.

Rob Manfred, baseball's commissioner, eventually imposed an abbreviated sixty-game schedule that green-lit the most bizarre "Made for TV" season imaginable, with players receiving pro-rated salaries to play in empty ballparks and most postseason games scheduled for warm-weather or domed neutral sites. It mattered little where the games were played; there could be no home-field advantage without fans in the seats. Gerrit Cole made the first start of a fresh nine-year, $324 million contract opposite the Washington Nationals' Max Scherzer on July 23, at an eerily silent Nationals Park in Washington, D.C. One of the few observers not in uniform was Dr. Anthony Fauci, taking a moment from his duties as a lead member of the White House's coronavirus task force to toss the season's ceremonial first pitch.

The fans were back in the spring of 2021, albeit in smaller numbers, under orders to maintain social distancing in seating pods roped off by plastic zip ties. Ushers roamed the grandstands, repeatedly barking masking instructions that never seemed enforceable, considering the teams were also trying to make up for the financial fallout of a shuttered season by slinging popcorn, sodas, and beer. The players engaged in their "new normal," even as President Joe Biden's administration lobbied the league to delay Opening Day to address safety concerns. The games went on as scheduled, most players received vaccinations, and MLB entered 2022 expecting a much smoother ride from a health and safety perspective.

Now it was just about the money, with the league and union haggling over compensation for young players and limitations on clubs tanking to receive higher selections in the amateur draft. It was baseball's first work stoppage since the 1994–95 strike that dashed the World Series, and the first player lockout since 1990. With Judge and his teammates barred from communicating with team personnel (the league set up a tip line to report infractions like phone calls or text messages), the players trained independently, as most did during those first dark months of the pandemic. Judge opted to use the University of South Florida's facilities, a short drive from his apartment on Tampa's Bayshore Boulevard, part of a workout group that included big leaguers Tim Beckham, Mike Ford, Richie Martin, and Luke Voit.

With each batting practice lick, Judge exorcised lingering angst from an embarrassing defeat in the previous autumn's American League Wild Card Game. An injured Cole attempted to gut his way through a hamstring injury and recorded just six outs in a 6–2 loss to the Red Sox that never felt within reach for the visitors. Minutes after his club's season ended, manager Aaron Boone set up shop for his postgame media responsibilities at a laptop in the cramped visiting quarters at Fenway Park. Most teams had moved on from the Zoom era by then, but with clubhouses still closed to reporters, the idea of Boone passing through the exiting Fenway crowd in full uniform to the fourth-floor press conference room made little sense. "The league has closed the gap on us," Boone spat. "We've got to get better in every aspect."

The Yankees had not played a World Series game since 2009, when they bested the Philadelphia Phillies to hoist the franchise's twenty-seventh championship trophy. That roster aged toward retirement, with icons like Derek Jeter, Mariano Rivera, Jorge Posada, and Andy Pettitte finding their way out of the game within the next few seasons. They

desperately needed to spark a new era apart from the "Core Four," a realization that became more evident each passing season. The "championship or bust" mantra once instilled with desk-pounding intensity by the
club's former principal owner, George M. Steinbrenner, needed to pause.
In 2016, general manager Brian Cashman swallowed hard and told the
Boss's successor, Hal Steinbrenner, that his $213 million roster was not
good enough to win the ultimate prize. Cashman's recommendation was
to dismantle what they'd built, off-loading veterans and big money in
hopes of a stronger tomorrow.

That conversation might have prompted a firing or tongue-lashing
in Steinbrenner's hottest heyday of the 1970s and '80s. Fortunately for
Cashman, Hal Steinbrenner favored a cooler, more analytical mindset,
his experience as an amateur pilot prompting his cockpit view of the
organization from a perspective of thirty thousand feet.

"I think about that a lot; what would my dad do?" Steinbrenner said.
"I can be impatient, as much as a pilot should never admit that, because
it's not a good trait. We have differences; there's no doubt about it. He
was very, very hands-on in every intimate part of what goes on, and I'm
a little bit more [geared to] delegation of authority, even though I'm very
involved. There's differences, but the passion to win and the understanding of what our fans expect is definitely something we have in common."

As such, Cashman would be allowed to make moves with an eye toward the future, but "tanking" was a dirty word. They would never follow
a model like the Astros, who had put forth an awful product in 2013 and
'14, rolling out a barely competitive team of "Dis-Astros" that generated
0.0 Nielsen television ratings for some games.

That was the fastest way to reload a roster for future success, but in
many ways, the Yankees still subscribed to the advice that Broadway
producer Jimmy Nederlander once offered the elder Steinbrenner in the
1970s: "Remember, we are a star-vehicle town. New York loves stars,
worships stars, so you've got to have some stars to draw the people."

Aaron James Judge was the biggest piece, literally and figuratively, of
whatever that future would become. The Yanks first spotted Judge in tiny
Linden, California, a pinprick of shady walnut groves, peach orchards,

and vineyards about one hundred miles northeast of San Francisco. Linden touted itself as the Cherry Capital of the World, a tight-knit community that boasted an annual jubilee each May, highlighted by a pie-eating competition and a 5K fun run. Patty and Wayne Judge were teachers at various schools across San Joaquin County, where they instructed students in physical education and leadership. The couple adopted Aaron the day after he was born in a Sacramento, California, hospital on April 26, 1992, bringing him home to meet an older brother, John, who had also been adopted.

"My greatest accomplishment and achievement in life has been the love and development of our family," Patty Judge said.

From Judge's first pediatric checkups, he ranked near the top percentile of his age group, with doctors taking note of his large hands and feet. The recommended four ounces of formula had not satiated the boy, who only seemed soothed when Patty and Wayne blessedly stumbled upon the solution of mixing oatmeal into his bottles.

"We kind of joked that he looked like the Michelin Tire baby," Wayne Judge said.

Years later, Judge would reflect upon his bucolic hometown as "a perfect environment to grow up in." Linden counted a population of 1,784 in the 2010 census; locals could shop at the Rinaldi's Market grocery store (established 1948), order a cheese pie from Pizza Plus, or sample the rib eye sandwich at Sammy's Bar & Grill. There were no stoplights along Linden's portion of State Route 26, but there were two churches, a volunteer fire department, countless fields of blossoming trees, and one imposing up-and-coming athlete.

Judge's T-ball opponents scattered toward the outfield grass and turned their backs when he came to bat, fearful of being smoked by a hard grounder or line drive. "It was just a small community," Judge said. "I had a mom in every single house down the street. I had people always looking out for me and people in the community looking out for me. Growing up in something like that was something special. I always had a place to go, and there was a friend on every corner you looked." He recalled his parents being "tough on me" when it came to his studies; if he wanted to go outside or play video games, Judge could count on being asked if he had completed his homework. "I didn't really like it as a kid, but looking back on it, I really appreciate what they did for me."

Said Patty Judge: "Aaron has a pretty good compass. At a young age, he knew the difference between right and wrong."

Though Judge has had no contact with his biological parents, he knows his biological father is Black and his biological mother is white. He was about ten years old when he came home with a question that his parents had long anticipated. "I think it was like, 'I don't look like you, Mom. I don't look like you, Dad. Like, what's going on here?'" Judge said. "They just kind of told me I was adopted. I was like, 'OK, that's fine with me.' You're still my mom, the only mom I know. You're still my dad, the only dad I know.' Nothing really changed. I never really asked any questions after that. There's no need to." When his parents asked if he had any questions, Judge replied: "OK, can I go out and play?"

Around that time, Judge experienced an even more life-altering moment. Wayne Judge volunteered as Linden High School's varsity basketball coach, and young Aaron enjoyed tagging along for the late-afternoon practices. While the team went through its squeaky-sneakered drills in the gymnasium, Judge would usually dribble a basketball off to the side or sit in the bleachers.

"At one practice, one of the guys said, 'We're doing a layup drill. Come warm up with us,'" Judge said. "I was in the layup line with them. They were passing the ball to me, high-fiving me. That little moment didn't mean anything to the players, but to me, those three minutes was something I'll never forget."

More than a decade later, Judge would look into the seats near his position in the outfield or the on-deck circle, frequently using spare moments to establish a personal connection with younger fans. He recognized the ripple effect that any interaction—a brief game of catch, a souvenir baseball, or even a fist bump—could create.

"That's what it's all about," Judge said. "If I can touch ten kids' lives or one hundred kids' lives, if I can inspire them to do something special or chase their dreams, that's amazing."

———

A standout three-sport athlete who played baseball, football, and basketball for the Linden Lions, Judge stood six foot three as a high school sophomore, shooting up another four inches by senior year to fill out his blue, white, and gold uniform.

"Here we are in the Mother Lode League, and there's a 6-foot-7 tight end matched against a 5-foot-nothing defensive back," said Mark Miller, a longtime teacher and football and softball coach at Linden High. "It probably should have been illegal. But you never saw Aaron get boastful, despite the difference in talent. He was respectful of teammates and opponents."

Thick smears of eye black were already part of his game day routine, as were loud batting practice sessions. As a senior first baseman, Judge hit .500 with 7 home runs in 74 at-bats, also compiling an 0.88 ERA in 48 innings pitched. His secret weapon was a splitter; years later, as he recalled his pitching days, Judge remarked: "That's the one they didn't know about." He set a school record for touchdowns, catching 54 passes for 960 yards and 17 touchdowns as a senior, and paced the basketball team by averaging 18 points per game.

"All the way through high school, I was playing three sports and just enjoying it," Judge said. "I wasn't too serious about any of them. To be honest, I would get tired of the sports. Once it got near the end of football, I'd say, 'I can't wait for basketball season to get here; I'm tired of getting hit every day.' Then once I got to the end of basketball, it was, 'I'm tired of running up and down the court; when does baseball start?'"

There were several games where opponents had refused to pitch to Judge, prompting Coach Joe Piombio to set up the cage so Judge could put on a show for visiting scouts; since the rest of Judge's teammates had showered and gone home, it would be up to the scouts to slap on gloves and roam the outfield, shagging balls after each echoing ping of his aluminum bat. The Oakland Athletics were the first organization to take a swing at Judge, calling his name in the thirty-first round of the 2010 draft. Jermaine Clark, an Oakland-area scout, filed a report that described Judge as an "untapped monster."

As a teenager, Judge attended a workout at the Oakland Coliseum; he parked batting-practice balls into the suite level, prompting observers to ask Clark what college he played for. The afternoon experience was thrilling, but Judge had doubts about signing a professional contract straight out of high school. His parents largely left the decision up to him, but they coaxed him to consider the value of continuing his studies.

"Both of them are teachers, and to them, education came first," Judge said. "It was the right decision. And to be honest with you, I wasn't ready to go out into the world. I needed to go to college. I needed to mature."

Despite his gaudy amateur statistics, teams were not convinced that Judge was ready to play professionally, sensing that he had the makings of a big fish in a small pond. When Clark had attempted to file reports on Judge, he was frustrated to learn that Oakland's database could not even recognize the Mother Lode League, which included Linden and little-known opponents like Calaveras, Summerville, and Bret Harte. Tim McIntosh was then a Yankees scout who lived about ten minutes from Linden, and he came away largely unimpressed after attending five or six of Judge's games. For McIntosh, a former big-league catcher, writing the organization's first report on Judge had been a chore.

"I just put him in the system in case something crazy happened," McIntosh said. "And then something crazy happened."

So this is not exactly Derek Jeter's origin story, where Yankees scout Dick Groch stamped his foot about the gangly shortstop at Michigan's Kalamazoo Central High School, insisting that Jeter was headed for Cooperstown. But McIntosh did play an important role by pestering Kendall Carter, then a Yankees national cross-checker, to park behind home plate for some of Judge's games at Linden High.

Carter described Judge as a "newborn giraffe" who needed to grow into his body and would benefit greatly from an opportunity to play against higher-level competition. In a brief conversation with Damon Oppenheimer, the Yankees' director of amateur scouting, Carter remarked that the kid might be someone to look at down the line.

Seemingly every day, the Judges' mailbox contained another invitation on crisp white collegiate letterhead. Stanford, Michigan State, and Notre Dame were among the programs that envisioned Judge suiting up as a wide receiver or defensive end; a UCLA coach told Judge they would probably ask him to put on thirty to forty pounds and convert him into a tight end.

Mike Batesole, Fresno State's head baseball coach, wanted desperately to keep Judge off the gridiron. When Judge visited Fresno State's campus for a baseball workout, Batesole saw about three swings before pegging Judge as a Dave Winfield clone. The comparison was apt; also drafted by the NBA's Atlanta Hawks, the ABA's Utah Stars, and the NFL's Minnesota Vikings, Winfield chose baseball, believing the sport would be easier on his body.

Winfield landed in the Hall of Fame, and Judge's father ensured his son knew Winfield's story. "My dad has always talked about him," Judge said.

As Judge toured the campus, Batesole assigned star first baseman Jordan Ribera to accompany the prospective freshman to a football game.

"I'm like, 'Who is this six-foot-seven donkey? Like, is he going to take my spot?'" said Ribera, who was then the NCAA's reigning home run hitter. "The next day, Judge was like, 'I'm going to Fresno State.' That's my claim to fame with Judge."

Ribera was assured that his grip on the starting first-base job was intact, and Judge learned that his choices would be between playing the outfield or riding the bench. Batesole patiently explained to Judge that if he could run down a football, there was no reason he couldn't do the same with a baseball. That made sense to Judge, who agreed to lace up his spikes and jog toward the outfield. Judge experienced bouts of homesickness during that first season, but said he adapted to life on campus quickly.

"It was the first time being away," Judge said. "You're on your own, learning the things that your parents did for you. Now you're on your own, and nobody is there for you. You've got to grow up and adapt and learn. Otherwise, you're going to sink and have a miserable time in college."

Batesole soon recognized that Fresno State was gifted a unique talent in Judge, named a Louisville Slugger Freshman All-American and the Western Athletic Conference's Freshman of the Year. Each fall, Batesole organized a touch football league to help his baseball players maintain conditioning, with the gridiron running from the right-field foul pole across the outfield grass. It was no suburban backyard Turkey Bowl; they had wristbands with plays, kept statistics, and even wore uniform jerseys. Then weighing about 230 pounds, Judge dominated the six-on-six games from the first snap.

"His freshman year, I'm out there running it," Batesole said, "and the first throw they make is a wide receiver screen, and it was like Barry Sanders. They couldn't touch him. This is touch football. Division I athletes cannot touch him. That's how light and agile, and freakish of an athlete he is. I saw that in one play, and I said, 'This kid's going to play in the big leagues as long as he wants.' It's just a different animal."

Fresno State eventually had to keep Judge out of the flag football games, as Batesole feared someone might blow a knee trying to keep up with Judge. During those drills, Batesole began referring to Judge as "Big Ass Judge," and still greets his former outfielder as "Big Ass." In 2019, when big leaguers were allowed to choose nicknames to be stitched on the backs of their alternate Players Weekend jerseys, Judge opted for "BAJ."

"I was a freshman in college, battling for an outfield spot," Judge said. "Our first game comes up, and the lineup's posted. I go and check it; I'm looking and looking, and I don't see my name. I went down to the clubhouse, and I'm getting ready to hit in the cage. All of a sudden, another outfielder is like, 'Hey, man, you'd better start getting ready for the game.' I said, 'I'm not playing.' He said, 'Go check the lineup again. You're batting seventh.' I go and check the lineup, and all that was written was 'BAJ.'"

Judge played left field and right field as a freshman at Fresno State, then center field in his final two seasons, earning a reputation as a solid defender and hard worker. His power had yet to translate into game action. At one point, Judge believed it was because the thirty-four-inch, thirty-one-ounce metal bats he was using were too light and short for his swing, saying he "felt like I was swinging a toothpick." He'd sought a bigger and longer customized bat, but could not acquire one. "I feel like I can hit for more power and still be a (high) average guy."

Though Judge stole twice as many bases (36) as he hit homers (18) in a Bulldogs uniform, there were glimpses of what Judge would become, including a memorable batting-practice session during a Cape Cod League showcase at Fenway Park in July 2012. Standing in the same batter's box once occupied by fearsome right-handed Red Sox sluggers like Jim Rice and Manny Ramirez, Judge drove pitches to the deepest corners of the park, thwacking the thirty-seven-foot-tall Green Monster with rockets that demanded observers pay attention.

John Altobelli was tossing batting practice that day. The manager of the Cape Cod League's Brewster Whitecaps, Altobelli was a celebrated coach at Orange Coast College in Costa Mesa, California, who tragically perished in the January 2020 helicopter crash that also killed basketball star Kobe Bryant and seven others.

Altobelli once recalled that "a lot of guys were going max effort, grunting as they tried to hit them over the Monster so they could have something to talk about. The ease of his swing, the way the [hits] sounded—especially with no fans in the stadium—it was a different sound than everyone else."

Matt Hyde, a Yankees scout assigned to the New England region and the Cape Cod League, had filed effusive reports on Judge before his junior season at Fresno State. So had Brian Barber, a national scout who had seen Judge in the lineup for the Cape Cod League's Brewster Whitecaps on at least four occasions that season.

In one game, Judge was playing center field when he hit what Barber described as "an absolute mammoth home run"—the opposing shortstop leaped to try and catch Judge's drive, which kept soaring past the left-field fence.

"It was like, 'All right. Wow. That's how superstars hit them,'" Barber said.

A pitcher for the St. Louis Cardinals and Kansas City Royals in the late 1990s, Barber filed a report that suggested a definite first-round pick. Scouts utilize a scale of 20 to 80, where 20 is the lowest possible grade, and 80 is the highest. Barber had Judge with a future forecast of 55 hitting ability and 70 power, with high grades also affixed to his running and throwing.

"He just did something at the park every day that made you like him more and more," Barber said. "It wasn't just the power. He was playing center field. He was a quality defender out there. He knew what he was doing, and he could really throw. The last piece of the puzzle was this guy is six-foot-seven with really long limbs, and he's able to keep his swing halfway short and get the balls on the inner half. I played ten years before scouting, and when you saw a guy that big, the first thing you'd try to do is exploit him inside. You couldn't do that with this guy."

When the Yankees returned to the Fresno campus for a fresh look at Judge, they saw a player who had traveled light-years from Linden High. Judge compiled a monstrous 1.116 OPS and was an All-American as a junior, a season that impressed area scout Troy Afenir. A former first-round pick who appeared in forty-five big-league games for the Houston Astros, Oakland Athletics, and Cincinnati Reds in the late 1980s and early '90s, Afenir was one of the Yankees' toughest graders. As he began a new role in 2013, his first year scouting in Southern California, Afenir was awed by Judge's sheer size and athleticism.

"I don't know exactly what I've got here, because I'm new to this," Afenir told Oppenheimer. "But people aren't going to hit it any harder. They're not going to hit it any farther."

On Afenir's recommendation, Oppenheimer trekked through security at San Diego International Airport on a Sunday morning in February 2013, boarding a flight north to see Fresno State against Stanford University. Judge went 5-for-5 with three RBIs, including a long home run to left field leading off the seventh inning. Watching from the seats behind home plate at Stanford's picturesque Sunken Diamond, Oppenheimer thought: "Wow. What else do I need to see?"

"It's not just home runs or the batting practice before the game," Oppenheimer said. "We saw that he was a really good outfielder at Fresno State, that he played hard, that he used the whole field to hit. It was the baserunning. All of that stuff that we looked at and watched him do at Fresno State, you thought, 'All right, this is what this guy could be.'"

The questions that remained were ones Judge could not answer himself. Big-league comparisons provide a safety net for scouts, and in Judge's case, there had not been many successful players with his physique. Dave Winfield had stood six foot six when he'd begun a Hall of Fame career a generation before; Giancarlo Stanton had just broken into the majors with the Marlins, still going by the first name Mike at the time. Could Judge join their ranks? The Yankees intended to find out.

The organization dispatched Chad Bohling, their director of mental conditioning, across the country on a research mission. Bohling spent about an hour with Judge at a restaurant near Fresno State's campus, probing the prospect's mindset and background. Of note, Bohling reported, was Judge's team-first orientation. Judge seemed reluctant to speak about himself, echoing a rule instituted by Batesole at Fresno State, fining players a dollar if they used the words "I," "me," "my," or "myself" during an interview. In three seasons as a Bulldog, Judge had not surrendered a single buck.

"If you listen to Judge talk in his interviews, it's never about Judge," Ribera said. "That's one hundred percent credited to Batesole. It's never about you. It's about what your team did, who came in and delivered. If you make it about you, you're doing it for the wrong reasons. And Judge, you see him to this day carry that out. It's why he's the face of New York."

Batesole said, "I love that. That comes from Mom and Dad. That's already in him. We tried to put him in a place where that kind of character can flourish, but that was all Mom and Dad. And I think fans gravitate to him because he's one of us."

The first day of the 2013 MLB Draft took place on June 6, and Judge and other top amateur players were invited to MLB Network's studios in Secaucus, New Jersey. The Yankees' decision-makers navigated a cluttered war room of dry-erase boards and binders at Steinbrenner Field, where they had ranked Judge as one of the top collegiate hitters on the board. New York owned the No. 26, No. 32, and No. 33 selections in the draft, having acquired compensatory picks when outfielder Nick Swisher and pitcher Rafael Soriano signed with the Cleveland Indians and the Washington Nationals, respectively.

The Yankees loved Judge, but the sentiment was not universal across baseball. For example, Notre Dame's Eric Jagielo was a more conventional pick, a left-handed hitter with power who profiled well at the infield corners. Oppenheimer suggested that they take Jagielo at No. 26, believing that Judge would still be there at No. 32. The picks ticked down as the Yanks waited for their next to arrive: outfielder Phillip Ervin went to the Reds, followed by pitcher Rob Kaminsky (Cardinals), pitcher

Ryne Stanek (Rays), shortstop Travis Demeritte (Rangers), and pitcher Jason Hursh (Braves).

"I've had a lot of guys since that have told me that they really liked him, but there was a split camp with their clubs," Oppenheimer said. "Some teams had scouts that really liked him, and some that weren't on him. For us, we were lucky in that we didn't have a split camp. Guys went and saw him, Aaron was good, and our guys saw what he could be. They saw that future. There was still a long way for him to go, but the big kicker was the makeup. The makeup set him apart as somebody that we thought could reach those lofty projections."

Dressed in a charcoal suit with a gray shirt and purple tie, Judge fidgeted in his assigned seat, occasionally whispering to his parents. As Hursh's selection was announced by Bud Selig, baseball's commissioner at the time, Judge considered excusing himself for a bathroom break. He decided better of it, waiting to see if the Yankees would call his name. It was no lock, in Judge's mind. The trip had marked his first visit to the New York City tristate area, including an opportunity to tour Yankee Stadium; Judge had peered out at the field from the first-base dugout, later recalling that he had thought, "This would be an amazing place to play at some point."

Yet, at that moment, the fantasy did not include pinstripes. Judge's initial read of the Big Apple was that it had been "too busy; seems hectic." Overstimulated by a stroll past the M&M'S store and scruffy knockoff Elmos of a Disney-fied Times Square, he had told a *Fresno Bee* reporter the day before the draft that he was "not sure if I could ever live here." He later recalled: "Coming here from a small town in California, there's no one on the sidewalks back home. Here, it's crowded, and you're shoulder to shoulder with people. That was probably the first thing I noticed."

The Yankees believed Judge would fit in fine. Selig announced the selection, identifying Judge as a center fielder from Fresno State. The pick took Judge by surprise, and he embraced his mother in a bear hug. As Judge tried on a Yankees uniform top for the first time, MLB commentator Harold Reynolds said, "I don't think that jersey fits. This kid is *big*." On the air, Reynolds added: "The only thing that'll be interesting in New York is, do the [NFL's] Jets or Giants want him? That's how big this kid is."

Said Oppenheimer: "The size was never a concern for us because there was a grace to the way he did things. There was fluidity. It wasn't like where you were talking about somebody who was gawky and struggling. He was playing center field in college, and that gives you confidence in the athleticism."

Agreeing swiftly to a $1.8 million signing bonus, Judge intended to begin his Yankees career with the Charleston RiverDogs of the South Atlantic League, but a torn right quadriceps muscle kept him off the field. Instead, the team assigned him to a training facility in Tampa, Florida. It was not the start he'd envisioned, but one that allowed for an auspicious meeting. Judge recalled sitting at his locker one day, when Derek Jeter walked through the clubhouse, having just completed an on-field workout.

That year was a nightmare for Jeter, who was grinding to return after fracturing his left ankle in the previous year's American League Division Series. Jeter sized up the youngster in his line of sight, extended his right hand, and said, "Hey, Aaron, good to meet you." Judge was stunned; he could not believe that Jeter knew his name.

"I've always remembered that, because he could have just walked by me, and he didn't," Judge said. "I've tried to learn from that and treat teammates the same way."

The quadriceps healed over the off-season, and Judge was back on the field at the beginning of the 2014 season. He made his professional debut with Charleston and was soon promoted to the Tampa Yankees of the Florida State League. James Rowson was the organizational hitting instructor at the time and recalled that Judge seemed inquisitive about the art of hitting, even at age twenty-two.

"He always wanted to know 'Why?,' which I think is the most important question a young hitter can ask," Rowson said.

Tyler Wade became one of Judge's closest friends during their time together in Charleston, referring to Judge and teammate Michael O'Neill as his "big brothers." Wade was nineteen then, not far removed from clutching his diploma on graduation day at Murrieta Valley High School in Murrieta, California. Wade said that even at that early stage, players in the RiverDogs clubhouse recognized that Judge appeared to be headed for more impressive things.

"That was my first time playing with someone like that," Wade said. "The way he carried himself, there was that stardom. He gave off a presence. You always felt like he was going to be something special. The way his mind works, saying how he wants to get better and how his vision is. You know how some guys say things just to say things? When he says things, he firmly believes it, and that's what he's going to do. I was like, 'Damn, man, this guy has got big things coming.'"

Judge earned selection to the Arizona Fall League, a showcase for top minor leaguers, then split his 2015 season between Double-A Trenton and Triple-A Scranton/Wilkes-Barre. Those summers of highway travel, greasy bags of fast food, and stays in budget hotels taught Judge how to play the game the right way and not take his opportunities for granted.

"Even when I was in Charleston, Trenton, Scranton, I was preparing myself as if I was in Yankee Stadium," Judge said. "When you're in the minor leagues, and you've just got done traveling for twelve hours on a bus, it's pretty tough to get motivated. But then when you think, 'Hey, I'm not in Charleston, South Carolina, I'm in the Bronx in Yankee Stadium, playing in front of 50,000 people,' that gets you going."

Aaron Hicks recalled his first encounter with Judge in 2015, when they were both playing at the Triple-A level. Then a member of the Minnesota Twins organization, the switch-hitting Hicks already had some big-league service under his belt and was rehabbing an injury with the Rochester Red Wings.

"I was playing center field and he hit a ball to me. It got to me so quick," Hicks said. "I was thinking, 'This kid has some serious power if the ball is getting to me this fast.' Once he learned to properly hit the ball in the air, he was going to be scary. I think it was the first time I ever said this to somebody; I was like, 'Damn, bro, why are you hitting the ball so hard?' He was just like, 'Trying to do my job, man.'"

By spring 2016, Judge drew attention at Yankees camp, ticketed to begin the year at Double-A Trenton. Hall of Famer Reggie Jackson, then a special advisor with the team, watched Judge strike the top of the scoreboard in left field during batting practice and remarked that the youngster had "power like [Willie] Stargell." Judge's measured demeanor also impressed.

"I remember doing a long one-on-one interview with him in spring training of 2016," said Pete Caldera, a veteran reporter for the *Bergen (NJ) Record*. "There was attention around him, but we were led to believe that Greg Bird and Gary Sánchez would have better careers than Judge at that point. He was so unique because of his size. He had the body of an NFL tight end, but he really wanted baseball. He loved the cerebral part of the game; I remember him saying that he loved the chess match of batter versus pitcher, which drew him to baseball."

Promoted to Triple-A that summer, Judge found Nick Swisher giving his career one last shot. The boisterous, switch-hitting outfielder spent over a decade in the big leagues, including a career highlight as a key cog of the 2009 Yankees club that notched the franchise's twenty-seventh World Series championship. Swisher had been released by the Atlanta Braves in the spring of 2016, wobbling on a pair of surgically repaired knees, and his chances of getting back to the Show were not looking great.

Swisher signed a minor-league contract to return to the Yankees, attempting to squeeze a bit more daylight into his career, while offering assistance to the next generation. He had become a regular at the Waffle House restaurant on Davis Street in Scranton, Pennsylvania, where he'd order his hash browns "smothered, covered, and chunked" (onions, cheese, and ham) and invite teammates to put breakfast on his tab. Judge was among those who took Swisher up on his offer.

With the clatter of dishes and the hum of two-lane roadway traffic serving as background ambience, they spoke often, and Swisher sensed then that Judge would succeed.

"He knows the man that he is; he knows what he stands for," Swisher said. "I think that's his parents. They built such a good man. As a role model, now that I have kids myself, that's the kind of guy that I want my children to look up to." As Swisher entertained future "Baby Bombers" like Judge, Gary Sánchez, and Luis Cessa, the big-league Yankees were sputtering toward a fourth-place finish in the American League East, the third time in four seasons that manager Joe Girardi's club failed to qualify for postseason play. It was time for a changing of the guard, one that took place on August 12 as the Yankees showed Alex Rodriguez the door, ushering their star-crossed slugger into retirement.

Through gritted smiles, both A-Rod and club officials pretended all was well in their respective universes, though Rodriguez (at age forty-one and four home runs shy of 700) still believed deep within his bones that he could continue playing.

As public address announcer Paul Olden read from a script lauding Rodriguez's career, a lightning bolt flashed across the sky, accompanied by a loud thunderclap. Rodriguez jumped. The skies opened seconds later, in a delicious metaphor that sent Rodriguez, Steinbrenner, and others dashing toward the first-base dugout. Still, it was a surprisingly gracious exit for A-Rod, considering he'd threatened the club with legal action before being hit a 162-game performance-enhancing drug ban just three years prior.

Around midnight that evening, highlights of Rodriguez's final game—a 6–3 Yankees win, in which he'd stroked a run-scoring double off the Tampa Bay Rays' Chris Archer—flickered across a television screen in Rochester, New York. Judge was seated with his parents and then-girlfriend Samantha at a Dinosaur Bar-B-Que restaurant. Their table was surrounded by kitschy restaurant decor, including vintage beer advertisements, a potentially pilfered railroad crossing sign, and a signpost indicating that they sat 362 miles from "NEW YAWK."

Judge poked at a bacon cheeseburger, complemented by heaping helpings of macaroni and cheese and baked beans, as he clocked Scranton/Wilkes-Barre manager Al Pedrique moving with purpose across the wooden floor. Pedrique had played parts of three seasons with the Pittsburgh Pirates in the late 1980s, a light-hitting infielder who entered the coaching ranks in the early 2000s. As a Houston Astros special assistant in 2007, Pedrique had championed a diminutive Venezuelan infielder, voicing his conviction that José Altuve deserved a look.

Now Pedrique was in his first season managing Scranton/Wilkes-Barre, and he told Judge: "Hey, you might want to speed your dinner up a little bit. You've got to go play right field in New York tomorrow."

Judge blinked. "Rochester is in New York, isn't it?" To that, Pedrique laughed. "Nah, you're going to be playing right field at Yankee Stadium," the skipper proudly reported. Judge had gotten the call. Patty and Wayne hugged, tears streaking from Judge's mother's eyes. At that moment, Judge's first thoughts concerned travel logistics. The Yankees had an afternoon game the next day, scheduled for 1:05 p.m. against the Tampa Bay Rays.

There were no remaining flights from Rochester that evening, and Judge's parents decided that the quickest route to New York City would be to pack their rental car as quickly as possible, then drive through the night. The road trippers arrived at a Parsippany, New Jersey, hotel around 6:00 a.m.; Judge had unsuccessfully tried to steal some sleep in the back seat, no easy task for a passenger of his size. When the hotel's fire alarm went off about an hour later, Judge decided to report early for his first day at the new office. It was a good day to arrive ahead of the crowds; on a sweltering afternoon with temperatures in the mid-nineties, the team was honoring its 1996 World Series championship roster, with Jeter, Rivera, Pettitte, Posada, and Bernie Williams all on hand to bask in their glories of yesteryear.

The No. 99 emblazoned across the back of Judge's size fifty-two jersey ensured that he stood out right from the start. Judge liked No. 44, but it was retired in honor of Hall of Fame outfielder Reggie Jackson, and pitcher Michael Pineda owned his second choice, No. 35. Credit Rob Cucuzza, the team's clubhouse manager, for selecting the now-iconic No. 99 instead. It took Judge some time to warm up to the number; he'd even briefly considered asking for No. 13, vacated by A-Rod's departure just hours earlier.

"[Judge] was like, 'Should I keep 99?'" CC Sabathia said. "[I said], 'Fuck yeah, you keep 99. Nobody's like you, bro.' Now every Little League team that I see has a No. 99. That didn't happen before."

Judge's first major-league at-bat started with a bang: not one of his own, but a drive off the bat of Tyler Austin, his fellow first-day rookie teammate. Austin had received the call earlier than Judge, but a canceled flight pushed the Yankees to usher the twenty-four-year-old outfielder and first baseman to the Bronx via a five-hour car trip. He hadn't slept much more than Judge, and adrenaline surged through both players. Facing right-hander Matt Andriese in the second inning, Austin lifted a fly ball down the right-field line that reached the first row of seats, just over the 314-foot marker for a home run. Austin pumped his right fist as he charged around the bases, and as he waited at home plate, Judge thought: "Don't make a fool of yourself. Put the ball in play and get on to the next one."

He did more than that. With the crowd still buzzing, Judge made history, unloading on a 1-2 changeup for a mammoth 446-foot drive to deep center field. Those were depths rarely tested since the opening of the new Yankee Stadium seven years earlier. Judge became the third player to hit a ball off or over the glass panels above Monument Park, joining the Seattle Mariners' Russell Branyan in 2009 and the Houston Astros' Carlos Correa earlier in the 2016 season.

He and Austin were the first teammates to homer in their first big-league at-bats in the same game; as Austin would proudly recall after Judge had been crowned the AL's Most Valuable Player. "I went first. I couldn't believe that it happened for myself, much less when he did it back-to-back," Austin said. "That was unbelievable, especially because it had never been done before [by rookie teammates]. I was just super excited for him."

Years later, Judge still recalls that first at-bat as a career favorite.

"I'm losing my mind on deck, high-fiving, and now everyone's looking at me like, 'Hey, man, you've got to go out there and hit now,'" Judge said. "Then, getting a chance to hit another back-to-back home run with my friend Tyler Austin, it was a pretty special moment that I'll never forget. Having my family and friends there in the stands was something that meant so much to me."

Michael Kay called that afternoon's game for the YES Network and said that his first thoughts concerned Judge's size, wondering if any player so large could succeed in the majors. Then Kay introduced himself to Judge, got to know him a bit, and thought: "He gives off a lot of Jeter vibes."

"I see that with a lot of players that are raised by a strong family," Kay said. "Buck Showalter told me about Jeter after the first time he came to the stadium and he got drafted. He said: 'Well, he's never going to embarrass the Yankees. His parents, they're strong people, and strong people raise strong children.' I've met [Judge's] parents and talked with them a lot; they're impressive people. I got that vibe from him, that he was not going to do stupid things."

Judge's debut stint ended earlier than expected due to an oblique injury sustained on September 16 against the Los Angeles Dodgers. Aside from that first-day homer, Judge's first twenty-seven games in the majors showcased few indications of a future home run king. He ended the season with 4 homers, strikeouts in 42 of his 84 at-bats, and a .179 batting average. There was no sugarcoating it: Judge had been humbled.

As he returned home to Linden, where he'd help his parents around the yard between workouts and visits to high school basketball and football games, Judge clicked on the Notes app on his iPhone. All season, he'd kept a digital log of team meetings, phone calls, batting cage sessions, goals, milestones, and fleeting thoughts. In bold letters, he typed ".179" at the top.

"I've still got it there," Judge said years later. "It's turned into a baseball notes page, but still at the top is .179, followed by different stuff I like to see; goals I've written down or quotes or tidbits I've written down to help get me through the year."

Judge would be better prepared in 2017, and the key to unlocking his potential would come from a most unlikely source.

2

◆

LAUNCH QUICKNESS

David Matranga knew what it felt like to hit a home run in the big leagues—precisely one.

That shining moment had come in his first at-bat as a member of the Houston Astros on June 27, 2003, when he'd borrowed a bat from Triple-A teammate Alan Zinter and entered a game as a fifth-inning pinch hitter. Facing the Texas Rangers' Joaquín Benoit, Matranga looked at a called strike and a pitch out of the zone.

The next offering came in at his knees, and Matranga barreled a drive that cleared the left-field wall at Minute Maid Park, landing in the stadium's Crawford Boxes.

Only eighty-three previous players had homered in their first big-league at-bats, though that feat alone hardly guaranteed future success. For every Will Clark, Gary Gaetti, or Tim Wallach, there were more than a few like Mitch Lyden, Dave Machemer, or Gene Stechschulte, relative unknowns who'd never go deep again. Matranga, then a twenty-eight-year-old second baseman, would fall into the latter category.

A standout at Orange (California) High School in the shadows of Anaheim's Angel Stadium, Matranga turned enough heads at Pepperdine University to garner the Astros' sixth-round selection in the 1998 draft. Unable to edge stars like Craig Biggio, Jeff Kent, and Adam Everett for playing time, Matranga had five more at-bats without a hit for Houston in 2003, then resurfaced for one plate appearance with the Angels two years later. After bouncing around Triple-A with four different organizations, Matranga was ready for his next chapter.

When an opportunity to continue playing in Japan fizzled, Matranga's agent, Page Odle, suggested a different way to remain in the game. Matranga joined the representation ranks, learning the ins and outs at Odle's firm, PSI Sports Management. Odle was a former player, too; he'd been an outfielder and first baseman in the Pittsburgh Pirates farm system in the mid-1980s before founding his agency in 1992.

Working from the company's modest headquarters in Ventura, California, Matranga's experience in spikes served him well in understanding athletes' needs. His first client was Arizona State outfielder Kole Calhoun, who made it to the big leagues with the Angels in 2012; they'd counted shortstop Jack Wilson, pitcher Doug Fister, and pitcher James Shields among their stable, a school of small fish swimming in a big pond dominated by superagents like Scott Boras. PSI Sports also represented Aaron Judge. As the young Yankee began training for the 2017 season, Matranga was thinking about Richard Schenck, a swing doctor he'd found via an internet message board a dozen years prior. Matranga found Schenck fascinating, and though it had been too late in his playing career to apply Schenck's lessons fully, he wondered if the self-proclaimed "Teacherman" had the tools to unlock Judge's swing.

"Aaron struggled so bad in 2016, and it was clear that his mechanics were really going to hinder his ceiling, what he could really truly be," Matranga said.

Schenck had only seen professional pitches from the grandstands or on television, never advancing higher than Division II college baseball. Since 1989, Schenck had spent his days as the owner and operator of a billiards hall in the St. Louis suburb of St. Peters, where the one-time social studies teacher offered lessons on controlling the cue ball. He had a knack for instruction and a natural curiosity concerning the art of hitting, especially once his children began playing. He considered Barry Bonds to be baseball's best player, and Schenck wondered if secrets could be found in the San Francisco Giants superstar's swing.

Like a mad scientist, Schenck distilled Bonds's essence in his base-ment workshop. He would record at-bats on video, load them on a computer, and attempt to sync Bonds's swing to his own, hitting off a machine that spat out golf-size plastic balls. As Bonds batted in a Sep-tember 2006 game against the St. Louis Cardinals, Schenck reached for his TiVo remote and hit pause, advancing the image one frame at a time. Schenck recognized that Bonds's bat barrel would snap backward with every swing before it went forward, forming a blur behind Bonds's head. A left-handed swinger, Schenck fiddled with his stance in the basement and was delighted to discover that—even in his mid-fifties and with some paunch spilling over his denim jeans—he could now square up everything the pitching machine offered. He called it "launch quickness," which Matranga wanted Judge to try.

"I was a little nervous, because I'm just a guy from St. Peters, Mis-souri," Schenck said. "I've never played professionally, and here I am with a first-round draft pick that's had a cup of coffee in the big leagues. But I felt good, because David gave me a good recommendation."

They first met in November 2016, with Schenck setting up shop at the state-of-the-art D-BAT facility in Peoria, Arizona, located in a quiet office park two miles from a spring training home shared by the Seattle Mariners and San Diego Padres. After shaking hands and exchanging small talk with Judge and Matranga, Schenck broke the ice by asking Judge to try what he called a "command drill," where a hitter assumes a loaded launch position and swings when he hears the word "Go!" Schenck placed two balls on tees, one for him and one for Judge. Standing behind them, Matranga gave the command. Each time, Schenck connected first.

"I was sixty-two, he was twenty-four, and he couldn't beat me," Schenck said. "I beat him to the ball every time. Finally, he looked at me and said, 'What are you doing?'"

There was no comparing their power, but Schenck's drill reinforced that there was something Judge could do to reach the baseball more rap-idly. Over the next week, Schenck instructed Judge to envision his swing as an oscillating fan turning on its pedestal, with the bat functioning as the blade and the hands as an angle. Schenck illustrated the point further with a pink fidget spinner, then showed a video contrasting Judge's swing against Bonds and Manny Ramirez. One swing at a time, Schenck made Judge a more dangerous hitter. Not only could Judge get to the baseball faster, but the extra milliseconds also offered a better chance to halt a swing if fooled by an unappealing pitch. Schenck said he had seen similar mechanics in Dustin Pedroia, Ichiro Suzuki, Albert Pujols, and Mike Trout, hitters of various body types and batting stances.

"I didn't invent it, but I learned how to teach it," Schenck said. "In my opinion, all the great hitters—almost all of the Hall of Famers and almost anybody that's worth a darn in the big leagues, they've been doing this. They might have stumbled onto it, or maybe some other coach taught them. Once they get from the loaded launch position to contact, they all look the same."

The Yankees provided each player with personalized and detailed workout plans before each off-season, and they were not enthused to learn one of their top prospects had spent the winter training with an outside contractor. When Judge arrived at the team's complex in Tampa, Florida, and attempted some of Schenck's drills, hitting coach Alan Cockrell scoffed, instructing Judge to knock it off. Marcus Thames, the club's assistant hitting coach, recalled watching Judge try a few oddball exercises in the batting cages underneath the first-base grandstand at George M. Steinbrenner Field, thinking: "What the hell?" Judge quietly seethed as he caught glimpses of other coaches standing behind him, shaking their heads. Joe Girardi, entering his tenth and final season as the club's manager, was not completely sold, either. Judge was competing with Aaron Hicks to break camp with the team, and the organization had not ruled out a return to the minors. But Judge believed in Schenck, telling the coaches: "I've tried this all off-season, and it feels really good."

"There was a lot of negative feedback, people saying, 'It won't work. You shouldn't do it,'" Judge said. "But you've just got to have faith. It's my career. It's nobody else's career. If I'm going to fail, I'd rather fail my way."

The swing changes not only helped Judge win a starting outfield job over Hicks, but they set him on a path to begin a remarkable 2017 campaign that saw him set a rookie record with 52 home runs (later eclipsed by the Mets' Pete Alonso), earning unanimous selection as the American

League's Rookie of the Year and finishing second in the AL Most Valuable Player race.

"'17 was crazy," Judge said. "That's another year that people ask me,
'Man, you hit all these homers; you must have been feeling great every
single time you stepped up to the plate. There was times after the All-
Star break where I was the worst player in baseball. I didn't even want to
step in that box. I was like, 'It's going to be 1-2-3 and I'm going to walk
right back to the dugout and right field.' I leaned on my teammates a lot."

Aaron Boone wore a media credential that spring, fulfilling his on-
camera role as an analyst for ESPN's *Baseball Tonight*. As he observed
Yankees camp in Tampa, Boone said that Judge's demeanor reminded
him of how people around the Boston Red Sox had reacted when slugger
David Ortiz appeared in uniform.

"I was standing in the home dugout, and I knew he was one of the
stories of the camp," Boone said. "You're first struck being around him
by the size, but then you watch how he interacts and touches different
people. That's something that stood out to me right away, like, 'Oh, wow.'
The buzz around him and the gentleness that Aaron treats people with
when he sees kids and stuff like that, it's always stood out."

As Judge headed north, his place on the team was still uncertain.
He opted to spend the first few homestands in a Times Square hotel,
unwilling to fork over a sizable deposit on a New York apartment with a
return trip to Triple-A still seemingly possible. After games, Judge would
sometimes roam among the tourists, occasionally searching for frozen
yogurt to indulge his sweet tooth. Brett Gardner didn't love the sound of
that, and the veteran outfielder invited Judge to spend a week in the guest
room of his family's rented home in suburban Armonk, New York, telling
him, "New York isn't all tall buildings and flashing lights."

"I remember Dave Robertson stayed with Johnny Damon for a little
while; same type of deal," Gardner said. "But my house was empty. My
wife and kids weren't up here, so he learned some things from me. Maybe
I learned some things from him, too, so it was good. We had a good time
together. He cleaned up after himself; good, proper etiquette. He puts
his dishes in the dishwasher and takes the trash out. I put him to work
while he was there."

Judge loved the peace and quiet, saying the home reminded him of a cabin in the woods. But his chances of a permanent invitation disappeared after Judge helped himself to some leftover Easter chocolate, to the dismay of Gardner's young sons. "His boys weren't too happy about that," Judge said.

Judge had to go back to the city anyway; more and more, it appeared that he would be staying for a while. "I never saw 62 [home runs] coming," said Reggie Jackson, then a special advisor for the club. "I will say that, in '17, they were wondering if he could come and play in the big leagues. Everybody got their chance to talk. I said, 'If he's going to be okay striking out two hundred times, he's going to hit thirty baseballs in the air that are going to be outs for most people. If he can manage the strikeouts, then he's going to be a hell of a big league player.'" Within weeks, Judge had appeared on the cover of *Sports Illustrated* and appeared in a taped segment for NBC's *The Tonight Show Starring Jimmy Fallon*, where he sported a pair of Clark Kent glasses and a blazer to quiz unsuspecting passersby in New York's Bryant Park about the Yankees' new right fielder. Some recognized him; most didn't: one oblivious fan identified him as "Adam Judge." By late May, the Yankees were unveiling a "Judge's Chambers" seating area in Yankee Stadium's Section 104, three rows beyond the right-field wall.

"They just brought it up to me and said, 'Hey, this is what we're going to do,'" Judge said. "When you come to a game, it's supposed to be fun for the players and the fans. I feel like it might be something that's fun for the fans out there."

Framed by faux wood paneling and fashioned to fit eighteen fans, each of whom wore black judicial robes with No. 99 on the back, the addition was an instant hit—and an exciting departure for an organization that had always taken a more conservative approach in marketing its young talent. There had been no such semipermanent tributes erected for Derek Jeter in the late 1990s, for example, but the club was beginning to relax and recognize the importance of providing unique attractions as it moved into the Instagram era.

Everyone wanted to be part of the fun. Before long, the Judge's Chambers had even attracted an actual judge: Supreme Court Associate

Justice Sonia Sotomayor, who took in a game against the Boston Red Sox
from the unique vantage point.

"I had the best time in the whole world," the Bronx-born Sotomayor
said.

One of Judge's season highlights came in his victorious performance at
the Home Run Derby at Miami's Marlins Park, where he outslugged
the Marlins' Giancarlo Stanton and others by slamming a jaw-dropping
forty-seven balls over the walls, including four drives of five hundred feet
or more. Stacked end to end, Judge's homers would have traveled nearly
four miles from home plate into adjacent Biscayne Bay. The largely pro-
Stanton crowd initially booed Judge, but by the night's end, Judge had
seemingly won everyone over. "He's so quiet and simple," marveled Colorado Rockies outfielder Charlie Blackmon, "that he looks like a contact
hitter trapped in an ogre's body."

The derby theatrics, as Judge later revealed, came at a price. His exhibition aggravated a left shoulder injury sustained weeks before while crash-
ing into an outfield wall, eventually requiring surgery in the off-season.
Judge vowed he'd only participate in another Home Run Derby before an
All-Star Game at Yankee Stadium; it was last held in the Bronx during
the summer of 2008, a farewell to the original "House That Ruth Built."

Even though Judge's shoulder injury sapped his power in the second
half, there was no better advertisement for Schenck, whose client list
rapidly expanded. The "Teacherman" counted the Philadelphia Phillies'
Scott Kingery and the Chicago Cubs' Ian Happ among his new pupils.
Professional athletes were willing to look past Schenck's acerbic online
sparring with those who doubted his methods—Jeff Frye, a big leaguer in
the 1990s and early 2000s, was among Schenck's most vocal Twitter critics. Schenck frequently returned fire, criticizing Frye's swing (a throwback to when players were encouraged to put the ball in play, rather than
prioritizing launch angle) and referring to the former infielder as "Judy."

The Yankees cared little about what Schenck posted on the internet;
their concern was ensuring that Judge continued developing into one of
the game's most dangerous hitters. Around this time, Schenck received
a phone call from Thames, who asked: "Hey, could you give me some

pointers to help Aaron during the season?" Since that day, Schenck said, no one from the Yankees has contacted him.

"It works perfectly, so we've got no complaints," said Dillon Lawson, the Yankees' hitting coach. "Aaron is extremely professional, and the Rich in person is different from the Rich online. We want to understand the thought process behind all that, because it's what Aaron believes."

The Yankees' unexpected advance to the American League Championship Series that autumn produced a seemingly adorable story line, allowing photographers to capture the six-foot-seven Judge standing on second base alongside the five-foot-six José Altuve. It was a warm-and-fuzzy message to Little Leaguers everywhere that all shapes and sizes of athletes can make it, but that soured with revelations of the Astros' sign-stealing scandal. Initially gracious after finishing second to Altuve for the MVP, Judge scrolled back through his Instagram feed to delete a post he'd made congratulating the Houston infielder.

Judge "felt sick to his stomach" reading quotes from Mike Fiers, a pitcher on that 2017 Astros team, who blew the whistle on the scheme in November 2019. As Fiers detailed to *The Athletic*, a television monitor was installed outside the Houston dugout with the center-field camera feed on it, allowing for real-time decoding of opponents' signs. Players would bang on a trash can with a bat or massage device known as a Theragun to signal if a batter should be ready for a curveball or offspeed pitch. There would be no audible bang if the next pitch was believed to be a fastball.

"To find out it wasn't earned and that they cheated, it didn't sit well with me," Judge said.

Those Astros, slapped with fines and losses of draft picks, but no suspensions to active players, would continue to be a thorn in the sides of Judge's Yankees. 2018 ended in heartbreak and disappointment at the hands of the Boston Red Sox in the AL Division Series. It was the Astros again in 2019, an ALCS that incredibly ended again with Aroldis Chapman giving up the winning blast to—who else?—Altuve. A loss to the Tampa Bay Rays in the weird neutral-site and empty-ballpark ALDS followed in the COVID-19–shortened 2020 season. As he prepared for the 2021 season, Judge felt so good in a winter workout, he had boasted to Schenck, "I'm going to hit fifty again this year." Schenck agreed, but Judge's prediction was a year off. He hit 39 in 148 games before the Yanks' season ended in that Wild Card Game disaster at Fenway. Judge had become a superstar, fulfilling Rob Manfred's prediction from late in 2017, when the commissioner said that Judge could be "one of the faces of our game." He was certainly that, having signed endorsement deals with companies like Pepsi, T-Mobile, Adidas, and Oakley, while appearing on the cover of the popular *MLB: The Show* video game. Though critics still questioned Judge's durability, noting that injuries limited him to 390 of 546 possible regular season games from 2018 to 2021 (71.4 percent), 2022 would be a different story. Judge was sure of that, if the league and the players union would just let him get on the damn field.

The players were locked out, and forty-three agonizing days passed without talks. It was a costly game of chicken, played across conference tables in a series of marathon sessions held at Roger Dean Stadium in West Palm Beach, Florida, the shared spring home of the St. Louis Cardinals and Miami Marlins. The timing, for Judge at least, wasn't the worst. He was still in the afterglow of a honeymoon with the former Samantha Bracksieck. They'd met and fallen in love at Linden High School, where Samantha was one year behind Aaron, and attended Fresno State together. A kinesiology major, Samantha performed her master's thesis on the prevalence of ulnar collateral ligament injuries among baseball pitchers. That knowledge of athletic movements provided a great teammate for Judge, who would reflect on her ability to "continue to push me and motivate me, day in and day out, even if it's 2:30 in the morning and we're sitting on the couch, breaking down my film. You're right there with me." The couple wed in December at the Montage Kapalua Bay hotel on Maui, with close family and friends on hand. Gerrit Cole, Corey Kluber, DJ LeMahieu, Gleyber Torres, Tyler Wade, and Luke Voit were among the current or former Yankees who made the invite list.

"We had a blast," Judge said. "We always enjoyed going out to Hawaii during the off-season every now and then, checking it out and getting away from things. So we just thought that'd be the perfect destination to do our thing."

Judge had stared down scores of big-league pitchers without fear or trepidation. He expected that would translate to his wedding day, telling friends and family before the ceremony: "I've played in playoff games. I've been in big situations like this. This is just another day."

"I was just going to be stone-cold; let's do our thing and get to the party," Judge said. "But, man, right when I saw her coming down the aisle, the photographers didn't have my back. They caught me with tears coming out of my eyes. They got me, but I couldn't help it. You try to resist it, and you've got so many different emotions flowing. It kind of all hits you at once."

As the soon-to-be Judges exchanged their vows, pods of whales breached in the picturesque waters of Namalu Bay, drawing astonished gasps from the attendees. The day was peaceful, relaxing, and intimate, according to Wade, who was part of Judge's wedding party. "It was very beautiful; very well done," Wade said. "I applaud Sam for that one. She definitely set the standard."

The newlyweds plotted their future as baseball's labor negotiations dragged on. For years, position players had griped that seven weeks of exhibition games were too many, scheduled to provide extra time for pitchers to build stamina. Now the hitters would get their wish. Ninety-nine days after the league instituted the lockout, a deal was struck and players hustled for an abbreviated spring training. The originally scheduled opening series was lopped off the schedule and moved to the tail end; for the Yankees, that meant that instead of opening against the Rangers in Arlington, Texas, they'd begin at home against the Red Sox.

The Yankees' roster had not changed much since their last assembly. The most significant moves before the lockout had been a reshaping of Boone's staff, with three new hitting coaches, an additional pitching coach, and a new third-base coach and first-base coach. Dillon Lawson, one of the hitting coaches, said that his first workout with Judge felt like an interview. As they huddled behind the batting cage, Judge seemed less interested in seeking assistance than in quizzing Lawson about how he would fix teammates' problems in different scenarios.

"He believes that if he gets into a good initial position, as long as he's swinging at a strike, then he's going to be pretty damn successful,"

Lawson said. "He really doesn't waste time in the cage; he's super ef-
ficient. He'll do lead-up drills off the tee, get those feelings, and make
sure things are dialed in. We'll get some video for him so he can check
some things out, but he's at the point where you can let him be. He can
coach himself at times."

Brian Cashman and the Yankees had disregarded a loaded crop of
free-agent shortstops, allowing Carlos Correa, Corey Seager, Marcus
Semien, and Trevor Story to land elsewhere. They pointed instead to the
rising tandem of Oswald Peraza and Anthony Volpe, a duo of fast-rising
prospects whom Hal Steinbrenner touted as future stars. If the Yankees
could find a gem in the youngsters, it might mean more money in the
coffers to satisfy a long-term extension due for Judge, who was slated to
become a free agent after the 2022 season.

As Opening Day approached, Judge and most of the veterans gathered in Boone's office, shutting the heavy steel door behind them. The
cinder-block-walled room was packed, with almost all the space filled
around the manager's desk, a circular office table, and a couple of leather
couches that had hosted the backsides of Yogi Berra, Reggie Jackson,
Ron Guidry, and every other pinstriped dignitary over the past few decades.

They spoke for about three hours about their personal lives and goals
for the season. The idea was not to delay a meeting until they faced adversity. It was far better to begin building that camaraderie from the start,
with lofty goals in place.

"When you look around Yankee Stadium, you don't see division
championships or 'we made it to the playoffs this year,'" Judge said. "You
see World Series championship banners everywhere. To be here from '16
on and still not have a banner up that you've contributed to, it's tough
and frustrating, but it's also motivation to go out there and make this
year special."

3

ON THE CLOCK

The first pitch of the regular season was less than three hours away, and the possibility of Aaron Judge becoming a Yankee for life still seemed to hang in the air.

It was the morning of April 8, cold and wet in New York, and the slugger was hiking his navy-blue socks underneath pinstriped pants at his Yankee Stadium locker. He'd just moved into prime clubhouse real estate, occupying a space previously assigned to outfielder Brett Gardner, who was spending his Opening Day at home for the first time in over a decade.

Judge had a little more storage in his new spot, appreciating its direct line of sight to a pair of flat-screen televisions that were usually tuned to ESPN or MLB Network, but it also meant that everyone had a better view of him. A group of about twenty reporters waited awkwardly. Their assigned mission: to sniff out any indication that a Judge contract extension might be in the works.

"Your guess is as good as mine," he said, adding a wink and a sly grin. Judge wasn't about to spill the beans, but he already knew that he had placed the bet of his life—gambling on his talent, performance, and health by rejecting a seven-year, $213.5 million extension offer. General manager Brian Cashman made multiple overtures to Judge's camp over the final three weeks of spring training, all of which were rejected. Somehow, the negotiations stayed quiet, an astonishing achievement considering the fishbowl nature of baseball in New York.

At Judge's insistence, there would be no more proposals once Gerrit Cole threw the season's first pitch. Judge told agent Page Odle that in his heart, he wanted to remain with the Yankees. But this was business, and Judge was prepared to enter free agency if his camp did not receive an offer they desired. They agreed that if talks were to continue during the season, it would serve as a massive distraction.

"The last thing I wanted to do," Judge said, "is to be in the middle of May after a good series and people talking, 'Oh, you going to sign an extension?' Or after an 0-for-4, 'You should have signed that extension.'"

Yankees manager Aaron Boone had already submitted his lineup card for the opener against the Boston Red Sox, a contest pushed back one day by inclement weather in the New York tri-state area. Still, at that time, few outside of a tight circle knew of Judge's decision to play out the season as a free-agent-to-be. As Judge laced his spikes and painted reflective eye black above his cheekbones, he faced down the possibility this could be his last season opener in pinstripes.

He'd wrestled with the team's proposals, understanding that each represented generational wealth. No one back home in Linden could have imagined that windfall, even in their wildest Powerball fever dreams, let alone turning it down. But in professional sports, athletes equate money with respect, and Judge's camp believed the offer sat short of his actual market value.

At $30.5 million per season, Judge would have become the franchise's highest-paid position player in terms of average annual value, eclipsing the $27.5 million Alex Rodriguez averaged over his final deal. It also would have represented the largest extension the team had issued to that point, eclipsing those agreed upon by Derek Jeter (ten years, $189 million) and CC Sabathia (five years, $122 million).

But it wouldn't have given Judge top billing on the Yanks' roster; that would still belong to Cole, who agreed to a $324 million pact before the 2020 season. Judge and Odle were seeking one of the largest deals ever issued to an outfielder, a group that featured Mike Trout (twelve years, $426.5 million), Mookie Betts (twelve years, $365 million), Bryce Harper (thirteen years, $330 million) and Giancarlo Stanton (thirteen years, $325 million).

With input from his parents, Patty and Wayne, and his wife, Samantha, Judge swallowed hard and said, "Thanks, but no thanks."

It was a considerable risk. The Yankees had factored in Judge's health and forecasts of how he might fare over the life of that contract. Judge had missed nearly a quarter of his team's games (164 of 709) since the beginning of the 2017 season, though some injuries could be excused. After Judge's 2016 debut campaign was cut short by an oblique strain, he needed arthroscopic surgery on his shoulder during the 2017–18 off-season, part of the price for his winning performance in that summer's Home Run Derby.

In July 2018, a fastball thrown by the Kansas City Royals' Jakob Junis fractured Judge's right wrist; the team's medical team provided a laughably optimistic forecast of three weeks for Judge's return. That experience had been incredibly frustrating for Judge. He, not the doctors, saw the reporters hovering near his locker at each home game, seeking explanations for why Judge was behind the club-announced schedule to get back on the field. Judge sustained another oblique strain during an April 2019 game against Kansas City; cursing himself for not correctly stretching, he'd miss two months, resolving to be more diligent with his pregame preparation in the future.

From that point forward, Judge focused on core strength and flexibility, performing planks, taking boxing classes, and working out on Pilates machines. He'd received some good advice from Edwin Encarnación, a three-time All-Star who spent half of the 2019 season with the Yankees as a designated hitter and occasional first baseman. Encarnación suggested that Judge needed to cut down on his extra cage work. "You don't need to take a thousand swings. Less is more," Encarnación had said. Judge listened, hoping it would help him stay healthier.

There was another freak injury in the spring of 2020, though it traced back to a September 2019 game against the Los Angeles Angels of Anaheim, when Judge's chest thudded hard on the Yankee Stadium outfield grass while he was attempting to catch a sinking line drive. Judge felt the effects of that play for the rest of the season, and he hoped a winter of rest would cure the lingering discomfort in his right shoulder and pectoral area. Agonizing jolts still accompanied each of Judge's first swings of the new year. In the weeks before the COVID-19 pandemic shuttered baseball, Judge was diagnosed with a stress fracture in a rib and a collapsed lung. Had the season started on time, Judge would have missed months.

There were also calf strains and lower-body soreness that, at least on one occasion, Boone blamed on uncomfortable airplane seats. No one would dispute that six-foot-seven frames are not what Boeing's engineers have in mind, but the club flew alone on customized Delta jetliners that offer poker tables and other amenities (though, as *Sports Illustrated* embarrassingly revealed, players and coaches still needed to cough up $9 per flight for Wi-Fi service). As the Yanks crisscrossed the country, Judge could stretch out across three seats in his assigned row—he wasn't exactly Steve Martin wedged next to John Candy in the opening scenes of *Planes, Trains and Automobiles*.

"Even the years he's gotten hurt, he's put up a full season of numbers that are massively MVP-like, in four months rather than six," said Yankees general manager Brian Cashman. "So if you look back at some of the years that he was short-circuited because of rib cage or calf or whatever it was in the past, and you add on numbers that he could have had if he didn't get hurt—I mean, I don't know if it would take him to 62 [home runs], but it takes him to pretty spectacular heights. So the bottom line is when he's able to go out there and post, he's going to put up numbers."

Coming off his healthiest season since 2017, Judge felt he was making the right choice in turning down the extension, but it had not been a slam-dunk decision. Judge found a sounding board in teammate Giancarlo Stanton, the other half of the club's twin towers, whose similar frame and long-ball prowess provided hints about opposing pitchers' game plans. In this case, Stanton could call upon his experience reaching a massive extension with his original franchise, the Miami Marlins.

The thirteen-year, $325 million pact that Stanton agreed to in November 2014 set new benchmarks and displayed incredible loyalty on the team's part. Stanton was only months removed from sustaining facial lacerations, multiple fractures, and dental damage, having been hit in the face by a pitch from the Milwaukee Brewers' Mike Fiers in September. (Yes, the same Fiers who blew the whistle on the 2017 Astros.)

Stanton would later describe the gruesome scene of laying motionless at home plate, finding some of his teeth floating in the blood rapidly pooling in his mouth. No one who saw Stanton carted off the field that day could say with authority if Stanton would ever return as the same player. Baseball history is littered with cautionary tales like Tony Conigliaro, the promising Boston Red Sox outfielder whose career was cut short by an errant pitch in 1967. Just twenty-two at the time, Conigliaro's injury helped usher in the protective earflap that is now required to be worn by all batters, but he should have made a more significant mark on the sport.

Pitchers showed Stanton no mercy upon his return; buzzed up and in with fastballs, Stanton had to prove that he wouldn't flinch. He succeeded, rewarding the Marlins' faith with a 59-homer performance in 2017. Stanton earned National League Most Valuable Player honors just weeks before the unprofitable franchise's new ownership group moved Stanton and $265 million of his contract to the Bronx—a decision made with Derek Jeter installed as a chief operating officer, fulfilling his long-voiced desire to help call shots from the front office.

The Yankees envisioned Judge and Stanton as a modern-day version of Mickey Mantle and Roger Maris, a pair of front men who would power the Bombers back to the World Series, as the "M&M Boys" had done in the summer of 1961. The duo's first four bites at the apple had not yielded the intended result, but as Judge negotiated his deal in the spring of 2022, Stanton said, "It's been great playing with him, watching him grow as a player and a person. I hope the rest of our careers are together. And I think we'll get it figured out."

Judge's 2022 paycheck was still unsettled, and the Yankees were playing hardball. It was Judge's final year of eligibility for arbitration, the process by which salaries for players with three to six years of big-league service time are determined. Judge had requested $21 million from the club, representing a 48 percent raise over his 2021 salary of $10.175 million. The Yankees countered at $17 million, and the matter appeared headed for a courtroom. To put Judge's proposed figure in context, Atlanta Braves first baseman Matt Olson, Los Angeles Angels pitcher Noah Syndergaard, and Los Angeles Dodgers shortstop Trea Turner each earned $21 million in 2022. Players earning $17 million included pitchers Lance McCullers Jr., Clayton Kershaw, and Nathan Eovaldi, and the Dodgers' Cody Bellinger and Justin Turner.

Arbitration matters are typically settled during spring training. During Judge's first full season in 2017, the Yankees triumphed over right-handed reliever Dellin Betances in a dispute over the relatively paltry sum of $2 million. The formal part of those ninety-minute proceedings went cordially enough in a conference room at the Vinoy Renaissance in St. Petersburg, Florida; Betances was disappointed, but not upset. Later that day, though, team president Randy Levine called a press conference to spike the football, announcing over a speakerphone that Betances had been "a victim" of agent Jim Murray's "half-baked" attempt to alter the pay scale for relief pitchers.

"In effect, it's like me saying, 'I'm not the president of the Yankees; I'm an astronaut,'" Levine said. "Well, I'm not an astronaut, and Dellin Betances is not a closer, at least based on statistics."

That did not sit well with Betances, a six-foot-seven flamethrower whose gentle demeanor masked his New York toughness. Born in Washington Heights and raised in the Lillian Wald housing project on Manhattan's Lower East Side, Betances starred at Grand Street Campus High School in Brooklyn and still possessed his $7 ticket stub from David Wells's 1998 perfect game. The joy that the ten-year-old had felt in the bleachers that afternoon—Beanie Baby Day against the Minnesota Twins—was a distant memory as Betances fumed. He'd said that Levine's outburst forced him to recognize that baseball was a business. Then preparing for his first full season in the majors, Judge took note.

"I think both sides want to avoid getting into that situation, having to go into that room and have to fight each other and bring out the boxing gloves," Judge said. "I learned back then when Dellin went through it; I talked to him about that process and got a heads-up about how that works."

Because the lockout had condensed the spring, hearings were scheduled during the season; Judge wondered if the team would have him wake up early on a game day to hear lawyers argue about his flaws. It seemed to be a perplexing nickel-and-dime argument, considering that *Forbes* had just published an analysis of Major League Baseball's franchise values, showing the Yankees again topping the list at the $6 billion plateau, joining the NFL's Dallas Cowboys (an estimated $6.5 billion) as the most valuable global franchises. For anyone keeping score at home, *Forbes*'s estimates suggested that the Yankees had produced a 59,900 percent rate of return from George Steinbrenner's original $10 million investment in 1973.

Judge reiterated that he wanted to stay with the Yankees, but he added: "If it comes to it that it doesn't, I'll enjoy my memories here." The baseball industry had just watched a shocking breakup between first baseman Freddie Freeman and the Atlanta Braves, the defending World Series champions. Freeman's return to Atlanta seemed to be a lock, until it wasn't; now he was in spring training a coast away with the Los Angeles Dodgers. Forever was promised to no one.

Cashman promised to keep negotiations with Judge "as private as we can," and other items were on the general manager's agenda. Because the lockout had frozen rosters across baseball, Cashman and his competitors were now in hurry-up mode. There was a free-agent frenzy representing more than $3 billion (with a *b*) in contractual commitments; Freeman went to L.A., shortstop Corey Seager to the Texas Rangers, shortstop Carlos Correa to the Minnesota Twins, first baseman Kris Bryant to the Colorado Rockies.

It was a wild shootout, and the Yankees mostly watched from the sidelines. Their most significant move was to re-sign first baseman Anthony Rizzo to a two-year, $32 million deal with an opt-out. Rizzo's pact represented the twenty-seventh largest commitment in the free-agent class, which Cashman defended by pointing out that the Yankees were already "running out the highest payroll we've ever had in our history."

But there was a blockbuster trade with the Minnesota Twins simmering on the back burner. The clock had expired on the team's patience for Gary Sánchez, a power-hitting catcher with a rocket arm who set an American League record by reaching the 100-homer plateau in just 355 games. That All-Star version of Sánchez had been missing in action for some time; now he seemed utterly lost, batting .187 over the last two years while offering fans in the pricey Legends seats too much face time as he chased passed balls.

As Cashman worked the phones, the Minnesota Twins expressed interest in Sánchez, dangling third baseman Josh Donaldson. Cashman believed that Donaldson, who had won the 2015 American League Most Valuable Player award with the Toronto Blue Jays, still had thunder in his bat and could contribute Gold Glove–caliber defense at the hot corner. He also thought that Donaldson could counteract any complacency in the clubhouse; a prickly, take-no-crap hard-ass from the Florida Panhandle, Donaldson had a reputation for irking teammates and opponents with his outspokenness and swagger.

And therein was the thorny issue that needed to be resolved. The previous year, Donaldson had been one of the league's most outspoken players against pitchers using "sticky stuff" to improve their spin rates, and he had mentioned Gerrit Cole by name. Donaldson's comments helped prompt a league-wide crackdown in which umpires regularly checked pitchers' hands, hats, belts, and gloves between innings.

Pitchers had previously utilized a mixture of sunscreen and rosin to improve their grip on the baseball; for years, it was common to see bullpens stocked with Bull Frog sunscreen, which surely had nothing to do with combating UV rays during night games or contests played in domed stadiums. Hitters regularly used pine tar, but it was not permitted for pitchers, as the Yankees' Michael Pineda memorably learned in an April 2014 ejection at Fenway Park, when the hurler had brazenly slathered a thick swath across his neck.

Spider Tack, a super-sticky paste intended for use by competitive weight lifters, worked even better. Studies showed that the goop not only helped in controlling pitches, but could also increase the ball's revolutions per minute, creating the DNA of a nastier and more unhittable pitch. Donaldson's claim spurred an awkward press conference in the basement of Minnesota's Target Field, during which a reporter asked Cole point-blank if he had ever used Spider Tack. Cole stammered and repeatedly blinked, pausing for six arduous seconds before finally replying: "I don't know quite how to answer that, to be honest."

Cashman considered the trade carefully, finally deciding that Donaldson was "an uber-competitor that's not afraid, and that's something that maybe we were lacking," adding, "Maybe we need a little more edge." Donaldson would never apologize for his fiery personality; as the Yankees would soon learn firsthand, he sometimes intentionally needled opponents to create a performance advantage.

"The sport that we're playing, you do it so much that you can be just going through the motions at times," Donaldson explained. "You've just got to find that mechanism that's going to say, 'Hey, I've got to dial it in.' You say things like, 'I don't like how he wears his uni. I hate how he's wearing his hat. I'd love to knock his fucking hat off.' Those are real thoughts that are going through your head."

Cashman buzzed Cole's cell phone late on a Sunday evening, mentioning Donaldson's name and asking for the hurler's opinion, if not his explicit blessing. It had not been uncommon for Cashman to fill Cole in on news before it hit the wire, and in this case, the pitcher's response came quickly: "I'll be fine." The Yankees had remade the left side of their infield. Sánchez and third baseman Gio Urshela were going to Minnesota in exchange for Donaldson, shortstop Isiah Kiner-Falefa, and catcher Ben Rortvedt, a move that would allow Gleyber Torres to shift from shortstop to second base, a position for which the team believed he was better suited.

Donaldson wasted no time getting started. As Sánchez and Urshela trudged south to the Twins' spring complex in Fort Myers, Florida, Cole and Donaldson were shaking hands in Boone's office at Steinbrenner Field, an exchange described as brief and cordial. Donaldson said that he and Cole "felt very good about where it ended," which was to recognize each other as teammates in pursuit of a title and flush their previous war of words. Cashman believed that Cole and Donaldson would proceed as professionals, just as his 1999 team had embraced Roger Clemens after a blockbuster trade sent away the immensely popular David Wells. The Yankees detested Clemens, who'd made a hobby of plunking their hitters with inside fastballs, embracing his reputation as an intimidating villain.

Nine days into Clemens's pinstriped tenure, Derek Jeter and Chuck Knoblauch had provided levity, strapping on full catching gear before digging into the batter's box. Clemens laughed, jokingly buzzing a pair of pitches behind the heads of his new teammates. "I knew something was going to be up," Clemens said then. "I thought it was a good move by them. And to make them feel right at home, I had to throw those ones behind them." As it turned out, Clemens helped the Yankees to two World Series titles and three pennants, which was precisely what Cole and Donaldson hoped they could do together.

"I wanted to hear him out, and I wanted him to hear me out," Donaldson said. "After that, after the meeting, it's over. That was important to me. Me and him are boys now. My fiancée hangs out with his wife. Our kids had a playdate. I love baseball; Gerrit loves baseball. He loves to talk baseball, and so do I. At the end of the day, we're going to have conversations, which is cool."

The Yankees had reloaded, and their competitors were raring for the fight, especially the Toronto Blue Jays. "Last year was the trailer. Now you guys are going to see the movie," boasted infielder Vladimir Guerrero Jr., one in a constellation of talents who cemented the Jays' status as the sexy pick in the American League East.

Young, bold, and studded with marquee names like Guerrero, Cavan Biggio, and Bo Bichette, all of whom carried the swagger of their All-Star fathers' achievements, Toronto and the perpetually nimble Tampa Bay Rays looked to be the division's favorites; the "win-forever" Yankees seemed to sport the agility of a cruise liner, building their game plan around three-run homers. Oddsmakers forecasted every team except the rebuilding Baltimore Orioles to post a winning record, and Cole observed that the AL East would be "no messing around."

Opening Day approached, and with it, Judge's self-imposed deadline. Between at-bats, Judge checked his phone for updates from his agents. He remained optimistic, though as he stood at his Steinbrenner Field locker one March morning, Judge noted, "It's a short window. We'll see what happens." The turmoil prompted a brief conversation between Judge and Boone in the manager's office, where Boone was pleased to find that Judge's focus had not wavered.

"The bottom line is, there is a business side to this sport, and we all understand and respect and navigate our way through it," Boone said.

A misstep by Carlos Beltrán, making his debut as a color commentator for the YES Network, added intrigue. During an April 4 exhibition against the Phillies, Beltrán seemed to hint that he knew something the audience didn't.

"I'm just glad to see him being able to create this new contract with the New York Yankees and being able to extend his stay here in New York," Beltrán said.

What had Beltrán heard? As a retired outfielder who once spent a spring lockering next to Judge and served a brief stint in the Yankees' front office as Cashman's special advisor, Beltrán certainly had the right connections to score a scoop. The comment set off alarm bells, but Beltrán swiftly called Cashman to apologize, and clarified that he had only intended to say that he *hoped* Judge and the Yankees would reach an agreement. It was arguably the first, but not the last, piece of misinformation that would be floated concerning Judge's contract.

"Carlos, he's my man," Judge said. "I think he was just looking out, trying to have my back a little bit there."

As a pair of trucks loaded with Yankees equipment raced the auto carriers moving the players' vehicles on Interstate 95 north from Tampa to New York, the Yankees had made their last, best offer of the spring. They would go no further than seven years and $213.5 million; in the months that followed, some members of the front office would question if any number could have brought the deal to the finish line at that time.

Rain fell in New York City on the slate-gray morning of April 6. Seated behind his desk at Yankee Stadium, Brian Cashman glanced over the intersection of Jerome Avenue and the Macombs Dam Bridge. Opening Day would be a washout, and the general manager burned a few minutes by flipping through a thick packet, prepared daily by the club's media relations department. Poring over the hodgepodge of xeroxed newspaper clippings and internet printouts, Cashman was surprised to see that none of the outlets regularly covering the Yankees had reported the details of the offer to Judge. It was only a matter of time before someone leaked the numbers, he thought.

Cashman had spent the better part of his quarter century as a GM tightening the Yankees' infamously leaky information spigot. The turning point had come in a mid-2000s showdown with George M. Steinbrenner, when Cashman insisted on silencing the faction of the club's splintered hierarchy closest to the Boss. For years, Cashman and his deputies in New York could—and would—be overruled by Steinbrenner's favored lieutenants in Tampa, Florida. Cashman never seemed sure who had the Boss's ear on any given day; that had to change if he was to perform his duties correctly. Some Tampa old-timers were phased out after October 2005, while other benched voices were brought back into the fold. One was Gene "Stick" Michael, an infielder of the 1960s and '70s who served stints as a GM, manager, and superscout. Michael was widely credited with helping build the late 1990s dynasty, possessing the fortitude and vision to hold on to talents like Bernie Williams, Derek Jeter, and Mariano Rivera while Steinbrenner served a suspension. Cashman went to bat for him, telling Steinbrenner and general partner Steve Swindal that Michael's voice needed to be added back to the inner circle.

Then came November 2008. In failing health, Steinbrenner officially ceded day-to-day control of the club to his sons, Hank and Hal. As early as 2003, Steinbrenner had spoken of a day when he might "let the young elephants into the tent," and now the time had arrived. Hank Steinbrenner showcased his dad's bluster, swigging from bottles of Heineken with a cigarette in hand, opining like a sports talk radio caller on moves the team could or should make. Hal Steinbrenner was younger and more fastidious, having cut his financial teeth by overseeing a collection of seven profitable hotels in Florida and Ohio, catering to travelers under corporate umbrellas like Marriott, Fairfield Inn, and Holiday Inn. By 2009, when the Yankees christened their new $1.3 billion stadium with a championship, Hal Steinbrenner was firmly in control—the one who took to the field to receive the Commissioner's Trophy.

Hal watched the bottom line closely, mindful of exceeding luxury tax thresholds and repeatedly remarking that no team should need to field a $200 million payroll to contend for a championship. Inflation and the game's health shifted that stance slightly by the spring of 2022; Steinbrenner would now allow that $300 million should be plenty to field a team with title aspirations. As they discussed the Judge offer, Cashman told Steinbrenner that the figures would leak out, given the scrutiny of their media market and the player's importance. It could come from someone connected to the Yankees, the Judge-Odle camp, or perhaps someone in the inner circles of Major League Baseball. "I just know there's no secrets," Cashman said. Cashman suggested the team take control by announcing the numbers, volunteering to do it himself. Steinbrenner told him to go ahead.

"I think Cash's idea was, it's going to get out anyway," Steinbrenner said. "Let's be transparent about it so the correct information gets out there for our fans, because our fans want to know. They wanted to know that we were making a real effort."

Cashman told Jason Zillo, the club's director of media relations, that he wanted to speak to the media before the first pitch was thrown on Opening Day. A press conference was hastily scheduled for 11:15 a.m., and reporters hustled from the playing field and press box to hear what some anticipated could be an announcement of a Judge extension. Instead, Cashman stunned the group by revealing the offer with unprecedented clarity. Cashman initially announced the rejected terms as eight years and more than $230 million, a bit of creative accounting on the club's part; it included a $17 million salary for Judge in 2022, so the actual extension was $213.5 million over seven years.

"I think as an industry, people were like, 'That's a really high offer,'" Cashman said. "Aaron turned it down, moving forward and betting on himself."

Considering it would likely be his only opportunity to cash in at the highest levels, Judge thought the offer was too low. A seven-year deal would take Judge through his age-thirty-eight season. By that time, he might be in the twilight of his career. At six foot seven and 282 pounds, he was the largest player in the big leagues. In baseball history, only six position players who weighed at least 250 pounds were still playing at age thirty-seven: designated hitters Jim Thome and Miguel Cabrera, and four catchers: A. J. Pierzynski, José Molina, Erik Kratz, and Corky Miller. None were outfielders. But who really could say how Judge, already an outlier among outliers, would age?

Judge was unlike almost anyone else in other ways, too. Only four homegrown players have ever hit 300 home runs in a Yankees uniform: Lou Gehrig, Joe DiMaggio, Yogi Berra, and Mickey Mantle; Mantle was the most recent, having hit No. 300 on July 4, 1960. Mantle played his final game in 1968, so even with all the titles in the late 1970s and the late '90s, an entire generation of fans had not seen the franchise develop a home run hitter like Judge.

In the press conference room, there was frantic scribbling in notebooks, then rapid tapping on cell phones as the beat reporters raced to be the first to drop the terms of the offered contract on Twitter. As Cashman continued to speak in his peppy monotone, a few reporters exchanged glances of surprise and raised eyebrows.

"As Cash was talking, I was thinking, 'Holy shit. This is not going to end well. Judge is not going to be happy about this,'" said Kristie Ackert of the New York *Daily News*. "It seemed like they were going to war."

"$213.5 million is a lot of money," said Brendan Kuty of *NJ Advance Media*. "But we don't know what he means to the Yankees from a box office standpoint. He's not Mike Trout; he's Arnold Schwarzenegger. He's Brad Pitt, Bruce Willis. People go to the movies because their names are on the title, and Aaron Judge is that guy for the Yankees."

Cashman said that he briefed Odle of the club's plan to announce the figures, but Judge was furious at the turn of events. "I don't like talking numbers. I like to keep that private," he said. Judge vowed to test free agency at the end of the season, when he'd invite all thirty teams to make their best offers.

"We kind of said, 'Hey, let's keep this between us,'" Judge said. "I was a little upset that the numbers came out. I understand it's a negotiation tactic. Put pressure on me. Turn the fans against me; turn the media on me. That part of it, I didn't like."

Most of the 46,097 fans filtering through Yankee Stadium's maze of metal detectors were blissfully unaware of the contract developments. Only cheers were heard when public address announcer Paul Olden gleefully announced Judge's name and position in the starting lineup, an octave or two higher than he had rattled off the identities of the Boston Red Sox.

The Yankees were again staring across the field at the Red Sox, a rematch of the Wild Card Game that saw Cole's first "normal" season in New York end on a sour note. An intensely serious student of the art of pitching, one who could leave teammates mystified after detailed dugout conversations, Cole also had a goofy side. Southern California born and bred, Cole was passionate about fine wine and Italian cuisine.

He had fully embraced life as a not-quite-so-cool dad in the two years since he and his wife, Amy, welcomed a son, Caden, during the lockdown days of the pandemic. In describing the Red Sox as a formidable opponent, Cole said that he saw the historic rivals as "two stags locking up in the forest; somebody's going to break an antler every once in a while, but nobody's certainly going to back down."

And it was a good show; this one decided in the eleventh inning as Donaldson stroked a bouncing ball past two diving Red Sox defenders, leaving Boston second baseman Trevor Story rolling gloveless on the outfield grass. Isiah Kiner-Falefa slid home with the winning run as the Yankees celebrated a gritty 6–5 win over their archrivals.

"The energy in the stadium, the atmosphere was pretty electric," Donaldson said. "It doesn't get any bigger than this."

There were plenty of firsts, including pinstriped debuts for Donaldson and Kiner-Falefa, among others. After two pandemic-affected Opening Days, it marked a return to normalcy in the Bronx—perhaps with too much pomp and circumstance for Cole, who barked, "Let's go! Let's go!" as pregame ceremonies (including actor and comedian Billy Crystal's first pitch, low and outside) ran four minutes long.

Cole called the micro-delay "an unforeseen challenge," as was Boston's loud contact in the first inning, an unwelcome flashback to the Wild Card Game. Cole heard boos as J. D. Martinez doubled home Xander Bogaerts with the third Red Sox run, then righted himself to offer four innings and sixty-eight pitches—close to his limit, given the abbreviated spring.

The Yankees powered back, flexing their muscle. Anthony Rizzo launched a two-run homer in his first at-bat of the season, then Giancarlo Stanton awed the crowd with a 116.3 mph rocket that left the playing field in 3.5 seconds. DJ LeMahieu homered in the eighth, and the normally stoic infielder felt the moment, screaming as he rounded the bases. Gleyber Torres rode the bench as the odd man out in a crowded infield mix, then was summoned for a crucial opportunity in the tenth inning, battling encroaching shadows to lift a key sacrifice fly.

"That," Judge said, "was one of the best Opening Days I've been to here at Yankee Stadium. The place was rocking. It almost felt like kind of a playoff game. Hats off to the fans. I think they'd been missing some Yankees baseball."

'61 FLASHBACK: THE MVP

Roger Maris wore a polo shirt, corduroy jeans, and white buckskin shoes as he stepped off the airplane at New York's LaGuardia Airport early in 1960, collecting his bags and readying to begin a new chapter with the Yankees. Entire rosters of athletes have grown up lusting for an opportunity to wear the storied pinstripes, honing their skills with aspirations to play under the brightest of lights.

Maris was not one of them. After breaking into the majors with the Cleveland Indians early in the 1957 season, Maris had been enjoying his time with the Kansas City Athletics, making his first All-Star team the previous summer. He, his wife, Pat, and a growing family would have been just fine continuing to live in their comfortable and spacious Raytown, Missouri, home.

That changed on December 11, 1959, when the Yankees and A's consummated a seven-player trade—yet another installment of a lopsided transaction list between the clubs, prompting many of the era to view Kansas City as just another Yankees farm team. The A's received outfielder Hank Bauer, pitcher Don Larsen, first baseman Marv Throneberry, and outfielder Norm Siebern in exchange for Maris, first baseman Kent Hadley, and infielder Joe DeMaestri.

Maris got the news while greeting customers in an Independence, Missouri, supermarket, part of an offseason gig with a Kansas City meatpacking firm.

"A customer walks up to me and tells me how nice he thinks it is I'm getting a break with the Yankees," Maris said. "I thought the fellow was kidding and I phoned my wife to find out if she had heard anything. She told me she had just heard it on radio and she was so surprised she could barely talk."

Assigned uniform No. 9 by Pete Sheehy, who'd overseen the clubhouse since Ruth's days, Maris scored no points for tact when he arrived for spring training in St. Petersburg, Florida, and told the press that he was "not all that happy" coming to the Yankees. "I liked Kansas City," he said. "I expected to play out my career there." Mickey Mantle was the golden boy in New York, the superstar center fielder and the latest in a four-decade line of succession that could be traced from Babe Ruth to Lou Gehrig to Joe DiMaggio.

Despite his down-home Oklahoman drawl, Mantle played the part. A fair-haired superman, the Mick flashed thick wads of cash and dressed in a tailored wardrobe he stashed at Yankee Stadium. Fueled by black coffee and Camel cigarettes, Maris preferred seersucker jackets from Sears Roebuck and a flattop crew cut—New York's barbers gave out a "glamour boy" look that Maris couldn't stand.

In short, Roger Eugene Maris—born in Hibbing, Minnesota, and raised in Grand Forks and Fargo, North Dakota—was a ballplayer, through and through. "Big Julie" Isaacson was a friend of several players and writers, a heavyset six-foot-three Brooklynite who had volunteered to drive Maris from the airport to a hotel at 43rd Street and Eighth Avenue. This was the 1960 of Don Draper's *Mad Men*. Gentlemen wore jackets, hats, and ties, especially in New York City.

Eyeing Maris's white shoes, Isaacson remarked, "Listen, kid. Yankee players don't dress like you. You've got these Pat Boone shoes. They've got to go."

As they arrived at the hotel, Maris asked Isaacson if a Thom McAn shoe store was nearby —a moderately priced chain that enjoyed its heyday with back-to-school shoppers in the 1960s and 1970s. Over Isaacson's objections, Maris bought two more pairs of the Pat Boones, just to prove his point.

"The hell with them," Maris said. "If they don't like the way I look, they can send me back to Kansas City."

New York was still very much Mantle's town as Maris stood near Yankee Stadium's home plate on a raw and windy Tuesday afternoon, Opening Day of the 1961 baseball season. A meager crowd of 14,607 filed in, with many potential patrons scared off by an ugly forecast. It was the first game for the Minnesota Twins, who stood in the visiting dugout wearing crisp red, navy, and gray. The American League had expanded from eight teams to ten, and the Twins and Los Angeles Angels were the new uniforms on the scene.

The Twins were just the rebranded Washington Senators, who had moved from the nation's capital. The expansion team was a different Senators outfit, one that would eventually become the Texas Rangers. To maintain a balanced schedule, the regular season was extended by eight games, from 154 to 162. Some two dozen pitchers who wouldn't have cracked a 1960 roster were now big leaguers, an appetizing recipe for increased offensive production.

Not that Maris was aiming for Ruth's record. He'd been asked about it during a January appearance in Rochester, New York, speaking at a local Press and Radio Club dinner.

"Nobody will touch it," Maris said. "Look up the records and you'll see it's a rare year when anybody hits 50 homers, let alone 60 as Ruth hit in 1927."

Maris was deeply uncomfortable in front of audiences and came to detest the banquet circuit; he vowed not to accept any such engagements after the 1961 season.

Seated in a box next to home plate were the "first ladies of baseball." Mrs. Babe Ruth, Mrs. Lou Gehrig, and Mrs. John McGraw looked on as Maris prepared to receive the 1960 American League Most Valuable Player Award. It had been a razor-sharp vote the previous November, with Maris edging Mantle, 225 points to 222. Maris hit .283 with 39 home runs and 112 runs batted in during the 1960 season, leading the American League in RBIs and slugging percentage (.581), while winning a Gold Glove in right field.

"The pitching is so tough and the defense is so good that you are doing pretty good if you hit .280 and get your share of home runs," Maris said. "Fellows who have been around a long time like Ted Williams, Yogi Berra and Mantle will tell you the same thing. You don't see any .400 hitters any more."

"I think Mickey helped him a lot," Tony Kubek said. "Mickey took him under his wing in New York; Roger was MVP the year before, so there were a lot of expectations for Roger going into '61."

But Maris couldn't understand why it had to be so black and white, with someone always having to be the bad guy. As he'd later tell Mike Shannon, a teammate with the St. Louis Cardinals, Maris had resolved to take his frustration out on the American League's pitchers.

When Maris arrived for spring training in '61, there was a new face in the manager's office. Casey Stengel was out, the ever-quotable "Old Pfessor" deemed too long in the tooth after his Yankees lost a crushing World Series to the Pittsburgh Pirates in seven games. The Yankees had attempted to spin Stengel's exit as a retirement, but Stengel revealed the truth almost immediately.

"I'll never make the mistake," Stengel said, "of being seventy again."

Ralph Houk held the reins now, promising more stability than Stengel, whose constant lineup shuffling, platoons, and love of pinch-hitting had upset the veterans. Nicknamed "the Major" for his army service during World War II, when he received the Bronze Star, the Purple Heart, and the Silver Star, the cigar-chomping Houk was a former backup catcher who would be no pushover. There would be hell to pay, Houk promised, if any of his players were found on a golf course the day of a night game. He disliked his men playing poker, dice, or consuming hard liquor in public. But Houk promised to pick a lineup, stick with it, and speak to his players face-to-face. Previously, most Yanks had to read a newspaper to know how Stengel felt about them.

The addition of Los Angeles thrust the Yankees into the jet age; they had been the last team in the American League to adopt air travel, still traveling by rail as far west as Kansas City. Now they were flying high in more ways than one. Houk knew the clearest path to a championship was to have Maris and Mantle healthy, hitting back-to-back in the lineup.

Keeping Mantle on the field was no simple task. He played almost all of his eighteen-year career with a torn anterior cruciate ligament, sustained when his spikes got caught in a storm drain while chasing a Willie Mays fly ball during the 1951 World Series. DiMaggio had called Mantle off, and the rookie dutifully ceded to the graceful legend.

"I was running as hard as I could to get over to it, because Casey had told me before the game how Joe had slowed up a little bit, he thought," Mantle once said. "Well, anyway, when I get there, Joe is already standing under the ball. He said, 'I got it.' And you don't want to run into Joe DiMaggio. So when I tried to stop—I was going as fast as I could—my back cleat in my spike stuck in a rubber drain, and when it did, my knee went right out through the front of my leg, and I just folded up on the field."

Mantle had said that his right knee was "destroyed" by the injury; the outfielder underwent several operations to repair the ACL, medial collateral ligament, and meniscus injuries that essentially went undiagnosed and unrepaired by surgical methods of the era.

Oh, what Mantle would have given to play his career with today's medical advances: when forty-two-year-old Mariano Rivera sustained a similar injury in May 2012, he'd returned as good as ever, posting a 2.11 ERA in his final season before tearfully handing the baseball to Derek Jeter and Andy Pettitte on the Yankee Stadium mound.

Alas, the swaggering Mantle limp, practiced lovingly by scores of schoolboys like Billy Crystal of Long Beach, New York, was no act. The uniform pants hid Mantle's mummified tape job, wrapped in rubber from the thigh to the ankle. It was not uncommon for Mantle to be reduced to helplessness on days when his achy legs flared up; a teammate might have to grab Mantle's wrist and pull him out of a taxicab, for example.

"There are a lot of things I wish I could do over," Mantle said in 1986. "Hey, if I knew I was still going to be alive now, I'd have taken care of myself. When I had knee surgery in 1951, I never did the exercises. Maybe if I had, my legs would have lasted longer. I don't know. I was young. I figured it was never going to end."

Early in 1961, Houk was asked how the expanded schedule might affect his star.

"I hope he plays 162 games, and if he hits 60 homers and Maris hits 59, they'll make me a hell of a manager," Houk said.

That was telling. Even in Houk's wildest fantasies, Ruth's record could only be tied, not eclipsed.

◆

4

SWINGING BIG

The season was less than a week old, and Aaron Judge feared he had made a mistake.

As he stood in right field at Yankee Stadium on the evening of April 12, five games and twenty at-bats into the season, his home run total rested at zero. He'd hit a few balls hard, including an eighth-inning double that helped the Yankees to their third win of the year. Still, as he kicked at a freshly sodded patch of Kentucky bluegrass, Judge could hear a selection of unfiltered comments from the Bleacher Creatures behind him, second-guessing his decision to turn down the cash.

"It was tough in the beginning, definitely in April," Judge said. "There is a little doubt that creeps in your mind about it. You're sitting there in the outfield, thinking, 'Man, I should have taken that deal.' I'm hitting .240, and I've got no homers. I'm like, 'Oh man, I think they're right.'"

Anthony Rizzo, Giancarlo Stanton, and DJ LeMahieu all slugged homers in the extra-inning Opening Day win over the Red Sox, followed by Rizzo and Stanton again the next night, then Aaron Hicks in a win over Toronto. Judge was being left out of the fun.

He paused, reminding himself why he and agent Page Odle had chosen this path. He'd personally spent long hours weighing the package with his parents, Patty and Wayne, and even more time discussing the future with his wife, Samantha. He'd prayed often, then leaned upon trusted teammates like Rizzo, LeMahieu, Cole, and Stanton, each of whom sprinkled their opinions and past experiences into the mixture.

Trust the process, Judge told himself, and it would work out.

"After a couple of weeks of talking with my teammates, talking with my family, you say, 'Hey, clear all that. Go out there and play and just be yourself, and everything's going to work out the way it's supposed to,'" Judge said. "It's all out of your hands, out of your control. Just have the faith to go out there and play your game."

It was the fifth inning, and as Cole zipped a fastball past the Blue Jays' George Springer for a strikeout, Judge pounded his glove and jogged toward the first-base dugout. Due up third that half-inning, Judge watched intently from the on-deck circle as Rizzo looked at a curveball out of the zone from right-hander José Berríos. That was the norm for Berríos, a twenty-seven-year-old from Puerto Rico who'd been around a while, relying primarily on his curveball, four-seam fastball, and sinker to navigate seven previous seasons, mostly with the Minnesota Twins.

Catcher Alejandro Kirk flashed his right index finger, suggesting a four-seam fastball, and Berríos nodded. Kirk dropped to a knee, placing his glove below Rizzo's kneecaps. Berríos missed the target badly, pumping a 93 mph offering at the top of the strike zone. It might as well have been on a tee. Rizzo launched the drive into the bleachers beyond the right-field wall, no cheap shot. Now the Yankees trailed Toronto, 3–1, and Judge wanted to keep the line moving.

The crowd was still buzzing as Rizzo placed his helmet into a cubbyhole above the bat rack. Digging his size 17 spikes into the right-handed batter's box, Judge heard a few beats of his walk-up song, Pop Smoke's "Hello." Judge craved a fat pitch, the kind of hit-me offerings that prompted him to remark that most homers are "thrown, not hit." Those had proven to be in short supply, but that was about to change. Berríos went into a windup and delivered his next pitch, a 91.9 mph sinker. Judge was ready.

HOMER #1: April 13 vs. Toronto Blue Jays' José Berríos (5th inning, solo)
Exit velocity: 108.4 mph. Distance: 413 feet. Launch angle: 27 degrees. HR in 30 of 30 MLB parks.

Like the previous pitch to Rizzo, Berríos's offering had missed its location, sailing toward the middle of the strike zone on the inside corner. Judge took a mighty cut and sent a drive toward the bleachers; Raimel Tapia, patrolling left field for Toronto, merely kicked his spikes at the dirt of the warning track. The Yankees had gone back-to-back (and, as long-time radio announcer John Sterling would say, "belly to belly"). More important, Judge was on the board, rounding the bases as the LED stadium lights twinkled above Yankee Stadium's white frieze.

"The first one, No. 10, 20, 30, the big numbers are usually the toughest ones," Judge said. "It's all the numbers in between that come in bunches."

The blasts from Rizzo and Judge cut the deficit to a run in a game they'd lose, 6–4, landing on the wrong side of an otherworldly Vladimir Guerrero Jr. performance. Appropriately, it was forty-four years to the day that the Yankees handed out chocolate bars at the turnstiles to honor Reggie Jackson, paying homage to his nickname-clinching feat of belting three home runs in a World Series game the previous October.

When Jackson went deep in the first inning of that home opener, thousands of the orange-wrapped, caramel-and-nougat treats had rained from the seats in tribute. Yankees pitcher Jim "Catfish" Hunter voiced the best line about that product: "When you unwrap a Reggie! bar, it tells you how good it is."

Across the street from where pounds of Mr. October's chocolate had once littered the turf, Guerrero put on a 3-homer show to remember, one decidedly less sweet for those in pinstripes. Two blasts were off Gerrit Cole, who literally tipped his cap to the young Jays star. "Did you see his night?" a stunned Cole remarked. "If you had a cap, you'd tip it, too."

New York completed their season-opening homestand a night later with a rain-delayed 3–0 victory, sending the club on the road to Baltimore's Oriole Park at Camden Yards, a jewel that ushered in the retro ballpark craze three decades earlier. Judge had long considered the ballpark one of his favorite hitting backdrops, having done plenty of damage in Charm City over the years, with 14 homers in just 35 career games. But that didn't translate in the first series there; Boone gave Judge a scheduled rest day in the opener, later remarking that he hadn't adequately considered the significance of the date—April 15, Jackie Robinson Day.

The Yankees lost two of three games over the weekend in Baltimore, traveling to Detroit to enjoy their first off day of the year. Judge saw an opportunity to get some swing work in, inviting Richard Schenck to fly in from Missouri. They agreed to meet in Waterford Township, Michigan, a community of plentiful lakes about thirty-five miles northwest of Comerica Park. Schenck had connected with Nick "Swanny" Swanson, director of the USA Prime Michigan Baseball & Softball Training Center.

"He looked on Google and found our place," Swanson said. "He was like, 'Hey, man, we're in town—my name's Richard. We're looking for a place to hit. Do you mind if I bring Aaron up there?'" At the time of their phone call, Swanson had one eye on a baseball tournament at Central Michigan University, watching young pitchers attempt to impress scouts. "Aaron who?" he replied, and Schenck offered the name of his famous client. "Holy crap," Swanson replied, dropping everything. "Absolutely, man. I'll see you on Monday."

Swanson kept a CLOSED sign on the door for Judge, who rode in an Uber from the team hotel with his wife, Samantha, carrying their miniature dachshund, Penny. As Judge and Schenck went through their checkpoints in the cage, Penny ran free on the artificial turf of the indoor facility, thrilled to have some space to burn energy.

"I swear to God, his wife is the nicest person I've ever met," Swanson said. "She was talking to us about life on the road. And so they came in, and they hit for forty minutes."

When Judge completed his session, he asked Swanson and a couple of other employees what they had thought. "We all kind of laughed, and we said, 'Pay the man!'" Swanson said. "He was dying laughing." Judge and Samantha called an Uber, waiting outside the facility, the former site of a thrift store nestled in a rusting strip mall between a Rent-A-Center furniture/electronics outlet and a shop offering sales and service on garage door openers.

"They're outside in our parking lot, throwing snowballs around, playing with their dog until their Uber came," Swanson said. "And I'm like, this is so cool."

As for Schenck? There were no snowballs tossed. His Motown visit was all business.

"We're teacher and student," Schenck said. "I'm old enough to be his grandpa, so we don't hang out. We don't go to dinner or have a drink together. I go to the city and find a place to hit. I'll go to the game if I get tickets from him; watch him play and take video. If I see something important, I'll text him, but our relationship is just about hitting."

The conditions were miserable for that series in Detroit; 43 degrees with 19 mph winds in the opener, a day that reminded the Yankees why travel agents never suggested the Motor City in early spring. Judge managed three hits, including a double, as the Yanks took two of three. Asked about his home run production, Judge offered a bit of foreshadowing, remarking: "They'll come. It's just a matter of time, but they'll come." With thirteen games in the books, the Yankees carried a 7-6 record back to New York for their second homestand. It was going to be a fun one. For one thing, Judge's thirtieth birthday was coming up; Yankees players and staffers whispered excitedly about the event, which promised to be an all-out banger. First, they needed to take care of business on the field, welcoming the Cleveland Guardians to town.

It was Cleveland's first visit to New York since the franchise scrapped their "Indians" moniker, nixing a nickname that had drawn decades of demonstrations by Native Americans and their supporters. The club's red, white, and navy blue colors remained the same, but their grinning Chief Wahoo logo was in mothballs. A Tom Hanks–narrated video announced that the club would now honor the Guardians of Traffic, a set of art deco monuments that overlooked the east-west movement on Cleveland's Hope Memorial Bridge since 1932.

No matter what they called themselves, manager Terry Francona's club seemed overmatched as they arrived in the Bronx, committed to a youth movement. Cleveland had not celebrated a World Series championship since 1948, the plotline of the movie *Major League* remaining relevant nearly four decades after its theatrical release. Burn on, big river: by all indications, this wouldn't be their year.

Boone thought he noticed something different as he made his rounds in the clubhouse before the game, performing his routine check-ins to ask about sore legs or arms. His focus locked upon Judge. "He kind of had that look in his eyes," Boone said. "Sometimes he tells me that he's got us. And he gave me that look right before the game, like, 'I got this.'"

> **HOMER # 2**: April 22 vs. Cleveland Guardians' Eli Morgan (3rd inning, two-run)
> *Exit velocity: 112.0 mph. Distance: 397 feet. Launch angle: 34 degrees. HR in 25 of 30 MLB parks.*
> **HOMER # 3**: April 22 vs. Cleveland Guardians' Tanner Tully (5th inning, solo)
> *Exit velocity: 112.0 mph. Distance: 364 feet. Launch angle: 19 degrees. HR in 24 of 30 MLB parks.*

There was no score in the third inning as the Yankees came to bat, with clear skies and temperatures in the mid-sixties. Eli Morgan was on the mound, a Gonzaga University product beginning his second big-league season and standing less than a month shy of his twenty-sixth birthday. Primarily a fastball-changeup artist who occasionally sprinkled in a slider, Morgan issued a five-pitch, two-out walk to DJ LeMahieu, bringing Judge to the plate.

Morgan fell into a 3-1 count and had to challenge, rearing back to throw a 91 mph fastball. Judge connected, sending a drive toward the right-field bullpen for his second home run of the year. The Yankees had an early lead, and as Judge remarked, "With our pitching staff, we've just got to get them one run, and I feel like we're in a good spot." The weekend fun was just getting started. Judge contributed on defense, making a strong fifth-inning throw from center field to third base that cut down an over-aggressive Andrés Giménez, then stood on deck for his third at-bat.

New York led, 3–1, as Judge eyed Tanner Tully, a twenty-seven-year-old left-hander making his debut. It had been a long and winding path to the majors for Tully, a twenty-sixth-round pick from Elkhart, Indiana. He had benefited from an early-season rules change that permitted clubs to carry twenty-eight players rather than the usual twenty-six, a nod to the effect that a lockout-abbreviated spring might have on pitchers' stamina. After years of bouncing from places like Lake County to Lynchburg to Akron to Columbus, the six-foot-two hurler was on the mound at Yankee Stadium. LeMahieu grounded out to shortstop, bringing up Judge, who worked the count full.

Tully pumped a 92.3 mph fastball toward the outside corner, and Judge lashed a low line drive toward the short porch in right field for his second home run of the night, its four seconds of hang time scarcely offering outfielder Josh Naylor more than a cursory glance. From a coast away, Mike Batesole had to chuckle. As his phone lit up with text messages from Fresno State alumni that read things like "Big Ass Blast!" the former head baseball coach knew that "BAJ" had gone deep again.

"He's made for Yankee Stadium," Batesole said. "There's always a thirteen-year-old kid in Little League who makes the field look small, and his line drives go over guys' heads or out of the ballpark. That's what Judge does in the big leagues. That right-field porch is an accident; you don't have to get sixty percent of it, but what are you going to do?"

The Yankees would celebrate a 4–1 win, and though Judge was now hitting .280 with 3 homers through 14 games, he was still striking out too frequently for his taste. He stood in the center of the oval-shaped home clubhouse, in front of a pull-down backdrop that showcased the club's interlocking "NY" logo, and seemed nonplussed.

"You can't base how the season will go off fourteen games," Judge said. "I just happened to get a hold of a few tonight."

The next day brought the Yanks' first big on-field controversy of the season. With Cleveland looking to close out a one-run lead in the ninth inning, Isiah Kiner-Falefa lashed a drive that sent rookie left fielder Steven Kwan in pursuit. Kwan crashed into the wall, sending Tim Locastro racing home with the tying run. Kiner-Falefa pulled into second base with a double, and Kwan staggered around the warning track, requiring medical attention to evaluate a possible concussion. The fans in left field celebrated his injury, jeering Kwan, who was bleeding from his chin and forehead. Myles Straw, Cleveland's center fielder, took issue with some of the comments, climbing the outfield fence for a face-to-face confrontation.

"Some of the things that were said to him, just for me, they weren't going to fly," Straw said. "My emotions got to me a little bit."

When play resumed and Gleyber Torres followed with a walk-off single to right field, fans in the right-field seats began throwing beer cans, ice cream, and other leftover concessions at Straw and right fielder Oscar

Mercado. It was an ugly scene, prompting Judge, Giancarlo Stanton, and others to abandon their celebration in shallow right field, running to the outfield wall in hopes of calming the situation. They were too late; the damage was done. Mercado called the display "classless," and Straw went further, calling the Bronx faithful "the worst fan base on the planet."

"I didn't know what was going on, but that can't happen," Kiner-Falefa said. "I love the atmosphere; I love the fans. I love everything about them, but we want to win with class. That's something that this organization is about; it's about class. We'll fix it next time, I hope."

Extra security was hired for the series finale, where Straw was mercilessly booed in a 10–2 thumping, the Yanks coasting to their first true laugher of the season. Straw would later recount receiving death threats from some claiming to be Yankees fans; he'd shrugged them off, saying, "People say all kinds of stuff all the time." Cole, enjoying his first win of the year, quipped: "Everybody can breathe today, right?" Yes, it sure felt that way.

Good timing, too, because a milestone birthday party was on the agenda. Samantha led the charge in planning the event, renting out a New York venue and selecting a large cake with four six-inch sparklers breathing fire. Guests had been asked not to share content on social media, but, of course, a few clips and photos leaked. Judge donned an orange Hawaiian shirt as he was presented with the cake, Drake's "Ratchet Happy Birthday" blasting over the loudspeakers. Judge beamed, planting a kiss on Samantha. With thirty on the horizon and a new marriage taking shape, Judge sure seemed to have met a new level of focus and security—impressive for a man who'd already been one of the game's best.

"Having someone every night that I could go home to and be like, 'Hey, I've got some things on my mind,' she was that rock in my life," he said.

Judge was thrilled by the turnout for the event, which included many of his teammates. Like CC Sabathia in years before him, Judge believed in the importance of developing relationships and uniting the clubhouse, which meant prioritizing finding ways to spend time together away from the field. Team dinners were frequent, especially on the road; on Judge's watch, the Yankees would never be confused with the 1978 Boston Red Sox, of whom Peter Gammons memorably wrote: "25 players, 25 cabs."

"When everyone finds out you're on the Yankees, their first question is, 'What's Aaron Judge like?'" said pitcher Michael King. "He's unlike anybody I've ever met, because he's such a superstar, but he treats everyone like they're the star. I remember I got called up in 2019 and didn't really know anybody. He came up to me in the trainers' room and said, 'About damn time you're here, Kinger!' It made me feel so good about myself. I absolutely love that about him. It's not about him; he just wants us to be a team."

HOMER #4: April 26 vs. Baltimore Orioles' Alex Wells (8th inning, solo)
Exit velocity: 98.5 mph. Distance: 392 feet. Launch angle: 34 degrees. HR in 29 of 30 MLB parks.

The Orioles arrived in town on Judge's actual birthday, April 26, and the series opener proved to be a slugfest. Eight homers were hit in the game, highlighted by the first 3-homer game of Rizzo's career. Acquired from the Chicago Cubs at the season's midpoint in 2021, Rizzo had almost instantly seemed like a good fit in pinstripes, joining a legacy of slugging left-handed first basemen that featured names like Don Mattingly, Tino Martinez, Jason Giambi, and Mark Teixeira.

Since the switch-hitting Teixeira retired at the end of the 2016 season, the Yanks had employed a revolving door at the position. They weren't wholly unproductive; the top buttons of his uniform jersey perpetually unbuttoned, Luke Voit had led the majors in homers during the pandemic-shortened 2020 campaign. But though he was beloved by teammates, Voit was a burly football player–type in baseball pants; Rizzo seemed like he'd been sent from central casting, showcasing a stroke and temperament custom-built for the Bronx.

"I was lucky to play in Chicago and be groomed in a big market," Rizzo said. "There's a different level to the big market, and you need to learn how to maneuver that. Playing baseball isn't enough; there are a lot of other things that come with that, and I enjoy doing those things. I enjoy taking the responsibility to do those things to stand up to talk to the media, good, bad, or indifferent. I think that teaches you a lot about this game of baseball and teaches you valuable lessons in your own life. Everyone loves you when you're good. The coaches, the media, your friends, everyone, you're the greatest thing on earth. But when things go bad, you find out who you are."

In Chicago, Rizzo had once seemed like part of the Windy City furniture, like Ferris Bueller, deep-dish pizza, and "Da Bears." He'd hoped to retire as a Cub, where he was a three-time All-Star and won four Gold Gloves. Rizzo bought an apartment in Chicago for the 2014 season and squeezed the last out of the 2016 World Series, the Cubs' first title since 1908. But negotiations on a contract extension had stalled, with Rizzo turning down offers of $60 million over four years, then $70 million over five. The Cubs dismantled the championship core that had delivered victory to Wrigley Field; Rizzo was traded to the Yankees, shortstop Javy Báez went to the Mets, and infielder-outfielder Kris Bryant landed with the Giants. Judge and Rizzo quickly sparked a friendship, the pair perpetually chatting away in the dugout and taking it off the field as well, hanging out and keeping things loose by wearing dog-themed Hawaiian shirts on travel days. Judge had clamored for the Yankees to re-sign Rizzo during the abbreviated off-season, staging an aggressive text messaging campaign.

"One thing I picked up a lot from Anthony through the past couple of years was how, from day one, he treated teammates and thinks ahead in games," Judge said. "He was somebody that I was like, 'OK, I can't wait to continue to learn from this guy and pick his brain.' For me, it started out just by watching and being around someone who's done a lot of great things."

Held to a seventh-inning single through his first four at-bats of the evening, Judge stepped in with two outs in the eighth inning, the Yankees ahead by two runs. On the mound was left-hander Alex Wells, navigating his second inning of relief. This marked the twelfth big-league game for the twenty-five-year-old Wells, a soft-tossing lefty from Australia—the thirty-sixth ever big leaguer to come from a land down under. The first pitch was an 87.3 mph fastball that miraculously snuck past Judge for a swinging strike. Catcher Robinson Chirinos had no desire to press his luck, flashing two fingers for a curveball. Wells delivered a breaker that hung, and Judge launched the 72.4 mph floater into the half-empty seats in left field.

"There were so many times I hit a homer, and I'd look to the guy on deck, which would usually be Anthony Rizzo," Judge said. "Everybody else has their hands in the air; they're cheering, they're going crazy. And I just see Anthony sitting there; he's getting his [bat weight] donut off and just not really smiling. I got no excitement out of him. So we've got to work on that a little bit. I don't know if [Rizzo was] mad at me for taking the RBI. I don't know what's happening."

Responded Rizzo: "No, I'm in my routine. I'm in my zone getting ready, because if you don't get the job done, it's on me. If I celebrate then and there, I'm not going to be doing my job. I have to try to stay focused."

So now it was Rizzo's turn, and as he lifted a ridiculously high drive toward right field, he stood in the batter's box for a few extra beats. It was definitely a foul ball, he thought, but there would be no harm in watching it. Then it started to slice ever so slightly, and . . . could it be? Rizzo tossed his bat aside, laughed as the ball clanged against the foul pole, and began trotting around the basepaths with the first 3-homer game of his career. "I was just shocked," Rizzo said. "I've never hit three homers in a game." The fans offered their approval with an honor that Rizzo said he would never forget: "A curtain call here at Yankee Stadium, that's special."

"He came as advertised, to be quite honest," said general manager Brian Cashman. "We knew he was beloved, not only by the Cubs' fan base but his teammates. We knew he was a tremendous defensive first baseman. We knew he was a great contact hitter from the left side with power. He's checked all of those boxes. We knew he had leadership capabilities and qualities, so he's been everything and then some."

The Yanks had won four in a row, making it five the next day behind Jordan Montgomery's solid start and more strong relief from King, who was quickly becoming a valuable multi-inning force out of the bullpen. A thoughtful right-hander who spent most of his childhood in Warwick, Rhode Island, breaking his father Jim's heart by choosing to purchase a Yankees cap during Game 5 of the 2003 American League Championship Series at Fenway Park, King wasn't shy about voicing his preference for starting. Boone had no desire to change a formula that worked so well, and King gamely accepted his assigned role.

"I think first things first is wins," King said. "So if Boonie thinks that I'm more valuable doing this, then I will gladly do it. If the time comes where he wants me to start, I will gladly do it. I just want to help the team win in as many ways as possible."

HOMER #5: April 28 vs. Baltimore Orioles' Paul Fry (8th inning, three-run)
Exit velocity: 113.6 mph. Distance: 415 feet. Launch angle: 23 degrees. HR in 30 of 30 MLB parks.

It was a getaway-day matinee in the Bronx, one the Yankees seemed to have well in hand. With New York leading by four runs, left-hander Paul Fry's goal was to record a few quick outs and get his teammates on their flight back to Baltimore.

It wouldn't be that simple. A walk, stolen base, hit by pitch, and a fielding error by shortstop Jorge Mateo loaded the bases for Judge. The twenty-nine-year-old Fry, a fastball-slider artist, missed badly with a wild pitch that sailed to the backstop as Tim Locastro trotted home with the Yanks' seventh run of the day.

Fry was all over the place, and with a 3-1 count on Judge, he was in trouble. The choice was a slider, and it wasn't a terrible pitch, dotting the strike zone low and inside. Judge was just better, and he clobbered it, sending fans down a stairwell in the left-field seats in pursuit of the three-run blast.

Though rookie Ron Marinaccio scuffled in the ninth, allowing three runs and prompting Boone to summon Lucas Luetge in relief, the Yanks held on for a 10–5 win. Judge was hitting .296 with 5 homers, and his team had posted six consecutive victories, their perfect homestand moving them into first place in the American League East. Judge's blast and postgame commentary were the clips that led the nightly sports recaps.

"From the beginning of the year, we saw Aaron take on more of a vocal leadership role," said Meredith Marakovits of the YES Network. "He was really becoming the face of the team, as far as somebody that was speaking to the media. Look, you could talk to Aaron Judge every day, just like you could have talked to Derek Jeter every day. People want to hear from them, regardless of what they do in the game."

Rizzo called it "a full team homestand" and said he believed "playing well at home is going to energize our fan base more and more throughout the summer, especially as it warms up." That made for a happy flight to Kansas City, where they opened a three-game series with the Royals the next night at Kauffman Stadium.

They were off and rolling early in the opener, as Rizzo and Giancarlo Stanton homered in a three-run first inning off starter Kris Bubic. Nestor Cortes twirled five innings of one-run ball before the Yanks salivated at the prospect of facing the soft underbelly of the Kansas City bullpen.

"We saw in there in the first inning; they already had a guy warming up after just four or five batters," Judge said. "Just continue to have quality at-bats, man. We do that, you know, good things are going to happen."

HOMER #6: April 29 vs. Kansas City Royals' Dylan Coleman (7th inning, three-run)
Exit velocity: 105.4 mph. Distance: 389 feet. Launch angle: 34 degrees. HR in 30 of 30 MLB parks.

Judge stood on deck as DJ LeMahieu stroked a liner toward shortstop Nicky Lopez, who booted the ball for a run-scoring error, giving New York a two-run lead. On the mound for the Royals was Dylan Coleman, a twenty-five-year-old from Potosi, Missouri, a city of about 2,660 in the suburbs of St. Louis. Coleman's first pitch was a 97 mph fastball that Judge swung through; the righty wouldn't get away with a second.

Coleman reared back and generated a little extra oomph on the next pitch, clocking 98.2 mph. Judge was ready, barreling it toward right-center field. Kansas City outfielder Edward Olivares raced toward the wall, seemingly having a bead on the drive as he approached the warning track. Olivares attempted a leap against an advertisement for National Car Rental, and Judge's drive had just enough gas in the tank. Olivares lost his cap as the ball clipped the top of the wall, ricocheting into a standing-room section for a three-run blast that put New York up, 7–2.

"That," Aaron Boone said, "was a big boy homer."

As Judge rounded the bases, Kansas City sounded like Yankee Stadium Midwest, a sizable contingent of the heartland having embraced the opportunity to see the Yankees on their turf. A torrential thunderstorm encroached upon the ballpark and sent fans scattering for cover; the game was called after eight innings, giving the Yanks their seventh straight win in a 12–2 decision. Judge rested the next day as the Yanks ran their win streak to eight, and though having Judge absent from the lineup was a bummer for the ticket-buying public, those one-day respites had historically re-energized Judge.

"I don't get it," Judge said with a laugh. "I think the biggest thing is keeping the body fresh, and when I swing at pitches in the zone, I feel like I can do some damage with them."

That proved to be the case almost immediately on a sunny Sunday afternoon.

HOMER #7: May 1 vs. Kansas City Royals' Daniel Lynch (1st inning, solo)
Exit velocity: 113.5 mph. Distance: 453 feet. Launch angle: 27 degrees. HR in 30 of 30 MLB parks.
HOMER #8: May 1 vs. Kansas City Royals' Josh Staumont (9th inning, solo)
Exit velocity: 106.8 mph. Distance: 395 feet. Launch angle: 35 degrees. HR in 30 of 30 MLB parks.

The Royals were unveiling their snazzy City Connect uniforms, paying homage to Kansas City's reputation as the city of fountains (said to have more such fixtures than Rome), and Daniel Lynch was trying not to get soaked. A six-foot-six lefty, Lynch was one of the Royals' better prospects, having merited a $1.7 million signing bonus out of the University of Virginia in 2018.

This was the nineteenth big-league start for Lynch, and it got off to a loud start. Lynch missed high with a heater for a ball, then tried another—a 93.9 mph offering grooved right down Broadway. Judge tattooed it, striking the 12-story center-field scoreboard shaped like the Royals' crest with a towering drive. In the YES Network broadcast booth, Carlos Beltrán (no stranger himself to long drives on that Kansas City diamond and elsewhere) marveled: "He makes it seem pretty easy." Ryan

Lefebvre, the Royals' play-by-play announcer for twenty-four seasons, said, "That's a first for me, and that's hit into a crosswind."

"The way he cleaned that first one out, man—it's hard to hit one more pure," Boone said.

Judge would later joke: "I pick my days at Kauffman. I've got to find the days when [the wind] is blowing out a little bit." As prodigious as the blast off the high-definition screen was, Judge's check-swing ground-out in the seventh inning was just as effective, a dribbler that sent Isiah Kiner-Falefa home with the tying run. Josh Donaldson followed with a fielder's choice that put the Yanks ahead.

With closer Aroldis Chapman throwing in the bullpen, preparing to protect a one-run lead, Judge aimed to provide more breathing room. Josh Staumont was on the mound, a twenty-eight-year-old from La Habra, California, about halfway between Los Angeles and Anaheim. He tried a couple of curveballs; Judge bit on neither. Now behind in the count, Staumont fired a 98 mph sinker over the heart of home plate. Judge clipped it, sending right fielder Hunter Dozier back to the wall, helpless to stop Judge from notching his second multi-homer game of the year.

"What can I say?" Luis Severino said in the visiting clubhouse. "The guy is a monster."

As Severino spoke, his teammates hurriedly prepared for their first visit north of the border, zipping their travel bags and fiddling with the ArriveCAN customs app on their cell phones to prepare for Canada's more stringent rules regarding COVID-19. Proof of vaccination was required for entry, which had offered the Blue Jays an unexpected home-field advantage for their games at Toronto's Rogers Centre. Unvaccinated Oakland Athletics and Red Sox players had already left their teams shorthanded for the trip across the border.

But the Yankees, Boone proudly reported, would not be missing anyone on their active roster. That was a topic during spring training, when it appeared unvaccinated Yankees and Mets might be barred from suiting up for home games.

New York City mandated individuals performing in-person work within the five boroughs to be vaccinated against the virus; notably, Brooklyn Nets guard Kyrie Irving refused the jab, prompting his bench-

ing for all home games and practices within the city limits. A survivor of
Hodgkin's Lymphoma who underwent six months of chemotherapy as a
Boston Red Sox prospect in 2008, Rizzo refused the vaccine during the
2020 and '21 seasons, saying he was "taking more time to see the data."
Judge similarly sidestepped inquiries about his status.

But when Mayor Eric Adams reversed course by easing the mandate
for professional athletes in late March, Irving returned to the hardcourt
in Brooklyn, while Judge, Rizzo, and any other Mets or Yankees would
be available to play in the Bronx or Queens. Greeting reporters at his
Steinbrenner Field locker that morning, Judge quipped: "I told you guys
that I wasn't too worried about it. If the mandate's not there, then I guess
it's good for Kyrie. He can play some home games and help the Nets out
a little bit."

Irving had not put the Nets over the top; their season had ended
in disheartening fashion eight days prior, swept out of the playoffs by
the Boston Celtics. But the Yankees were sizzling hot. Gleyber Torres's
two-run homer helped New York to a 3–2 victory in the series opener,
extending the winning streak to nine games. A six-run explosion in the
next night's game would push that to double digits, playing host to one
of the most electrifying, then heartwarming, moments of Major League
Baseball's 2022 season.

HOMER #9: May 3 vs. Toronto Blue Jays' Alek Manoah (6th inning, solo)
*Exit velocity: 114.9 mph. Distance: 427 feet. Launch angle: 25 degrees. HR in 30 of
30 MLB parks.*

A misty rain fell from the slate-gray sky outside Rogers Centre as
Mike Lanzillotta downed a cold pregame beer with a friend, Nigel Singh.
A theft management specialist for a chain of department stores in the
Toronto area, Lanzillotta clutched a couple of tickets for that night's
game against the Yankees. As they moved upstairs to the stadium's 200
level, the pals joked about how many "Loonie Dogs" they might put
down; the Jays' popular promotion set the price for each hot dog at just
one Canadian dollar.

They checked, then double-checked, their seating location. They'd purchased seats Nos. 3 and 4, but found that those were occupied. They plopped instead into seats Nos. 1 and 2, right on the aisle, and soon took notice of a young boy and his father cheering for the road team—loudly. Derek Rodriguez, age nine, was wearing his only article of Yankees attire, a freshly purchased shirsey with Judge's No. 99 screen-printed on the back.

A conversation was struck up, and Rodriguez's father, Cesar, filled in the blanks—he'd watched the dynasty-era Yankees on television for years before moving from Venezuela to Toronto, mentioning that his son had been named after Derek Jeter. Lanzillotta recalled that he had once snagged a foul ball as a twelve-year-old; he'd reached over the railing to grab a slow roller, with his grandfather holding his ankles to pull him back into the seats.

"I promise you, we're going to get you a ball tonight," Lanzillotta told the boy.

It was a tall order. They sat a few stories above the left-field wall, more than a football field from home plate. Lanzillotta and Singh shouted at the outfielders between each half-inning, but no warm-up balls were sent toward their seats. Lourdes Gurriel Jr., Toronto's left fielder, lobbed a toss about twenty-five feet away, where another fan snapped it up. At that point, young Derek was discouraged, turning his attention back to the game action.

Alek Manoah, the Blue Jays' fiercely demonstrative ace, had held the Yankees to two hits through five innings. A twenty-four-year-old from Homestead, Florida, Manoah had been the eleventh overall selection in the 2019 draft, receiving a $4.547 million bonus to leave the West Virginia Mountaineers a year early. Manoah vs. Judge was a heavyweight battle in more ways than one, interrupted briefly as Aaron Hicks was caught stealing second base by a strong throw from catcher Alejandro Kirk.

On the eighth pitch of the at-bat, with the Rogers Centre crowd applauding and standing, Manoah geared up for a 96 mph fastball. Judge hushed most of the audience, sending a rocket toward the second deck in left field. It cleared the fence for a game-tying blast, then kept soaring, heading directly for Lanzillotta's seat. He tracked the projectile intently, a beer spilling from his grasp as he yelled, "I got it! I got it!"

The ball clipped one of Lanzillotta's bare hands, glanced off Singh's cheek, then plopped right into their shared tray of Loonie Dogs. The hot dogs had been loaded with mustard and ketchup, and now they were soaked in beer, but miraculously none of the condiments appeared to have touched the ball.

"Judge hit that ball right to us," Lanzillotta said. "It couldn't have been more perfect. That was probably one of the most memorable moments of my life."

That baseball transformed from a run-of-the-mill souvenir to a touching, viral internet clip because of what transpired next. Lanzillotta did not hesitate; he'd given his word. He presented the baseball to Rodriguez, telling him: "Someday, you're going to be in my shoes and can make a kid happy. Promise me you'll pay it forward." The fourth grader agreed, embracing the stranger in the tightest of hugs as tears streaked his tiny cheeks.

"I was so happy. All I can remember is I said thank you, and I hugged him," Rodriguez said.

Judge's homer had sparked a six-run outburst, and the Yankees coasted to a 9–1 victory. By the time Judge stood in front of his locker, the clip of the homer's aftermath was already bouncing around the world, racking up hundreds of thousands of views in just a few hours. Told about the exchange that night, Judge grinned.

"That's what's special about this game, man," Judge said. "It doesn't matter what jersey you wear. Everybody is a fan; everybody appreciates this game."

Baseball knew it had a good story. At the invitation of the Blue Jays and Yankees, Lanzillotta and the Rodriguez family were on the field the next day for batting practice. Speaking quietly but confidently behind the batting cage, Rodriguez called Lanzillotta his "best friend" and detailed how he'd brought the baseball to school that morning, impressing his teacher and classmates. Everyone was invited to see the ball, but Rodriguez had been the only one allowed to touch it.

"I still can't believe it," Rodriguez said. "It's so amazing."

The Yankees invited the Lanzillotta and Rodriguez families to join them in the Bronx later in the season, where both would be seated in the right-field Judge's Chambers. Blue Jays outfielder George Springer rewarded Lanzillotta for his generosity with an autographed jersey, and when Judge later completed his rounds in the batting cage, he gestured toward Rodriguez, waving him into the visiting dugout. The boy reacted with the timidity of a child approaching Santa Claus's chair. Their brief chat delivered smiles, a big hug, and a few more tears as Judge crouched at the boy's eye level.

"I asked him who his favorite player was, and he turned around to show me his little jersey," said Judge, who signed the home run baseball and gave the boy a pair of his batting gloves. "That still gives me goose-bumps to this day, to see little kids wearing my number, wearing my jersey. I used to be in his position, that little kid, rooting on my favorite players and teams."

For an instant, Judge revisited his days of sports fandom, when he'd counted the San Francisco Giants as his preferred club. Barry Bonds was unquestionably the team's best player of that era, in the midst of four consecutive Most Valuable Player Awards and on a mission to eclipse Babe Ruth and Henry Aaron on the all-time home run list. Yet the young Judge thought he identified most with infielder Rich Aurilia, a fifteen-year veteran who made his lone All-Star appearance with San Francisco in 2001. Judge recalled that he liked Aurilia mostly because he wore No. 35, which had been Wayne Judge's preferred number. As such, the tallest kid in the Linden Little League used to emulate the crouched, compact batting stance of a lifetime .275 hitter.

"When I was looking up to some of my favorite athletes, how they acted and treated their fans and teammates, I wanted to be the guy that was always putting the team first, putting other people first," Judge said. "That's kind of how I was raised. It's what my family always told me to do, what my parents told me. Put the team first, put others first, and be a good team player. Being a role model is just something I take a lot of pride in, doing things right on the field and off the field."

The Yankees' eleven-game winning streak snapped that evening, featuring hot-tempered fireworks near home plate, an old-school act that began with manager Aaron Boone whipping a wad of chewing gum across the artificial turf. Ejected by home plate umpire Marty Foster, Boone had barked one too many times about low strikes called on Judge, a recurring theme for a player who had seen more than his share of those over the years.

In this particular sequence, Boone was irked by back-to-back at-bats where questionable pitches rung Judge up on called third strikes in the sixth and eighth innings. Judge was not one to show up an umpire; as a big leaguer, he has never engaged in theatrics like the ones Boone showcased that night, though Judge admits he had a few moments like that during his college days. "My college coach [Mike Batesole] told me, 'You're not an umpire; you're a hitter. Focus on hitting, and don't be complaining about calls.'"

Since then, Judge adjusted to make his comments quietly while digging into the box à la Derek Jeter. He was pleased that his manager went to bat for him.

"I appreciate it," said Judge. "I voiced my opinion to Marty during the game and let him know what I was thinking about the calls. At that point, that's all I can do. That's why I have a manager to stick up for me. If I get tossed in that situation, it's going to hurt us. He stood up for us and for me, and I appreciate it."

So about that winning streak, which began on April 22 against the Guardians—a string of sweeps over Cleveland, the Orioles, and the Royals, with New York then handing Toronto its first series loss of the year. It was a special blend of hitting, pitching, and defense, and players made contributions up and down the roster, but Judge was performing at an otherworldly level. He'd hit .357 (15-for-82) with 8 homers, 17 RBIs, and 12 runs scored during the streak.

A few days earlier, Boone had looked at Judge's numbers and thought, "Wait until he really gets going." Indeed. He now stood at .303 with 9 homers, in less than a month of play.

"It just speaks to how good of a player he is, and how good of a hitter he is," Boone said. "It just seems like he's kind of doing fine, and he hasn't even gone to that [level] where he really gets going, like Judgie can. Then it's scary. He's such a good hitter that prepares really well. The experience he's gained over the years, he uses it the right way, and it makes him a better, smarter all-around player."

The balanced Bombers led the American League in runs scored, home runs, and earned run average, striking out less and hitting the ball harder. The early returns on Brian Cashman's off-season objective of upgrading the club's run prevention were immensely positive. Pitchers like Nestor Cortes, Clay Holmes, and Michael King were showing that their '21 campaigns were no fluke, taking advantage of much tighter infield defense. "Generally speaking," Boone said, "we've been in the game every time they've taken the mound."

With an off night in New York, Judge, Anthony Rizzo, and DJ LeMahieu attended the New York Rangers playoff game against the Pittsburgh Penguins, clad in authentic Broadway Blueshirts jerseys and chugging beers on the Madison Square Garden video screen. According to LeMahieu, that was just one example of how the 2022 Yankees continued to bond as a unit, even when they were away from the diamond.

"Judge and Rizz, they tried to get everyone to do something off the field," LeMahieu said. "That just makes it a lot of fun to come to the field. Going to concerts or games, stuff like that, they're always thinking about, 'What can we do?' Judgie has always been a leader, and people follow him, but he became *the* leader of the team. He did more off-the-field stuff, trying to get the guys together and not have it be a repetitive season. It's such a long season, so it keeps it fresh, doing things off the field and keeping it loose. Bringing his personality onto the team a bit more is great for us."

Inclement weather washed out the next two games in New York, setting up a Sunday doubleheader and a Monday makeup game against the Texas Rangers; Nestor Cortes carried a no-hitter into the eighth inning of the finale, with the Yanks taking two of three games in the series. That brought the Blue Jays to town for a memorable series, one that would finally see a Judge long ball have the last word.

HOMER #10: May 10 vs. Toronto Blue Jays' Jordan Romano (9th inning, three-run, walk-off)
Exit velocity: 112.5 mph. Distance: 414 feet. Launch angle: 31 degrees. HR in 30 of 30 MLB parks.

Judge had hit 167 previous home runs in the big leagues, but he'd never belted one to end a game; in fact, the first walk-off hit of Judge's career hadn't come until the final day of the 2021 season, when his infield single had clinched the Yanks' Wild Card spot. That would change on a cloudy Tuesday evening in the Bronx, a moment that Judge's teammates would almost unanimously select as their most memorable homer of his 2022 season.

"I feel like it was the fourth or fifth big homer he'd hit that month," said DJ LeMahieu, "and it was just like he was on a different level. That's when I think it became very real."

It had been a spirited affair between division juggernauts that Boone described as a "heavyweight game in May," having already seen three ejections—Blue Jays pitcher Yimi García, pitching coach Pete Walker, and manager Charlie Montoyo were all watching from the visiting clubhouse, the result of a sixth-inning García pitch that drilled Josh Donaldson squarely on his left upper arm, immediately following a Giancarlo Stanton homer that sliced against the wind to squeak into the right-field porch.

"When Josh got hit, I think that kind of locked us all in and said, 'OK, it's go time,'" Judge said. "Especially me. It got me going a little bit."

The Jays had punched across a couple of eighth-inning runs against Chad Green, and the Yanks' challenge was to respond against closer Jordan Romano. Earlier in the season, the hard-throwing righty from Markham, Ontario, had established a new Toronto record by converting his twenty-sixth consecutive save opportunity, a feat that had come on April 11 in the Bronx. Clad in a T-shirt and workout shorts, the twenty-nine-year-old had stood near the third-base line to showcase the milestone baseball for photographers, drawing the Yankees' attention.

Romano fanned Isiah Kiner-Falefa for the first out, and as Jose Trevino gripped his bat tightly in the batter's box, the catcher thought: "Get A.J. up, give us a chance to win the ball game." Judge had ducked down the runway from Yankee Stadium's home dugout, where he was training his eyes against a high-velocity pitching machine: hissing fastballs and hellacious sliders, cranked as high as the gears would allow. Making eye contact with coaches Desi Druschel and Casey Dykes, Judge said: "If I get an opportunity to end this thing, it's over."

Trevino worked a six-pitch walk, prompting Judge to move toward the on-deck circle. Still under the fluorescent lights of the batting cage, Dykes told Druschel: "He said it, so I'm pretty sure it's going to happen." When Romano lost DJ LeMahieu to a free pass on five pitches, the Jays huddled on the mound, a meeting during which pitching coach Pete Walker detailed how they might best attack Judge. A strikeout would be swell; a double-play grounder even better. Romano nodded, accepting a pat on the rear from catcher Zack Collins. Chomping on a larger-than-usual chaw of Dubble Bubble, Judge looked at a slider for a called strike, then softly chopped the next pitch foul past third base. Romano went to the slider again, failing to tempt Judge on a pitch that Collins blocked in the dirt. Romano next tried a fastball and slider, tough pitches that Judge wasted foul.

"It's funny how people think you can jinx things," said Michael Kay, the YES Network broadcaster. "Right before that pitch, I said, 'Aaron Judge has never hit a walk-off home run in his career.'"

Romano returned to the slider for his sixth pitch and immediately regretted the execution, leaving an 84.1 mph hanger near Judge's belt buckle. Judge swatted it high and far toward left field, taking a good look as the baseball landed in the second deck. Months later, Judge's teammates spoke with excitement and larger-than-usual eyes as memories flooded back of that drive.

"I remember being on second base," Trevino said, "and I think the wind was blowing in that night. I was like, 'Oh man, I don't know if I should run, this ball might not get out.' And then I remember coming in and watching it, and I was like, 'Whoa. That ball went *far*.'"

Said Kyle Higashioka: "I feel like everybody just knew that it was going to happen. I feel like we even knew what pitch it was going to be on. We were like, 'If he hangs a slider here, he's going to hit it really far.' And then it happened, and it was just great. Second deck, he just crushed it. And we like beating the Blue Jays."

The Yankees deliriously vaulted out of the first-base dugout, ready to embrace their hero. Judge chuckled as he approached third-base coach Luis Rojas, then removed his batting helmet, performing his version of the "Griddy" dance that Minnesota Vikings receiver Justin Jefferson had turned into a favored touchdown celebration in the National Football League.

"It's a weird feeling," Judge said. "You hear the crowd going crazy, you look at your bench and you see your guys jumping over the railing, just getting all excited. It's a special moment that I got to share with them."

Giancarlo Stanton waited with double-fisted bottles of Poland Spring, dousing his pal as the rest of the club clapped Judge's back. In the players' cafeteria, Luis Severino whooped and hollered, having seen performances like this one from his fellow Baby Bomber many times over. "Everybody knows who Aaron Judge is," Severino said that night. "He is a great hitter, a great player. In situations like tonight, you know that Aaron Judge is going to come through."

In the press box, writers scrambled to edit their copy, shaking their heads at a remarkable season in which anything seemed possible as long as the Yankees kept a bat in Judge's hands.

"Especially when we were under pressure and had the chance to win the game or come back from being down, it seemed like he just stepped up and hit a huge home run every time," Higashioka said. "There were so many moments during the year that he stepped up in clutch situations and did whatever it took to help the team win."

5

◆

BEST VIEW IN THE HOUSE

It had been a dozen years and counting since the Yankees' most recent World Series appearance, marked by a brisk November 2009 evening when the Core Four of Derek Jeter, Mariano Rivera, Jorge Posada, and Andy Pettitte stood upon a podium in center field to claim their fifth and final championship title. That night, veterans like CC Sabathia, Alex Rodriguez, and Mark Teixeira tasted ultimate victory for the first and only time in their careers.

The organization had come close since then, losing a heartbreaking American League Championship Series to the Astros in seven games in 2017, then bested again by Houston in a six-game 2019 ALCS. Some in the Yankees hierarchy still grumbled about the sign-stealing scandal of '17, and continued suspicion of more misconduct in '19; as one longtime staffer remarked, "The fucking Astros cheated us."

But this 2022 squad, off to its best start in decades, felt like it could author a different conclusion. It was a team beginning to draw comparisons to the vaunted 1998 Yankees, widely regarded as one of baseball's most dominant wire-to-wire clubs. That squad, managed by Joe Torre, had recovered from losing four of its first five games to set a new American League record with 114 victories, steamrolling the San Diego Padres in a World Series sweep to claim the franchise's twenty-fourth title.

Though the 2001 Seattle Mariners would eclipse their regular-season win total with 118, Seattle had been unable to finish the job, upended by Torre's squad in the ALCS. When discussing the best teams in sports history, and certainly in baseball lore, the '98 Yankees were a benchmark. That group had their muscle memory from the 1996 title, having stunned the Atlanta Braves in the Fall Classic, boasting Jeter and Rivera coming into their prime alongside a veteran cast of All-Stars and future Hall of Famers.

It was early, sure. But as they approached the quarter post of the 2022 season, these Yankees seemed to have some of the same dominant DNA. For example, eight previous Yankees clubs started a season with twenty-five wins in thirty-four games, as the '22 team did. Eight had won the pennant, with six World Series titles. Aaron Judge was the thumping heartbeat of these Bombers, crushing fastballs with regularity, blasting homers to all parts of the ballpark, and now taking over as the everyday center fielder.

Judge loved center field, a place he called "the best view in the house." It was the position he'd played back at Fresno State, fittingly located just off California's Route 99, when the Yankees took him thirty-second overall in the 2013 draft. Center field had also been where Judge stood during his first workout with the Yankees on June 11, 2013, a fresh-faced draftee invited to spend time with big leaguers during a visit to the Oakland Coliseum. Judge recalled being awestruck as he entered the visiting clubhouse, where Andy Pettitte extended a meaty paw, saying in his Louisiana/Texas hybrid twang: "Hey, my name's Andy. Great to meet you, Aaron."

Judge had stammered; five-time World Series champion, three-time All-Star, most postseason wins in history? Yeah, he knew who Pettitte was. When veteran Brett Gardner jogged out of the dugout, Judge grabbed his glove and followed closely. Coach Rob Thomson stood near second base with a fungo bat and a bucket of balls, stroking grounders to the outfielders. Judge's first chance took a bad hop and skidded through his legs; his freckled cheeks burned as he chased it toward the center-field wall.

"It rolled right under him," Gardner said. "He just completely missed it; completely whiffed on it. Thoms has got a great sense of humor; he threw his bat down and maybe even kicked some dirt. He made Aaron think that he was mad at him or upset with him, and I was out there laughing. It was a pretty cool moment to see him that very first day."

Then Judge stepped into the batting cage, and suddenly no one in the ballpark was snickering about the way-too-tall kid with the gap-toothed grin. Vernon Wells, a veteran of fifteen big-league seasons with the Toronto Blue Jays, Los Angeles Angels of Anaheim, and Yankees, watched Judge's display that day with curiosity. Stone-faced, Wells told hitting coach Kevin Long: "It's probably time for me to retire."

The Yankees had moved Judge to right field in the minors; the idea of someone Judge's size manning center field simply too unimaginable, too unprecedented to be considered for the pro ranks. There was a six-foot-seven center fielder named Walt Bond in the early 1960s, but he'd played only eleven games there, for the Cleveland Indians and the Houston Colt .45s/Astros.

"The first thing they told me once I got drafted was, 'I know you played center field in college, but we've got [Jacoby] Ellsbury there in center, and he's going to be there for a long time,'" Judge said. "'So if you want to make this major league team at some point, you've got to learn to play right.' So I said, 'All right, I'm fine with that.'"

For years, the Yankees had been reluctant to revisit that discussion, treating it as a break-in-case-of-emergency option. His first start at the position generated headlines in 2018, nine uneventful innings on Toronto's artificial turf. Boone wouldn't rip that Band-Aid again until 2021, when Judge made twenty-one starts in center field. Boone still considered Judge a right fielder masquerading in center, but he'd appeared there eleven times in the Yankees' first thirty-four games of 2022, providing the manager with additional lineup flexibility as Opening Day center fielder Aaron Hicks continued to struggle.

As Judge walked through the visiting clubhouse at Chicago's unfortunately named Guaranteed Rate Field, home of the Chicago White Sox, he eyed his name on the lineup card posted on the set of large steel doors that led to the dugout. In Judge's mind, there was no question about where he belonged.

"I love right field," Judge said. "But I'm definitely a center fielder."

HOMER #11: May 12 vs. Chicago White Sox's Ryan Burr (7th inning, solo)
Exit velocity: 114.0 mph. Distance: 456 feet. Launch angle: 25 degrees. HR in 30 of 30 MLB parks.

It was a steamy scorcher on Chicago's South Side, with the first-pitch temperature registering eighty-eight degrees, and the Yankees came out swinging early. Giancarlo Stanton hit a pair of early two-run homers off White Sox ace Dylan Cease, who lasted only four innings, and New York held a 6–4 lead as Judge came to bat in the seventh inning.

Ryan Burr was on the mound for the Pale Hose, and the twenty-seven-year-old had appeared to be on the verge of big things after posting a 2.45 ERA in thirty-four appearances for the White Sox in 2021. But his pitches had lacked snap and bite so far in '22, and there was a good reason for that. Burr had been masking pain in his pitching shoulder since spring training, receiving cortisone injections in a doomed attempt to get through the season.

He'd make only three more appearances before ultimately opting for surgery, with doctors discovering a partially torn labrum. Rehabbing ballplayers can usually count upon a lengthy, tedious recovery process at club training complexes in Arizona or Florida. Not so in Burr's case. The day after undergoing surgery in June, Burr was released by the White Sox, leaving the pitcher "devastated, embarrassed, and heartbroken."

"Facing surgery to fix your shoulder is one thing," Burr said. "But to do it without the support of the team whom you hurt your arm pitching for cut very deep. Literally."

As such, Burr's showdown against Judge would be one of his last of the year. Judge looked at three straight pitches out of the strike zone, then took a fastball down the middle for a called strike, unusual for a player who'd long ago earned the freedom to swing freely in a 3-0 count. And then he looked once more, a pitch near the knees running the count full.

Burr's luck expired as he grooved a 94.9 mph fastball, which Judge clipped to the back of the left-field seating area. "Hammered and way gone!" White Sox broadcaster Jason Benetti roared. "Wow. Absolute mammoth strength." Later, Judge's two-run single helped spark a seven-run eighth inning as the Yanks coasted to a 15–7 rout. As the beat writers filtered into the clubhouse, Judge made it clear that he only wanted to talk about Stanton, whose six RBIs represented a career high.

"Those were some pretty swings," Judge said. "What that guy is capable of doing every single night, he's a game changer. He can take over a game, just like he did tonight."

HOMER #12: May 13 vs. Chicago White Sox's Vince Velasquez (4th inning, solo)
Exit velocity: 103.8 mph. Distance: 355 feet. Launch angle: 31 degrees. HR in 13 of 30 MLB parks.

The Yanks continued to pound on the ChiSox the next night as Judge and Stanton each homered, pushing the duo toward rarified air in the franchise record book. Through thirty-two games, only the tandems of Babe Ruth and Lou Gehrig (1930), and Mickey Mantle and Yogi Berra (1956), had both tallied 10 or more homers so quickly. Stanton lifted a two-run homer that helped build an early five-run lead against starter Vince Velasquez. The White Sox still had Velasquez in the game by the fourth, attempting to soak up innings and save the bullpen. Velasquez got ahead of Judge with a couple of strikes, then tried to catch the outside corner with a 93.3 mph fastball. Judge clipped it, sending right fielder Leury García back to watch the drive rattle in the Chicago bullpen. Judge led the majors in homers, and the Yankees were on their way to a 10–4 rout.

"If you don't execute, they're going to capitalize," Velasquez said that night. "Look at the standings, look at what they're doing."

It was hard to imagine for a team coasting to a 24-8 start, but the series would mark a critical juncture in the season. Back on the diamond under cloudy skies on a pleasant Saturday afternoon, Josh Donaldson and White Sox shortstop Tim Anderson came together on a first-inning tag play that would demand reinspection in a week's time.

Catcher Jose Trevino snapped a throw to third base, where Donaldson applied a tag on Anderson, using his left knee to keep the runner from the base. Umpire Chris Guccione was on top of the play, barking at Donaldson: "You pushed him off!" Anderson and Donaldson were separated by the umpire as both benches cleared, though to the observer's eye, there was little more than jostling and shouting. Later, Donaldson copped to having "leaned on him a little bit, not intentionally, to make the tag," saying that the dustup with Anderson had been "just two guys competing, trying to make a play happen right there."

There were no other sparks that weekend, though it was notable that Donaldson had also ruffled feathers in New York days earlier, in the game when Judge had hit the first walk-off homer of his career. Donaldson and Blue Jays catcher Tyler Heineman exchanged "pretty strong words" in the sixth inning of that contest, according to a report filed by umpire Alfonso Marquez, who ejected pitcher Yimi García after Donaldson was hit squarely on the upper left arm by a pitch. Donaldson himself did not share words with the pitcher, but the Yankees' dugout did, including a torrent of expletives from the ordinarily stoic DJ LeMahieu. Donaldson remarked dismissively of the thirty-year-old Heineman after the game: "I don't even know the guy. Never heard of him."

The Yanks left Chicago having taken two of three, dropping the middle game when Aroldis Chapman surrendered a walk-off single to Luis Robert, then winning the finale behind a Nestor Cortes gem. Now it was back to Baltimore for a four-game series. The weather was warming, and better crowds would be on hand; droves of fans motored down Interstate 95 from New York, New Jersey, and Connecticut, overtaking Camden Yards as a Yankee Stadium South.

Judge sat for the opener, a Yankees win, setting the stage for a memorable contest the next night. Remember, Judge had a knack for turning in big offensive performances after a day out of the lineup. He had never enjoyed a 3-homer game in the majors, and if not for the ill-advised outfield reconstruction that neutralized right-handed power in one of his favorite venues, he'd have achieved it in Baltimore.

HOMER #13: May 17 vs. Baltimore Orioles' Spenser Watkins (3rd inning, solo)
Exit velocity: 105.5 mph. Distance: 410 feet. Launch angle: 29 degrees. HR in 27 of 30 MLB parks.
HOMER #14: May 17 vs. Baltimore Orioles' Joey Krehbiel (5th inning, solo)
Exit velocity: 112.2 mph. Distance: 422 feet. Launch angle: 25 degrees. HR in 27 of 30 MLB parks.

When the Orioles pushed their left-field wall back twenty-six and a half feet and raised it to thirteen feet, incorporating a quirky angle they nicknamed "Elrod's Corner" in honor of longtime bullpen coach Elrod Hendricks, they celebrated the likelihood of odd and interesting bounces. Judge quickly proved the point on this day.

Facing O's starter Spenser Watkins in the first inning, Judge clobbered a hanging slider to deep left field, the ball smacking near the top of the fence and ricocheting back into play. MLB's Statcast system claimed the drive would have been a home run in every other big-league park.

"I knew it didn't have a chance, but I was hoping for good old times' sake, it might get out," Judge said.

There was motion all around the field. DJ LeMahieu chugged home from first base as left fielder Austin Hays chased the ball, which was rolling back toward the infield. Judge rounded second and turned toward third base, daring Hays to throw him out. The throw came in strong on a bounce, where third baseman Tyler Nevin gloved it and slapped down a tag before Judge could grab the base with his left hand. Called out by third-base umpire Chris Conroy, Judge slammed his right fist into the infield dirt.

His uniform now heavily soiled, Judge was upset both about the wall and his decision to go for third base—the old axiom, which he'd learned as a Little Leaguer in Linden, California, was that a player should never make the first out of an inning at third base. His third-inning solution was to avoid the wall entirely. With a 2-1 count, Watkins pumped a 91.6 mph fastball right down the middle, the baseball equivalent of flipping a chunk of red meat into a lion's cage. Judge pounced, clubbing a drive that landed about five rows deep into the center-field seats.

"I learned my lesson," Judge said, "and decided to go to right field after that."

Baltimore took its first lead of the night in the fourth inning, as second baseman Gleyber Torres booted a slow bouncer up the middle for a run-scoring error and Nevin lifted a go-ahead sacrifice fly. Their advantage wouldn't last long. Joey Krehbiel relieved Watkins for the top of the fifth; a righty from Florida who'd already had big-league stints with the Arizona Diamondbacks and Tampa Bay Rays, his first assignment was to handle Judge. Krehbiel missed outside with a slider, then tried another that spun over the heart of home plate, all but screaming: "Hit me!" Judge obliged, dispatching a rocket that struck the batter's eye in center field. As he rounded the bases, chants of "M-V-P!" cascaded from the stands. No Yankee had won the American League's MVP award since Alex Rodriguez in 2007, and no Yankee outfielder had brought one home since Mickey Mantle in 1962. At this point, it wasn't outlandish to think that Judge might change that history, though he repeatedly said he still did not feel locked in.

"It's just about quality at-bats," Judge said. "I can't control the out-come. I can't control if I hit a homer or line out at somebody four times. It's just about me making sure I'm sticking with my plan, swinging at the right pitches, moving a guy over if I need to or driving a guy in if I need to. I'd drive myself crazy if I was searching for results this whole game."

There was still the matter of the first-inning double. In announcing the modifications, the Orioles had called it "a significant step towards neutrality." Boone preferred "Build-Your-Own-Park," and indeed, the remodeled Camden Yards looked like something a teenager could have dreamed up as a custom stadium in the *MLB: The Show* video game. Judge was also salty.

"It's a travesty, man. I'm pretty upset," Judge said. "It looks like a Create-A-Park now. I didn't like it, because I always liked coming here and playing here. Hopefully, in a couple of years, they can move it back in. We'll see."

The Yankees enjoyed a relatively peaceful ride through six weeks of regular season games. They were remarkably healthy, Judge led the majors in home runs, and the clubhouse seemed to be meshing nicely. Judge said that the vibe among the players was "fun," a group that wanted "to play two games a night, if we could." They were about to hit their first speed bump.

On the day that Donaldson joined the Yankees, making a two-hour drive up Interstate 75 from the Minnesota Twins' spring home, general manager Brian Cashman had spoken about the necessary "edge" that the veteran would bring. Cashman believed that the room lacked fire; even mild-mannered Aaron Hicks had spoken to that mentality, saying that the team's mantra should be to "have some fuck you." Donaldson provided that agitator quality, but it came at a price.

Nicknamed the "Bringer of Rain" for his propensity to hit home runs, Donaldson was the 2015 American League MVP with the Toronto Blue Jays, when he'd batted .297 with 41 homers, leading the AL with 123 runs batted in. For the better part of a decade, Donaldson had provided the Blue Jays, Oakland Athletics, Atlanta Braves, and Minnesota Twins with big-time power and a reliable glove at third base.

Donaldson was a three-time All-Star, a two-time Silver Slugger, and received MVP consideration in six separate seasons—yet he also had a reputation for wearing out his welcome, viewed as abrasive by some teammates, many opponents (ask Gerrit Cole), and others within the game's hierarchy.

While with the Twins in 2021, Donaldson had sparked a spat with the White Sox when he appeared to yell, "Hand's not sticky anymore!" after homering off Chicago's Lucas Giolito, a reference to baseball's crackdown on illegal substances used by pitchers to increase spin. In postgame remarks, Giolito called Donaldson "a fucking pest" and "classless," which prompted a parking lot confrontation between the players.

Donaldson was about to find himself in another firestorm, this time accused by Tim Anderson of the White Sox of making a racist remark. Eight days had passed since Anderson and Donaldson scrapped at third base in Chicago, and as the White Sox arrived in town, a two-year-old issue of *Sports Illustrated* was on Donaldson's mind. In a May 6, 2019, article, Anderson told journalist Stephanie Apstein that he felt a responsibility to help break what he called baseball's "have-fun barrier," the remnants of a stodgy old (and predominantly Caucasian) guard.

"I kind of feel like today's Jackie Robinson," Anderson said in the interview. "That's huge to say. But it's cool, man, because he changed the game, and I feel like I'm getting to a point to where I need to change the game."

It was May 21, a sunny and humid Saturday in New York. Donaldson arrived at second base in the second inning, having reached on a fielder's choice before advancing on a single. Looking in Anderson's direction,

Donaldson said: "What's up, Jackie?" Donaldson said he intended to have Anderson crack a smile, hopefully defusing any remaining tension from the series in Chicago. The comment had the opposite effect. Anderson ignored Donaldson, then returned to the dugout after the half-inning, telling his teammates what had been said.

"I spared him that time," Anderson said. "Then it happened again."

When Anderson and Donaldson crossed paths again after the third inning, Donaldson repeated: "What's up, Jackie?" This time, Anderson snapped back, volleying a few choice words. Anderson and Donaldson had to be separated, with Boone escorting Donaldson back to the home dugout and White Sox third-base coach Joe McEwing pointing Anderson toward the visiting side. When Donaldson came to bat again in the fifth inning, Chicago catcher Yasmani Grandal emerged from his crouch, screaming in Donaldson's face.

Donaldson stepped backward, asking, "What are you talking about?" Grandal spat back: "You know what you said." More words followed, and home plate umpire Nick Mahrley moved from his position, trying to defuse the situation. Both benches and bullpens cleared, and tempers were scorching hot. Though restrained by Chicago slugger José Abreu and infielder Gavin Sheets, Grandal continued to shout at Donaldson throughout a five-minute exchange that felt much longer. Grandal said the White Sox had heard enough from Donaldson.

"This game went through a period of time where a lot of those comments were made, and I think we're way past that. It's just unacceptable," Grandal said. "I thought it was a low blow, and I'm going to make sure I've got my team's back. There's no way you're allowed to say something like that. It's unacceptable."

There were no ejections. The final interaction between Anderson and Donaldson came in the seventh inning, when Anderson chose to turn an unassisted double play with Donaldson running. The players knocked legs briefly, and Anderson again spat words at the smirking Donaldson. In his postgame comments, Anderson said that Donaldson "made a disrespectful comment," mentioning the Jackie Robinson phrase. From behind his desk in the visiting clubhouse, White Sox manager Tony La Russa said that Donaldson "made a racist comment, and that's all I'm going to say. That's as strong as it gets." When a reporter from a New Jersey media outlet attempted to follow up, La Russa cut off the questioning, growling: "You're not going to let it go? I just said, that's all I'm going to say. I'm not saying anything else about that. Nothing. There ain't anything else to say."

Spirits were no better in the Yankees clubhouse. Minutes after Clay Holmes completed a perfect ninth inning for his fourth save, Donaldson was summoned to Boone's office. Judge, Giancarlo Stanton, and Aaron Hicks were in the room, and a lengthy discussion followed in which Donaldson offered his side of events. Yes, he'd called Donaldson "Jackie," citing the *Sports Illustrated* article. But in Donaldson's version of events, it had been an attempt at good-natured fun with Anderson, just a couple of pals sharing a laugh. In a revelation that did not help his case, Donaldson pointed out that he'd called Anderson "Jackie" on multiple occasions.

"In 2019, when I played for Atlanta, we actually joked about that," Donaldson said. "I don't know what's changed. If something has changed from that, my meaning of that is not in any term trying to be racist. It was just off an interview what he called himself. We said that before, we joked about it. Obviously, he deemed that it was disrespectful, and look, if he did, I apologize. That's not what I was trying to do."

Anderson had no interest in hearing that, or anything, from Donaldson. Neither did White Sox pitcher Liam Hendriks, a one-time teammate of Donaldson's with Toronto, who said, "Usually you have inside jokes with people you get along with, not people who don't get along at all. So that statement right there was complete bullshit." Chicago hurler Dallas Keuchel called Donaldson's remarks "very sad," adding, "There's no room for that here or anywhere in the game."

Michael Hill, MLB's senior vice president for on-field operations, found no dispute over what was said on the field. Regardless of intent, the league viewed Donaldson's comments toward Anderson as "disrespectful and in poor judgment, particularly when viewed in the context of their prior interactions." The league's punishment of a fine and one-game suspension left the White Sox wondering how Donaldson had evaded firmer discipline.

Pitching coach Ethan Katz took to Twitter to express his displeasure: "Just one game. We all saw his malice at third a week ago, then this comment with the ridiculous excuse that followed. What's the point or message behind a one game suspension? This is incredibly disappointing and plain frustrating." Katz would delete the tweet, but the sentiment lingered.

Meanwhile, the Yankees fretted about how to extinguish a budding public relations nightmare. Boone said that he did not believe Donaldson had "malicious intent" with the comment, though he added: "This is, just in my opinion, somewhere [Donaldson] should not be going." Judge prided himself on being a good teammate, but as a Black man who grew up in a white area (Linden's African American population was 0.6 percent, according to the 2010 census), the racial component gave him pause.

"It's a tough one," Judge said. "Joke or not, I just don't think it's the right thing to do there, especially given the history. The series in Chicago, kind of a little bit of beef between Anderson and J. D. Anderson is one of the best shortstops in the game and he's a big part of MLB and what's going on here, how we can grow the game. J.D. made a mistake, owned up to it, and now we've got to move on." Donaldson was stung, and not just because the team's de facto captain had seemingly backed an opponent over a teammate. Donaldson said it was "extremely hurtful" to be accused of racism, adding, "That's definitely not who I am, by any stretch or manner." There were wounds concealed within Donaldson's caustic exterior. His father, Levon, spent fifteen years in prison on charges of sexual battery, false imprisonment, and aggravated battery; Donaldson was between the ages of three and five for those violent episodes, some of which he can vividly recall, and wishes he could not.

"At one point, the cops were looking for him, and he asked me, 'Who do you want to go with, me or your mom?'" Donaldson said. "I was four years old. I obviously picked my mom."

Donaldson said he spoke to his teammates immediately after the Anderson interaction, attempting to explain his intentions.

"I think everybody responded to what I had to say," Donaldson said. "They know my heart, and that wasn't my intention at all. I do feel bad for the Robinson family. I never wanted them to feel [disrespected]. Their name should never be regarded in a bad light."

Reflecting upon the situation, Cashman acknowledged that it had been "a difficult circumstance for a period of time" within the clubhouse and front office.

"Josh Donaldson, to this day, I don't think he's racist," Cashman said. "It was just something that happened and took on a different tone. I didn't know how this was going. I just knew it was a very serious circumstance and it was creating a lot of uncomfortableness. Having to work through that, talk through that, live through that was obviously very difficult for everybody involved from New York to Chicago."

Cooler heads needed to prevail, and a splash of "out of sight, out of mind" helped. Donaldson was shuffled to the COVID-19 injured list, though he never tested positive; the pandemic-era rules provided a new loophole where a player could land on the injured list with no minimum stay, simply by stating that they were experiencing symptoms. While away, Donaldson took advantage of the opportunity to receive a cortisone injection in his troublesome right shoulder, which had been an issue since the spring.

Ultimately, as numerous conversations transpired within the clubhouse walls and hours turned into days, Judge came to consider the matter closed.

"We're grown men," Judge said. "He stood up and owned up to what he did, and that's all you can ask, especially when we're playing games every day. You can't sit here and dwell on something that happened. You've got to learn from it. He made a mistake, and now it's time to move on and keep playing baseball."

HOMER #15: May 22 vs. Chicago White Sox's Kendall Graveman
(8th inning, solo)
Exit velocity: 111.1 mph. Distance: 431 feet. Launch angle: 28 degrees. HR in 30 of 30 MLB parks.

Even with Donaldson absent, the Yankees seemed to be dragging, held to just one run over eighteen innings of doubleheader action on a steamy Sunday afternoon. That run came in the eighth inning of the first game, as Judge took an 0-2 Kendall Graveman slider into the second deck of the left-field stands for a game-tying shot. The rest of the contest was awful for the home team; they learned that reliever Chad Green needed season-ending Tommy John surgery, and Aroldis Chapman melted down again, surrendering a go-ahead homer to A. J. Pollock and a run-scoring double to Adam Engel.

In his postgame remarks, Boone struck a confident tone, saying, "With what we've been getting from our starting pitching, we'll be OK." But would they? Their bullpen no longer felt like a strength.

The weekend ended in a sweep, and Anderson got the last laugh in a dismal nightcap, one in which Chicago right-hander Michael Kopech carried a perfect game into the sixth inning. Booed by Yankees fans each time he stepped to the plate, Anderson hushed the crowd with an opposite-field, three-run homer in the eighth inning, drawing an index finger to his lips after rounding the bases. Anderson opted not to speak to the media after Chicago's 5–0 victory, but a hot ESPN microphone captured his words and intent just fine: "Making motherfuckers shut the fuck up."

The dream season had come off its rails, and someone needed to step up. Guess who?

HOMER #16: May 23 vs. Baltimore Orioles' Jordan Lyles (1st inning, solo)
Exit velocity: 112.0 mph. Distance: 418 feet. Launch angle: 22 degrees. HR in 29 of 30 MLB parks.
HOMER #17: May 23 vs. Baltimore Orioles' Jordan Lyles (5th inning, two-run)
Exit velocity: 103.1 mph. Distance: 405 feet. Launch angle: 32 degrees. HR in 30 of 30 MLB parks.

It was going to be a long summer for the Orioles, who needed someone to eat innings. Jordan Lyles was up for the challenge; a twelve-year veteran who owned a losing career record and was wearing his seventh big-league uniform, the South Carolina native would lead the young Baltimore pitching staff in innings, strikeouts, and victories.

Gerrit Cole set the O's down in order in the top of the first, and most of the crowd was still finding their seats as Judge got the Yankees off to a quick start. Lyles's third pitch to Judge was a 90.3 mph sinker that Judge pounced on, drilling a drive into Yankee Stadium's visiting bullpen. Sharp through two innings, Cole struggled to limit traffic on the basepaths, and Baltimore held a two-run lead when Judge's spot in the batting order came around in the fifth inning.

Lyles got ahead in the count, 0-2, then tried a slider and a sinker, failing to entice Judge to swing at either. Lyles returned to the slider again, and Judge crushed it into the left-field seats. Yet even a 2-homer performance wasn't enough, as the Yanks chewed on a 6–4 loss. In boiling down an eleven-strikeout, no-walk loss that he described as "peculiar," Cole couldn't help but crack a broad grin when asked about Judge's performance.

"Sometimes I feel like he's salivating for something, gets it, and drills it," Cole said. "And sometimes I feel like he's just being a good baseball player, staying up the middle, and drills it the same way. Not all the things are going his way, he's not looking for slug all the time. He's just putting better swings than guys are throwing. He's just—better."

Judge's multi-homer performance inspired an article in the next day's edition of the *New York Times*, asking, "Will Aaron Judge Hit 60 Home Runs This Season?" Comparing Judge's performance to the eight players to previously hit 60 or more homers in a season, Judge's 17 long balls through 40 games were more than Ruth (13) in his first 40 games of 1927, and more than Maris (11) through his first 40 games of 1961.

He was ahead of Sammy Sosa's paces from 1998 (7), 1999 (13), and 2001 (14), had matched Mark McGwire's clip from 1998 (17), and was ahead of McGwire's 1999 pace (12). Judge stood 5 short of where Barry Bonds sat after 40 games in 2001 (22). The article noted that the keys to Judge reaching rarefied air would be durability and consistency. In baseball's previous eight 60-homer seasons, the sluggers had averaged 156.8 games.

"I sometimes take it for granted, but not right now," Boone said. "He's a really special player, and he's really carrying us offensively."

Jose Trevino woke on the morning of May 24, glanced at the calendar, and knew it would be a difficult day. It was his late father's birthday.

Shuffling into the kitchen of his rented New York apartment, the catcher brewed a Keurig coffee pod and reached for a ceramic mug like the one that had been Dad's favorite, with Mickey Mantle's 1952 Topps rookie card printed on the side.

Nicknamed "Bugé," a nod to his energetic affinity for the dance floor, Joe Trevino had passed away in 2013 following a lengthy illness. His son could still picture the version of "Yankee Stadium" they'd constructed in Ben Bolt, Texas, the acre-long lot with a large oak tree, where left field and right field were short and drives toward center field could roll all day. There, Dad pumped thousands of tennis balls into the strike zone, his son still able to recall his instructions for running the bases: "Open your arms like you're flying." Hundreds of times, Bugé had repeated one other thought: "I'm preparing you to be a Yankee."

"From a young age, he never forced me to play baseball, but when I wanted to, he was always there," Trevino said. "It's just crazy that he would put me in that scenario."

So Trevino's heart was already heavy as he commuted to the Bronx, memories of his father sharing space with Jordan Montgomery's game plan against the Orioles. It was in the early afternoon hours that Trevino's cell phone buzzed with breaking news: there had been a tragedy in his home state, where a lone gunman had slain nineteen students and two adults at Robb Elementary School in Uvalde, Texas. It was yet another despicable act in a country where gun violence had become all too familiar.

As he squatted behind home plate, Trevino's heart ached for the small town. Upon season's end, Trevino would rent out the Six Flags Over Texas in Arlington for the Uvalde Little League team, a token of his support for the community. When Trevino walked toward home plate in the eleventh inning, he wondered if his father's spirit was in the building. It was a comforting thought. Staring at a 1-2 pitch from reliever Bryan Baker, Trevino lashed a hard liner past diving third baseman Ramón Urías, the ball rattling toward the left-field corner. The winning run came home, and as he rounded first base, Trevino could hold back his emotions no more. "Papi! Papi!" he cried, bellowing in the center of the infield. His eyes glassy and red following the hard-fought victory, Trevino clutched a wireless microphone and spoke to the crowd, his words reverberating over the public-address system.

"I just want to start by saying my thoughts and prayers are with everybody in Uvalde, Texas, tonight," Trevino said. "I know y'all saw some tears, and there's a reason behind it. My dad was a huge Yankees fan. He would always put me in these scenarios; he always said, 'Ninth inning, down one, you need a base hit to tie the game or win the game at Yankee Stadium.'"

There had been little fanfare when the Yankees acquired Trevino less than a week before Opening Day, swapping pitchers Albert Abreu and Robert Ahlstrom to the Texas Rangers. He had hardly been their first choice; the Yanks came up short in wooing free-agent catcher Manny Piña, and general manager Brian Cashman intended to enter the regular season with Kyle Higashioka as the starter behind the plate. His backup would have been Ben Rortvedt, a square-jawed, muscular backstop acquired from the Twins along with Donaldson and Kiner-Falefa. But Rortvedt had re-aggravated an oblique injury during spring training, shoving the Yankees back into the catching marketplace.

The Yankees knew about Trevino's reputation as an excellent pitch framer, the art of nudging umpires to see borderline pitches as strikes. It was a skill that Trevino had honed since his first days catching at Oral Roberts University in Tulsa, Oklahoma, when he'd moved from third base after a first-team freshman All-American campaign. Sixty feet and six inches from a machine firing 100 mph pellets, his coaches had barked: "Catch it! Make it look easy!" It was certainly not, and Trevino earned the bruises to prove it, but those rough beginnings led to something special on the defensive side. Yet as Cashman recalled later, Trevino's greatest attribute in the spring of 2022 boiled down to three words: "He was available."

The Trevino deal had been consummated from a podium at Cashman's alma mater, the Catholic University of America in Washington, D.C., where he was being inducted into the college's Hall of Fame. On an unseasonably mild spring day, ideal for taking in the pink and white clouds of the capital's cherry blossom trees, Cashman multitasked. He prepared his remarks while communicating with the Rangers about Trevino, and also with Mets counterpart Billy Eppler about a budding swap for right-handed reliever Miguel Castro.

"I was supposed to go watch my college baseball team play that day," Cashman said. "I had to call the coach and say, 'Listen, you don't have any pregame ceremonies, right? I'm not throwing out a first pitch?' He said they didn't, and I said, 'Good, I've got two deals I'm working on. I'll see you at the ceremony, but I can't go to the game.'"

As he eyed a packed house at Maloney Hall, the centerpiece of the campus's school of business, Cashman briefly considered putting Texas general manager Jon Daniels on speakerphone to tell the audience they were working on a trade. Cashman wondered how long it would have taken for that stunt to reach social media, thinking better of it. As Cashman and Daniels continued to work out the parameters, nervous showrunners nudged the GM to tell him, "Hey, you're up next." Cashman waved them away, telling them, "Oh, I know. I'll be there. Don't worry." Minutes later, Trevino was a Yankee. Bugé's dream had come true.

"At worst, we knew we're getting a really good defensive catcher," Cashman said. "We knew we were at least getting a quality backup catcher, somebody that we felt good about. He blew away expectations. He's a rat. He loves the game, loves to prepare, and loves to study. He loves to find where we can have an edge."

The next night, the Yankees were in the air, bound for their first visit of the season to Tropicana Field. The much-maligned home of the Tampa Bay Rays had opened in 1990 as the Florida Suncoast Dome, intended to lure the Seattle Mariners, Chicago White Sox, or San Francisco Giants to relocate to the Sunshine State. It would begin life as a perpetual bridesmaid. All three of those clubs flirted with the city of St. Petersburg before securing new parks in their respective home cities. Miami got its expansion franchise first, with the National League welcoming the Florida Marlins in 1993. St. Pete settled for arena football, a few seasons of Tampa Bay Lightning hockey, sporadic bookings for rock concerts, and way too many tractor pulls.

It would be five more years until the Trop hosted a big-league game, where the Tampa Bay Devil Rays took their first breaths as the perennial long-in-the-tooth loser of the powerhouse American League East. The franchise's most iconic moment was the image of a forty-one-year-old Wade Boggs kneeling to kiss home plate after homering for his three thousandth hit. Tampa Bay wouldn't post a winning season until 2008, the same year the team instituted a name change to the Rays and dispatched the garish green, black, and purple of their former identity.

A fresh blue, white, and yellow sunburst color scheme represented a new look in more ways than one. The Rays' baseball operations team had developed a reputation for making more from less, though winning performances in ten of fourteen seasons had never done much to improve the club's sparse attendance. The club's strong local TV ratings suggested interest in the team's fortunes, but few fans clamored to watch games in an outdated, drab facility that was difficult to reach from Tampa and other points north. Efforts to build a new ballpark in downtown Tampa and a concept to play some home games in Montreal had flopped. For the present and immediate future, the Rays seemed tethered to their artificial turf, where the raised roof and its accompanying catwalks reminded observers of a turn-of-the-century circus tent.

When Jameson Taillon and Clay Holmes combined on a shutout in the series opener, played in a breezy two hours and twenty-three minutes, Boone joked that he still had time to make it to Bern's Steak House—a lavish red-meat Tampa landmark that players and coaches loved to frequent during spring training. In the home clubhouse, Taylor Walls was in no kidding mood. A utility infielder who would finish the year batting .172, Walls jabbed at the rivals, saying that he viewed the Yankees as "very beatable, and we know we can beat them." Walls backed up his boast by slugging a homer off Luis Severino and contributing a pair of highlight-reel defensive plays, helping the Rays notch a hard-fought split of the four-game series. But Taylor Walls? Really? The Yankees mostly shrugged. Yet at least the visitors wouldn't leave town without a big swing from their superstar.

HOMER #18: May 29 vs. Tampa Bay Rays' Colin Poche (8th inning, solo) *Exit velocity: 107.4 mph. Distance: 420 feet. Launch angle: 31 degrees. HR in 28 of 30 MLB parks.*

Judge was kept in the ballpark almost until the end of the series, stepping in against Poche as the Rays tried to lock down a 4–1 lead on a Sunday afternoon—not that you could tell what time of day it was. Like a second-rate casino, Tropicana Field had almost no visible windows to the outside world. It could be 3:00 a.m. or 3:00 p.m.; good luck being able to tell the difference.

Poche missed high with a fastball, then tried another, a 91.3 mph heater hovering over the plate. Judge crushed it toward right-center field, appearing momentarily as though it might land in the Touch Tank, the thirty-five-foot, ten-thousand-gallon Florida Aquarium exhibit where fans could reach in to pet a cownose stingray. There was no splashdown, but it sounded like a Yankees home game as Judge rounded the bases, most of the sellout crowd of 25,025 (the Trop once held almost twice that, but the Rays had tarped over the upper deck in 2019 due to lack of interest) pledging allegiance to the Bombers.

"We always fight until the very last out," Judge said. "There, my job as the leadoff guy is to get on base and get a rally going. I got a good pitch to hit and was able to put a good swing on it." But then Poche recorded the next three outs, working around a single and a wild pitch, and J. P. Feyereisen set New York down in order in the ninth to preserve a Rays win. The Yankees should have been eyeing a well-deserved day off, having just completed a grueling stretch of twenty-three games in twenty-two days, but Judge departed the Trop wishing that he and his teammates could go right back to the bat rack.

"I think everybody in here wants to play again," Judge said. "I think we've got a bad taste in our mouth. It doesn't matter how many games you've got in a row. Everybody in here is ready to go, every single day. I know it's been quite a few games in a row, but this team is hungry. We've got a lot to prove. Two months into it, we've still got a lot of games to go. We're in first place; it's better than being in second place, that's for sure."

Giancarlo Stanton was never supposed to be a Yankee. Shohei Ohtani was. At least, that was the original plan.

In August 2017, Cashman and assistant general manager Jean After-man flew to Sapporo and Tokyo to scout Ohtani, then a twenty-three-year-old stud with the Hokkaido Nippon-Ham Fighters, who boasted the rare combination of being a standout right-handed pitcher and a left-handed slugger. Ohtani's dynamic hurling and hitting hadn't been seen in the same package since the Red Sox moved Babe Ruth from the mound to the outfield in 1919. Afterman had been instrumental in ironing out the details that brought Japanese stars Hideki Matsui and Masahiro Tanaka to the Bronx. She intended to help bring in Ohtani, a player whom the Yankees had been eyeing since 2012.

The Yankees spent much of the summer of 2017 collecting international bonus pool money in trades, including $1.5 million from the Athletics, in a deal that brought right-hander Sonny Gray to New York. Media reports painted the Yankees as the favorites for Ohtani, a designation Cashman later said made him "cringe."

The bad news came on a Sunday evening in December as the general manager dressed as one of Santa Claus's elves to dangle off a twenty-two-story office building in Stamford, Connecticut, participating in the city's annual "Heights & Lights" holiday festival. There was coal in the Yankees' stocking (not *Cole*; that would come two years later). The Yankees had sent a stellar video extolling New York City's virtues and the historical significance of wearing the pinstripes, but Ohtani's representatives informed Cashman there would be no need for an in-person pitch. Ohtani had decided to play for a team on the West Coast, preferring a smaller market than New York.

"I knew that our presentation was excellent; the feedback from that was outstanding," Cashman said. "I can't change that we're a big market, and I can't change that we're in the East."

As the world learned three days later, Ohtani's choice was the Los Angeles Angels of Anaheim. Billy Eppler, a one-time Cashman lieutenant who had landed in the Angels' GM seat, felt his phone buzz and recognized the incoming call—the main line of Creative Artists Agency, which represented Ohtani. Exchanging pleasantries with agent Nez Balelo, Eppler closed the door to assistant general manager Jonathan Strangio's office, taking the call in private.

"Shohei Ohtani wants to be an Angel," Balelo told Eppler, who stood up, then tried to sit back down—and missed the chair.

"I whiffed," Eppler said. "I fell all the way to the ground. There's so much adrenaline pumping at the moment, I didn't feel it. I was just stunned. It was a pretty remarkable moment."

The Yankees pivoted quickly that week, reaching a blockbuster trade with the Marlins to bring in Stanton, fresh off a 59-homer campaign as the National League's Most Valuable Player. Miami's ownership group was looking to cut payroll, and Stanton and Judge had made fantastic theater standing side by side at the Home Run Derby that summer in Miami, where Stanton had remarked that Judge seemed to be "the twin you've never met: everyone's comparing us to each other."

New York had its Bash Brothers in Judge and Stanton, but Ohtani in pinstripes would always present a great "What if?" question. That was especially true when Ohtani won the American League's MVP award in 2021, a season in which he hit 46 home runs and posted a 3.18 ERA. Yet even with Ohtani's otherworldly performance and one of the sport's great superstars in outfielder Mike Trout, the Angels had finished fourth in the AL West and weren't faring much better early in 2022. The Yankees spanked them, 9–1, in the series opener, completing May with a league-best 34-15 record. A rainout the next night set up a doubleheader, in which Ohtani would pitch the opener.

Ohtani had never performed well at Yankee Stadium, and so perhaps his stated preference not to play in New York had been apt. The previous June, the Yanks had thumped Ohtani for seven runs, knocking him out of the game in the first inning. They had his number from the first at-bat once again, with Matt Carpenter taking Ohtani deep on the hurler's eleventh pitch of the game.

A mustachioed veteran who'd once been a three-time All-Star with the St. Louis Cardinals, Carpenter had been sitting on his living room couch less than two weeks prior, having been released by the Texas Rangers from his Triple-A contract. When Carpenter joined the Yankees during their series at Tropicana Field, he'd expressed his gratitude for another opportunity to play at the highest level, telling Aaron Boone that he was willing to "load the bags on the plane" if that's what the team needed. Then Carpenter had scurried off to a pregame hitters' meeting, still clad in the denim jeans he'd worn on the flight.

They never pressed Carpenter into skycap duty; the resurgent slugger had a much more important role, enjoying the fruits of a cross-country winter mission that rebuilt his swing. After a lengthy phone call with the Cincinnati Reds' Joey Votto, Carpenter checked into a cutting-edge baseball performance lab in Baton Rouge, Louisiana, hired a private hitting instructor in Santa Clarita, California, and took swings with former teammate Matt Holliday at Oklahoma State University. The journey had unlocked his previous skill set.

"I just knew I needed to go play," Carpenter said. "I was in Texas and I started to feel that kind of click; I went down to Triple-A Round Rock and swung the bat well, and I knew that I was trending in the right direction."

Now he was rounding the bases in the Bronx. Gleyber Torres also slugged a first-inning homer off Ohtani, and after rapping a single in his first at-bat, Judge was ready when his spot in the order came around.

HOMER #19: June 2 vs. Los Angeles Angels of Anaheim's Shohei Ohtani (3rd inning, solo)

Exit velocity: 109.9 mph. Distance: 405 feet. Launch angle: 21 degrees. HR in 30 of 30 MLB parks.

Seeing Ohtani well in both of his at-bats, Judge looked at a slider and fastball for called strikes, then laid off a bad splitter in the dirt. He flicked a heater foul to keep the at-bat going. Ohtani followed with a slider that hung, and Judge drilled it to the left-field seats.

"I was trying to get something up in the strike zone, because he's got a nasty splitter that he likes to use with two strikes, and a good slider and curveball," Judge said.

The Yankees went on to sweep the doubleheader by scores of 6–1 and 2–1, extending the Halos' misery in what would be a fourteen-game losing streak that eventually cost manager Joe Maddon his job. So desperate were the Angels to snap their skid, they'd resort to using a team-wide soundtrack of songs by the Canadian rock band Nickelback as their walk-up music during a home loss to the Red Sox; Ohtani selected the 2005 song "Photograph," not that Chad Kroeger's vocals helped much.

As he absorbed Ohtani's performance that day in the Bronx, Maddon mused about the ease in which the Yankees seemed to tee up his star. "They're really good at reading pitches; they're really good at it," Maddon said. "I'm not accusing anybody of anything, except that they're good at it. If you're able to acquire things through natural means, I think it's great. There are things that pitchers do that other teams can pick up on. We need to be more vigilant."

The Yankees were doing nothing untoward; this was not a redux of the 2017 Astros electronic sign-stealing scandal. Rather, they were more code breakers, able to crack Ohtani's preferred pitch sequence. Apprised of his counterpart's comments, Boone did not disagree.

"I think we are," he said. "We're going to hopefully continue to be good at it."

In the nightcap, Jameson Taillon retired the first twenty-one Angels, coming within six outs of the Yanks' first perfect game since David Cone's 1999 gem over the Montreal Expos. The tight 2–1 win polished off a series sweep, and the Yanks were due for a rout. They'd get one the next night, pounding the Detroit Tigers by a 13–0 score.

Gerrit Cole followed Taillon's gem with one of his own, not permitting his first hit until the seventh inning, as the ace squeezed out some revenge for an abbreviated and awful start earlier in the season at frigid Comerica Park. By that time, Judge had already left his mark.

HOMER #20: June 3 vs. Detroit Tigers' Elvin Rodriguez (3rd inning, solo)
Exit velocity: 104.2 mph. Distance: 378 feet. Launch angle: 29 degrees. HR in 29 of 30 MLB parks.

Trevino put the Yankees on the board with a solo homer in the third inning off Rodriguez, who would soon learn that he—as Maddon had hinted of Ohtani—was tipping his pitches. Rodriguez's tell was far more blatant, so much so that Jimmy O'Brien could pick it up from his sofa. A thirty-something who rose to online prominence with a hilarious lip-reading video of a fiery 2019 Boone ejection, O'Brien's latest Jomboy Media breakdown revealed that Rodriguez stared toward third base before throwing fastballs out of the stretch position, but would only glance toward third base or stare straight ahead on a non-fastball. If O'Brien could see it, so could the Yankees.

"I didn't realize I was doing that, but I saw the video. Yeah, they got me," Rodriguez would later confirm.

With two outs, up came Judge, who got ahead with a 2-1 count. There were no runners on base, so Rodriguez was pitching out of the full windup; no tell. Rodriguez offered a 94.4 mph fastball and Judge connected, driving it high to right field. Rodriguez's reaction—a bemused stare—foretold that he knew the ball wasn't coming back. So did right fielder Daz Cameron, who turned away before it landed in the seats, a few rows in front of the Judge's Chambers in Section 104. Dillon Lawson, the Yankees' hitting coach, couldn't help but marvel.

"He's so diligent and consistent," Lawson said. "I remember they would say this about Jeter; they add up all the good days. On a given day, you might be able to outperform Jeter. But he would string so many good days together that, at the end, it would equal greatness. Judge is incredibly talented, has as much firepower as anyone in baseball, and then he was also super consistent on top of that. It doesn't just add up to greatness. It adds up to historic."

'61 FLASHBACK: OLD-TIMERS' DAY

Bobby Richardson sat in the living room of a modest one-story ranch on the west side of Sumter, South Carolina, surrounded by walls that had stood firm since the spring of 1961. Still spry and active with a dollop of youth as he approached his eighty-seventh birthday, some five decades after his final big-league game, he marveled at the images flickering across his television screen. It was happening all over again.

Then the Yankees' starting second baseman, Richardson had been a firsthand witness as Mickey Mantle and Roger Maris captivated the nation with their pursuit of Babe Ruth's home run record. He had watched from across the clubhouse as his teammates handled an insatiable crush; about a dozen writers swarming Maris at his locker, then moving as a pack to encircle Mantle, then sometimes back again.

"At the time, we were pulling for Mantle to break Babe Ruth's record, because he had grown up in the Yankees farm system," Richardson said. "But when he couldn't, we were glad that Maris did it."

It had been Mantle, not Maris, who carried the 1961 Yankees in the early going. Manager Ralph Houk searched for a lineup that clicked, beginning the year with Yogi Berra hitting third, Mantle fourth, and Maris fifth. It wasn't until the middle of May that Houk settled on the lineup that is fondly remembered from that season, with Maris third and Mantle fourth.

Dan Daniel, a reporter for the *New York World-Telegram*, wrote that Maris "wasn't hitting the size of his breakfast check, which usually comes to $1.70." Houk surmised that Maris (batting .208 with 3 homers as late as May 16) would benefit from seeing meatier pitches to hit, batting third ahead of Mantle, who led the majors with 126 walks. (By comparison, Maris generated 94 walks, none intentional.) Maris was summoned to the Yankees' offices, located at 745 Fifth Avenue in Manhattan, for a chat with owner Dan Topping and GM Roy Haney. They walked around the corner to Reuben's Restaurant, a pleasant place on Fifty-eighth Street known for corned beef sandwiches, cheesecake, and beer.

"We want you to stop worrying about your hitting," Topping said. "We're not worried and we don't want you to fret about it. Forget your batting average and go out and swing for home runs. We would rather see you hit a lot of home runs and drive in runs than hit .300."

Then Topping mentioned that the Yankees wanted Maris to get his eyes checked; a car service was waiting to ferry him to an optometrist. Maris's confidence was shaken, but the Yankees picked him up. He roomed with Clete Boyer during road trips, and their friendship helped Maris settle in. They were playing crisp defense, Mantle had 14 homers by the end of May, and Whitey Ford had developed what he called a "controlled curve"—essentially, a modern-day slider. Houk believed Moose Skowron, Elston Howard, and Yogi Berra could still do plenty of damage hitting behind Mantle.

"No matter what you say, Roger still had to hit all them home runs," Mantle said. "Cut through the crap, and that's the important thing."

Richardson frequently thought about '61 in his home, the one with red brick and off-white vinyl siding at a sleepy stop-signed intersection. In the front yard, a garden shaped like an irregular pentagon greeted the mail carrier; his letters, bills, and occasional autograph requests went to home plate. A large wooden cross stood sentry in the front yard, reflecting Richardson's faith in Christ.

On the day Richardson and his wife, Betsy, picked out this plot of land, he was the reigning World Series Most Valuable Player—the only one to claim those honors in a losing cause, still stinging from Bill Mazeroski's homer in Game 7 against the Pittsburgh Pirates. No one used the term "walk-off" then; that would come later. Richardson's 1961 contract was for $22,500; when the home builders quoted a price of $28,000, Richardson had winced.

"Man, I won't ever be able to pay for this," he'd thought.

But the place was a good investment, providing shelter and happiness for children and grandchildren. They had enclosed the garage and added on to the back a little over the years, but essentially it still looked and felt the same as it had in February 1961, when Richardson had packed to travel south, rejoining Maris, Mantle, and the rest of the Yankees for spring training in St. Petersburg, Florida.

Richardson wondered what it was like for this new kid, Aaron Judge. Every time Richardson turned on the sports channels, one of the talking heads seemed to be yapping about Judge, their words providing the soundtrack over another of the big guy's home run trots.

"I always knew how many he had, and what the possibility was that he might break it," Richardson said. "I think Roger would have been tickled to death knowing that Aaron Judge, a man of his character and how good he has been to the fans, would be the one to break the record. And he would be pleased that steroids are not involved in it at all."

In '61, Richardson hit leadoff and shortstop Tony Kubek batted second, which gave the double-play combination one overriding responsibility when they swapped their gloves for a bat: to get on base and score runs when Maris and Mantle belted the ball.

The 1957 Rookie of the Year, Kubek enjoyed a nine-year career in the big leagues, featuring four All-Star selections and three World Series rings, then spent three decades in broadcast booths as an analyst for NBC, the Yankees, and the Toronto Blue Jays.

"Hitting second in front of Roger was one of the most thrilling things in my career as a baseball player," Kubek said. "I was on second base a lot and saw a lot of his home runs. Roger had unlimited potential, and he fulfilled it. I think he was misunderstood by a lot of people. Roger was very quiet; he was a small-town guy who was thrown into the big time, where the fans can be the biggest boosters and yet the biggest critics. That's what New York City is all about."

Enjoying retirement in Appleton, Wisconsin, as he neared his eighty-seventh birthday, Kubek said that he rarely watched baseball now, preferring to fill his hours with hobbies like beekeeping and tapping trees for maple syrup. Kubek said his phone still rang occasionally from a network of fans who had become friends at fantasy camps run by Skowron and Hank Bauer decades earlier in Florida. They kept him abreast while Judge chased Maris's record.

"I've never met Aaron Judge," Kubek said, "but I think players are protected a little bit more now than years ago. During batting practice, there were writers all around the batting cage, all wanting a piece of you. There was a lot more commotion, and Roger gave them pretty much free access."

Richardson tuned into Yankees games regularly, and he considered Judge a worthy successor to the right-field lineage of Ruth and Maris. Judge and Richardson had met once, at an Old-Timers' Day game in 2018 at the new Yankee Stadium. Standing five foot nine and weighing 170 pounds in his playing days, a bit softer around the midsection now, Richardson had gripped Judge's right hand and arced his neck straight back—as though he were taking in the Empire State Building from 34th Street.

"You're as big as I thought you were," Richardson said.

Judge had flashed his toothy smile, clapping a hand upon Richardson's shoulder. "Rich," Judge said, "I'm glad you're still well enough to come experience this and be a part of it." The Old-Timers assembled in the dugout that day, a group that included Ford and Don Larsen, and they nodded with approval. The Judge kid seemed to get it.

"He was gracious," Richardson said. "He was one that came out and talked to the Old-Timers. There are so many that just stay in the dugout. He came out on the field during our practices and dealt with everybody. He's so friendly. Knowing him, he'll be a great steward and honor the Lord in every way."

Yet as for his rooting interests in the chase, Richardson had learned not to get too heavily involved in debates about the single-season home run record. Once, while speaking at the Babe Ruth World Series in Jamestown, New York, Richardson referenced Maris's 61 homers. "But it took him 162 games!" a woman in the audience had shouted. Only later did Richardson learn that the comment had come from Babe Ruth's daughter, Julia Ruth Stevens.

◆

6

◆

"ADVERSITY IS COMING FOR YOU"

Aaron Boone was no wet blanket. If anything, relentless positivity had become one of his hallmarks as a big-league manager, vowing to have his players' backs through hell and/or high water. But as he surveyed the walls of his Yankee Stadium office in early June, there was too much baseball history within his bones to throw a victory party over two hot months. Titles were not won this early, and his family tree could tell the tale.

Overlooking his desk underneath the first-base grandstand, a hard right turn from a hidden navy-blue wall autographed by franchise greats past and present, hung a large black-and-white framed photograph of Boone's grandfather Ray. Frozen in time, the thirteen-year big-league veteran was kneeling and holding a bat, wearing his baggy wool flannel Detroit Tigers uniform sometime in the mid-1950s.

A two-time All-Star, Ray Boone logged one World Series at-bat, coming as a twenty-four-year-old rookie with the 1948 Cleveland Indians; he'd struck out as a pinch hitter against future Hall of Famer Warren Spahn. Also decorating the walls was a photograph of Boone; his grandfather; his father, Bob; and brother, Bret, in the home dugout during an Old-Timers' Day at Philadelphia's Veterans Stadium sometime in the mid-1970s. Those had been good times for the Boones, too, as they saw their chapter in the City of Brotherly Love come together in a championship.

The Boone boys had been constants in the Phillies' clubhouse, begging off classes across the Delaware River in New Jersey to tail their dad around Steve Carlton, Pete Rose, and the rest of the Phils. Even at age five, Boone would mimic slugger Greg Luzinski's lumbering gait or pantomime manager Danny Ozark's agonizingly slow trudge to the mound. The boy paid attention, so when he accepted the Yankees' managerial job in 2018 with no prior managerial or coaching experience, Boone felt confident enough to say, "In a way, I've been preparing for this job my entire life."

Boone knew how difficult it was to be the last team standing, especially in an era of Wild Cards and greater parity. Ray Boone got his ring in 1948, but never tasted another title. Bob Boone squatted into his forties, behind the plate for three decades of foul tips, but a hungover flatbed truck drive down Philadelphia's Broad Street with the 1980 Phillies marked his greatest day in the sun. Even Boone's most recognizable moment, the home run off a Tim Wakefield knuckleball in Game 7 of the 2003 American League Championship Series, had only secured a pennant—the Yankees had exhausted their World Series energy against the Red Sox. They came up flat against the Florida Marlins, who upended New York in six games.

The 2022 Yankees had the makings of greatness, Boone would allow, but there would be bumpier days ahead.

"I tell you guys all the time, adversity is coming for you," Boone said. "You've got to be able to weather the storm. The season doesn't stop for anyone."

And as the calendar turned to June, what had been a gloriously smooth ride began to bang into Major Deegan Expressway–sized potholes. There were injuries (Aroldis Chapman, Chad Green, Jonathan Loáisiga, Tim Locastro, Giancarlo Stanton), a trio of close calls concerning potential COVID-19 exposure (Josh Donaldson, Joey Gallo, Kyle Higashioka), and the uncomfortable distraction stemming from Donaldson's ill-advised taunting of Tim Anderson and the White Sox.

"Every team deals with issues and injuries," Aaron Judge said. "It comes down to, when you get punched, can you get back up?"

Fortunately, the Yankees still held the game's best record, and Judge was slugging homers regularly. As long as those two things remained true, Boone would happily continue to take his chances with the current group.

HOMER #21: June 4 vs. Detroit Tigers' Beau Brieske (1st inning, solo)
Exit velocity: 106.4 mph. Distance: 378 feet. Launch angle: 31 degrees. HR in 14 of 30 MLB parks.

Babe Ruth's name appeared as a starter on 2,398 big-league lineup cards; never once as a leadoff hitter. Roger Maris hit in the top spot for 19 of his 1,136 starts in the majors, all but four of those assignments coming with the 1958 Kansas City Athletics. Mickey Mantle did it 78 times, mostly for manager Casey Stengel, as he attempted to make his mark in the 1951 and '52 outfields.

The combination of Judge's height and bulk hardly fit the classic definition of a leadoff hitter, though Rickey Henderson—arguably the game's best to ever fill that role—did boast a special blend of power, speed, and on-base ability. Like his early-season shift from right field to center field, the challenge of setting the table atop the lineup was an assignment that Judge gamely added to his resume. Boone saw figures like Judge—who combined on-base percentage with power—becoming more prototypical in the leadoff spot, citing the Los Angeles Dodgers' Mookie Betts and the Toronto Blue Jays' George Springer as examples.

"I like to try and create as much balance as I can, and I certainly like him getting up there as many times as possible," Boone said. "He's enjoyed the leading off and playing center. It obviously becomes a valuable spot, depending on what the rest of the lineup looks like." Judge felt that his winter work had prepared him for the challenge.

"I really wanted to improve on baserunning, speed work," Judge said. "If I was hitting in the top of the lineup, I wanted to steal some bases and get in scoring position for the guys behind me, and also help free up our lineup if I could play center field and give certain guys like Aaron Hicks a break."

On occasions when the formula worked perfectly, Judge could provide immediate offense. That happened when he sat dead-red against the Tigers' Beau Brieske on a sunny Saturday afternoon, sending the rookie's first pitch out of the yard. A twenty-four-year-old making his eighth big-league start, Brieske fired a 95.3 mph fastball and Judge was ready, powering a fly ball toward right-center field.

"I just saw one I liked," Judge said. "I wasn't really going to swing, but as he was stepping back, I was like, 'Should I swing? Should I not?' Then I saw something I liked. I know he's got a great fastball; a good little offspeed pitch too. I was just trying to see something up and out, and it was up, so I went for it."

This was one of those homers where Judge's workout program, which included flipping six-hundred-pound truck tires, made a difference. For most hitters, a similar swing would have generated a routine flyout. This one kept going, sending outfielders Derek Hill and Willi Castro to the warning track, where they watched it land in the eighth row.

"The off-season is where I build my base and I build my strength," Judge explained. "I run through a lot of stuff, and I'm already a pretty big guy naturally, so I don't really need to get too big in the off-season. When I'm lifting heavy, doing squats, and doing upper-body workouts, it's mostly about core and stability. But I'll still do deadlifts. . . . I'm trying to maintain that strength in my core, and if I can maintain that I feel like it'll help my body and help me play a little bit extra."

With a sweep of the Tigers under their belts, next up on the schedule was a trip to Target Field for a three-game set with the Minnesota Twins, a franchise the Yankees had delighted in dominating over the years. No one could explain exactly why, but no matter the cast of characters, the Yanks always seemed to have the upper hand against Minnesota.

As they arrived in the North Star State, New York owned a lopsided 109-38 record against Minnesota, dating to 2002. Sure, much of that dominance belonged to the Jeter-era club, but the present-day Yankees had the most fearsome slugger on the planet at their disposal.

And the press was beginning to take notice. Roger Maris Jr. saw his cell phone buzz at his home in Gainesville, Florida. A reporter from New York was calling, sixty-one years after the M&M Boys dominated the news cycle. If anybody was going to surpass his father's single-season American League mark, Judge seemed to be an ideal choice.

"Dad always said records are meant to be broken," Maris said. "You don't want to see Dad's record go, but if it happened, I can't think of a better guy to do it. He's a great Yankee. To do it in New York, how cool would that be? First we had Ruth, then we had Dad, and then to have Judge, that would be pretty awesome. I can't think of a better storyline."

HOMER #22: June 7 vs. Minnesota Twins' Cole Sands (1st inning, solo)
Exit velocity: 107.7 mph. Distance: 431 feet. Launch angle: 31 degrees. HR in 30 of 30 MLB parks.

Cole Sands still remembers his reaction when Twins manager Rocco Baldelli informed him that the club needed him to make a start against the first-place Yankees: "No way!"

A twenty-four-year-old from Tallahassee, Florida, Sands had bounced between the majors and Triple-A St. Paul early in the 2022 season, making a couple of relief appearances and a decent spot start against the Tigers. The Twins needed him again, and as Sands scanned New York's batting order, he hoped to use the start as a learning experience.

The Yanks wasted no time taking the rookie to school. DJ LeMahieu led off with a single to bring up Judge, who worked the count to 2-2. The Twins' game plan had theorized about attacking Judge down and away; Sands's next pitch, a 93 mph fastball up in the zone, was a mistake. Judge made him pay, clobbering it into Target Field's "living wall," a batter's eye of more than 5,700 sea-green juniper plants.

One batter later, Stanton homered, too, outdoing Judge by reaching the second deck above the bullpens in left field. A month later, Sands was back riding buses in Triple-A with the St. Paul Saints, still chewing on those fat pitches to Judge and Stanton.

"I've learned to navigate through lineups; which guys are you going to let beat you?" Sands said. "I had to learn the hard way, because Aaron Judge and Giancarlo Stanton got me."

The Yanks were off and rolling, surviving a three-error performance in a 10–4 win that made them the majors' first team to forty victories, against 15 losses. Every starter had at least one hit in what Judge said was "all around, a good night," noting that "the bottom of the lineup is picking up the top and then when the top comes back around, we're kind of picking everybody up."

Nestor Cortes took a loss the next night, but the bats broke out to rescue Gerrit Cole in the finale, a contest that saw the ace surrender homers to each of the first three Twins batters: Luis Arraez, Byron Buxton, and Carlos Correa. In over a hundred years of action, the Yankees had never seen one of their pitchers allow homers to the first three batters of a game. It wasn't exactly the type of history Cole had hoped to author.

"Boy, that was tough," Cole said. "Just really poor execution, and not great stuff."

As Cole returned to the dugout in the middle of the first inning, outfielder Joey Gallo sidled up to the hurler, promising him: "We've got you. We've got you." A swing-from-the-heels monster who cared little about his sub–Mendoza Line batting average, Gallo's New York experience had already been cemented as a bust, but this would be remembered as one of the few good days. Gallo homered twice, and Aaron Hicks and DJ LeMahieu also went deep in a 10–7 slugfest win.

Around this time, a group of Yankees instituted a new clubhouse rule for games on the road—they wouldn't leave for the bus until Judge was ready.

"It wasn't just two or three of us—it was like eight, nine, ten of us," Cortes said. "I thought that was pretty cool, that we just said, 'We're not leaving until Judge is ready.' So if Judge was getting treatment in the training room, we were just sitting down, waiting for him. Rizzo started waiting for him, then Big G started waiting for him, then I would. It became this thing where we wouldn't leave until he did."

Clint Frazier couldn't wait to walk back into Yankee Stadium. He had a few scores to settle.

When the Yankees had acquired Frazier from the Cleveland Indians in July 2016, part of the haul for dominant left-handed reliever Andrew Miller, general manager Brian Cashman had lauded the big-swinging outfield prospect for his "legendary bat speed." The fifth overall selection in the 2013 draft, Frazier seemed to have the ingredients for big-league stardom, including swagger.

His lustrous, poofy red hair had been a running story line during spring training in 2017, drawing attention in a clubhouse where George M. Steinbrenner's 1973-era grooming standards were still the law of the land. The fuss eventually prompted a conversation with manager Joe Girardi, who acknowledged that while Frazier's hair did not explicitly violate team policies, Girardi's opinion was that it had "become a distraction." Frazier grumbled as he submitted to the barber's chair, his hair chopped back to its seventh-grade level.

A couple of years into his career, he'd constructed a room in his Atlanta-area home to house his collection of expensive Nike sneakers; CC Sabathia referred to Frazier as "Canal Street Clint," part of a running clubhouse joke in which people around the team insisted that all of Frazier's shoes were cheap knockoffs. Frazier's attitude could rankle teammates, but it didn't derail his New York tenure as much as a series of career-altering concussions, the first of which he sustained in a 2018 spring training game against the Pittsburgh Pirates in Bradenton, Florida.

Released by the Yankees after batting just .186 in 2021, Frazier claimed that he had sustained another concussion while playing the outfield in a September 2020 game, one that he did not disclose to the club until the following June. As the series in the Bronx neared, Frazier cracked his knuckles and indicated he was looking forward to getting some thoughts off his mind. "[I] certainly don't miss some of the things over there," Frazier said. "You had to be a cookie-cutter version to be on that team. If not, then you were a really bad distraction, it seemed like. So I don't miss being told how I had to look for the last five years."

In an episode of unbelievable timing, Frazier never had a chance to take the field. As the Cubs prepared for batting practice, a cluster of New York reporters waited around Frazier's locker, which held a uniform jersey with the No. 77. As the apocryphal story went, Frazier had asked someone close to the Yankees if they "ever unretire numbers," stating his interest in wearing Mickey Mantle's No. 7. After that tale made the rounds, he'd requested double sevens, explaining, "Every time you see me, you're reminded that was a lie."

A staffer hustled Frazier to manager David Ross's office in the visiting clubhouse, where Ross broke the news that the organization had designated Frazier for assignment. The Cubs needed his roster spot to activate a pitcher, reliever Chris Martin. Frazier was "upset" and "emotional," according to Ross; Frazier spent the rest of his year with Triple-A Iowa, where he began going by his given first name of Jackson and dropped a few pounds because, as he said, "I'm a very picky eater, and being in Des Moines, all they have is corn and beer."

The series played on, and the Yankees overcame bleary eyes after their charter flight from Minneapolis landed in Newark just before sunrise, destined to play a four-hour, sixteen-minute marathon. It was not ideal, but Boone said that he had been struck by the buzz in the crowd, having peeked out of the dugout about twenty minutes before game time.

"Friday night, summer, Chicago Cubs in town," he said. "I felt like we fed off that energy a little bit. I thought the energy was really good, coming off a big comeback win and long travel, so I was pleased from that standpoint. That's credit to these guys, making sure they're ready to go and play for a lot."

There was another memorable Jose Trevino walk-off hit; each of the catcher's game-ending knocks had carried a measure of personal significance beyond the on-field celebration. His first came in 2018 with the Rangers, highlighting his first Father's Day with a newborn at home; the second had come in May, on what would have been his late father's birthday. June 10 marked young Josiah's fourth birthday, so Trevino should have known there would be something mystical at work as he walked to the batter's box.

In the thirteenth inning, Dad delivered the game-winning hit, lashing a sharp single that decided a 2–1 victory.

"I don't know what everybody believes in, but I know what I believe in," Trevino said. "I believe I got a little extra help every time something like that happens."

Josiah stayed up until the end, watching from the family's Texas home, chatting with Dad via FaceTime shortly after Trevino was mobbed by teammates between first and second base.

"He was kind of yelling at me, asking if I had won the game for his birthday," Trevino said. "He wanted the Yankees to win for his birthday."

HOMER #23: June 11 vs. Chicago Cubs' Matt Swarmer (1st inning, solo)
Exit velocity: 107.3 mph. Distance: 383 feet. Launch angle: 41 degrees. HR in 29 of 30 MLB parks.
HOMER #24: June 11 vs. Chicago Cubs' Matt Swarmer (5th inning, solo)
Exit velocity: 115.5 mph. Distance: 431 feet. Launch angle: 18 degrees. HR in 30 of 30 MLB parks.

It was a gorgeous Saturday evening in the Bronx, and Matt Swarmer understood the assignment as he walked to the mound. The Cubs desperately needed length, having used eight relievers the previous night, when starter Wade Miley had exited in the first inning with a shoulder strain.

Twelve days after making his big-league debut with a sharp effort against the Milwaukee Brewers, the rookie right-hander was being asked to contain a Yankees lineup with all the makings of a juggernaut. The top item on the agenda was Judge, again appearing in the leadoff spot while serving as the designated hitter. Judge measured the speed of Swarmer's first pitch, sailing outside for a ball. Judge obliterated the next one, an 89.7 mph fastball that came in about belt-high, giving the Yankees a quick lead with a blast to the left-field seats.

Giancarlo Stanton and Gleyber Torres cracked solo homers in the fourth inning. Stanton's 436-foot drive prompted his teammates and coaches to remark upon his freakish talent, a laser that struck an advertising board on the facing of the second deck before bouncing back onto the field. Boone called Stanton a "unicorn."

"We all just kind of looked at each other, and I'm like, 'You're weird,'" Boone said.

Trevino added a homer in the fifth, but Swarmer still had plenty of rope. Judge's spot came up again; Swarmer bounced a slider, then returned to the fastball. The result was much the same as the one he'd thrown in the first inning—this time, Judge hit it harder and farther, dispatching a rocket to the left-field seats overlooking the still-idle Cubs bullpen.

"Unreal," Stanton said. "It's fun to watch. We all have the best seat in the house to it. We all kind of laugh as well after he puts up nights like this."

Two batters later, Anthony Rizzo clipped the 6th Yankee homer off Swarmer, who'd captured a slice of ignominious history. Swarmer was the second pitcher in history to permit 6 solo home runs in a game, joining Hollis "Sloppy" Thurston, who had done it on August 13, 1932, while pitching for the Brooklyn Dodgers against the New York Giants .

The game was different then; Thurston won that day, pitching the Dodgers to an 18–9 victory at the Polo Grounds. Swarmer accepted his fate, saying that the Yankees "have a lot of power hitters, for sure," and that he needed "to make them feel more uncomfortable out there. It seemed they just saw the ball well."

As Judge completed his second trip around the bases, stamping his foot on home plate, loud chants of "M-V-P!" rang throughout the grandstand—it was becoming a common refrain from the paying customers. The clubhouse walls shook after the game, cranked to the highest ear-splitting volume the speakers would allow. For years, Judge had served as the club's in-house DJ, inheriting the auxiliary cord from Sabathia back when the players used an iPod Touch to supply their pre- and postgame music selections.

Judge painstakingly curated playlists on Spotify for each part of his workday; in the hours before first pitch, the clubhouse might be filled with high-energy hip-hop or rap from Migos, Kendrick Lamar, or Calvin Harris. Judge had a special loop that played after each victory, which he titled "Win Song 2022," featuring songs by artists Myke Towers, Kodak Black, and Kevin Gates, among others.

As he dressed at his locker that night, Judge's thoughts were on much more than music or thumping the Cubs.

"We've got a lot of guys in here that really haven't done much of anything," Judge said. "We have Rizzo, Chappy (Aroldis Chapman), a couple of guys with World Series rings—but this team collectively, we haven't. So we're not satisfied just winning the division. I want to go out there and bring the championship back."

"Win Song 2022" was back on the air the next day after another

ridiculous slugfest, an 18–4 rout in which the Yankees batted around
for five first-inning runs. Inserted into the lineup after Gleyber Torres
came down with a stomach bug, Matt Carpenter blasted two homers
and drove in seven RBIs, continuing to etch his name in the history
books.

Six of Carpenter's first seven hits in a Yankees uniform were homers
(the other was a bunt single), and he was the first Yankee to hit at least
six homers in his first ten games.

"I've played the game long enough to know what it feels like and
looks like when I'm right," Carpenter said. "This is certainly that. I feel
like I can have competitive at-bats every time I get in there. It kind of
got away from me the last few years; I didn't really have it. I was able to
put in a lot of good work and have a lot of people help me get it back. To
be able to do it in New York City, for the best team in baseball, it means
a lot. I'm enjoying it."

The Yanks had stumbled upon another heater, enjoying what would become a nine-game winning streak. Gerrit Cole induced a key double-
play grounder to help the Yankees win the opener over the visiting Rays,
on a picture-perfect Tuesday evening. They would improve their record
to a commanding thirty games over .500 the next night, which Boone
called "a drop in the bucket—a good deposit."

The mindset was similar to what former manager Joe Torre voiced
to his dynasty-era Yanks; focus on five-game "small bites" of the season,
getting to .500, then five games over, then ten. If they could do that, as
Torre's Bombers clubs often did, the standings would begin to take care
of themselves.

Nestor Cortes never played for Torre, of course; he'd been a freshman at Hialeah Senior High School near Miami when Torre managed
the final game of his Hall of Fame career in 2010, with the Los Angeles Dodgers. This was all new to Cortes, who said the achievement of
reaching thirty games over the break-even mark prompted conversation
behind closed doors in the players' lounge.

"I think this team can do a lot of great things," Cortes said. "The way
we carry ourselves in here translates out there. Night in and night out,

there's always a different guy stepping up to the occasion." One answered more than his share of those calls.

It was about five hours before the scheduled first pitch as Judge boarded an elevator outside the home clubhouse at Yankee Stadium, invited to visit the Yankees Museum on the ballpark's main level. Judge curiously eyed the exhibits, a *Yankees Magazine* editor observing as he perused artifacts like the uniform jersey Babe Ruth wore when he called his shot in the 1932 World Series, Thurman Munson's preserved locker from the old stadium, and nearly nine hundred baseballs autographed by current and former players.

Brian Richards, the museum's curator, keyed open an exhibit case and handed Judge a Rawlings fielder's glove that Mickey Mantle had worn during the 1963 season. Judge unfolded the fifty-nine-year-old leather and ran his fingers inside the pocket of Mantle's old gear, an experimental XPG-6 model. Judge was thrilled, but he couldn't imagine how The Mick used it. "To be honest, this is like an infield glove," Judge said.

"When I handed him Mickey Mantle's glove, he got this very sweet, innocent smile and said, 'Is it OK?'" Richards said. "He held it in his hands and looked at it, and then he looked up and had this look of pure joy on his face. His eyes were just sparkling because he felt this sense of wonder, that he was connected with Mickey Mantle by holding this glove."

Judge scanned the room, spotting his pinstriped No. 99 jersey hanging in an exhibit alongside those worn by Ruth, Mantle, Roger Maris, and Reggie Jackson. "What's that last one doing in there?" he asked. Judge started toward the exit, until Richards raised an index finger, coaxing his guest to wait for just a moment. Richards hurried to a storage vault, emerging with a forty-five-ounce Louisville Slugger bat that Ruth had swung during the 1922 season, when the Yankees still played their home games at the Polo Grounds.

Compared to modern equipment, Ruth's choice was a telephone pole, massively long and thick. Richards offered the bat to Judge, who asked: "I can touch it?" Richards affirmed that Judge could, inviting him to place his hands where the Babe once had.

"Oh, this feels great," Judge said. "I might take this out there tonight, if you guys don't mind. There's definitely some magic still left in this."

As he departed, Judge turned to Richards and asked: "Can I come back sometime?" Richards was reminded of a scene in the 1989 film *Field of Dreams*, where Ray Liotta's "Shoeless Joe" Jackson character asks if he will be allowed to return to the magical Iowa cornfield.

"I thought, 'Yes, I built this for you,'" Richards said. "He was respectful, appreciative, thoughtful; just very much in tune with Yankees history. I remember walking away just so impressed, thinking, 'He's exactly what I wanted him to be.' He's this combination of Mickey Mantle's tremendous power and Derek Jeter's personality, where he's comfortable in the spotlight and says the right things."

HOMER #25: June 15 vs. Tampa Bay Rays' Shane McClanahan (1st inning, solo)
Exit velocity: 104.1 mph. Distance: 364 feet. Launch angle: 24 degrees. HR in 1 of 30 MLB parks.

Judge used his own bat, not the Bambino's, as he stepped into the box that night against Shane McClanahan. A twenty-five-year-old left-hander, McClanahan was off to a terrific start as Tampa Bay's ace, on the receiving end of some early Cy Young Award chatter thanks to a 7-2 record and 1.87 ERA across his first twelve starts.

With one out in the first inning, McClanahan set to work against Judge, who worked the count full by spitting on a couple of pitches and fouling one off. McClanahan tried a curveball that lacked the intended bite, floating into dangerous territory. Judge connected and drove the ball to right-center field, where outfielder Manuel Margot ran out of room on the warning track.

"I just relied on my teammates, relied on our scouting reports," Judge said. "Especially against [McClanahan], I haven't had much success off him. He was running that fastball to 99 or 100; I'm just trying to battle and put something in play. I got a curveball hanging that I was able to put out to right."

It was a Yankee Stadium special, an extra-base hit or out in any of the other twenty-nine ballparks. In the Bronx, it was a homer. After Judge returned to the dugout, he conferred with Rizzo, who had a mischievous twinkle in his eye. "Hey," Rizzo said. "Get 30 before the All-Star break. We've got two weeks left. You've got this."

Judge grinned. Challenge accepted.

"Sometimes it's that guy next to you saying, 'Hey, come on, you've got this. Let's push it a little bit,'" Judge said. "Just having someone to manifest your goals with you, that positive reinforcement next to you, it keeps pushing you and helping you along."

The Yanks won that night and the next, when Rizzo had launched a walk-off homer in the ninth inning. Rizzo gestured as though he was securing the team's jewel-encrusted, wrestling-style belt across his waistline, a token for the game's most significant contributor.

As he clutched the real thing in the clubhouse five minutes later, Rizzo made the requisite closed-door speech to teammates and coaches, announcing that a championship season would take contributions from everyone.

"There's a lot of big names in this clubhouse, and you would never know inside," Rizzo said. "Everyone is treated on the same level, whether you have a couple of days in the big leagues or fifteen years. We keep it loose."

That win marked the club's fourteenth straight in the Bronx, an unprecedented run in the present-day incarnation of Yankee Stadium. "I thought Rizzo said it really well," Boone said. "It's something we say in spring training when the full group is there. Look around; even if you don't think you're going to impact us, there's a chance you might come up in a huge spot. One day, one week, whatever. Make sure you're ready."

Though Boone cautioned, "We ain't done nothing yet," Rizzo's bat continued sizzling, and the Bombers kept rolling. Rizzo hit a grand slam in a rout of the Blue Jays and Clay Holmes helped extend the winning streak to nine games with his twenty-ninth consecutive scoreless outing, eclipsing a franchise record previously held by Mariano Rivera. Holmes was humbled to be mentioned in the same sentence as the great Rivera.

"He's a guy that I grew up watching; I think everybody did," Holmes said. "Just to be in the same category for this one little thing he's done is pretty cool."

When Toronto salvaged the series finale, the Yankees embarked on a bus ride across the border. Because negative COVID-19 tests were still required to board international flights out of Toronto, some professional sports teams made a strategic two-hour detour to Buffalo Niagara International Airport in Buffalo, New York. The Blue Jays, Toronto Maple Leafs, Boston Red Sox, Oakland Athletics, and Philadelphia 76ers were among the other teams known to have bypassed Toronto's airports in favor of Buffalo, with COVID-19 testing no longer required to cross the border by land.

Safely on the ground in Florida, the Yanks reached another milestone the next night at Tropicana Field. Gerrit Cole took a no-hitter into the eighth inning as the Bombers became the majors' first team to fifty victories. New York's winning percentage stood at an otherworldly .746 as they shook hands on the turf that night, and watching from a suite high above the diamond, managing general partner Hal Steinbrenner was dreaming big.

"The club that Cash put together, that we rolled into Opening Day with, was one of the most dominant clubs in all of baseball—for months, not for weeks," Steinbrenner said. "For months."

Yet Cashman refused to take a victory lap; like Boone, he'd been through too many gauntlets, experiencing enough heartbreak to know that nothing had been achieved yet. From 2018 to 2020, the Yankees had lost more days than any other team to leg injuries—calves, hamstrings, and knees—prompting the hiring of health guru Eric Cressey before the '20 campaign. They'd suffered quite a bit in 2021, and prayed that their good health would continue through 2022.

"I've been in this game a long time," Cashman said. "So I've seen a lot of things go well early and not go well late. 162 games is so long, and unfortunately, there was plenty to go. I was very thankful for the time that I had a chance to get some sleep. It felt like we were magically healthy for a really long time; I mean, it was the longest I've ever had as a GM. Three months without any injuries is unheard of, for any club. And then, clearly, that changed."

HOMER #26: June 22 vs. Tampa Bay Rays' Shane Baz (4th inning, solo)
Exit velocity: 99.9 mph. Distance: 396 feet. Launch angle: 34 degrees. HR in 30 of 30 MLB parks.
HOMER #27: June 22 vs. Tampa Bay Rays' Colin Poche (7th inning, solo)
Exit velocity: 109.0 mph. Distance: 406 feet. Launch angle: 41 degrees. HR in 30 of 30 MLB parks.

Judge stood in the batter's box, his feet set widely apart, the bat cocked and still behind his right ear. The Yankees were down by three runs, with Tampa Bay having peppered Jordan Montgomery early, on homers from Rays infielder Isaac Paredes (his fourth in two games) and light-hitting infielder Vidal Bruján.

Now it was the second time through the batting order for Shane Baz, a twenty-three-year-old top prospect making his sixth start in the majors. Baz received a quick lesson in why not to leave sliders spinning over the heart of home plate as Judge pummeled a drive about twelve rows deep over the left-field wall, registering the Yanks' first run of the night.

Immediately after the swing, Baz swung his right arm across his waistline and muttered an expletive, not bothering to watch. He'd seen the last of that particular baseball.

Judge wasn't done yet. Facing lefty Colin Poche in the seventh, Judge clobbered a 1-2 curveball high over the left-field wall, losing track of the projectile as it hung in the air for 6.7 seconds and soared toward Tropicana Field's catwalks. Uncertain about how the ground rules would treat his blast if it were to dent one of those quirky pathways, Judge hustled out of the batter's box, then realized he could safely begin yet another trot. Glancing at first-base umpire John Tumpane while he rounded the bases, Judge sought confirmation that he'd indeed gone deep.

"I saw it the whole way through, but I don't know the catwalk rules," Judge said. "So I started running around the bases; I didn't know what would happen if it would hit one of those and drop back in. I was just trying to make sure I was on second base if it fell in play."

Jose Trevino belted a go-ahead, two-run blast in the eighth inning, providing the necessary margin of victory for the Yanks' eighteenth win in twenty-one games. As he spoke in the clubhouse, Trevino credited his new teammates for helping him reach his offensive potential, noting, "Learning from them has been huge, talking to them and being able to pick their brains. A guy like Judge is special."

To that comment, a passing Judge grinned, raising his right fist into the air—reminding at least one observer of Judd Nelson's character in the iconic closing scene of *The Breakfast Club*. Don't you forget about me, indeed.

The Yankees were heading home, about to test their mettle against the Astros. There was already a playoff atmosphere in the building as the turnstiles began spinning hours before game time, on a fine Thursday evening in the Bronx.

The fans had lubricated their vocal chords with parking lot Budweisers, intent on foully filling the eardrums of José Altuve, Alex Bregman, and the Houston Astros. For a considerable segment of the faithful, there would always be hell to pay for the sins of the 2017 sign-stealing scandal; chants of "Fuck Altuve!" frequently rang out, sometimes when the Astros weren't even in the same state. In that juiced environment, the Yankees rallied for a season highlight, stunning Houston with a furious ninth-inning rally.

New York trailed by three runs as Astros manager Dusty Baker handed the ball to Ryan Pressly for the ninth inning. The righty was a reliable ten-year veteran, but he couldn't hit his marks on this night, issuing walks to Giancarlo Stanton and Gleyber Torres. Watching from his perch near the top step of the dugout, Boone sensed a good level of focus, blended with calm, resolve, and energy.

"It was like, 'Let's go grind this thing out,'" Boone said.

Aaron Hicks's preseason prediction would fall short; that much appeared clear. During spring training, Hicks had boasted that he intended to post a 30-30 season, targeting 30 home runs and 30 stolen bases. As Hicks later learned, that was a feat that only two other Yankees had achieved—by Bobby Bonds in 1975, and twice by Alfonso Soriano, in 2002 and '03. Through his first fifty-nine games of the season, Hicks had managed two homers and seven stolen bases; his off-season plan of trimming weight had not yielded the desired combination of speed and power.

Yet this would be one of Hicks's best moments of the year, jumping on a 1-2 fastball to slug a game-tying home run over the right-field wall, transforming the bleachers and the dugout alike into a frenzied celebration. Pressly continued to struggle, prompting Baker to turn to reliever Ryne Stanek. With runners at first and second bases, Stanek offered a 3-0 cookie that Judge lashed to the left-field wall, celebrating a walk-off single.

"You saw up and down our lineup, guys working the at-bat, the moment not getting too big for guys," Judge said. "It's just believing in each other."

In a remarkable slice of timing, Judge's arbitration hearing had been scheduled for the next day—meaning that, less than twenty-four hours after lifting the team to victory over a despised rival, Judge braced for an opportunity to hear the Yankees' lawyers explain why he should be paid less.

Though Judge was in the midst of his best season yet, hitting .299 and leading the majors with 27 homers and 53 RBIs, the arbitration process demanded that time stop when Judge requested $21 million on March 22. No data from the 2022 season could be factored into the decision; he would either be worth $17 million, as the club contended, or $21 million.

The hearing was scheduled for noon on Zoom, and Judge arrived at the Manhattan headquarters of the Major League Baseball Players Association on time, dressed in a sharp suit and tie.

"Kind of bad timing," Judge said. "We were logged in, ready to go. All dressed up."

The hearing never began, delayed once, then again. By 12:45 p.m., the sides had agreed to meet at the midpoint, setting Judge's 2022 salary at $19 million. The team believed that they had the necessary ammunition to win the hearing, but common sense indicated that saving a few million bucks wouldn't be worth alienating their best player. Judge's new deal included attainable $250,000 bonuses if he was named AL MVP (as he would) and $250,000 if he were named World Series MVP. Still, by dragging things out to the last possible minute, the episode didn't necessarily inspire confidence that Judge's next negotiations would go smoothly.

"I was happy we were able to agree on a number and settle this thing and not have to go into court there," Judge said that night. "If I would have went in that room, I probably would have missed the game tonight, and that didn't really sit too well with me."

The next episode was a flashback, one the Yankees would have gladly skipped.

Almost nineteen years to the day, on June 11, 2003, six Astros combined to hold the Yankees hitless in an interleague game at the original Yankee Stadium. Those hurlers—Roy Oswalt, Peter Munro, Kirk Saarloos, Brad Lidge, Octavio Dotel, and Billy Wagner—had authored the first no-hitter against the Yankees since Baltimore Orioles knuckleballer Hoyt Wilhelm mystified the Bombers on September 20, 1958, at long-gone Memorial Stadium.

(Wilhelm, by the way, played a part in the Roger Maris home run chase—down two runs in the ninth inning on September 20, 1961, the Orioles used their closer to ensure Maris would not tie Babe Ruth's home run record within 154 games. Big league veteran Tom Candiotti would stand in for Wilhelm in Billy Crystal's *61**; Candiotti once recalled throwing Barry Pepper about fifteen straight knucklers, watching the actor playing Maris whiff at each one. Eventually, Crystal settled for rolling a ball up the first base line. Movie magic.)

It did not take long for Gerrit Cole to recognize that he was being challenged in a Saturday afternoon duel, putting up six consecutive zeroes against Houston's high-octane offense, then watching from the bench as young Cristian Javier did the same. After his previous start, Cole had remarked that he wasn't sure what "no-hit stuff" felt like. Javier gave everyone a glimpse of it in an impressive thirteen-strikeout performance, combining with relievers Hector Neris and Ryan Pressly to hold the Yankees hitless in a 3–0 loss that Josh Donaldson called "shocking."

At a career-high 115 pitches through seven innings, the twenty-five-year-old Javier had no chance of completing his gem without help—a preview of what was to come in Game 4 of the World Series, when Javier and three relievers would combine to no-hit the Philadelphia Phillies. The Astros joyously celebrated on the field, and though Cole claimed that the no-hitter stung no worse than a run-of-the-mill defeat, the game offered a jarring reminder. If the Yankees intended to win a championship, their path would likely have to go through Houston.

"That's certainly a fair outlook," Cole said. "They're a complete team. We all know that good pitching and defense win a lot of games in October. You've got to have clutch hitting and magical offense as well, but there's just not a lot of weaknesses over there. They can beat you in a lot of different ways—the same way that we can beat you in a lot of different ways."

HOMER #28: June 26 vs. Houston Astros' Seth Martinez (10th inning, three-run, walkoff)
Exit velocity: 112.0 mph. Distance: 417 feet. Launch angle: 20 degrees. HR in 30 of 30 MLB parks.

Now the Yankees were the "best planet on the team." Let us explain. As Judge stood in front of the first-base dugout at Yankee Stadium, the buzzing late-afternoon crowd still chanting his name, he attempted to collect his thoughts. He'd just drilled his second walk-off homer of the season, a three-run blast that landed in the visiting bullpen, helping to rescue the Yankees from the ignominy of having their offense silenced for a second straight day. In the annals of baseball history, no team has ever been no-hit in consecutive games, though as the Yankees sleepwalked through six innings against right-hander José Urquidy on a steamy Sunday afternoon, the possibility of that unthinkable occurrence was worth a double check.

Held hitless through fifty-two straight at-bats, the helpless vibe changed in a hurry; not only would they get a hit, but they were coming all the way back. Giancarlo Stanton visited Monument Park with a home run that shattered the no-hit bid and shutout. DJ LeMahieu launched a two-run homer to tie the game, and Judge stamped the conclusion with a three-run blast in the tenth, sealing a 6–3 victory over the Astros.

"What I marveled at," Boone said, "was just how easy he swung. It's like he's just trying to touch the ball."

Spotting director and New York superfan Spike Lee in the front row of seats over the first-base dugout, Judge slid the bat underneath the netting, and Lee reacted with the glee of an eight-year-old. Lee would later give Judge's bat prime real estate alongside the Cooperstown-worthy memorabilia collection in his Brooklyn office. He wasn't the only one caught up in the moment.

While speaking with Meredith Marakovits, the YES Network's clubhouse reporter, Judge's trademark media polish was missing . In fact, he seemed to be a bit tongue-tied. When Marakovits asked him where the Yankees' quiet confidence comes from, Judge replied, "Well, when you're the best planet on the team, how could you not?" The remark raised some eyebrows; some viewers swore that Judge had proclaimed himself "the best player on the team." That statement would not have been factually incorrect, but it would have represented an out-of-character declaration for Judge, whose default setting was modesty.

The *New York Post* rolled with it, publishing a story headlined: "Aaron Judge Shows His Confidence with Yankees 'Best Player' Statement." As he scanned the article on a reporter's iPhone the next day, Judge asked: "How could they print this without asking?"

After absorbing the text, Judge sighed. "I was trying to say, 'When you are the best team on the planet,' and I knew I messed it up," he said. "What I said was, 'When you're the best planet on the team.' And I thought to myself, 'I really messed that up.' And then I tried to say something about the fans, and that came out wrong too."

"Look, we've interviewed Aaron Judge a million times," Marakovits said. "The one thing we know about him is, he never likes speaking about himself. He always wants to put the team ahead of his individual accomplishments. So that comment would have been so beyond out of character for him. Even if those were the words that came out of his mouth, there's no way that was his intention."

Baker, Houston's manager, said that the series ended up "Judge 2, us 2." Having notched a hard-fought split of the four-game series with the Astros, the Yankees recognized they had met their most likely obstacle in advancing to the World Series. A softer three-game series against the woeful Oakland Athletics provided a welcome respite, with a rally and another strong spot start by rookie JP Sears fueling the first two wins.

In the finale of a battle between the haves and have-nots, there were three Oakland runs on the scoreboard after the top of the first inning. No problem. To hear Judge describe it, panic didn't fit with these pinstripes. Maybe they weren't "the best planet on the team," but these Yankees had cemented a reputation as kings of comebacks, especially in their home building.

HOMER #29: June 29 vs. Oakland Athletics' Cole Irvin (1st inning, two-run)
Exit velocity: 111.3 mph. Distance: 429 feet. Launch angle: 26 degrees. HR in 30 of 30 MLB parks.

Sure enough, the cavalry was coming in the form of two big swings, enough to secure yet another sweep.

Judge hit a two-run shot in the first inning and Stanton slugged a three-run shot in the third off Cole Irvin, who remarked: "Throwing a fastball down the middle to Judge is probably not the best idea." Irvin settled in, giving Oakland seven innings, but Jameson Taillon and the bullpen put the finishing touches on a torrid month.

The Judge and Stanton blasts gave the Yankees 57 home runs in June, eclipsing a previous mark (56) shared by the 2016 Orioles and 2019 Braves. But Judge said that no one in the clubhouse was satisfied yet.

"We know what's ahead of us," Judge said. "It's halfway through the year now, and we've still got a long way to go, but every win is important. There's been so many years [when] we look back in the end of September, fighting and clawing. I think guys are starting to realize the importance of, hey, we won the series, but this third game means a lot down the road."

Big swings and shutdown relief represented the latest ingredients in a delicious gumbo of home cooking. Their stats were pretty, but Judge nodded toward another one: 39,647, the sun-splashed tally of paid attendees on a Wednesday afternoon.

"It's the fans. The fans are coming out in numbers," Judge said. "It doesn't matter if it's a Wednesday day game or a Friday night where we're playing the Red Sox. The fans have been showing up and supporting us. The opposing teams, they feel that. It's a nice little home-field advantage we've got."

The month wrapped with a one-day trip to Houston's Minute Maid Park, making up a lockout-postponed game from April 4. A 2–1 loss sent New York on to Cleveland, where they arrived by the banks of the Cuyahoga River having claimed a new mantle. With Judge's potentially historic performance pacing the way, the Yanks were now the favorites in the eyes of the oddsmakers.

Caesars Sportsbook announced that New York had overtaken the Dodgers with +400 odds to win the World Series—the first time since July 2020 that Los Angeles had not been favored for the Fall Classic. The Yanks' terrific June, in which they'd won twenty-two of twenty-eight games, sealed the deal.

"After every big win, it seems like it's all Yankees future money on the bet ticker," said Eric Biggio, the lead baseball trader at Caesars. "They've definitely got it going."

Dragging a bit from their quick visit to Houston, the Yanks didn't complain about a Friday rainout, even though it spelled a long Saturday at Progressive Field. It was a solid day's work for the visitors, resulting in a doubleheader sweep. The Guardians salvaged the finale, sending the Yanks on to Pittsburgh, where Judge and several teammates took advantage of a rare Independence Day respite with a visit to the Roberto Clemente Museum.

The group outing had been scheduled by Taillon, who spent his first four seasons pitching for the Pirates and maintained a deep connection to Pittsburgh; an intense coffee aficionado, Taillon still partnered with a local java shop, Commonplace Coffee, on a nonprofit blend that benefited cancer treatments. Taillon invited his teammates to take a history lesson, and Gerrit Cole, Nestor Cortes, Judge, Anthony Rizzo, and Jose Trevino were among the present-day athletes learning about the fallen star's legacy.

A rocket-armed right fielder from Puerto Rico, Clemente tallied three thousand hits in an eighteen-year career, all with the Pirates. His contributions are hardly encapsulated by statistics alone. Clemente died in a 1972 New Year's Eve plane crash, having embarked on a humanitarian mission to deliver supplies to earthquake-ravaged Nicaragua. Clemente's body was lost at sea, and the Hall of Fame swiftly waived its usual five-year waiting period for induction.

As they toured the museum, an awestruck Judge was permitted to handle some of Clemente's game-used bats. Staffers offered to gift Judge a replica of the bat Clemente had used during his playing career, a thirty-six-inch, thirty-eight-ounce Hillerich & Bradsby model, larger than his usual thirty-five-inch, thirty-three-ounce lumber. Holding the stick in his hands, Judge was impressed by its physical weight and historical significance. He promised to use it in batting practice the next day, when he lashed several impressive line drives around PNC Park.

"You see the pictures of him, I'm thinking this guy is 6-5, 6-6," Judge said. "But you hear he was maybe 5-11, 5-10. It's pretty impressive he was able to swing something like this and produce the numbers he did." Judge also noted Clemente's love for the fans, especially a younger generation.

"That's something that's always been a passion for me, so I just kind of felt a connection," he said.

As Judge and the Yankees marveled over the bat, one of Clemente's former teammates ambled onto the playing field. Eighty-five years young, Bill Mazeroski had been the hero of the 1960 World Series, when he belted a ninth-inning home run off pitcher Ralph Terry to stun the heavily favored Yankees in a seven-game Fall Classic. Mazeroski's blast at Forbes Field sent left fielder Yogi Berra back to the ivy-covered brick wall, where he ran out of real estate in pursuing what remains the only Game 7 walk-off homer in World Series history. A portion of that wall still stands on the present-day campus of the University of Pittsburgh.

Elected to the Hall of Fame in 2001, Mazeroski had cut back on public appearances in recent years, but he made an exception with the Yankees in town.

"To get back here and see all these people, it gives me a thrill," he said.

That held true for some of the Yanks as well; Cole remembered his early days in camp as a Pirates prospect, when Mazeroski, Manny Sanguillen, and Bill Virdon would smoke cigars and talk shop, wearing old-school, long white underwear as they sat on stools in the Pirate City clubhouse in Bradenton, Florida.

"That's how I broke into this game," Cole said. "I'm never going to forget those types of things."

HOMER #30: July 6 vs. Pittsburgh Pirates' Manny Bañuelos (8th inning, grand slam)
Exit velocity: 114.7 mph. Distance: 419 feet. Launch angle: 24 degrees. HR in 30 of 30 MLB parks.

One of the Yankees' favorite stories of the season had involved Manny Bañuelos, once a celebrated pitching prospect in the organization who was part of a hyped "Killer B's" trio that also included Dellin Betances and Andrew Brackman. In June, Bañuelos finally got his chance to pitch in pinstripes, passing through the gate of Yankee Stadium's right-field bullpen.

"It's amazing," Bañuelos said. "My dream came true."

It had been 983 days since Bañuelos's most recent appearance in the majors, when he faced Cleveland as a member of the White Sox, and much longer since the opening chapters of his Yankees saga. Now thirty-one, Bañuelos originally signed with the Yankees out of the Mexican League in 2008 for $450,000. He pitched his way to big-league spring training in 2011, where he sheepishly asked Derek Jeter and Mariano Rivera to autograph baseballs for him.

Then the injuries hit; Bañuelos struggled to stay on the field in 2012, missing all of 2013 after undergoing Tommy John surgery. The Yanks traded Bañuelos to the Atlanta Braves in early 2015, a day that Bañuelos recalled as "very sad." Bañuelos spent the next few years drifting between Atlanta, the Angels, the Dodgers, the White Sox, and the Mariners. International stops in the Chinese Professional Baseball League, the 2020 Summer Olympics and the Mexican League had Bañuelos miles from the bright lights, but his original organization was still watching.

Signed to a minor-league contract, Bañuelos posted a 2.89 ERA in $9\frac{1}{3}$ spring innings. But the bullpen was crowded with talented arms, and Bañuelos was sold to the Pirates in late June, where he remained, as New York led by five runs in the eighth inning. Summoned for mop-up relief, the lefty notched a strikeout before permitting a hit and two walks, bringing Judge to the plate. Bañuelos would call Judge "one of the best teammates I've ever had," but at this moment, he was the enemy. Perspiration bathing the back of his neck, Bañuelos enticed Judge to swing and miss at his first pitch, a sinker out of the strike zone.

"When you face a good hitter like that, you want to show everybody how good you are," Bañuelos said. "Not because he's one of the best hitters in the league, but because you don't want to walk him. You want to strike him out."

The next pitch would be a souvenir, dispatched onto a left-field concourse beyond a row of yellow picnic umbrellas. As Judge rounded the bases with his third career grand slam, a large pro-Yankees contingent applauded. Clapping near the top step of the visiting dugout, Boone made eye contact with Carlos Mendoza, the team's bench coach.

"He's got 30 homers," Boone remarked, adding baritone as he spoke the number.

Boone, who hit 126 home runs over a dozen big-league seasons, simply could not fathom possessing that type of power. Few could.

7

HOLLYWOOD SWINGING

To borrow a phrase from an iconic 1959 compilation of Elvis Presley's chart-toppers, 3.7 million baseball fans couldn't be wrong. Aaron Judge was a lock for Los Angeles.

Far and away the leading vote-getter in the first phase of voting for the All-Star Game, the 3,762,498 digital checks next to Judge's name secured an automatic spot in the starting lineup for the July 19 Midsummer Classic at Dodger Stadium. To Judge's delight, he would have plenty of company.

The Yankees paced the majors with six All-Stars, all of whom would don charcoal-gray uniforms with golden trim as they posed for photographs across the stunning Bermuda hybrid grass of Southern California's mid-century baseball utopia. As Judge stood alongside Nestor Cortes, Gerrit Cole, Clay Holmes, Giancarlo Stanton, and Jose Trevino, squinting against the sunshine, he made certain to appreciate the moment's significance.

"That's a pretty big honor," Judge said. "It shows that a lot of fans are rooting for you, and I wouldn't be here without their constant support, motivating me to go out there and do my best. I have a passion and a gift, but I do it for the fans. I do it for the kids who are rocking my jersey in the stands and who one day hope to be playing at Yankee Stadium.

"That's what it's all about; to inspire those kids to do something special in their lives, whether that's baseball or anything else."

It was no surprise that the Yankees would be well represented at the All-Star Game, having arrived at the break with a commanding 64-28 record. At the YES Network command center in Stamford, Connecticut, the president of production and programming, John J. Filippelli, headed daily meetings in which producers and directors discussed topics to cover in each broadcast. There were twenty-six players on the Yankees' roster, but everyone couldn't stop talking about Judge.

"Aaron was dominating all of the storylines," Filippelli said. "The Yankees were winning at a pace that they'd hardly seen in their history, one of their best starts, and a lot of the winning was because of Judge. His offensive contributions were prodigious, his ability to play defense, on the bases and in the clubhouse and as a leader. In a lot of ways, home runs are the currency of this game. You put it all together, and he was the catalyst. The numbers started to pile up and we said: 'He's got a shot at this thing.'"

What no one could have sensed at the moment, least of all Judge, was that the 2022 Bombers had already played their best baseball. The Yanks' high-water mark was achieved on July 8 in Boston, when Josh Donaldson and Matt Carpenter homered to power a 12–5 victory, an old-fashioned, molasses-paced Fenway Park slugfest.

"The first half of the season, they were phenomenal," said Hal Steinbrenner. "We had starting pitching, bullpen, offense, leading the league in numerous categories. What I saw in that first half, we just had a really good, well-rounded team—and it was a team. This was a team that never thought they could lose a game. It didn't matter if they were down ten runs. I saw that in this team, more so than any in a while. That's a powerful thing, when they believe that."

The Yankees' lead in the American League East swelled to 15½ games with that July 8 win, which prompted manager Aaron Boone to proudly proclaim that his team seemed "better in every way" than the vanquished squad that entered its winter of discontent 275 days earlier. That night, having lost a Wild Card game in Fenway's ancient red-brick corridors, Boone had said in a pindrop-silent visiting clubhouse that the league had "closed the gap" on them.

There was little concern when the Yankees split a four-game series with the Red Sox, though it did seem curious when the last-place Cincinnati Reds took two of three games at Yankee Stadium. In the moment, though, it was viewed as little more than a blip. Baseball games aren't played on paper, but if they were, that would've been a series you'd pencil in as a win for the home team—the mighty Yankees against an unremarkable Reds club, which was already preparing to trade away its best pitcher in ace right-hander Luis Castillo. By any measure, Castillo aced his Bronx audition, holding the potent Yanks to a run and two hits over seven innings—an outing that made the Bombers, and their fans, salivate over what could be.

Said Judge of Castillo: "When you've got 100 [mph] and you're painting the corners, it's going to make for a tough day." General manager Brian Cashman frequently called starting pitching the "key to the kingdom," and he knew his club could use help, especially on a day when Luis Severino landed on the injured list with a right lat strain.

It was no easy sale to convince Severino to submit to an MRI examination; Severino experienced extreme claustrophobia and detested visits to that confined tube, but his subconscious interest in self-preservation had been telling him to hold back with his fastball. He'd been able to talk his way out of the machine before; not this time. To his chagrin, Severino wouldn't pitch again in the majors until September.

"I was not happy," said Severino. "I was not expecting that. But if that's the plan they have for me to come back healthy, you have to just follow that plan and work hard to come back."

HOMER #31: July 14 vs. Cincinnati Reds' Jeff Hoffman (8th inning, solo)
Exit velocity: 112.0 mph. Distance: 435 feet. Launch angle: 23 degrees. HR in 28 of 30 MLB parks.

The Yankees trailed by three runs as Judge came to the plate in the series finale against the Reds, facing Jeff Hoffman, a twenty-nine-year-old from upstate Latham, New York. A veteran of seven big-league seasons with the Colorado Rockies and Cincinnati, Hoffman was certainly a more welcome sight than the electric Castillo, whose talents would fuel a prospect-rich bidding war in just a few weeks.

Facing Hoffman, who liked to mix changeups and sliders with a fastball that clocked in the low-to-mid 90s, Judge saw two balls and a strike before the righty pumped a dead-red heater over the plate. Judge crushed it, pelting a red Toyota advertisement that overlooked the Yanks' bullpen in right field. The drive sparked a three-run inning as the Yanks tied the game, only to have late relief struggles spell their fall in ten innings; just their fourth series defeat of the season.

As Judge met the media in the clubhouse, a classic Bob Marley track blasted over the stereo system. Normally, the clubhouse was kept silent after a loss, limited to hushed mumbling and the occasional clink of forks against plates. This time, Marley's 1977 hit "Three Little Birds" seemingly had a message for the players: "Don't worry about a thing / 'Cause every little thing is gonna be all right."

"I liked our chances going into extra innings, especially with how our team handles big situations like that," Judge said. "We had an opportunity to win the game, but we just fell a little short. The Reds battled their butts off this whole series. We went back and forth, but couldn't pull that one out."

Marley's comforting reggaeton was only a momentary salve. There would be more frustration on deck; the Yanks flushed a winnable series opener against the Red Sox, in which Boone was again ejected after arguing pitches out of the strike zone called on Judge. As he exited, Boone whipped his gum toward the grass, a sidearm motion borrowed from his days patrolling third base. His players soon experienced similar anguish when Xander Bogaerts dashed home on a Michael King wild pitch.

Now the sound system was silenced, except for Trevino striking a glass-half-full note, opining: "A little adversity never hurts anybody. I think we'll be fine."

HOMER #32: July 16 vs. Boston Red Sox's Nick Pivetta (5th inning, solo)
Exit velocity: 102.6 mph. Distance: 401 feet. Launch angle: 26 degrees. HR in 30 of 30 MLB parks.
HOMER #33: July 16 vs. Boston Red Sox's Kaleb Ort (6th inning, two-run)
Exit velocity: 108.5 mph. Distance: 444 feet. Launch angle: 26 degrees. HR in 30 of 30 MLB parks.

At least the Carpenter and Judge show continued to roll. After Boston took the series opener, New York scored three first-inning runs off left-hander Chris Sale, who exited after a line drive fractured the pinkie finger of his pitching hand. Cole said that the Yankees "felt really bad about" Sale's injury, noting the former ace's efforts to return after missing most of the last two seasons due to Tommy John surgery. With the Red Sox tossing an unexpected bullpen game, the Yanks erupted for eight runs in the fourth inning, sending twelve men to the plate.

Carpenter received an emotional curtain call after clearing the right-field wall with a three-run homer off Nick Pivetta, then another three-run shot in the fifth off Darwinzon Hernandez. Already a cult hero in the Bronx who could find his mustachioed likeness on T-shirts—the best was one that depicted him and Cortes as Yankees versions of Nintendo's Mario and Luigi, the "Super 'Stache Bros."—Carpenter had belted thirteen long balls since the day he volunteered to help load bags on the team plane. Judge said that he was not surprised.

"Once I saw the way he worked, the way he prepared, I knew he was going to do something special with us," Judge said. "From his presence to the way he talks to younger guys, the way he just fit in from Day 1, there was no awkward period. He bought into our process."

Judge's mindset remained simple—to hunt strikes, and hit them hard. He teed off on a Nick Pivetta slider in the fifth inning, prompting the righty to drop to a knee on the mound as the ball sailed toward the left-field seats. Kaleb Ort tried almost the same pitch in the sixth against Judge, and the result was nearly identical; Ort stood with his hands by his hips, tracking the drive as it rattled into the Boston bullpen.

"I threw a first pitch slider to try to get ahead," Ort said. "I threw it right down the middle and he hit it over 400 feet. He's clearly locked in."

Three Red Sox sat nearby; not one moved as the ball struck an advertisement for Lotte Hotels, falling near the warm-up mounds. Only one Yankee had ever hit 33 homers before an All-Star break: Roger Maris, in 1961. Now there were two.

"There's some guys you watch where it's like, 'Man, this guy is just on it right now,'" said Clay Holmes. "Toward the midway point of the year, we were starting to look at the pace he was on, and it was like, 'Yeah, [62] is definitely attainable.'"

It was around this time that hitting coach Dillon Lawson sidled up to Judge near the bat rack; Lawson can't pinpoint the exact date or opponent, but he said the Yankees were winning big at home, which makes this 14–1 rout of Boston a solid educated guess. "I was just thinking about my kids, telling him, 'I'll be gone, my kids will be gone, and if they have kids—their kids will know you and talk about you like people talk about Maris and Mantle and DiMaggio and Ruth and Gehrig. It's crazy and amazing to think about.'"

Lawson described walking through the hallways underneath Yankee Stadium, where black-and-white photos appear primed to return to life, like the scene of a cigar-chomping Babe Ruth exiting a boy's closet in *The Sandlot*. In return, Judge had offered a sheepish, humble smile.

"You know how he is," Lawson said. "It was a very short remark back. But he's thankful, and he appreciates that. He's not ever going to tell you if he agrees with that. I think he goes there, definitely, behind closed doors."

Boone planned to spend the break vacationing with his family in the Hamptons, mentioning several times how he looked forward to holding a spatula and donning board shorts. His club was not off duty yet. A 13–2 rout of the Red Sox sealed the Yankees' sixty-fourth victory, establishing a new club record for victories before the Midsummer Classic. Yet that alone was no guarantee of greater things. Since baseball integrated in 1947, six big-league teams had won 64 of their first 92 games, with the 2022 Yankees joining the 1954 Indians (64-28), 1969 Orioles (64-28), 1970 Reds (64-28), 1998 Yankees (68-24), and 2001 Mariners (66-26). Only one of those clubs—the '98 Yanks—hoisted the World Series trophy at the year's end.

"It's pretty big; it's pretty cool," Cole said, "but we have bigger goals. We have a lot more baseball to play, so we're trying to keep it in perspective, in that regard."

As ESPN prepared to air the first installment of Derek Jeter's *The Captain*, a seven-part documentary offering a behind-the-scenes look at the Hall of Famer's career, a chartered jet delivered Judge and his teammates across the country to Los Angeles. Somewhere over a flyover state, Judge predicted to his fellow passengers that Stanton would "definitely" hit a home run in the All-Star Game. They were spectators for a winning

Home Run Derby performance by wunderkind Juan Soto—then of the Washington Nationals, but not for much longer.

Soto had recently rejected a monstrous fifteen-year, $440 million extension from Washington, and the Nats were weeks away from trading the twenty-two-year-old outfielder to the San Diego Padres. Judge had a few nuggets of advice for Soto, telling him to "focus on the game" and allow his agents to handle the big-money decisions to "help set up his family, grandkids, future kids down the road." His remarks to Soto represented a rare in-season window into Judge's considerations and process, with his own yet-to-be-negotiated contract percolating on the back burner.

Judge was more interested in discussing Soto's on-field talent. He could appreciate the slugger's efforts in besting Julio Rodriguez, the impressive Seattle Mariners outfielder and the eventual Rookie of the Year. Judge's 2017 Derby performance at Miami's Marlins Park was not easily forgotten; it had been so memorable, Judge insisted that he was probably a one-and-done in the home run hitting competition.

With his Derby calendar thus clear, Judge exuded Golden State cool as he walked a red carpet at the L.A. Live entertainment complex downtown, Major League Baseball's chosen venue to lean into Hollywood glitz and glamour. Clutching his wife Samantha's right hand and sporting black sunglasses, Judge offered photographers two fingers for a peace sign, outfitted in a tan double-breasted blazer over a white T-shirt with white pants and white sneakers. The shutterbugs clamored as Judge received the full movie star treatment. He was having fun, but he also felt as though he hadn't achieved anything yet.

"The minute I'm satisfied, or the minute I sit back and reflect on how far I've come, that's when you get complacent," Judge said. "I certainly don't want that to happen. There's a long way to go. I don't sit around in a comfortable chair thinking about the 33 home runs I've hit so far. You really have to stay focused on the immediate future, and that's what I'm doing."

It was a sunbaked eighty-seven degrees at three o'clock in the afternoon as Judge and Giancarlo Stanton advanced toward the batting cage, representing the first Yankees outfield duo to start an All-Star Game since Rickey Henderson and Dave Winfield in 1988.

By coincidence, Winfield was on the infield grass observing the festivities, and Judge told him with a wink: "We had our own little Home Run Derby during batting practice."

The Hall of Fame outfielder asked who had won. Now Judge offered that megawatt grin.

"Stanton," he said. "He did what he's been doing the whole season, just hitting clutch home runs."

It was a precursor of what was to come later that day. The All-Star Game represented a homecoming for Stanton, who grew up in the Tujunga area of Los Angeles, a three-sport athlete at Notre Dame High School in Sherman Oaks, California. His living room hadn't been far from Dodger Stadium—though, as Stanton recalled with a chuckle, "I'm like 30 minutes with no traffic, but we all know L.A. That's two hours."

He'd once dreamed of wearing Dodger blue, envisioning himself plying his trade in front of one of the sport's most picturesque backdrops, the palm trees and assorted flora of the Elysian Hills and San Gabriel Mountains overlooking decades of standout performances. A young Stanton counted Raul Mondesi, Mike Piazza, and Hideo Nomo among his favorite players, and he'd once called the ballpark "the place that made me love baseball."

The legendary Vin Scully voiced much of Stanton's summer soundtrack, and he'd frequently try to come to games when Barry Bonds, Mark McGwire, Sammy Sosa, and other great sluggers were in town—players that Stanton referred to as the "big bops." Sometimes, Stanton would wait in the parking lot until a few innings had been played, scoring discounts from scalpers so he could see the stars' last two at-bats.

Around age ten, Stanton had spent a particularly busy batting-practice session chasing those big bops' deep drives into the gold and blue bleachers when he told his father, Mike, "I'm going to hit one completely out of this stadium." Stanton had hit about four over-the-fence home runs in Little League to that point, and Dad laughed, replying, "Now that would be something."

"Kids say some wild things," Stanton said, "but I was dead serious. I thought about it every time I'd go there after that."

Only three players had slugged homers completely out of Dodger Stadium; the Pittsburgh Pirates' Willie Stargell in 1965, Piazza in 1997, and McGwire in 1999. Stanton would become the fourth, though it didn't happen quite as he'd intended.

George Genovese, a legendary Southern California–area scout, invited Stanton to show off his still-developing power in a predraft workout at Dodger Stadium. Genovese pushed hard for Stanton, urging Los Angeles to select him in the 2007 draft. The Dodgers passed on Stanton twice, using their first picks on pitchers Chris Withrow and James Adkins—neither of whom made much of an impact. Stanton, taken seventy-sixth overall by the Marlins, made his mark.

In 2015, a few months after committing to the thirteen-year, $325 million contract that was expected to keep him wearing the orange, black, blue, and red of the Miami Marlins forever, Stanton made good on his promise. Facing the Dodgers' Mike Bolsinger, Stanton tattooed a ball over the left-field pavilion and into the Chavez Ravine parking lot—a blast so prodigious that left fielder Scott Van Slyke didn't bother to turn around.

"Where was I going to go, try and catch it?" Van Slyke asked.

Childhood fantasies rushed back every time Stanton set foot in Dodger Stadium, especially while he patrolled left field as an All-Star Game starter.

"This brings back so many memories," Stanton said. "I just keep looking into the stands, and I see fathers sitting there with their sons. That brings me all the way back to when I was sitting out there with my dad. Being on the field today, it's all in reverse."

Judge, Stanton, and Cole had all experienced multiple All-Star Games, and the decorated trio relished seeing Cortes, Holmes, and Trevino savor their first trips to the Midsummer Classic.

A hidden camera installed on Boone's desk had captured the players' reactions as they were summoned, one by one, to the manager's office at Fenway Park a week prior. Boone relished each of those faux interviews, but took special delight in relaying the news of Cortes's All-Star selection. That spring, a conversation occurred between Boone and Cortes in the clubhouse at Steinbrenner Field, where Cortes asked for a temperature check on his chances of heading north with the club. Boone was caught off guard.

"Nestor," the manager said, "you're in the All-Star Game this year."

Cortes had chuckled, but he didn't believe it. Boone's prediction seemed more attainable when the mustachioed throwback delivered dollar-store ERAs early in the season: 1.50 through ten starts, 1.94 through twelve, and 2.74 as he sank into the well-worn leather couch parked underneath a vintage Fenway photo, dressed in an NBA-style sweatsuit with an interlocking "NY" over the left breast.

"Do you remember the conversation we had at your locker in spring training?" Boone asked.

Cortes nodded, a grin leaking across his face. He knew what this chat was about.

"You said," Cortes replied, "that I would be an All-Star this year."

Now Boone was nodding, leaning back in a leather recliner.

"Well, you've got to let all of Hialeah know," Boone said. "They've got to go to L.A. The legend of Nestor Cortes moves on to Hollywood. We've got bigger fish to fry, brother, but it's time to go celebrate what you deserve and earned."

It had been only a few months since Cortes had reached out to pitching coach Matt Blake, asking about his place on the roster by saying, "Am I on the inside looking out? Or am I on the outside looking in?" Blake had laughed, then realized that Cortes was serious. Despite holding opponents to a 2.90 ERA across ninety-three innings in 2021, it would perpetually be 2018 in the lefty's mind, when Cortes had made his big-league debut with four appearances for the cellar-dwelling Baltimore Orioles.

After allowing 4 runs and 10 hits in 4⅔ innings, a 7.71 ERA, Cortes was designated for assignment—essentially, baseball terminology for being fired. Cortes felt that his long-shot career had reached a tipping point. "I just got DFA'ed," Cortes recalled thinking, "by the worst team in baseball." If he couldn't pitch for the Orioles, an awful team headed toward a 115-loss season, then who would want him? To Cortes's surprise, the Yankees still did.

Cortes had been a thirty-sixth-round selection in 2013, when he'd accepted a relatively paltry $85,000 signing bonus from the Yanks. Cortes's parents, Nestor Sr. and Yuslaidy, wanted the boy they'd brought to Miami at 7 months old from Surgidero de Batabanó, Cuba, to be the first member of their family to attend college. The son of a forklift driver and a manicurist, Cortes wanted that, too, committing to Florida International University, while considering Miami Dade College as a backup.

He dreamed of following in the footsteps of local products like Anthony Rizzo, Manny Machado, and his baseball role model, pitcher Gio González, but there was no guarantee that a professional contract waited on the other side of campus. When area scout Carlos Marti dialed Cortes's phone number late on the third day of the draft, nine rounds remained, and Cortes ranked tenth on the list of players that the Yankees wanted.

Marti recalled following Damon Oppenheimer, the team's vice president of domestic amateur scouting, to the restroom in hopes of pleading Cortes's case: "I know he doesn't throw hard, and he's not very impressive to look at, but this guy is going to get a lot of outs."

Oppenheimer asked Marti if he'd stake his career on the pick. Marti shook his head.

"I just know that he's going to help us," said the scout, who'd later admit that he only envisioned Cortes's ceiling as being one of a back-end starter.

Other teams grabbed a few of the names that Oppenheimer desired, and Marti's request was granted. Standing a stocky five foot ten as he reported to rookie ball, Cortes did not light up the radar gun, spending three seasons at the lowest levels of the minors, while scraping the low 90s with his fastball. Cortes watched teammates with more talent become disillusioned and hang up their spikes. He would make someone tear the uniform off him, even if it meant struggling financially and eating Little Caesars pizza three times a week.

Cortes flashed enough moxie in the minors to tempt the Orioles in the 2017 Rule 5 Draft, a procedure granting Baltimore his contractual rights for six years, as long as they kept him on their major-league roster for the entire 2018 season. But Cortes's audition had flopped, and the Yankees welcomed him back. Boone called Cortes's number as a long reliever and one-time spot starter for thirty-three games in 2019, with Cortes pitching to a forgettable 5.67 ERA.

That November, Cortes's contract was sold to the Seattle Mariners for $28,300 in international bonus spending pool money. Cortes spent the lockdown portion of the COVID-19 pandemic tossing in his Florida front yard; when the shortened season finally began in July, Cortes made five appearances, and a bloated 15.26 ERA delivered Cortes to another career crossroads. Pitchers who towered and glowered with 97 mph fastballs got more chances; guys who looked like Cortes were more likely to be stuck hanging on in the independent leagues, if at all.

During a stint at Seattle's alternate site in Tacoma, Washington, Cortes sidled up to pitching coach Rob Marcello Jr., asking: "Tell me what I did in the minor leagues that helped me be so successful, and what I'm doing now that's not correlating." Marcello, a former minor-league pitcher, used a high-tech camera and reams of information to perform a deep dive into Cortes's mechanics. They decided that Cortes's cutter and changeup had the potential to be average pitches, but his fastball presented no challenge to the world's most talented hitters.

Marcello suggested that Cortes try a different grip to generate spin, turning the baseball into a clock. Instead of holding the ball with his middle and index fingers at his natural 10:45 setting, Cortes rotated to 11:30, which made the ball travel with more backspin. Now he had a weapon that could make hitters swing and miss. Encouraged by the early results, Cortes threw harder, though his average fastball still only registered slightly faster than a Cole changeup.

He might have to do it with smoke and mirrors, but Cortes resolved to sink or swim his way, mystifying hitters with various arm speeds and deliveries, precision and funk. It was too late to revisit his boyhood fantasies of becoming a marine biologist; Cortes needed to make baseball work, and he continued to fine-tune his newfound grip in the Dominican Winter League.

He'd been altering his pitching motion as far back as his high school days, incorporating herky-jerky pauses that befuddled hitters. He'd periodically trimmed that part of his arsenal during his early minor-league career, sensing pressure to fit in, but picked it up occasionally while pitching with the Double-A Trenton Thunder. Sometimes, Cortes wondered if the act made the decision-makers think of him like something of a sideshow. Now he wanted to stand out, skepticism be damned.

"He's really authentic," Blake said, "in who he is."

Against long odds, Cortes had become a star. He was even being noticed on the streets of New York more, though he believed that was more attributable to his old-school mustache than his pitching prowess. The "Super Mario" had been Cortes's most successful choice by far, much better than the clean-shaven, goatee, and full-beard looks he'd tried over his first few big-league seasons.

"I go out there every fifth day like it's the last time I'm going to pitch," Cortes said. "I think that's how I've handled my whole career, even the minor leagues. For me to be able to go out there, enjoy the moment and just be part of it, I think that's what keeps me level-headed—with that sense of urgency to do well every time."

Marti, the scout who'd once gambled his livelihood on the Hialeah Kid's success, had by then left baseball in favor of teaching government and economics at Cortes's alma mater. He frequently told students that no one would blink an eye if Cortes entered their classroom holding a ladder and wearing a maintenance shirt; surely, that would not be the case if Judge or Stanton stopped by to change a light bulb.

That everyman quality was part of Cortes's charm; he'd lobbied for the Yankees to adopt a turtle as a pet, which they named "Bronxie" and kept in the clubhouse during the club's 2021 postseason drive.

That winter, Cortes had a "Nasty Nestor" tattoo inked on his non-pitching hand, desiring a permanent reminder of what could be a fleeting moment in the sun. Even while dining with teammates, Cortes still sometimes looked around the table at faces of players like Judge, Stanton, Cole, and Rizzo, wondering what he'd done to finagle an invitation with that crew.

"I grew up in Miami," Cortes said. "I watched Stanton when he was on the Marlins. It's so cool to share a clubhouse. Sometimes, I see myself sitting on the couch with Anthony Rizzo. I'm like: 'Hey, what's up, dude? I can't believe I'm sitting right next to you.'"

Boone continued delivering good news as Carlos Mendoza padded across the cramped visiting quarters, the same room that Maris, Mickey Mantle, and every great American League player of the last century had inhabited, at least for a brief stay. Clay Holmes sat quietly at his locker, on the far wall. The bench coach summoned Holmes to the manager's office, walking past the perpetually mildewed shower, which had finally been protected from prying eyes by a clubhouse attendant's long-overdue decision to procure a $3 vinyl curtain.

Holmes wasn't sure what Boone wanted, and a curious expression was evident to everyone in the room. Knowing that his new closer wasn't much for chitchat, Boone cut to the chase, noting, "Well, the most dominant reliever in the sport gets to go to L.A. for the All-Star Game. You earned it, and we're all reaping the rewards."

Holmes nodded and cracked a smile, replying flatly, "Sweet. That's awesome. Awesome."

Once he exited the office, Holmes returned to his locker, dug out his cell phone to call his wife, Ashlyn, then sent a group text message to alert his family that they should begin pricing flights to Los Angeles. Wielding a nasty power sinker that Cole called "one of the best pitches in baseball," Holmes had assumed the closer's role when Aroldis Chapman was sunk by an early-season combo of ineffectiveness and injury. In forty-one appearances before the All-Star break, Holmes held opponents to a 1.31 ERA and .182 batting average, with sixteen saves. It marked an impressive turnaround for the twenty-nine-year-old, who'd hardly been a household name when the Yankees acquired him from the Pittsburgh Pirates in July 2021.

Clutching bottles of water and a fresh tube of toothpaste in the checkout lane of a Pittsburgh Target that day, Holmes had felt his cell phone buzz. Recognizing the number, he thumbed a green button to accept the call. Ben Cherington, the Pirates' general manager, eschewed pleasantries and cut to the chase. Holmes had been traded to the Yankees. He thanked Cherington, then spun and strode through the store aisles, searching for a razor.

Since that day, the six-foot-five, 245-pound Holmes looked like a diamond in the rough. Shawn Hill and Brandon Duckworth, a couple of former pitchers in the Yankees' scouting ranks, were credited with having looked beyond Holmes's high walk totals and ERA with Pittsburgh. They eyed his stuff and underlying performance, suspecting he'd benefit from a change of scenery. Hill's internal report said that trading for Holmes would be "a no brainer."

It was a full-circle moment for Holmes. As an eight-year-old in Slocomb, Alabama, a city of 2,094 and the self-proclaimed "home of the tomato," Holmes had pitched and played third base for a youth baseball team that borrowed the Yankees' nickname. Holmes's father, Wendell, was a local pastor who also served as the team's coach.

One day in 2001, Wendell Holmes mailed a letter to Yankee Stadium, asking if the team would donate souvenirs to the boys on his team. Two boxes soon appeared on the Holmes's doorstep containing Yankees caps with the World Series logo stitched on the sides. The kids cheered, and though Holmes grew up in Atlanta Braves country, Yankees memorabilia would forever adorn the walls of his childhood bedroom.

The tallest, and best, player on that youth Yankees team developed into one of Alabama's top prospects. Pittsburgh selected Holmes in the ninth round of the 2011 draft, handing over a $1.2 million signing bonus that kept him from attending Auburn University. Holmes's ascent toward the majors featured a 2014 season lost to Tommy John surgery and more than a few bouts of wildness, but he made it to the Show in 2018.

When injuries limited his 2020 season to a lone appearance, Holmes spent his downtime digging into pitch analytics, specifically focusing on his sinker—the ground ball–inducing pitch that, upon arrival in the Bronx, the Yankees' coaches instructed him to throw even more frequently.

"I've just started learning my best sinker and trying to throw that one more often," Holmes said. "The feel has definitely come along and I've been able to throw it to both sides of the plate if I need to. It's been a combination of things, but first is being in good counts with it so I can let the action do the work."

On the day Boone delivered buckets of good news to his All-Stars, Jose Trevino had been focused on scouting reports for the Red Sox lineup, preparing to guide Jameson Taillon through his seventeenth start of the season. As it did for Cortes and Holmes, a tap came for Trevino, who wore an expression of uncertainty during Boone's preamble.

"I know you're all about winning a championship. That's what we're here to do, right?" Boone said. "One of the reasons we're in this position that we're in right now is because of you."

Trevino swallowed hard and blinked. Worst-case scenario images of a trade, demotion, or release flickered through his mind. "So, there's a little break in the championship run next week," Boone continued, "and I think you should go to L.A. so you can be in the Midsummer Classic." Finally, Trevino exhaled, sporting a relieved grin as he cradled his cheeks in his palms. Twice, Trevino asked his manager if he was being serious.

"You're a major-league All-Star, and no one will ever be able to take that away from you," Boone replied.

Ambling onto the Dodger Stadium diamond, Trevino watched with a measure of bemusement as Shohei Ohtani, the Angels' magnificent two-way superstar, navigated a packed media horde behind home plate. Even with NEW YORK across his chest, Trevino could enjoy relative anonymity in this circle.

He wore custom spikes adorned with Yankee Stadium's iconic frieze and the famous phrase from Joe DiMaggio, "I'd like to thank the good Lord for making me a Yankee," the same words that had been printed on a sign above the clubhouse runway at Yankee Stadium, inviting a grazing touch from Derek Jeter before every home game.

"When I was growing up, I didn't dream about playing in the majors; I dreamed about playing for the Yankees," Trevino said. "I'm thankful to be here, and I feel like wearing the Yankees uniform has helped me reach my potential."

———

Forty-two years had passed since the last All-Star Game at Dodger Stadium, which featured eight future Hall of Famers in the starting lineups and ended with Ken Griffey Sr. claiming Most Valuable Player honors. That iconic number, 42, loomed large with a pregame tribute to barrier-breaking legend Jackie Robinson, narrated by actor Denzel Washington, who sported a replica of Robinson's Brooklyn uniform jersey.

Washington passed the microphone to Mookie Betts, the Dodgers' outfielder, who asked the crowd of 52,518 to mark the occasion of Rachel Robinson's one hundredth birthday by singing "Happy Birthday."

It was a spirited and competitive contest, and four Yankees made significant contributions. The National League grabbed an early two-run lead facing the Rays' Shane McClanahan, and a runner stood at first base with one out in the top of the fourth inning as Stanton stepped in for his second at-bat of the night. Stanton had yet to notch a hit in an All-Star Game, striking out four times, including once already on this night. Dodgers pitcher Tony Gonsolin started Stanton's second at-bat with a couple of strikes, but there would be no whiff this time. Stanton launched the righty's next pitch deep toward the left-field bleachers, the very same area where he'd once chased batting-practice bombs.

Stanton's 457-foot homer tied the game, a clout witnessed by at least fifty family members and friends for whom he'd left tickets, including his father. The night of the 2015 blast that hit the back canopy of the left-field pavilion, then bounced into the parking lot, Stanton had hugged his dad outside the visiting clubhouse as they laughed giddily. This moment was even better. Stanton had hardly settled back into the dugout when the American League took the lead, with the Twins' electric outfielder Byron Buxton also going deep off Gonsolin.

"He was telling us," Buxton said, "how he used to sit as a kid just a few rows from where he hit that home run. You couldn't be any happier for him."

The AL's relievers ensured that the lead held up, including Cortes, who partnered with Trevino to author a scoreless sixth inning. The Cortes-Trevino battery provided some of the evening's best entertainment; both players wore microphones for the FOX broadcast, capturing their on-field banter after the lefty opened his frame with a strikeout of the Braves' Austin Riley.

"You want this ball?" Trevino asked. Replied Cortes: "Yeah, why not?"

Trevino was still wearing his microphone when he stepped to the plate in the seventh inning, lashing a single off the Brewers' Devin Williams for his first All-Star Game hit.

"I need that ball; this is my first All-Star hit right there!" Trevino said. "This is unreal!"

Holmes appeared more even-tempered, but was no less excited in the eighth, facing three batters in his first All-Star appearance. Emmanuel Clase, Cleveland's fireballing closer, struck out the side in the ninth to seal the AL's victory, setting the stage for the on-field Most Valuable Player presentation—an award named after Ted Williams, the legendary Boston Red Sox outfielder. There was little debate; the hometown boy had earned the honor. Stanton held a commemorative bat high above his head with both hands, a moment that he said was "incredible."

"I think this is right up there with anything I've done personally," Stanton said. "I have some goals in terms of winning a championship and going all the way, but for the road I've gone on to get to where I am now, right where it all began for me as a kid, this is very special."

As Stanton returned to the AL clubhouse, his teammates chanted, "M-V-P!" To that, Stanton beamed.

"I can't really explain how special this is," Stanton said. "It's hard to put into words that this is reality right now. It's really cool."

'61 FLASHBACK: HALFWAY TO RUTHVILLE

It was not even Independence Day, and Roger Maris was already halfway to Ruthville.

When Maris slugged his 30th home run of the 1961 season on July 2, taking Johnny Klippstein of the Washington Senators deep, the Yankees were rolling. New York had won twenty-two of thirty-two games in June and appeared on a straight path toward another World Series, while discussion of Babe Ruth's record was becoming more common in the Yankee Stadium press box. Joe Trimble of the New York *Daily News* is believed to be the first writer to ask Maris about chasing Ruth.

"Listen, I don't give Babe Ruth a thought. Not now or ever," Maris said. "I don't think about the record, and I'm surprised I've got as many homers as I do."

Trimble raced to his typewriter at rickety Municipal Stadium in Kansas City, feeding a clean sheet of paper through the roller. Five years earlier, Trimble had stared at an empty diamond, hours after Don Larsen pitched the only perfect game in World Series history. His mind, he told colleague Dick Young, had gone blank.

Young clacked the keys, covering for his co-worker's unfortunate case of writer's block by crafting a memorable lede that would win awards under Trimble's byline: "The imperfect man pitched a perfect game yesterday." With fresh Maris quotes in his notepad, Trimble fired off a dispatch that was no love letter:

Kansas City, Mo., June 20—"Roger the red-necked Yankee" is almost the term used by other ballplayers to describe Roger Maris. But ballplayers being ballplayers and this being a nice newspaper, we've had to paraphrase the expression, anatomy-wise.

Maris doesn't take surly pills. He only acts that way. The Yankee slugger really is a nice man. It's just that he is perpetually sore.

"I was born red-necked and I guess I'll stay that way," the national game's angry man said Tuesday.

And that's the image of Maris that was delivered to the public, even before the chase was in full swing. If there was any question about Maris's state of mind, the writers could simply check the stool in front of his Yankee Stadium locker. On days when Maris didn't feel like talking, and those were growing more frequent, he would produce a plaster cast of a hand with an extended middle finger.

"That didn't endear him to the press," said Marty Appel, a Yankees author and historian who served as the club's public relations director during the 1970s. "These were guys who were covering the Yankees in the 1920s and '30s, so they weren't about to be disrespected. You had these afternoon papers like the *[New York] World-Telegram*, decrying Roger Maris as being a bad guy."

Maris's dismissal hardly doused excitement over the budding home run chase; Maris hit his 31st homer on July 4, while Mantle trailed close behind with 28. A few writers attempted to stir drama, suggesting that Maris and Mantle disliked each other. Teammates refute that in the strongest terms, painting them as buddies who spent time together away from the stadium and benefited from the competition.

They had more in common than outward appearances indicated; Maris and Mantle were both three-sport high school athletes from blue-collar backgrounds, North Dakota and Oklahoma, respectively, who married their high school sweethearts and now found themselves stars in the big city. As in the *61** movie, Mantle, Maris, and outfielder Bob Cerv really did spend that summer in a modest two-bedroom apartment off the Van Wyck Expressway in Queens, not far from Idlewild Airport (renamed John F. Kennedy International Airport following the president's 1963 assassination).

One too many of Mantle's alcohol-fueled, late-night Manhattan incidents spurred Maris to host something of an intervention, believing that the team's star player needed a break from his high life at the Hotel St. Moritz, which today overlooks Central Park as the Ritz-Carlton New York. Mantle was earning $65,000 in 1961, and it was disappearing fast. The St. Moritz alone charged $125 per night, more than $1,200 in 2023 dollars, and Mantle was running up thousand-dollar tabs all around town.

Maris laid the ground rules: there would be no partying, no women. Mantle had nodded, saying that he could use a summer like that. In their unassuming living space, Maris liked to cook breakfast; he'd fry bacon first, then make the eggs in the fat from the bacon, which would blacken the eggs. "Big Julie" Isaacson, one of Maris's best friends during his time with the Yankees, said: "I used to tell him this wasn't North Dakota, that no one in New York makes eggs like that. But Roger did, and I ate them. I'll say this, they weren't bad."

Maris, Mantle, and Cerv would spend hours putting golf balls into a small tin hole atop the living room carpet, playing for pennies. They rode to the Bronx in Maris's convertible, the top down and the wind in their faces. On one occasion, the M&M Boys went grocery shopping together, the sight of Mantle and Maris pushing a cart down a Queens supermarket aisle prompting a teenage stock boy to fall from his ladder. Cans scattered everywhere; Mantle and Maris had just laughed.

"I liked it in Queens," Mantle said. "The press couldn't find us. We had an icebox full of sandwiches and pizza. Roger liked his privacy. When we went out to eat, Roger didn't like to be bothered for autographs during the meal. He'd ask the person to come back when he was finished eating. Usually, I just signed it to get it over with. When I was with Roger, I followed his lead. Outside the park, Roger would stand there and sign as long as anybody, but he had a thing about being bugged in restaurants. That's why the apartment was perfect for him, and it was good for him. He wanted to get away from everything, and I needed to get away from it all, too."

It was the afternoon of July 18 when Commissioner Ford C. Frick—pressed by the surging interest in the race—made his ruling, suggesting that any record not broken within a player's first 154 games would be recognized as a new and separate record.

Frick suggested there would be a "distinctive mark" to show that a record like Ruth's was set in a 154-game schedule; it was Dick Young, the influential columnist at the New York *Daily News*, who suggested that there would be an asterisk applied. Young wrote that a record achieved in a 162-game schedule was akin to "permitting a man to run 95 yards to break a record in the 100-yard dash."

"Over the years, [Frick] came to be ridiculed and defiled over this decision," Appel said. "But if you put yourself in his position, baseball clung to tradition so strongly, and now he's faced with this possibility that every record could fall and we could have an entirely new record book. The home run record was getting everybody's attention, and he was thinking—not incorrectly—that the whole record book was in danger, and with it, baseball's heritage and legacy."

Coincidentally, Maris entered an 0-for-19 skid as Mantle briefly inched ahead in the race, but Maris homered four times in a July 25 doubleheader against the Chicago White Sox. The Yanks won twenty of twenty-nine games in July, and Maris finished the month leading Mantle, 40 to 39.

There was an interesting subplot to the Maris and Mantle chase concerning the baseball itself, which was manufactured at the time by Spalding. It was called the "rabbit ball," believed to be livelier than anything Ruth had swatted. Edwin L. Parker, the company's president, insisted that "the built-in characteristics of the ball haven't changed in 35 years."

The *New York Times* commissioned an investigation, hiring chemists and engineers to run tests on seven balls manufactured between 1927 and 1961. It appeared on the *Times*'s front page on August 14, below larger and much more important headlines concerning the East Germans and Soviet allies having encircled Berlin with a barbed-wire barrier, the predecessor of the Berlin Wall.

Three pages of charts and data, detailing "surgical dissection and batterings by an explosive-driven Remington Arms ram" and headings like "Impact vs. Travel," "Rotational Stability," and "Rebound Coefficient" yielded this finding: Was the 1961 ball livelier than Ruth's? "Maybe yes and maybe no."

In the clubhouse, the '61 Yankees had chuckled, considering the story ridiculous. It was the grandfather of the conversation that would arise in December 2022, when an *Insider* investigation claimed that three types of Rawlings baseballs had circulated during the previous year, with astrophysicist Dr. Meredith Wills conducting tests of 204 balls obtained from twenty-two different ballparks during the season.

Major League Baseball had previously acknowledged two different baseballs, one less lively than the other, citing a manufacturing issue at a Costa Rican plant during the COVID-19 pandemic. The report suggested that there was a third type of ball, which it called "Goldilocks"—not too heavy and not too light—that was largely found in the postseason, at the All-Star Game and the Home Run Derby. According to *Insider*, the only "Goldilocks" balls not bearing commemorative stamps were found in Yankees games.

MLB forcefully denied the story, stating that "the conclusions of this research are wholly inaccurate and just plain wrong." Meanwhile, people close to the Yankees said that pitchers did complain about some of the baseballs, but a sample size of 204 balls was too small to prove the distribution of the balls had not been random throughout the league.

The more things change, the more they stay the same. In 1961, it was Mantle who had said: "Maybe it's the players now who are livelier."

◆

8

WALK-OFFS AND MAGIC WANDS

Since the August 2016 beginning of the Yankees' Aaron Judge era, no place had brought them more heartbreak than Houston's Minute Maid Park.

The retractable-roof ballpark at the corner of Crawford Street and Texas Avenue opened its existence as Enron Field, that name lasting but two years before the energy and financial trading company became synonymous with embarrassment and scandal.

It was where CC Sabathia had wept in the visiting clubhouse after the 2017 American League Championship Series, and where Brett Gardner's voice had cracked during a heartfelt speech to his vanquished teammates at the end of their 2019 run.

Where Joe Girardi had marched through a service corridor in '17, jaw clenched, to deliver his final words as the team's manager. Where there had been awkward silence again in '19, punctuated only by the slaps of palms against shirtless backs as players absorbed defeat and wished each other well for the winter.

Oh, the Yankees hated that place.

The opening of the second half of the season offered little reason to change that stance. Once again, the Yankees returned disappointed from their sojourn to Space City, swept in a day-night doubleheader between

the league's top teams. Houston rookie J. J. Matijevic decided the opening contest with a walk-off single off Michael King, and things looked
bleak in the nightcap, too.

Yordan Alvarez and Alex Bregman slugged first-inning homers off
Domingo Germán, then added run-scoring hits off the righty in the
second inning.

"They're definitely our kryptonite," King said. "Even when we played
them during the regular season, it wasn't pretty."

Chas McCormick's two-run homer off JP Sears gave Houston a commanding 7–2 lead, but the Yanks had one last gasp in them.

HOMER #34: July 21 vs. Houston Astros' Brandon Bielak (9th inning, three-run)
*Exit velocity: 111 mph. Distance: 410 feet. Launch angle: 33 degrees. HR in 30 of 30
MLB parks.*

Brandon Bielak, a twenty-six-year-old righty from Metuchen, New
Jersey, was born on the same day that Derek Jeter made his first Opening
Day start. A generation of Yankees fans would speak fondly of the frigid
afternoon that Jeter announced his presence on the big-league stage
with a stellar performance in Cleveland, contributing a terrific over-the-
shoulder catch behind pitcher David Cone and slugging his first career
homer off veteran Dennis Martinez.

Bielak's assignment here in Houston had been to ice the Yankees,
and he was doing well, spinning three scoreless innings in relief as the
game plodded toward the end. Fatigue, and perhaps some nerves, were
setting in as manager Dusty Baker sent Bielak back to the mound in
the ninth. Isiah Kiner-Falefa and DJ LeMahieu opened the inning with
singles, and after Anthony Rizzo flew out, Bielak saw Judge come to the
plate. Bielak pumped a low sinker for a called strike, then missed out of
the strike zone. The next pitch, a slider, squirted through catcher Martín
Maldonado's legs for a wild pitch that advanced the runners. Now Bielak
went back to the sinker, and this one hovered around belt-high.

Judge crushed it deep to left field, where it landed on the train tracks
overlooking the ballpark, an homage to the ballpark's previous life as
Houston's heavily trafficked Union Station. Standing in the dugout,

Giancarlo Stanton smacked his palms on the padded dugout railing; the Yanks were back in the ball-game. But Rafael Montero entered to record the final two outs, inducing Matt Carpenter to hit into a game-ending double play, and the Yanks chewed on a 7–5 defeat.

Judge showered and paced toward the back left corner of Minute Maid Park's visiting clubhouse, the same stall he'd occupied back in October of 2019, when José Altuve's homer off a smirking Aroldis Chapman had dealt a death blow to the Bombers' postseason. The room was once again pin-drop quiet as Judge buttoned a dress shirt, face toward his belongings, then scrolled through text messages before nodding to a waiting media contingent.

Yogi Berra might have called it "déjà vu all over again," but Judge wasn't going there. This was 2022, and it had nothing to do with 2019.

"We've got the best record in baseball," Judge said. "They're a great team, and I'm not going to sit here and dwell on things that happened in the past, no matter what, good or bad. So we'll see what happens down the stretch, but I'm focused on this year and this team. We've got a great ballclub here. We've got to stay within ourselves, focus on ourselves, and I think good things will happen."

In the manager's office, Boone sounded exhausted—from traveling to Houston and the day-night twin bill, and also about questions concerning his team's seeming inability to answer the Astros. Judge noted that the Yankees still owned the majors' best mark (64-30), but Houston was hot on their tail at 61-32. Those losses mattered in the present, but Judge said he considered October a different animal altogether.

"So," he said, "this is just kind of a practice test. Every team we play is a little practice test to see how we stack up. Take your notes and then get ready for the real thing."

The narrative, Boone understood, would not change unless the Yankees toppled the Astros in October—when the games counted most.

"Ultimately, we may have to slay the dragon, right?" Boone said.

HOMER #35: July 22 vs. Baltimore Orioles' Tyler Wells (3rd inning, three-run) *Exit velocity: 108.6 mph. Distance: 436 feet. Launch angle: 26 degrees. HR in 30 of 30 MLB parks.*

HOMER #36: July 22 vs. Baltimore Orioles' Tyler Wells (5th inning, solo)
Exit velocity: 113.5 mph. Distance: 465 feet. Launch angle: 25 degrees. HR in 30 of 30 MLB parks.

There were no wakeup calls scheduled as the Yankees' plane touched down outside Baltimore in the wee hours of a Friday morning. Players and coaches shuffled wordlessly into their hotel, closing the blackout shades tight to avoid the approach of sunrise, just precious minutes away. When Judge finally awoke, he had a text message from his father, Wayne: "Hey, make sure you go to right field. They've got that big wall in left field."

Judge chuckled, rolling his eyes and leaning back into the pillow. How could he forget; that modified, deeper wall at Camden Yards had spoiled one of his favorite hitting backdrops.

"I might try to get one over that," Judge had replied.

Judge did better than that, enjoying his eighth multi-homer game in leading his club to a 7–6 win. In the third inning, Orioles righty Tyler Wells fell behind Judge with a 2-1 count. Judge pounced on a fastball up in the zone, clearing the Baltimore bullpen and reaching the distant visiting warm-up area, where the ball dented earth and rattled against a digital scoreboard touting an upcoming bobblehead night for retired slugger Boog Powell.

"It's actually really impressive to see how much his approach has changed and how much his swing has changed," Wells said. "For me, a lot of the time it is, 'Okay, how can we execute this pitch to where we can eliminate his power?' Last year, I felt like that was an up-and-in pitch to Judge and that's where I was able to get him most of the time, or a down-and-away slider. But this year, it seems like he's made those his strengths. He can get to the inside pitch. He can get to the low-and-outside slider."

A loud contingent of Yankees fans chanted "M-V-P!" for Judge, which was becoming a familiar and welcome occurrence. "When you give our team an early lead," he'd say later, "it usually comes out to a good outcome." New York was up, 3–0, and Judge had another big swing in the fifth, with Wells still in the game. Once again, Wells fell behind in the count two balls to a strike. This time, he tried a changeup, and Judge hit it even farther. This one cleared both bullpens, smacking off a fan before bouncing back among the Bombers' relievers; the third-longest homer ever clocked at Camden Yards. On YES, Ryan Ruocco exclaimed: "Aaron Judge is going to get on NASA's radar!"

Coincidentally, the six-foot-eight Wells was the only player that Judge (six-foot-seven) had homered off in the big leagues who was taller than him. "It doesn't help whenever you throw it down the middle to him," Wells said. "The first home run that I gave up to him, I was trying to go up there; just didn't get it in enough. The second one, he just took a pitch right down the middle and hit it a long ways. I think it just shows with Judge or that Yankees lineup, you miss in the middle, you're going to pay for it." The performance put Judge back on pace to equal Maris's 61 homers, with 6 in the Yanks' last seven games, and the mark seemed quite within reach, at least to his teammates. "At the rate he's going, he could definitely accomplish anything," Jameson Taillon said.

"The first time I really thought about it was in the second half," said Pete Caldera of the *Bergen Record*. "At that point, the Yankees had a ridiculous lead in the division and you're looking for other things to circle the calendar for. You take a real good look at Judge's home run total and you say, 'Oh my God, this guy's got a shot to hit 60.' I remember predicting 59, only because 60 is so mythic in Yankees lore and MLB history."

Though Judge's two blasts had sparked revelry in the clubhouse, the fun would be punctured by bad news. That afternoon, while shagging batting-practice fly balls, Michael King had confided in Clay Holmes. King told Holmes that his pitching elbow had been aching for weeks, to the point where he no longer suspected tendinitis. King had been gobbling anti-inflammatories in the trainers' room, and Holmes told King that he needed to go straight to the team's training staff when batting practice ended. King listened, nodded, then completely ignored his teammate. "After the conversation, I said, 'My velo has still been there. I'm still producing decent numbers. I don't want to shut it down,'" King said. "Our bullpen was struggling at the time, so we really needed the help. I would have felt really soft if I said, 'Hey, I'm actually hurt and I need to get shut down here.'"

Watching from the Yankees bullpen, Holmes agonized as he watched

King exit with one out in the eighth inning, pointing to his right elbow. Tests showed that King had fractured his pitching elbow and needed surgery, having likely aggravated a stress reaction by continuing to pitch. With a 2.29 ERA in thirty-four appearances, the twenty-seven-year-old King could have been the club's seventh representative at the All-Star Game in Los Angeles. Instead, he was gone for the year.

Cole tried to shoulder the load for a gassed bullpen and coughed up a three-run lead the next night, in a loss of missed opportunities that Boone called "frustrating." One reporter noted that the Yanks had lost eight of their last twelve, their poorest stretch of the season. Perhaps because the stretch was interrupted by the glitz of the Tinseltown trip, or because the Yankees still held a twelve-game lead in the American League East, Cole seemed surprised by the statistic.

"I didn't realize that," he said. "That's not very good."

Zoom out a little farther and they had been a more manageable 16-15 over their last thirty-one games, though they were rapidly falling off the pace of juggernauts like the 1998 Yankees and 2001 Mariners. Cashman acknowledged then that he was "concerned," painting his job as one in which he must always plan for the worst and hope for the best.

Behind the scenes, the Yanks were deep in talks with the Cincinnati Reds about ace right-hander Luis Castillo, and they had checked in with the Washington Nationals about a mega-deal for outfielder Juan Soto. The respective prices had been exorbitant; with no requests moving off top prospects like Anthony Volpe, Oswald Peraza, and Jasson Dominguez. They also seemed to be serious contenders for Kansas City Royals outfielder Andrew Benintendi, but they'd have to keep plugging away with what they had in house for the moment.

HOMER #37: July 24 vs. Baltimore Orioles' Dean Kremer (3rd inning, two-run)
Exit velocity: 111.1 mph. Distance: 456 feet. Launch angle: 31 degrees. HR in 30 of 30 MLB parks.

Judge was up for the challenge, extending his big-league home run lead by teeing off on a hanging curveball from Dean Kremer, a shaggy-haired twenty-six-year-old righty from Stockton, California. As Judge's shot to the left-field seats soared on a hazy, humid afternoon, O's catcher Robinson Chirinos dropped to his right knee and craned his neck. In Chirinos's view, Judge was the most dangerous hitter in the league.

"I don't think anybody should pitch to him," Chirinos said. "The guy is unbelievable. He's hitting good pitches. He's hitting mistakes. Normally when a guy's hot, he's hitting doubles and singles. He's hitting the ball out of the ballpark, and it's crazy. He's a good hitter. What can you say?"

Judge's two hits not only supported a winning Nestor Cortes effort but also raised his batting average to .294, which he considered a key area of focus. "I saw a lot of the greats—Albert Pujols and Miguel Cabrera— they always hit above .300 and the power just came with it," Judge said. "That's always been a goal of mine, to hit above .300, and we'll keep working towards it."

Around this time, Michael Kay approached Judge, not to garner a quote, just to share a chat. That spring in Tampa, Florida, Judge had given a pair of batting gloves to Kay's eight-year-old son, Charlie. It was a move that Judge had done numerous times before, believing that gifting an article of gear held much more significance than scribbling his name on a ball.

As Judge continued to slug homers in July, Charlie told his dad: "I just want you to know that if Judge leaves, I'm not going to root for the Yankees anymore." Kay was incredulous: "Really? Even though your father's the announcer?" Charlie replied: "Yeah. I'm out."

"The next day, I went into the clubhouse and told Judge that story," Kay said. "He had almost a sad look on his face. He really paused, longer than he usually pauses. And he said to me: 'Please tell Charlie not to worry.'"

HOMER #38: July 26 vs. New York Mets' Taijuan Walker (1st inning, solo)
Exit velocity: 112.1 mph. Distance: 423 feet. Launch angle: 29 degrees. HR in 30 of 30 MLB parks.

It didn't reflect reality for anyone who has swiped a MetroCard since the venerable subway token was phased out, but a segment of the population swears that New York is not really a Yankees town. The five boroughs have rich National League heritage, traced to the Brooklyn Dodgers' occupation of Ebbets Field and the New York Giants' finest seasons at the Polo Grounds, just across the Harlem River in Manhattan from where both iterations of Yankee Stadium have stood.

Soon after the Dodgers and Giants moved west after the 1957 season, the New York Mets came along to fill the void, a crew of lovable losers who shocked the world by winning a "Miracle" World Series in 1969—just a few months after Neil Armstrong set foot on the moon. Yogi Berra steered the Mets to an unlikely 1973 pennant, the rowdy Amazin's rode through the Canyon of Heroes in 1986, and there was the true Subway Series of 2000—the one after which Derek Jeter swore he'd have moved out of Manhattan, had the Yankees lost.

Yet that autumn was the outlier; for the most part, when one team is up, the other has been down. Still, since the dawn of interleague play in 1997, the Mets-Yankees rivalry had provided reasons to cheer and to dream. Should they ever meet again in October, as the Mets' Pete Alonso said, "The city will just be on fire." Judge appreciated those games, mostly because of the heated postseason atmosphere; fans swapping chants of "Let's Go Mets," "Let's Go Yankees," and several PG-13–rated variations.

That was the scene as Judge limbered in the on-deck circle at Citi Field, the 2009 replacement for dilapidated and outdated Shea Stadium. If Yankee Stadium was a living museum of the Yanks' rich history, Citi Field attempted to inspire intimacy, beginning with an entryway rotunda borrowed from the blueprints for long-gone Ebbets Field. Citi Field hardly seemed to honor the Mets at all—Fred Wilpon, the club's previous owner, had been a die-hard Dodgers fan and a one-time high school teammate of Sandy Koufax. Outcry eventually prompted change, from restoring the outfield walls to their traditional blue and orange to commissioning a stunning statue of Tom Seaver, the franchise's greatest player.

"I think our guys look forward to playing in this kind of environment," Boone said. "Especially as we enter the dog days of summer, it seems like it gives guys a little shot in the arm, a little life. I think most guys would agree that they enjoy playing on this kind of stage, with the amount of interest that is on the series within the city."

With this installment of the Subway Series underway, Judge stepped in to face Walker, a ten-year veteran who'd bounced between the Seattle Mariners, Arizona Diamondbacks, Toronto Blue Jays, and the Mariners again before landing by the shores of Flushing Bay. Walker's preferred uniform number was No. 99, and in this battle of ninety-nines, Judge saw five pitches, filling the count. The sixth left the yard, a four-seam fastball down the middle that Judge parked into the visiting bullpen, beyond the right-field wall.

Anthony Rizzo homered on Walker's next pitch, but the back-to-back blasts only served as an appetizer for the power show. The Mets pelted Jordan Montgomery for four runs in the home half of the first, including homers by Starling Marte and Eduardo Escobar; Montgomery needed seventy-one pitches to record seven outs, and when Boone came to the mound to retrieve the baseball, the lefty blinked and asked: "Why?" A brief explanation followed; Boone patted his hurler's chest in something of an apology, though the five runs already on the scoreboard told the tale. "I wanted to be out there, but I sucked," Montgomery said.

The Mets made it a Subway sweep the next night, with Max Scherzer performing marvelously on his thirty-eighth birthday, including three Judge strikeouts. Gleyber Torres smacked a game-tying homer in the ninth, but Marte answered with a walk-off single. Cashman had a response, too; minutes after the game, the Yankees announced that they'd acquired Andrew Benintendi from the Kansas City Royals for three minor-league pitchers.

Conveniently, Benintendi was already in town; the Royals had checked into a midtown Manhattan hotel that night, preparing to open a four-game series with the Yankees. Benintendi spent the next few hours playing cards with his former teammates, saying, "It's definitely a weird situation, lacing it up with them yesterday and going against them today."

HOMER #39: July 28 vs. Kansas City Royals' Scott Barlow (9th inning, solo, walk-off)
Exit velocity: 109.6 mph. Distance: 431 feet. Launch angle: 35 degrees. HR in 30 of 30 MLB parks.

Benintendi tried on his new pinstriped uniform with No. 18 stitched on the back, surveying his attire in a mirror affixed to the wall of the players' restroom. He looked sharp in crisp Yankees white. However, it would be a stretch to say Benintendi had ever envisioned being on this side of the rivalry, having grown up in a suburb of Cincinnati before playing his first five big-league seasons with the Red Sox.

His year and a half with Kansas City had blunted any shock of the transition, though. Benintendi had an opportunity to play the hero in his Yanks debut as the game proceeded scorelessly to the bottom of the ninth inning. New York had been held to one hit through the first eight frames, and as he dug in against Kansas City closer Scott Barlow, Benintendi got a pitch to hit—a 95 mph fastball right over the heart of the plate.

He whipped his bat through the zone and lifted a drive . . . that left fielder Kyle Isbel snagged in foul territory, the first out of the inning.

So a storybook ending wasn't in the cards for Benintendi on day one—not in Judge's season. Judge was the designated hitter that night. As Barlow warmed in the Kansas City bullpen, rookie reliever Ron Marinaccio had spotted Judge walking through the clubhouse on his way back to the dugout. "Let's get this thing done," Marinaccio told the slugger, who had replied with a wink.

About two minutes later, Judge clobbered a drive that pelted an advertising board at the back of Yankee Stadium's visiting bullpen for yet another walk-off homer. While watching from the weight room, the flashing Yankee Stadium LED lights caught Jameson Taillon's attention—a signal to rush for the field.

"We were just like, 'This dude did it again,'" Taillon said. "It's pretty unbelievable, but we've come to expect it. It seems like every big moment, he comes up there and he comes through."

Said Benintendi: "Seeing it from the other side, it's incredible what he's doing. Then to be a part of it, it's almost like it was drawn up exactly how he wants it."

Judge's three walk-off homers tied Mickey Mantle (1959) for the most by a Yankee in a single season; channeling the Mick, he'd swung hard and tried to hit one out of the park.

"Especially in that situation, I was [0-for-2] with two [strikeouts].

What's the worst that's going to happen?" Judge said. "I just go up there, try to do the job. Get something over the plate and make something happen for the guys behind me. Luckily it happened with the first pitch and we were able to get it done."

> **HOMER #40:** July 29 vs. Kansas City Royals' Kris Bubic (1st inning, two-run)
> *Exit velocity: 110.2 mph. Distance: 449 feet. Launch angle: 29 degrees. HR in 30 of 30 MLB parks.*
> **HOMER #41:** July 29 vs. Kansas City Royals' Jackson Kowar (8th inning, grand slam)
> *Exit velocity: 105.1 mph. Distance: 370 feet. Launch angle: 29 degrees. HR in 10 of 30 MLB parks.*

Should you ever wind up in a bar, quizzed about the identities of the three Yankees to hit 40 or more homers by the end of July, don't over-complicate the matter. It's Judge, Maris (1961), and Babe Ruth (1928). Here was a telling snapshot of Judge's historic summer: as he stood in the center of the Yankees' clubhouse late on a Friday evening, the slugger was asked to ponder if he preferred making a leaping catch over the wall or hitting a grand slam to help win a game. Of course, he'd done both in the same night.

As he had for pretty much the entire season, Judge starred on both sides of the ball in a rainy 11–5 victory over the Royals, helping out Gerrit Cole by bringing back a first-inning homer, then joining pinstriped royalty with his 40th and 41st home runs.

"Ooh, they're close," Judge said. "Robbing [a home run], you've got the crowd excitement, helping out a pitcher who's working his butt off. It's pretty cool. Then, you've got the same thing when you hit one, helping your team add some runs to the board. Hitting a homer is still above robbing one for me right now."

Said Cole: "I wish I could have my phone on the bench like the rest of the fans, taking video of every one of his at-bats."

Boone found 41 homers before the end of July "hard to process," while noting, "Nobody is better equipped to go through it and handle it than him." The multi-homer game, Judge's ninth of the year, had put him on pace to hit 66. "There is going to be a generation," said Paul O'Neill, "that looks back and reminds their kids: 'You know, you remember Aaron Judge in 2022?'" He had 11 homers in his past thirteen games alone. Yet, even in the afterglow of a six-RBI performance, he whisked the topic away—just like the magic wand that Cole said Judge seemed to be waving every night, calling it "a steady dose of amazingness."

"When he started creeping up there over 40, I was saying, 'This guy's got a real chance to do it,'" said Clarke Schmidt. "Every day, he was hitting one or two, and you couldn't stop him. I was grateful to be on the same team as him; I was glad not to be on the other side facing him, that's for sure."

On a night when one fortunate soul struck a billion-dollar Mega Millions jackpot at a Des Plaines, Illinois gas station, the wager that Judge placed back in April seemed even more like a sure thing. The offer of $213.5 million wasn't yesterday's price, nor was it today's or tomorrow's. When fans chanted "M-V-P!" after each highlight-reel contribution, it was a shorthand plea for the front office to pay whatever it took to keep Judge in pinstripes. Judge never saw turning down the extension as a bet on himself, but if it had been one, Judge was winning big time.

"It was never a gamble for me, because no matter whether we got a deal done or didn't get a deal done, I was still going to be playing with the Yankees this year," Judge said. "In my mind, there was no gamble. I'll be playing for the Yankees, working as hard as I can to help us win a World Series. All that other stuff, that's why I've got an agent."

Though Aaron Judge stole twice as many bases (thirty-six) as he hit homers (eighteen) during his three seasons at Fresno State University, there were glimpses of the superstar he would become. "This kid is going to play in the big leagues as long as he wants," said head baseball coach Mike Batesole.

The Yankees selected Aaron Judge with the thirty-second overall pick in the 2013 MLB Draft, a choice announced by Bud Selig, baseball's commissioner. The day before the event, held at the MLB Network studios in Secaucus, New Jersey, Judge had told a reporter that he was "not sure if I could ever live" in New York.

Aaron Judge announced his presence on the national stage with a winning performance in the 2017 Home Run Derby at Miami's Marlins Park. Judge slammed forty-seven balls over the walls, including four jaw-dropping drives of five hundred feet or more. "It was a blast. I enjoyed every minute of it," he said.

How popular was the Yankees' big-swinging right fielder? The club constructed a "Judge's Chambers" seating area in Yankee Stadium's Section 104, three rows beyond the right-field wall framed by faux wood paneling and fashioned to fit eighteen lucky fans.

Brad Penner / USA TODAY Sports

Having found his place as one of the game's biggest stars, Aaron Judge reached new heights early in 2022. Many teammates identified his May 10 walk-off against the Blue Jays as their favorite Judgeian blast. "That's when I think it became very real," said DJ LeMahieu.

Dustin Rabin

Aaron Judge connects with a Tim Mayza sinker for his 61st home run on Sept. 28, 2022, tying Roger Maris's sixty-one-year-old American League record for home runs in a single season. Judge gifted the milestone ball to his mother, Patty, saying, "She's been with me through it all."

Aaron Judge's 62nd home run ball was caught by Cory Youmans, a thirty-five-year-old Dallas native seated in Section 31, Row 1, Seat 3 of Globe Life Field. Youmans opted to list the ball at auction, where it sold for $1.5 million. "I'd never caught a ball at a game before, let alone a home run ball," he said.

Aaron Judge celebrated with his family and several trusted associates after belting his 62nd home run in Arlington, a group that included his father, Wayne; mother, Patty; wife, Samantha; and his representatives at PSI Sports, Page Odle and David Matranga.

ABOVE: Aaron Judge and his Yankees teammates celebrated clinching the American League East on September 28, 2022, coming in a 5-2 victory over the Blue Jays at Rogers Centre. "What a year it's been so far; we're definitely not done, but this is a great first step," Judge said.

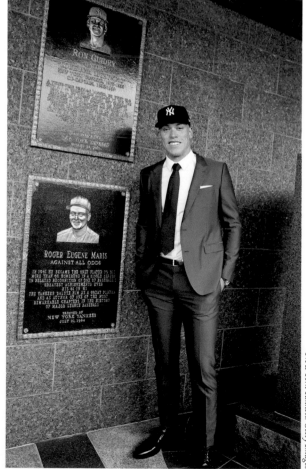

RIGHT: Having been freshly minted as the sixteenth captain in franchise history, Aaron Judge ventured out to Yankee Stadium's Monument Park, posing with Roger Maris's plaque. "Having my name next to someone who's as great as Roger Maris, it's incredible," Judge said.

Aaron Judge hit his 62nd home run of the 2022 season on October 4, 2022, connecting with a 1-1 slider from the Texas Rangers' Jesús Tinoco. Judge's blast came off the bat at 100.2 mph and traveled 391 feet, eclipsing Roger Maris's sixty-one-year-old single-season American League record.

Aaron Judge was honored as the American League's Most Valuable Player on January 28, 2023, with his hardware presented by Spike Lee at the New York Baseball Writers' Association awards dinner. Judge said the season showed him that "no matter what you're trying to accomplish, or anything you're going through, you're never alone"— especially in New York.

Roger Maris hit his 61st home run on October 1, 1961, off Tracy Stallard of the Red Sox at Yankee Stadium. The only three players in American League history to hit sixty or more homers in a single season have been Yankees right fielders: Babe Ruth in 1927, Maris in '61, and Aaron Judge in 2022.

One of the most heartwarming moments of Aaron Judge's 2022 season came on May 3 in Toronto, when Blue Jays fan Mike Lanzillotta gifted a Judge home run ball to nine-year-old Derek Rodriguez. Judge greeted Lanzillotta, Derek, and his younger brother, Cesar, in the Rogers Centre dugout the next day.

Stockton Record – USA TODAY NETWORK

Marly Rivera

ABOVE: Raised in Linden, California, Aaron Judge was a standout athlete in high school, starring in baseball, basketball, and football. Several top-flight college football programs pursued Judge as a wide receiver or tight end, but his heart was on the baseball diamond. "I love this game, that little chess match you get to play," Judge said.

LEFT: Patty Judge, Roger Maris Jr., and Yankees broadcaster Suzyn Waldman share a moment outside the Rogers Centre visiting clubhouse on Sept. 28, 2022, shortly after Aaron Judge hit his 61st home run off the Blue Jays' Tim Mayza. Maris was impressed by his meetings with the Judges. "You can see the apple doesn't fall far from the tree. The family seems very grounded," he said.

9

HEROES AND GHOSTS

A vintage copy of *Life* magazine, dated August 18, 1961, and carrying a cover price of twenty cents, rested on the carpet of Aaron Judge's locker at Yankee Stadium. The grinning color visages of Roger Maris and Mickey Mantle greeted Judge, placed over a black-and-white photograph of Babe Ruth and below a red, white, and blue banner that promised: "Will Yank Sluggers Reach 60 Homers? The Real Odds."

For some reason, the magazine's editors placed the Maris-Mantle teaser below one for an Ann Landers article: "Frank Talk on Youth and Sex," in which the finger-wagging columnist had used her space to admonish teenagers against the dangers of necking and petting in parked automobiles. "Of course sex is natural. So is eating," Landers wrote. "But would you sit down at the dinner table and pull the leg off a turkey or scoop up the mashed potatoes with your hands?" Decades after that text landed in mailboxes, one was reminded of Ned Flanders, the normally straight-laced neighbor on *The Simpsons*, whose tongue was loosened by a sip of blackberry schnapps, prompting a declaration to his horrified wife: "Ann Landers is a boring old biddy."

Judge flipped through the yellowed pages, past advertisements for General Electric refrigerators, White Owl cigars, and Kellogg's Corn Flakes, and scanned the text of the article about Maris and Mantle. The magazine, left as a gift for Judge by YES Network president John J. Filippelli, provided a time-capsule window into the world of his predecessors.

"I had it from childhood," Filippelli said. "I'm a baseball historian, and I have been since I was a child. My father ran a bar across the street from Ebbets Field. I was 10 years old in 1961, and I became a big Roger Maris fan. The whole world was rooting for Mickey Mantle to break the record. I was rooting for Maris. He still is my favorite player of all time, because I love the way he conducted himself. His humility really struck me."

Life's readers were treated to a convoluted interpretation of a mathematical formula in which the magazine opined that Mantle's chances of breaking Ruth's record was "50-50," while noting that the odds were running 4-1 against Maris. The combined probability of one, or both, breaking the record was 3-2 in favor. The article, which did not have a byline, recounted a game against the Los Angeles Angels (a quick search identifies the contest as August 7, 1961) in which Maris stepped to the plate with Bobby Richardson on third base and two outs, with the Yankees trailing by a run.

The Angels had played the infield back, expecting Maris to swing away against pitcher Ken McBride. It was the third inning, and Maris had 41 homers; why would they think differently? But the Angels didn't know that Maris had nudged manager Ralph Houk in the dugout that half-inning, asking, "Ralph, what do you think about me bunting for a hit?" Houk had given his approval, and Maris dropped a superb bunt down the third-base line, scoring Richardson with the tying run. Yogi Berra would hit a go-ahead homer in the sixth inning and the Yanks won, 4–1.

As *Life* wrote, "Maris had decided that tying up the game was more important than Ruth's record." Judge thought the magazine was "pretty cool," especially the part about Maris's bunt—team first, all the way. "That's what it's all about," he said. He'd skipped the Landers article, though it generated a good laugh for the beat writers.

That nostalgia was in the air as the Yankees assembled on the afternoon of July 30, celebrating the return of Old-Timers' Day, a popular event benched for two years because of the pandemic. The traditional three-inning game had yet to return, but thanks to the video highlights accompanying each entrance to the playing field, headliners like Ron Guidry, Tino Martinez, Willie Randolph, and Bernie Williams could remain forever young. As members of the greatest teams in recent history milled about in Monument Park, inspecting plaques and retired numbers, one name continued to spill from their lips. Those assembled alumni marveled at the special season Judge was enjoying, while also wondering aloud about his pinstriped future.

"I'm just so proud of him," Randolph said. "I got a chance to spend some time with him in spring training. We got together and talked about a lot of different things, just baseball in general. The way he stepped up, I'm not really surprised. But he's having a phenomenal year. I just hope that he continues to stay healthy." Randolph added: "I'm surprised they pitch to him as much as they do. I mean, what are you doing? The guy's six foot seven; you don't notice he's here?"

Williams, who posed for camera phone selfies in front of his Monument Park plaque, said he sensed that Judge felt "the allure and greatness of remaining a Yankee." Williams could relate. He had been at a similar career crossroads after the 1998 season, when he turned down a five-year, $37.5 million extension, prompting general manager Bob Watson to remark, "This is star money for a non-star player." Far coarser than anything Cashman said in April, the remark stung the introspective and sensitive Williams.

Like Judge, Williams vowed to test free agency. Soon after the World Series sweep of the San Diego Padres, Williams discovered his true market value by flirting with the Boston Red Sox, who floated $91.5 million to install Williams as their center fielder for the next seven years. Williams strongly considered Boston, where he would have been a switch-hitting centerpiece of a lineup powered by Nomar Garciaparra and Mo Vaughn.

Williams discovered that, deep in his heart, he couldn't picture himself playing eighty-one games a season at Fenway Park. Besides, who wanted to jump ship just as a dynasty was getting rolling? When negotiations to import temperamental free-agent slugger Albert Belle collapsed, the Yankees finalized a seven-year, $88.5 million pact with Williams. That deal ensured Williams would never be without his pinstripes, gradually transitioning from baseball into a successful musical career after the 2006 season. He hoped that Judge could also be a forever Yankee. "Every time I see him talking on TV, he just says the right things all the time," Williams said. "He's a good ambassador for the team. I think if he signs a long-term deal, he'll probably be in line to be the next captain. There's no doubt about that in my mind."

HOMER #42: July 30 vs. Kansas City Royals' Jonathan Heasley (2nd inning, two-run)
Exit velocity: 105.2 mph. Distance: 364 feet. Launch angle: 22 degrees. HR in 1 of 30 MLB parks.

Since the Old-Timers hadn't played their customary three innings, there was no ice required to aid creaky joints, though they were enjoying some as they clinked glasses upstairs in a suite overlooking the playing field. Judge gave them something to cheer about, fouling off a couple of pitches against Kansas City starter Jonathan Heasley before sending a low laser out toward right field, where it just cleared the wall over the head of outfielder MJ Melendez.

The ball was caught on the fly in the front row of Section 103 by a young man wearing an unbuttoned pinstriped Yankees jersey and dark sunglasses, who celebrated wildly as Judge rounded the bases. It was the kind of clout that prompted Martinez, the affable first baseman of three Yankees World Series–winning teams in the Joe Torre dynasty, to predict that Judge would surpass Maris's record.

"As long as they keep pitching to him, I believe he can do it," Martinez said. "He's got a short swing. He puts the ball to bat and it goes a long way. If he keeps doing what he's doing, I think he will get there."

Matt Carpenter also hit his 15th homer as the Yanks rolled to a convincing 8–2 victory, one in which the sloppy Royals committed three errors. With 12 homers in his last fourteen games, Judge left the stadium on pace to hit a staggering 67 home runs. He waved the numbers away, saying, "You can't look at it.

"I've just got to keep working hard, keep my head down and do what I can to help this team win games," Judge said. "At the end of the year, we can talk about what we finish at."

Also of significance: Judge's shot was the 200th homer of his career, coming in his 671st career game—only Ryan Howard (658 games) reached the milestone quicker than Judge, who joined Jorge Posada (275), Derek Jeter (260), and Don Mattingly (222) as the only players drafted by the Yankees to hit 200 or more homers with the franchise.

Judge joked that he'd been racing against Aaron Hicks, who was closing in on his 100th career homer at the time. With help from the Yankees' security team, Judge obtained the ball from what he called "a good family" with a simple swap. Like his first home run ball, Judge planned to give No. 200 to his parents.

"I told him, 'You'll see that home run a lot for the rest of your life,'" Yankees manager Aaron Boone said. "When they're marking back from whatever the final number ends up being, they'll go back and say, 'Here was his 200th.' It was a wall-scraper for him, but he smoked it. I told him, 'The right fielder would have been moving in if I hit that same ball.'"

The next day, Jordan Montgomery made what would be his final start as a member of the Yankees, thumped for four runs in four innings. Unbeknownst to Montgomery, general manager Brian Cashman had been working on an under-the-radar acquisition for weeks, eyeing St. Louis Cardinals center fielder Harrison Bader. Talks between the clubs had been so promising, Cashman dispatched one of his baseball operations staff members to quiz Carpenter about his former teammate.

"That guy can't be available," Carpenter told the staffer. "He's the best center fielder I've ever played with."

The Yankees pressed for more information. Carpenter grinned, sporting the bushy W. B. Mason mustache that had become a trademark during his brief Bronx tenure. "He's a gamer. Gamer. This guy is unbelievable. If you can get him, you should get him." The Cardinals' asking price never came up in that chat with Carpenter, who surely would not have given the move a thumbs-up if Montgomery's name was mentioned.

A six-foot-six left-hander who had acquired the college nickname "Gumby" for his gangly frame and a general lack of coordination, Montgomery had grown up in Sumter, South Carolina—Bobby Richardson territory—and came to the Yankees as a fourth-round pick in 2014. As well-liked as anyone in the room, Montgomery had unassuming charm and a dry sense of humor. He also had no reason to suspect a trade was in the works. He'd proposed to his fiancée, McKenzie Dirr, on the Yankee Stadium diamond weeks earlier. Many of his current and former teammates were on the invite list for the couple's wedding, set for December.

The Yankees weren't actively shopping Montgomery, but the Cardinals were asking, and they were persistent. Cashman also weighed the wear and tear of having Judge pressed into regular duty as the center fielder. That had never been part of the original plan, and as it appeared unlikely that Hicks would reclaim the position, there was appeal in the idea of bringing in a Gold Glover to man the position for years to come—a move that would also return Judge to the relatively safer confines of right field.

August 1 had already been a busy day in the Bronx, the clock to baseball's trade deadline ticking in the backdrop. Cashman's day opened by acquiring right-handed reliever Scott Effross from the Chicago Cubs, though he'd hoped to accomplish much more. Luis Castillo was the top pitcher available, and the Yankees wanted the electric right-hander desperately—even more so after Castillo had dazzled in his July 14 gem in the Bronx.

Reflecting months later, Cashman said that the Yankees "were dead serious" in their aim to acquire Castillo. They had put a lot on the table; switch-hitting outfield prospect Jasson "The Martian" Dominguez was offered to Cincinnati. The Reds insisted on shortstop Anthony Volpe and more. According to MLB Pipeline, Dominguez was the Yankees' No. 2 prospect; Volpe, a confident and clean-cut twenty-one-year-old who'd earned lofty comparisons to Derek Jeter, was No. 1. Cincinnati GM Nick Krall promised he would get back to the Yankees. There was radio silence, and Cashman sensed Castillo was on the move. Finally, Krall's call came in: "We traded him. He's gone."

Cashman stammered. "He's gone?" Krall apologized, telling Cashman, "We just had an offer that we could not refuse." Castillo had been traded to the Seattle Mariners for shortstop prospect Noelvi Marte, plus shortstop Edwin Arroyo, and right-handed pitchers Levi Stoudt and Andrew Moore. With three of Seattle's top five prospects, it was a haul for Cincinnati, and Cashman said his baseball operations department quickly understood why Krall hadn't returned their call.

"Once we heard what they got, it made sense," Cashman said. "They did a great job."

So the Yankees were on to their plan B, having identified Oakland Athletics right-hander Frankie Montas as the second-best starter on the block. The price would be a few ticks lower, as recent injury issues added an element of risk. Montas had pitched well against the Yankees in a June 28 game in the Bronx, but he exited his next start after one inning with discomfort in his pitching shoulder. Eighteen days passed before Montas next appeared on a big-league mound, outings in which he'd performed well against the Detroit Tigers and Houston Astros.

Reviewing Montas's medical records, the Yankees gambled that his shoulder issues were behind him. It was a call that would prove disastrous. In the moment, they had been enticed by Montas's success against the Houston Astros, recognizing that their most likely path to a championship would be through the 713 area code. Montas owned a 3.40 ERA in fifteen career games (thirteen starts) against Houston, including two strong victories at Minute Maid Park in 2021.

"When he was flying high with Oakland, he would handle Houston and navigate their lineup really well," Cashman said later. "We thought, 'This is somebody who has success against them and could play an instrumental role.'"

In exchange for the twenty-nine-year-old Montas, the Yankees sent pitchers Luis Medina, JP Sears, and Ken Waldichuk, plus infielder Cooper Bowman, to Oakland. The A's included right-handed reliever Lou Trivino in the deal, reminding Luis Severino about a confusing moment he'd had earlier in the season. Upon hearing that the Yanks traded for catcher Jose Trevino in April, Severino had assumed they were acquiring Trivino, the reliever. He had been surprised when Trevino arrived at camp, lugging his Texas Rangers equipment bag. Now both Trevino and Trivino resided in the same clubhouse.

Cashman also convinced the Los Angeles Dodgers to take outfielder Joey Gallo, whose Yankees tenure ended with a .159 batting average in 140 games, ranking alongside Ed Whitson and Hideki Irabu for some

of the worst Bronx imports in recent memory. Judge said he hadn't had
time to read much about the moves; he'd save that for later in the night,
planning to log on to Twitter before bed. But he would always greet his
new teammates, hoping to ease their transition and build relationships.

"For me, the first thing is just going out and introducing myself, because I understand how difficult it is," Judge said. "If you're a new kid
at school, it's tough making friends, you don't know anybody. It's a different environment. I treat it the same way in the clubhouse when I see
somebody new come in, if it's a rookie we just called up or somebody we
traded for. I want to go over there, introduce myself and try to be a familiar face. 'Hi, I'm Aaron, great to meet you. If you've got any questions
or you need anything, come to me.'"

HOMER #43: August 1 vs. Seattle Mariners' Marco Gonzales (2nd inning,
two-run)
*Exit velocity: 105.5 mph. Distance: 420 feet. Launch angle: 29 degrees. HR in 29 of
30 MLB parks.*

The YES Network microphones perched behind home plate at Yankee Stadium were picking up chants of "M-V-P!" as Judge came to bat in
the second inning against Marco Gonzales, a thirty-year-old lefty who
survived on a diet of fastballs and changeups. Judge had won two consecutive American League Player of the Week Awards, and he seemed
off to a good start in pursuing a third, pouncing on an 87.4 mph cutter
that landed in the visiting bullpen.

"To me, hearing Player of the Week back-to-back weeks—even for
a guy in the middle of an MVP season, that's like, 'Wow,'" Boone said.
"There is a level of awe."

It was a power party in the Bronx, a 7–2 win that included a three-run
Anthony Rizzo blast and Jose Trevino's first career multi-homer game,
helping the Yankees become the season's first club to reach seventy victories.

"Judge is doing something that's beyond special in this day and age
of baseball, everything that he's doing for this franchise," Rizzo said. "It's
fun to be a part of."

Judge once again deferred to his teammates in postgame remarks, saying he was just trying to "match what they're doing." In particular, Judge lauded DJ LeMahieu, saying that because the team had the infielder "up there at the top of the lineup hitting close to .300, constantly on base and constantly working the count—it helps everybody."

Having added his trademark "See ya!" call to yet another Judge homer, Michael Kay removed his headset between innings and shook his head. Kay had called multiple World Series championships and the greatest moments of a few Hall of Fame careers, but he wasn't sure if he'd ever experienced anything like this.

"I remember in the beginning of August, I told Boone, 'He's going to end up with 64,'" Kay said. "Boone didn't say anything back, but I think he felt good about it as well. I actually thought at one point that he could finish with 70. I was just amazed that in July and August, teams were still pitching to him."

To borrow a phrase from Cashman, August 2 marked "pencils down." When the clock struck 4:00 p.m. Eastern time, all thirty major league clubs could no longer make trades involving players on their forty-man rosters. If your team needed to import a pitcher or a slugger for the postseason run, or had a high-priced veteran to shed, it was now or never.

Cashman tapped a pen against the desk in his Yankee Stadium office, eyeing a large board that included the surnames of every notable player in the organization. In recent days, magnets reading BENINTENDI, MONTAS, TRIVINO, and EFFROSS had been added. The Cardinals were still calling about Montgomery, and Cashman leaned toward saying yes.

The wrinkle was that Bader wouldn't help the Yankees tomorrow, next week, or even next month. The twenty-eight-year-old hadn't played for the Cardinals in over a month; he was wearing a protective walking boot on his right foot, stemming from a nasty case of plantar fasciitis that made running impossible. Cashman discussed the injury with his medical staff, who cited historical studies suggesting Bader would return sometime in September, with enough time to be an impact player during the postseason.

The pen tapped a little more rapidly now. Cashman liked Montgomery, but he scanned the starting pitchers on that magnetic board—Cole, Severino, Cortes, and now Montas. Cashman did not envision a scenario where Montgomery would be needed to make a postseason start. He sure could imagine Bader running around Yankee Stadium chasing fly balls as though his shaggy red hair was on fire, though.

It didn't hurt that Bader was a local product, having grown up a few miles from Yankee Stadium in Bronxville, New York. He seemed to have a flair for showmanship; Bader's cousin, Chris Baio, did not shy away from the stage as a bassist for the rock band Vampire Weekend. Nor did his first cousin once removed, actor Scott Baio, best known for heartthrob roles on 1970s and '80s television series like *Happy Days* and *Charles in Charge*. Joanie loved Chachi, and Cashman wanted Bader.

"I would say, my confidence in making that move came from me being in this position for as long as I have. I'm not sure how many GMs would be willing to take that risk," Cashman said. "But once we walked through the medicals with our entire medical team, I had assurance that Bader would come back from that injury. The only worry would be if he blew a tire or something else took him off-line. As good as Jordan Montgomery could be, we felt Bader would play a bigger role than Montgomery would if our roster stayed the same. It was a very difficult decision; I think it worked out for both teams, although it was devastating to trade Jordan."

The Yankees were preparing for a game as the deadline struck, and there was confusion and shock in the clubhouse. Montgomery was brought to Boone's office and told he'd been traded to the Cardinals. Montgomery asked what the Yankees got in return; the news was so fresh that Boone didn't have an answer. Montgomery choked back tears as teammates said goodbye to one of their favorite starting pitchers, and it was not the best time for Jameson Taillon to tie his season high in runs allowed, seeing six Mariners cross the plate on his watch.

"That trade hurt; caught me off guard," Taillon said. "He was definitely a best friend for me here. We sat next to each other on the flights, shared a love for bourbon and coffee. We were pretty much inseparable at the field."

There was one more move on the burner, but it appeared to be rapidly cooling. The Yankees had been volleying proposals with the Miami Marlins concerning right-hander Pablo López, a twenty-six-year-old who'd posted a 3.41 ERA over his first twenty-one starts of the season.

But López's last outing had been awful, hammered by the Mets for six runs and twelve hits over 2⅔ innings, and that scared the Yankees off as much as Miami's request for infielder Gleyber Torres. The Yankees weren't actively shopping Torres, whose future had dimmed a few shades after back-to-back All-Star campaigns in 2018 and '19, but they would listen. The sides played chicken until 4:00 p.m. arrived, neither team willing to budge enough to reach a compromise.

"The God's honest truth is, what they asked us for, we said no," Cashman said. "What we told them we would do, they said no. So if that's considered close, I guess we were close."

For better or worse, the 2022 Yankees were now complete. Cashman slid a new magnet with BADER atop his center-field depth chart and watched his team come up two runs short against the Mariners. They lost again the next night, and the night after that. It was like the plot of *Austin Powers*: Had the Montgomery trade robbed the Yankees of their mojo?

The painful stretch delivered five straight losses after the deadline, including Castillo's return to the Bronx in his Seattle debut, when Cole heard boos after allowing six first-inning runs—including three homers. Then they endured a miserable three-game sweep in St. Louis, where players sweltered under triple-digit conditions and had their bats shut down by Montgomery's winning effort on a Saturday afternoon. Seeing Montgomery in Cardinals red was "a little funky," as Judge put it, but the lefty felt right at home in his new duds.

"I was always worried about getting booed off the mound in New York," Montgomery said. "I mean, the pinstripes are heavy. Not everyone can handle it. I feel like I handled it OK. I could have been better, but there were a lot of things going into that. Here [in St. Louis], I'm just being myself and pitching the way I want to. The Yankees were good to me for seven years, so I'm not going to say anything bad about them. I always thought I was going to be a Yankee lifer."

Before the Yankees departed St. Louis, Judge continued a conversation that he'd started at the All-Star Game with Paul Goldschmidt, the Cardinals' standout first baseman and the eventual National League MVP. They exchanged cell phone numbers and texted frequently, looking to glean information that could boost their respective games. Judge's interest was in improving his contact rate with two-strike counts, seeking to mimic Goldschmidt's no-stride approach. Judge toyed with it occasionally throughout 2022, and again the following spring.

HOMER #44: August 8 vs. Seattle Mariners' Ryan Borucki (9th inning, solo)
Exit velocity: 107.7 mph. Distance: 423 feet. Launch angle: 23 degrees. HR in 27 of 30 MLB parks.

Team meetings always make for interesting story lines, at least offering an optic that a manager and players are grinding behind closed doors to correct a skid. Some would argue that they are little more than eyewash, but that's a debate for another time. Back in 1998, the Yankees were in Seattle when manager Joe Torre called a meeting five games in, telling his star-studded roster that he had been disgusted by their play. Then David Cone spoke, and Paul O'Neill did, too. They won fourteen of the next fifteen games, claimed first place by the end of April, and never let go.

"To me, winning is a by-product of doing everything right," Torre said, years later. "We just weren't playing well. I've always preached, 'Don't lose this game. Make somebody beat you.' We were losing games because we weren't playing up to our ability. I was upset with it. I was very upset in that meeting."

Pacing the carpet in the visiting clubhouse at Seattle's T-Mobile Park, the retractable-roof building that spent two decades known as Safeco Field, Boone wasn't as chapped as Torre had been in '98 at the old Kingdome. But as Boone spoke to his players that afternoon, he stressed that the dust of the trade deadline had settled. August needed to be go time, and as he looked around the room, he saw the faces of the men who would determine how far this roster could go.

"This is our group now," Boone told his team. "We have everything we need in this room. We've got everything in the room to get through this and realize our goal of being a champion."

Taillon, who started that night, called the pregame meeting "a nice little get-together" and said the team "went out there with a ton of energy." Judge had nodded. He'd noticed that the Yankees had not won since his last home run, and sensed that his teammates were looking for someone to lead.

Judge banged a ground-rule double in his first at-bat of the night, but Andrew Benintendi and Josh Donaldson did most of the heavy lifting, combining for six RBIs. Judge put the cherry on top in the ninth, parking a Ryan Borucki slider over the center-field wall to seal a 9–4 rout.

Not everything sparkled in the Emerald City, though. That evening marked the expiration of Matt Carpenter's magical run in a Yankees uniform, seeing him painfully limp off the field after fouling a ball off his left foot. X-rays revealed a fracture, and he was promptly fitted for a walking boot. Carpenter had batted .307 with 15 homers and 37 RBIs in just 127 at-bats, but he'd have no more in the regular season and would struggle greatly against postseason pitching, removing an unexpectedly valuable contributor from the lineup.

As the series continued, Seattle bested the Yanks in a grueling thirteen-inning contest, a 1–0 decision that featured Cole and Castillo going toe-to-toe deep into the night. The aces were overpowering, and Mariners manager Scott Servais called it "one of the best major league games I've ever watched." Cole and the Yankees just considered it another loss, especially when baserunning miscues hurt their chances. The Mariners were legitimate, Boone thought, and they'd be an unappealing matchup in the postseason.

"They're really good," Boone said. "They can pitch, obviously have some good starters, but their bullpen is about as good a bullpen as we've faced."

HOMER #45: August 10 vs. Seattle Mariners' Penn Murfee (7th inning, solo)
Exit velocity: 105.2 mph. Distance: 412 feet. Launch angle: 32 degrees. HR in 30 of 30 MLB parks.

As the Yankees concluded their visit to Seattle, Judge's remarkable campaign conjured one of the great mysteries of his career, which took place on that same field during Judge's rookie season. On July 21, 2017, Judge had crushed one of the longest homers ever hit at what was then called Safeco Field, just a row or two from completely leaving the stadium. In an era when technology could pin numbers to every swing, miss or hit, that particular drive toward left field off Andrew Moore remains a glitch, a homer that went unrecorded by MLB's Statcast system.

As such, it seemed to gain some of the mythology that Mickey Mantle created in 1953, when a mammoth drive at Washington's Griffith Stadium coined the phrase "tape-measure home run." Reports of the time indicate that Mantle's shot off Chuck Stobbs soared over the 391-foot marker on the fence, cleared thirty-two rows of bleachers in left-center field, and struck an advertising sign 460 feet from home plate before continuing to roll. Arthur "Red" Patterson, the Yankees' press secretary, trekked from the press box and found ten-year-old Donald Dunaway, who showed Patterson where he'd discovered the ball resting in the backyard of 434 Oakdale Street. Based on Dunaway's account, Patterson made the unscientific calculation that Mantle's drive had traveled 565 feet. For his part in the tale, Dunaway is said to have received a crisp dollar bill. (Alternate retellings have the payment at seventy-five cents, five dollars, ten dollars, or nothing at all.)

Judge's drive was Mantle-esque in that way, eluding the radar and cameras that are used to calculate home run distances. CC Sabathia gawked in the visiting dugout, gesturing animatedly toward the top of the stadium to show Judge where the ball had landed. Alan Cockrell, the hitting coach at the time, had been with the Mariners for three years from 2008 through 2010. Even Cockrell raved that he'd never seen a ball hit farther in Seattle. "It's not fair," said David Robertson, a Yankees reliever at the time. "It's like he's playing in a little kid's park."

We will never know exactly how far Judge's drive traveled that day in 2017, but at least the systems had eyes on him as he tacked on another Seattle souvenir. Facing Penn Murfee, a twenty-eight-year-old rookie, Judge sent a slider into the left-field seats. The drive built a 3–1 lead, but Seattle rallied, with veteran Carlos Santana hitting a go-ahead blast off Albert Abreu (the main piece of the trade for catcher Jose Trevino having been reacquired after a brief stint with the Texas Rangers). Judge was hitting .304 with 45 homers and 99 RBIs, but as he stretched across a row of seats on a chartered jet, his team had lost eight of ten games. It was a quiet flight across the country.

"Superstars have the ability to carry a team by themselves," said Kyle Higashioka. "We don't want to put them in that situation; we want to take all the pressure off them that we can and just have everybody always firing on all cylinders. But that's just the nature of a true superstar, picking us up when eight of the nine of us are going bad. Big G did that for us in 2018 for like two months after Judge broke his wrist, and we were really banged up. [Stanton] is an MVP caliber player. So is Judge. It's just what the superstars do."

HOMER #46: August 12 vs. Boston Red Sox's Nathan Eovaldi (3rd inning, solo) *Exit velocity: 113.8 mph. Distance: 429 feet. Launch angle: 31 degrees. HR in 30 of 30 MLB parks.*

The Yanks enjoyed an off day before getting back on the field at Boston's Fenway Park, where they had an early one-run lead against Nathan Eovaldi. A hard-throwing right-hander, Eovaldi happened to come from Alvin, Texas, home of the ultimate hard-throwing righty. As a Yankee in 2015, Eovaldi had beamed on the field in Houston as he pressed palms with Nolan Ryan, a pitcher unlike any other. Over twenty-seven years with the New York Mets, California Angels, Houston Astros, and Texas Rangers, Ryan racked up more strikeouts (5,714) and walks (2,795) than anyone in history.

"Growing up for me, I connected to baseball with him," Eovaldi said. "In our town, it was Nolan Ryan everything. You'd go to any restaurant and his memorabilia and everything was there."

Durability had been Ryan's hallmark; Eovaldi was not so blessed. His Yankees tenure ended with the second Tommy John surgery of his career, and he'd only twice made thirty or more starts over his eleven seasons. Rizzo singled home Judge to build a first-inning lead, and Judge notched his 100th RBI a frame later, blasting a drive that cleared the Green Monster and came to rest atop a parking garage on Lansdowne Street.

"We were trying to go up and in right there—it's just, he's on fire right now," Eovaldi said. "He's locked in at the plate. I felt like I located that pitch."

Eovaldi, who'd been in Yankees pinstripes for Judge's big league debut in 2016, said that he was rooting for Judge to break Maris's record—though he'd wished not to have become a footnote in the chase.

"When you have a guy who goes out there and bets on himself, you want those guys to do well," Eovaldi said. "Obviously not against us, but he's doing it well and it's impressive to watch. One of the best things about him is, he's not selfish in any way. He's going to do what it takes for the team and that's why he's one of the leaders over there."

There was a gut punch to come. Clay Holmes had lost his dominant touch, blowing his fourth save as the Yanks fell, 3–2, in ten innings. Boone acknowledged that he was considering removing Holmes from the closer's role. Though his Yanks hardly resembled the first-half juggernaut that steamrolled its opposition nightly, Judge was doing everything he could to strap the club across his broad shoulders.

"He gets a lot of credit for the home runs, obviously," said DJ LeMahieu, "but he's a complete baseball player. He can hit for average; he's a complete hitter that hits home runs. And his defense isn't always appreciated, because he hits home runs. He's a complete player who takes pride in all of the aspects of his game."

Judge had 46 home runs as the Yanks took the field in Boston the next night, which meant Judge and Isiah Kiner-Falefa had combined for . . . 46.

Though the team had forecast that swing changes and friendlier dimensions in the Bronx might unlock double-digit home run power, Kiner-Falefa was still looking for his first long ball in a Yankees uniform. A distant relative of Hall of Fame slugger Ralph Kiner, Kiner-Falefa had called the Yankees "my dream team," having fantasized about playing Derek Jeter's position when he posed for a boyhood photograph in the right-field bleachers at the old Yankee Stadium while on a family trip from his native Hawaii.

But his year on the field had been more trying than anyone could have imagined. The low point came when a fan attacked Kiner-Falefa's father, Fili, in a haunting Twitter message, claiming that the shortstop had been "shot dead in the Bronx." Though the comment turned out to be from a kid being stupid, Kiner-Falefa was understandably upset.

"If they don't like me, they don't like me," said Kiner-Falefa, whose intense demeanor was well received in the clubhouse. "The only thing I can do is play better. It's kind of my fault."

Privately, Kiner-Falefa's teammates were furious and protective on his behalf. They had hated seeing how players like Joey Gallo and Aaron Hicks were treated by the home fans, believing that there was too much swirling negativity amid a special season, and family members being subjected to what could be perceived as death threats was completely unacceptable.

"When that type of stuff happens, it sucks. It's on us in the clubhouse to make sure you're loved and protected," said Anthony Rizzo. "When you hear outside noise, it's hard to ignore it. But as professionals, you ignore it and you do the best you can. The atmosphere you create in the clubhouse is the most important thing."

Kiner-Falefa's first Yankees homer finally came in the fifth inning of a 3–2 win, caught by a young fan sitting atop the Green Monster. "This," Kiner-Falefa said, "is everything I've ever wanted in my life. To get the opportunity to come through tonight feels good."

When a club security official scaled the Monster seats hoping to broker a swap for Kiner-Falefa's milestone baseball, the kid asked for an autograph—not Kiner-Falefa's, but Judge's. Fair enough; the deal was struck, and Kiner-Falefa understood.

"Who wouldn't want a Judge ball?" Kiner-Falefa said.

Another three-game skid began with Judge handcuffed in an 0-for-4, three-strikeout performance at Fenway, snapping his string of fourteen straight games reaching base. Then there were two subsequent defeats to the Rays; though Judge said that it was better to hit a skid in August than in the first week of the playoffs, it sure would have been preferable not to have one at all.

The Yankees dressed in their pinstripes early on the afternoon of August 17, organizing to take the annual team photo in center field ahead of that day's game against the Rays. Judge had also agreed to participate in a different photo shoot that day, and the photographer asked him to bring a bat and batting gloves out to the field.

With the entire team assembled in three rows, Judge stood on a riser at the back and center, with the roster facing toward the 408-foot marker in center field. He playfully held the bat over his right shoulder for a few takes, then dropped it out of sight. Only later did team photographer Ariele Goldman Hecht discover what Judge had done. She loved it. When editors evaluated their options, they decided that the official team photograph should have Judge holding a bat. In 120 years of Yankees photographs, there had never been one like it.

"Had another player tried to pull a similar stunt, the photo might never have seen the light of day," said Nathan Maciborski, an executive editor at *Yankees Magazine*. "But Judge was having fun, as he is wont to do, and during such a magical season, we felt him holding his bat for the team photo was rather appropriate."

On the night Judge surreptitiously inserted his bat into the team photo, Josh Donaldson hit a memorable walk-off grand slam that stamped a victory over Tampa Bay, but another three losses followed—all at the hands of the Blue Jays. Boone had reached his boiling point, seething as he found a seat at the front of Yankee Stadium's press conference room, obligated to unpack another loss—their fifteenth in nineteen games. They were getting booed at home, and the manager's patience had worn thin.

"We've got to play better, period. And the great thing is," Boone said, pausing mid-sentence for effect. He raised his right hand and slammed the table in front of him, jarring a microphone and a plastic bottle of Poland Spring water. For those in the audience, it almost felt as though one of your elementary school teachers had finally been pushed too far.

"It's right in front of us! It's right here!" he continued, now circling his right index finger and thumb into an OK sign, gesturing animatedly.

"And we can fix it. It's right here. It's there and we can run away with this thing. And we've got the dudes in there to do it. We've got to do it. If we don't score, tough to win. And I'll answer these same questions—am I perplexed? Yeah. I am."

Said Cashman: "I've got to give managers credit. They have the pre- and postgame [interviews] every day. It's rinse and repeat sometimes. Whether you're a player or a manager, it's not easy while you're going through adversity to address and fill in the blanks when questions are coming in. Sometimes the answers don't appear as easily as you'd like."

The fans were just as frustrated, voicing their displeasure by jeering Cashman during a pregame ceremony to retire Paul O'Neill's uniform No. 21, during which the YES Network analyst received a Gatorade watercooler impaled by a bat; O'Neill kicked it. Appropriately for the hot-tempered O'Neill, there were fireworks with the Jays; Toronto ace Alek Manoah hit Judge in the left elbow with a fastball.

Judge ambled up the first-base line slowly, registering his displeasure. Judge's teammates trickled out of the home dugout, stragglers awaiting their cue, but Judge waved them off. Later, in the dugout, he told team- mates that the "game was too close" to risk ejections. Benintendi would club a two-run homer, his first long ball in a Yankees uniform, to avert a sweep.

"We've got to have that mentality of, 'Hey, every time we step up to the plate, I'm going to be the guy that goes out there and gets it done,'" Judge said. "It's about us picking ourselves up and not forgetting we're the New York Yankees. We've got to go out and show people that."

HOMER #47: August 22 vs. New York Mets' Max Scherzer (3rd inning, solo)
Exit velocity: 109.6 mph. Distance: 383 feet. Launch angle: 26 degrees. HR in 30 of 30 MLB parks.

Max Scherzer was gunning for his two hundredth career victory as he walked to the mound at Yankee Stadium on a pleasant Monday evening, the three-time Cy Young Award winner enjoying a dominant first season with the Mets. Given the Yankees' recent struggles, the pitching matchup looked like a mismatch. Judge ensured that it wouldn't be, providing a big blow after DJ LeMahieu nicked Scherzer for a first-inning sacrifice fly. In this fifteenth spin through the circuit, the thirty-eight-year-old Scherzer still brought it as one of the game's best, and he relished the challenge of taking on Judge.

"I recognize how good of a hitter he is," Scherzer said. "He can hit me. I'm not going to sit here and act like I'm better than him. He can definitely take me deep. I also believe I have the stuff to get him out."

Scherzer started Judge with a fastball that sailed low and away for a ball, backhanded by catcher James McCann. Scherzer went into his deep windup again, hands over his head as his left leg pumped high, dotting the bottom of the zone with another heater for a called strike. Now Judge's mind was racing, trying to stay ahead of Scherzer and McCann. Scherzer had a slider, changeup, cutter, and curveball in his arsenal, making it impossible to be confident in a guess. Judge decided to stay geared for the fastball, and Scherzer grooved one right over the plate.

Judge powered it to right field, and as Starling Marte charged toward the wall, Scherzer stood at the front of the mound with his hands on his hips. The odds had all been in Scherzer's favor; Judge was 2-for-11 with seven strikeouts against Scherzer lifetime, and battling a 4-for-32 slump, not having homered in nine games. But there was no way the stadium would hold this one, the ball landing about five rows in front of the Judge's Chambers.

"That's one of the reasons why I love this game, that little chess match you get to play," Judge said after the Yanks' 4–2 win. "To have a future Hall of Famer that you get to do that with, it's electric. You've got the crowd on your feet for every pitch right along with you. It's fun. I'll look back on moments like that."

HOMER #48: August 23 vs. New York Mets' Taijuan Walker (4th inning, solo)
Exit velocity: 115.9 mph. Distance: 453 feet. Launch angle: 26 degrees. HR in 30 of 30 MLB parks.

Judge's second homer in as many games sparked the attack against Taijuan Walker, who once again landed on the wrong side of a showdown between players who favored uniform No. 99. Working the count full, Judge pounced on a 94.7 mph sinker and drove it deep to the back of Yankee Stadium's left-field bleachers, rounding the bases with a skyward point as an air-raid siren played over the speakers. The Yanks held on for a 4–2 win and a Subway sweep, riding a bullpen high-wire act with

Clarke Schmidt pushed to a season-high sixty pitches before Wandy Peralta extinguished a bases-loaded jam by inducing a Francisco Lindor flyout.

"That," Judge said, "was as close to a playoff atmosphere as you're going to get."

Indeed, it did seem like they might have reached a turning point, providing a pleasant journey back to the West Coast, especially when Giancarlo Stanton returned from the injured list to help the Yankees paste the Athletics by a 13–4 count the next night. Stanton's MVP performance in the All-Star Game had come at a price, aggravating an Achilles' strain. The crumbling Coliseum was easily the worst of all thirty big-league parks, yet Judge always felt comfortable there; maybe it was because of that first workout day in 2013, when he'd played catch before the game with Brett Gardner and been invited to chat over lunch with CC Sabathia.

But the national media had descended on the Judge chase—ESPN was tagging along until he hit 50, then would rejoin if and when he got closer to 61. More and more reporters angled for one-on-one interviews with Judge: just fifteen or twenty minutes of your time, please? The numerous extra bodies filling Oakland's outdated visiting clubhouse spurred Judge to spend more time than usual in the trainers' room before first pitch, seeking solitude away from prying eyes (the exact move that Maris had leaned on sixty-one years prior, when he had ten to fifteen reporters crowding his locker each day).

Said Kristie Ackert of the *New York Daily News*: "It was exhausting, for him and everyone around it. I mean, it kind of shows you really how hard it is to do, because those last two or three weeks—that march to 62 was just excruciating. It was so intense."

When Judge did emerge to speak, he leaned on one of his interview trademarks—a thoughtful pause of one or two seconds preceding a response.

"It does get tough day after day standing up there, good days and bad days," Judge said. "It's a lot. One way that I handled it is, I try to take my time up there. I try to really think about what I'm going to say. If you just get up there and start rambling or saying this and that, you're like, 'What did I even just say?' I always try to pause, think about it, and come up with a genuine answer. You've got to be honest with these guys, because they can see through it when you're giving them a made-up answer or something fake. Just be honest with people."

As Clarke Schmidt said: "When you watch his interviews or anything he's doing, you're like, 'Is this fake? Is he really like this in person?' The way he carries himself, it's so consistent."

HOMER #49: August 26 vs. Oakland Athletics' JP Sears (5th inning, three-run) *Exit velocity: 109 mph. Distance: 427 feet. Launch angle: 31 degrees. HR in 28 of 30 MLB parks.*

The Yankees were happy to see JP Sears once again. A slight twenty-six-year-old lefty, he'd provided the Yankees with seven sharp outings, including two spot starts, before being packaged to the Athletics in the Frankie Montas trade. Now Sears was wearing green and gold, and more surprisingly, he was still clean-cut: one of the few ex-Yankees not to immediately grow a beard. In fact, Sears seemed to be settling in nicely, having won two of his three starts since joining Oakland.

Like the trip to Pittsburgh in early July, when Manny Bañuelos found himself on the wrong end of Judge's historic march, Judge wasn't about to show mercy to a former teammate.

It was clear that Sears wanted to work carefully; he walked Judge on seven pitches in the first inning, then put him aboard intentionally in the third, setting up a Stanton double play. But there was no room for error in the fifth, as rookie Oswaldo Cabrera and DJ LeMahieu opened the frame with sharp singles. At the far end of the visiting dugout, Anthony Rizzo nudged Nestor Cortes, who was standing with his hands in the pocket of a hooded sweatshirt.

"Nestor, he's about to hit a home run," Rizzo said. "When he hits the home run, just drop your head like you're pissed."

Sears exhaled, coming set as he eyed Cabrera dancing from second base. The pitch, a slider, came out of his left hand. It hung, and Sears immediately knew he was about to watch a souvenir. Judge's drive sent center fielder Cal Stevenson racing back, back, back—the ball struck about halfway up the batter's eye, bounding back onto the playing field.

"I hadn't seen the slider yet," Judge said. "He showed me the fastball, he showed me the changeup . . . I was talking with a couple of guys and was like, 'I might see a slider here first pitch, let's see what happens.'"

As instructed, Cortes dropped his gaze toward the concrete floor, while Rizzo covered his eyes with his right hand, as though he was experiencing a sudden migraine.

"On the replay, you get the side angles, and the side camera picked us up," Rizzo said. "So he hits the home run, everyone's cheering, and you just see Nestor and I like, 'All right.' Those are the little fun games you interact with throughout the year; just the little kid jokes that help you make it through the 162 [game] grind."

Judge laughed when he saw the replay. He called No. 49 "just another number," but the blast thrilled a personal cheering section for Judge, a gathering of friends and supporters from St. Andrews Lutheran Church in Stockton, California, about twelve miles from his hometown of Linden.

"The stadium in Oakland, a third of it had Judge [apparel] on. It was incredible," said Jordan Ribera, a former Fresno State teammate who attended the series as a fan. "You start seeing what he means to the game and the fan appreciation; he is doing something special. To do it in New York, I can only imagine the daily temptations or invites."

Though Gerrit Cole starred on his side, striking out eleven in the Yanks' 3–2 win, he seemed most impressed by his slugging teammate. "I get to have the best seat in the house every night for The Aaron Judge Show," Cole said, "which is one-of-a-kind right now."

With Judge on the precipice of joining Babe Ruth and Mickey Mantle as the only Yankees to hit 50 or more homers in two or more separate seasons, the YES Network approached Patty Judge to gauge her interest in wearing a microphone for the last two games of the A's series.

"She said, 'No, I don't want the camera on me right now. You can start filming me when he hits 60,'" said Troy Benjamin, a producer at the YES Network. "She knew he was going to do it."

HOMER #50: August 29 vs. Los Angeles Angels of Anaheim's Ryan Tepera (8th inning, solo)
Exit velocity: 111.1 mph. Distance: 434 feet. Launch angle: 34 degrees. HR in 30 of 30 MLB parks.

The bats had gone ice-cold again: a five-game winning streak snapped by consecutive poor showings against Adam Oller and Adrián Martínez, a pair of Oakland starters with bloated ERAs over 6.00. Judge said that "this is the time of year when it's kind of a grind," challenging his teammates to "step up and respond" as they moved down the California coast to Anaheim for a new series with Shohei Ohtani and the Angels.

This was also the portion of the schedule where the AL MVP debate had gone into full swing, with little more than a month remaining for Judge and Ohtani to state their respective cases. Judge's offensive numbers were better, holding an advantage in the triple-slash line categories of batting average, slugging percentage, and on-base percentage, along with the edge in stolen bases and runs batted in.

But Judge did not pitch, and that added value seemed to provide pause. At the time, Ohtani owned a 2.67 ERA with 176 strikeouts over 128 innings. Ohtani was a unicorn; there would be a case for him to win the MVP every year, since no one did what he could. Tyler Wade, who played sixty-seven games with the Angels that season, said that he loved having Ohtani as a teammate but believed Judge's season deserved the MVP award.

"I'm not trying to be biased," Wade said, "but when you're breaking records like that and leading the team to a division title, and he was chasing the Triple Crown for a little bit, too—I don't think we're going to see a year like that for quite some time. I think the writers got it right in the end. [Judge is] more deserving of it than anybody, on and off the field."

Voters on each side of the aisle had new ammunition to support the argument as the superstars traded homers in a Monday-evening showdown. Ohtani struck first, belting a two-run shot in the fifth inning off Montas, who had raised some eyebrows earlier that afternoon by having alterations performed on a new lime green suit in a reception area outside the visiting clubhouse. Surely, there must have been a better time to schedule a tailor. He now owned a 7.01 ERA through five starts with New York—hardly the difference-maker Cashman and his staff envisioned. Montas would later acknowledge that his shoulder "wasn't fully 100 percent" at the time of the trade, saying he "was trying to pitch through it. I got traded to a new team and wanted to show what I could do."

Judge was walked intentionally in two of his first three plate appearances, prompting more than forty-four thousand voices to fill the air, booing lustily. They made no secret about what had drawn them across Interstate 5's congested lanes on a picture-perfect SoCal evening: history.

With the bases empty and one out, interim Angels manager Phil Nevin gave reliever Ryan Tepera the green light to face Judge, who clobbered a slider off the rock waterfall beyond center field. "It's hard to wrap your mind around just how incredible of a season he's had to this point," Boone said. "The one time they pitch to him, he hits it off the rocks." Judge's 50th homer trimmed the Yankees' deficit to a run, but the comeback stalled there, with the visitors accepting a 4–3 loss.

"You couldn't get a fastball by him, and if you hung anything, you're not getting it back," said reliever Lou Trivino. "It was a fun experience for me to witness something like that firsthand. Everyone talks about how Barry Bonds would get one pitch to hit. I feel like I saw that with Judge. If I'm pitching, I don't want to give him anything to hit—I probably go in, in, in, and see if it gets him to chase. He made sure that he put the barrel on it."

The West Coast trip delivered hints of the media fuss dramatized by Billy Crystal's *61**, including a brief skirmish between a writer and a television camera operator, who elbowed for position in front of Judge's locker in the Angel Stadium visiting clubhouse. Judge watched that scene develop, an expression of confusion and annoyance spilling across his gaze. As he navigated the scrum, he made it clear that homers in losing efforts offered no joy, even if they were nice round statistical milestones.

"I'm not downplaying it, but I just don't like talking numbers," Judge said. "It doesn't mean anything because we lost. We can talk about numbers and all that kind of stuff when the season's over with; we can review it. But for right now, the most important thing for me is getting some wins."

'61 FLASHBACK: THE M&M BOYS

The biggest obstacle keeping the Yankees from reaching the World Series in 1961—their version of the Houston Astros, if you will—had been the Detroit Tigers. The Motown team was stacked, led by Al Kaline, Norm Cash, Rocky Colavito, and Jim Bunning. Despite an incredible August, in which the Yankees won twenty-two of thirty-one games, they had yet to shake Detroit in the race.

As September dawned, Maris had benefited from a lengthy chat with hitting coach Wally Moses, transpiring in a most unlikely place as the Yankees rode the rails down to Washington, D.C. "I ran into Roger in the men's room on the train, and we started talking," Moses said. "I know it's hard to believe, but we spent four hours in the men's room talking hitting. Roger was worried about losing his confidence and didn't want to fall off down the stretch, like he had in 1960."

Maris had a mental block about hitting in Griffith Stadium, the Washington Senators' home park. Moses helped unlock it; Maris homered in all four games the Yanks played in D.C., then hit 3 homers in his next two games against the White Sox. Maris entered September with 51 homers, while Mantle had 45.

"I just hope," manager Ralph Houk said, "both of my guys do it."

Detroit arrived at Yankee Stadium on September 1, beginning a three-game set. New York swept them, swelling their league lead from 1½ games to 4½. The Yankees were off and rolling, rattling off a thirteen-game winning streak as Detroit lost eight straight. The pennant race was effectively over, but the series came at a price. Mantle strained a muscle in his left forearm on a checked swing, yet still homered twice in the finale to reach 50.

All of the focus was now squarely upon Maris and Mantle, who received ovations just for taking batting practice. In an era when fans could exit via the playing field, security guards had to hold ropes at the final out just so Mantle and Maris could reach the dugout without incident. In the clubhouse, teammates witnessed the chase's strain. Mantle had spent years in the spotlight; he was used to having every movement or syllable parsed. He'd also had a big home run year previously, slugging 52 homers to lead the majors during his Triple Crown season of 1956. Maris's career high was 39 homers in 1960, a number he'd topped by July 1961.

"Roger smoked a lot of cigarettes, unfortunately, before the game and after the game," said Tony Kubek. "But once he got through batting practice and his work, getting into the clubhouse, he'd just think about the game on that particular date and the pitcher. That's what Roger Maris was all about. He was a baseball player, not born to be a hero, but he became that. I don't know how many guys could have handled it, with all the duress he was under."

The M&M Boys were neck and neck through a September 10 doubleheader against the Cleveland Indians, with Maris at 56 homers and Mantle at 53. Mantle was ill, suffering from a heavy head cold, respiratory infection, and eye infection. The symptoms lingered through a road trip to Chicago, Detroit, and Baltimore. Mel Allen, the Yankees' broadcaster, mentioned that he knew a doctor who could fix everything.

Dr. Max Jacobson ("Miracle Max," as Allen called him) was known as a Dr. Feelgood for the jet set, having treated the likes of President John F. Kennedy, Eddie Fisher, Johnny Mathis, and Tennessee Williams with concoctions of amphetamines and vitamins. Mantle visited Jacobson in New York on September 25, a team off day. The doctor filled a syringe with smoky liquid, then plunged the needle into Mantle's hip.

The shot missed the mark; Mantle described the feeling "as though he'd stuck a red-hot poker into me." Mantle arrived at Lenox Hill Hospital days later, suffering from a 104-degree fever. The wound was infected; in some retellings, the resulting abscess in Mantle's hip was large enough to fit a fist; others say a golf ball. All agree that it was not conducive to playing baseball at its highest level. Mantle would return to hit one more homer and played sparingly in the World Series, but for the most part, it was now Maris vs. Ruth.

"I thought I had a chance at the record in '61," Mantle said. "I had been there in '56 when I hit 52. Roger was having a great year, I was having a great year. What everybody forgets is that Ruth hit seventeen in September. So you're ahead of the pace in July and you're still ahead of it in August, and all of a sudden, it seems like you've got to hit one about every day because that's what Ruth did."

The press contingent thickened; Bobby Richardson recalled seeing fifty to seventy writers covering a game. Whether or not Maris homered, they kept prodding, seemingly asking the same questions on a loop. Even though he'd heard some variation dozens of times before, Maris sat quietly in his locker, sucking on a beer and waiting for the inquiries to end.

"There were so many games when Roger would say, 'Why don't you guys talk to Ellie Howard? He's hitting .350,'" said pitcher Bob Turley. "Talk to Whitey; he's won twenty games. Talk to Luis Arroyo. Talk to Bobby Richardson; he never plays a bad game."

It was a momentous time in baseball history, but the key figure could not enjoy it. Bob Fishel, the Yankees' public relations director, expressed regret that daily press conferences did not exist. Fishel died in 1988, but he saw how Pete Rose navigated a pursuit of Ty Cobb's all-time-hits record in 1985, believing that Maris would have benefited from a more structured environment.

"Bob was a class act and came to take the blame for what Maris went through, when he needn't," Marty Appel said. "It just wasn't done. He would have been inventing something that nobody had thought of at the time. The NFL started the interview rooms [in the 1970s], and baseball followed for All-Star Games and the World Series. Individual teams weren't doing it at all."

The chase had physical manifestations, leaving bald patches in Maris's crew cut as mysterious rashes appeared on his body. Tony Kubek, the Yankees' shortstop in 1961, said that he believed no athlete in any sport had endured more pressure than Maris over a prolonged period.

"I'll tell you, I felt bad about what some people said and wrote about Roger," Mantle once said. "You could see him holding it all inside, see his hair falling out. He had rashes all over the place. And Roger would never really drink. I mean, he'd have a few beers, but that's not the kind of drinking I'm talking about. I remember telling Roger, 'You can't hold all this inside you, or you'll blow up. You gotta release it somehow. Let's go get a few drinks.' But on the road, Roger stayed in his hotel room."

Moments of serenity were difficult to come by, and Maris savored them when he could. The Yankees had been in Detroit on September 17, when Maris hit No. 58. Kubek danced off second base as Maris batted in the twelfth inning, the score tied, 4–4. Maris stepped out of the box and fixed his gaze on the upper deck in right field, where a flock of about 250 squawking Canada geese were approaching.

Maris took off his cap, wiped his brow, and watched the geese; home plate umpire Nestor Chylak permitted Maris as much time as he wanted, as pitcher Terry Fox stood impatiently on the mound, rubbing the baseball. When play resumed, Maris drove a homer into the upper deck in right field, just under where the geese had flown.

"I can still see those geese," Maris told Kubek decades later. "Watching them was so peaceful."

No. 59 came on September 20 in the Yankees' 154th game, fittingly played in the city where Babe Ruth had been born. Batting practice had been washed out on a damp, chilly day, and Maris spent the pregame hours smoking and pacing at his locker, occasionally ambling up the runway to peek at the field. That day, Mantle had bowed out of the race, telling Maris: "That's it. I'm through. We're all behind you."

Facing righty Milt Pappas, Maris flew out to deep right field in the first inning, then scorched a 2-1 fastball to right field in his second at-bat. The wind had been gusting in, but Maris overpowered it, reaching the bleachers about 380 feet from home plate. As he rounded the bases, Maris thought: "That's 59. I have two, maybe three more shots at it." But Maris struck out and flew out in his next two at-bats, with Baltimore manager Luman Harris calling on knuckleballer Hoyt Wilhelm in the ninth.

As Maris came to the plate, catcher Gus Triandos said: "Well, this is your last shot." Maris replied: "Don't think my collar isn't tight." Maris checked his swing on a Wilhelm floater, nubbing a soft roller back to the mound. Later that night, Maris said: "Commissioner Frick makes the rules. If all I'm entitled to is an asterisk, then it will be all right with me."

There was a brief postscript regarding Maris's 59th. A thirty-two-year-old Baltimore man named Robert Reitz caught the ball and posed for photos with Maris, who offered two new baseballs in trade. Reitz declined, and Maris wished him good luck. A day later, Reitz contacted the Yankees to demand two World Series tickets, then four; he then indicated that he wasn't quite sure what he wanted. The team offered $25; Reitz countered at $2,500. Maris told Reitz he could keep the baseball, and he did.

"I'd like to have it," Maris said, "but I'm not looking to get rid of that kind of money for it."

◆

THE GREATEST SHOW ON DIRT

Just as the likes of Yogi Berra, Elston Howard, and Moose Skowron had watched with rapt attention during the summer of 1961, witnesses to history while Roger Maris and Mickey Mantle traded blows in pursuit of Babe Ruth's home run record, Aaron Judge's Yankees teammates felt as though they were fortunate to own a front-row seat for baseball's most compelling one-man show.

With 50 homers in the team's first 129 games, Judge sat ahead of Maris's 1961 pace and Babe Ruth's 1927 pace. A new American League record was well within his reach.

"Once he got into the fifties, it was all Aaron Judge, all the time," said Meredith Marakovits of the YES Network. "It was impossible for that not to be the story. At that point in time, we just pushed all the chips in and said, 'This is it. What the people are interested in is Aaron Judge.' We covered the team, but he was the leading story, regardless of the results on the field."

It was wild. Few individuals could say they had experienced anything like what Judge was going through, but Giancarlo Stanton could.

In 2017, as a member of the Miami Marlins, Stanton had led the majors with 59 home runs—until Judge exploded upon the scene, only Stanton and Ryan Howard had flirted with 60 in the post-steroid era.

Reflecting on the end of that season, Stanton pointed out that he could have hit a few more—Nos. 58 and 59 came on September 28 against the Atlanta Braves, and the Marlins had three games remaining. Though Stanton stroked five hits in those contests, he produced only one extra-base hit, a double.

"It all goes into the dynamic of the game; who you're facing, if they're in the playoff race, if the game's out of hand," Stanton said. "There's a lot of things going on. Who's batting behind you? As the game develops, you could get two chances, you could get four, or you could get none. It's on to the next one. If you strike out or hit a homer, you've got more work to do. You're never satisfied."

As Judge absorbed becoming the third Yankee to enjoy multiple seasons of 50 or more homers, joining Babe Ruth (1920, '21, '27, '28) and Mickey Mantle (1956, '61), Stanton felt confident Judge's chase would end differently than his own.

"I think he's going to do something incredible. He already has," Stanton said. "We've got a month more to watch."

For all the jaw-dropping drives, Stanton was most impressed by Judge's work behind the scenes, which took place hours before the game, out of view of the fans and television cameras. "I watch him work every day, just seeing when he doesn't feel his best," Stanton said. "None of you guys are going to know that, but the guys who see him every day can tell. He's still out there producing; he's still out there showing up. I'd say that's the biggest thing, besides the numbers."

"Probably one of the most impressive things on my end about him was the way he stuck with the consistency of his routine," added Casey Dykes, the Yankees' assistant hitting coach. "He took care of his cage work, but also had flexibility with it, knowing what series were coming up, what travel was coming up, what type of sleep he was getting. I think that was a huge part of him being able to play a full season healthy."

"Load management" had become the NBA's hottest term a few years prior, and the concept made a lot of sense for Judge. He'd learned that lesson the hard way earlier in his career, later coming to recognize that there was a price to pay for taking hundreds of extra batting-practice swings or defensive reps over a 162-game season. He also had expanded his thinking to focusing on rest and recovery, counteracting the cumulative effects of games played.

"When you first get called up, you're young. You play a game, shower and leave and you're ready for the next game," Judge said. "Talking with a lot of guys away from the field at the places I work out during the season, they helped keep my body right. I'm not twenty-four, twenty-five, running around anymore. I'm only getting older. I'm just focused on doing the little things, making sure my body is prepped and ready to go, playing the nine innings today and then recover, stretch out, do anything I need to do for the next one."

HOMER #51: August 30 vs. Los Angeles Angels of Anaheim's Mike Mayers (4th inning, three-run)
Exit velocity: 107.5 mph. Distance: 378 feet. Launch angle: 36 degrees. HR in 6 of 30 MLB parks.

The Yanks' stay in Southern California was proving to be a productive one.

Anthony Rizzo and Andrew Benintendi hit early homers as they snapped their three-game West Coast slide, but it was Judge's drive that had a crowd of 42,684 buzzing. The celebration in the stands was nothing compared to what transpired in the visiting dugout, with Judge clipping a high fastball from the Halos' Mike Mayers to the opposite field, clearing a high wall in front of the right-field bleachers.

It was just Mayers's third opportunity as a traditional starter; he'd had a disastrous nine-run outing as a rookie in 2016 with the St. Louis Cardinals, spelling his assignment to the bullpen. The Angels had pressed him into duty six days prior against the Tampa Bay Rays, with decent results; his Yankees audition hardly inspired future opportunities. "They get paid to hit, just like we get paid to pitch," Mayers said. "They were better than I was."

Mayers said he regretted the pitches to Rizzo and Benintendi, but he'd executed the pitch to Judge just as intended. "He's in a groove right now," Angels interim manager Phil Nevin said. "You can just see watching his swing from the side, how on time he is. Everything's in a good place. He's hard to pitch to." Jameson Taillon agreed, saying it felt like Judge had a chance to do something special every time he came to bat. "I've never seen anything like it. It doesn't matter what scouting report you have or whether you execute your pitch or not," Taillon said. "He's just so good that you can make a good pitch and he can still hit it out of the park. It's special, it's fun to be a part of, and it's fun to watch. He just shows up every day and prepares, and goes about it the right way. He's extremely neutral. He doesn't let it get to his head or anything. He's a great guy."

Judge was now just ten big swings away from equaling Maris's record, on pace for 63, and he still had a full calendar month to be played. Like Stanton, Rizzo marveled about Judge's daily process, calling it "the most special thing about him."

"His routine, getting to watch him every day and talk to him, it's so fundamentally sound," Rizzo said. "That's the most enjoyable part. The results are amazing, but the way he goes about it is even better."

Judge was the most dangerous hitter in the majors, but the team was flagging badly, having endured a particularly brutal August. A 3–2 loss in the finale sealed another series loss, and they zipped back to the East Coast having dropped four of seven games to the Athletics and Angels, a couple of California clubs well out of the race. New York's advantage in the AL East, once 15½ games, had been shaved to 6.

Even with Judge doing his best Lightning McQueen impression, attempting to drag his flat-tired club across the finish line into the postseason, the Yankees had managed just ten victories in their last twenty-eight games. That resulting .357 winning percentage marked the club's worst calendar month since September 1991, when they limped to the finish with a 9-19 mark that spelled the merciful end of the Stump Merrill era. Still, Judge stood tall, projecting confidence.

"We've got everything we need here in this room," Judge said. "Nobody on the outside is going to help us; nobody is going to feel sorry for us. It just comes down to that attitude; if you're not feeling good, a little banged up, you've got to bring it."

September started poorly, too. Disgust was palpable as Boone walked to the mound in the eighth inning of a game at Tropicana Field, seeing nine runs littered across the scoreboard, more runners still on the basepaths, and a position player walking out to lob a few pitches.

In 2009, on that same diamond, Nick Swisher had enjoyed his only career pitching appearance a bit too much during a blowout loss; years later, Swisher could still recall the "daggers" he'd felt from Jorge Posada's eyes, letting the newcomer know in no uncertain terms that the Yankees didn't find losing funny. That was still the case more than a decade later; Marwin González took no joy in his one recorded out, cleaning up a torturous eighth inning with three runs charged apiece to relievers Greg Weissert and Anthony Banda behind broken-bat hits, errors, and bases-loaded walks.

Chewing on the 9–0 loss to the Rays, Boone said his team should be "pissed off and embarrassed," and that those nine innings had better represent their "rock bottom." If it wasn't, everyone in the visiting clubhouse was in for a rough ride.

"We've set a much better standard in that room," Boone said, "that we've got to start living up to."

But even before Weissert and Banda struggled, hopes of a rally seemed remote, as the offensive doldrums continued. Adding injury to insult, Andrew Benintendi was lost, feeling a violent pop in his right wrist after a third-inning hack.

Benintendi had fractured the hook of the hamate bone, which was baffling to Benintendi, because he believed that particular bone had been surgically removed after a similar injury during his freshman year at the University of Arkansas. The surgeon had not completed the removal, and the bone eventually grew back. Though Benintendi attempted to speed his rehab, he could not return, ending his Yankees tenure with a .254 batting average in thirty-three games.

"That was frustrating," Cashman said. "Who would have thought, that from an old hamate surgery, it could grow back? It's very rare, and it snapped on our watch. He was an important piece we could have utilized. I appreciate everything Andrew did to try and be ready and get back as soon as he possibly could."

HOMER #52: September 3 vs. Tampa Bay Rays' Jason Adam (9th inning, solo)
Exit velocity: 103.5 mph. Distance: 392 feet. Launch angle: 26 degrees. HR in 23 of 30 MLB parks.

The trip to Tropicana Field had been a bust, and now the Yankees were down to their last three outs, their lineup still gasping for production as Judge carried his bat toward home plate. Throughout a second-half slide that threatened to create the wrong kind of history, Judge's at-bats were always their best chances to put numbers on the scoreboard.

Judge delivered, crushing No. 52 to remain ahead of Maris's pace, but his teammates again were unable to help. The next three batters were retired in order as the Yankees absorbed a 2–1 loss, seeing their advantage in the American League East shrink to just four games—their slimmest lead since May 11.

"It's baseball," Judge said. "You're going to have those moments where nothing goes your way, or those moments where everything goes your way. The in-between is where you make your money and really what defines a team. Going through those tough times where we get our butts kicked for a couple of weeks, I think all that it does is make a team stronger."

It had been two weeks since Boone exhibited one of his most intense press conferences, when he slammed his palm on a table and shouted: "It's right in front of us!" Though his talking points remained largely the same after the loss at Tropicana Field, Boone's tone sounded more like a deep sigh than a fiery explosion.

Boone acknowledged that a sizable portion of the fan base was "really mad," and the limping offense was to blame—in recent weeks, his coaching staff had pointed to a cocktail of underperformance, pressing, injuries, and lack of focus to explain why the Yankees weren't scoring runs.

For the first time, Boone seemed to acknowledge the possibility that this Yankees season—once so magical and promising—might not end with a parade.

"Injuries and [having] guys beat up is a real factor, but everyone deals with that," Boone said. "We've still got to find a way to put points on the board right now. So the best I can tell you is, we're in control of that. On the whole, we've done a good job. If we don't dig ourselves out, you'll have a great story to write."

HOMER #53: September 4 vs. Tampa Bay Rays' Shawn Armstrong
(1st inning, solo)
Exit velocity: 115.3 mph. Distance: 450 feet. Launch angle: 30 degrees. HR in 30 of 30 MLB parks.

Though he claimed to not be paying attention to his growing home run total, Judge was acutely aware of where he measured against Maris's 1961 pace and his own 2017 pace.

That year, Judge had hit 52 home runs as the American League's Rookie of the Year, and having matched his career high, he voiced a desire to collect any of the homers from that point forward. Eddie Fastook and Mark Kafalas, a burly pair of New York Police Department alumni who had spent years serving as the team's security detail, were tasked with the assignment.

When any Yankee slugged a milestone ball into the seats, be it Derek Jeter's three thousandth hit or a rookie's first long ball, Fastook or Kafalas would identify the fan who secured it and offer a reasonable trade—usually a signed baseball, a bat, or a clubhouse meet and greet. There have been exceptions: when noted ball hawk Zack Hample snagged Alex Rodriguez's three thousandth hit in 2015, there were two weeks of negotiations before the club agreed to make a $150,000 charitable donation, along with inviting Hample to participate in a press conference, with memorabilia, tickets, and other perks.

So Fastook and Kafalas were on alert as Judge stepped to the plate in the first inning at Tropicana Field. They didn't have to wait long for action; batting leadoff, Judge set the tone by swatting opener Shawn Armstrong's second pitch to the top deck in left field for No. 53.

"My job at the top of the lineup is just trying to get on base for the guys behind me," Judge said. "That's all I'm trying to do there in the first inning, especially with a guy like Armstrong, who's got a good little sinker-cutter combo. I tried to put something in play and was lucky to get something over the plate."

"He was so dialed in, and made it look so easy," Marakovits said. "I'd joke with him occasionally, like, 'Oh, only one home run today? That's all you've got? Slow day for you.'"

Judge's blast proved enough, as Frankie Montas hurled five one-hit innings before Clay Holmes survived late drama to seal the club's eighti-eth win. Holmes surrendered three hits before pinning the go-ahead and winning runs on base, ringing up Yandy Diaz with a called third strike that the Rays believed was low.

At 101.7 mph, it was the fastest pitch Holmes had ever thrown in the big leagues; the game on the line, Holmes said that he had decided: "If he was going to beat me, he was going to beat me on my best bullet."

Even if the pitch was a tick or two out of the strike zone, it repre-sented a much-needed break to conclude a rough road trip. Watching on television after a fifth-inning ejection, Boone joked that his pacemaker (installed during spring training in 2021, a scary episode when his heart rate had dipped below fifty beats per minute) "was kicking into over-drive."

Holmes said, with a smirk: "I thought it was a great pitch."

HOMER #54: September 5 vs. Minnesota Twins' Trevor Megill (6th inning, two-run)
Exit velocity: 109.6 mph. Distance: 404 feet. Launch angle: 34 degrees. HR in 03 of 30 MLB parks.

It was Labor Day as the Yankees returned to the Bronx, hosting the Minnesota Twins to begin a four-game series. As he had done many times before, Gary Sánchez was making a slow trot around the base-paths. The excised catcher may have enjoyed this one more than the rest, savoring each moment of the 473-foot drive he'd parked to the back of the bleachers. For all the polarization that Sánchez's inconsistency had created within the fan base and at higher levels of the Yankees organiza-tion, no one could debate this: when "El Gary" got a hold of one, it still traveled a long way.

It took all of one inning for Sánchez's onetime Baby Bombers team-mate to respond. Facing righty Trevor Megill, Judge belted a 3-1 slider down the left-field line; Megill, in his second big-league season, dropped his shoulders and stared at the infield grass. The ball landed in the second deck, marking a piece of franchise history; now Judge and Alex Rodriguez were the only two right-handed Yankees to hit 54 homers in a single season, with A-Rod having done it during his 2007 AL MVP season.

It was three straight games with a homer for Judge, putting him on pace for 65 with twenty-seven games left. "Just trying to do what I can every single day," Judge said after the Yanks' 5–2 win.

"That sealed it for me," said Brendan Kuty, a beat reporter for *NJ Advance Media*. "It felt like it was an inevitable march toward history at that point. He was on fire, healthy, he seemed nonplussed, like he was just shrugging this off his shoulders while we're looking at the calendar and the record books, saying, 'Oh man, this is going to happen. This is unbelievable.'"

Even Boone was beginning to find himself at a loss for words to describe Judge's exploits. Teams were pitching around Judge, not issuing intentional walks—at least, not yet—but focusing on him as the force in the Yanks' injury-ravaged lineup whom they could not let beat them. "What am I going to do, slam my bat down?" Judge said. "It is what it is."

Sooner or later, they gave him a pitch to hit, and Judge always seemed ready for it.

"He's our leader," Isiah Kiner-Falefa said. "He goes about his business the right way. Everybody sees it, everybody feeds off his energy and just the way he does things. Everybody notices it. I'm excited for what's to come for him."

HOMER #55: September 7 vs. Minnesota Twins' Louie Varland
(4th inning, solo)
Exit velocity: 102.1 mph. Distance: 374 feet. Launch angle: 28 degrees. HR in 21 of 30 MLB parks.

Opposing pitchers seemed helpless to slow Judge's torrid pace, but Mother Nature still could. Heavy rain prompted a postponement, delaying the inevitable before Judge homered for a fourth straight game. New

York City schools were not reopening until the next day, but the stadium was still mostly empty for the first game of a doubleheader, a Wednesday afternoon.

It marked the big-league debut for Louie Varland, a twenty-four-year-old righty plucked out of the Twins' backyard in St. Paul, Minnesota. Months later, Varland would still salivate about the postgame spreads delivered to the visiting clubhouse, recalling the bounty of shrimp, mussels, scallops, and rib-eye steak his teammates were served. Oh yeah, and he remembered going up against Judge.

Fielding questions from a group of youth athletes, Varland heard one boy call out: "Aaron Judge hit a home run against you." Yes, indeed he did.

Varland struck out Judge in their first matchup, but he wouldn't be quite so fortunate the next time. Judge was ahead in the count, 2-1, and Varland left a changeup hovering over the outer part of the plate. Judge hammered it, clearing the left-field fence, where two fans in the front row collided and knocked the ball back to the warning track.

"I was happy to get a run on the board," Judge said. "The rookie was making his debut and kind of had us shut down there for a little bit. He had a good quick pace, working all of his pitches. It kind of got some stuff going, got this offense going a little bit."

Judge's blast sparked a comeback from three runs down, coming in a game where the Yanks' injury-depleted lineup looked a lot like the type of squad they'd have brought on the road for a spring training game. Five players wore uniform numbers in the nineties: Judge (99), Oswaldo Cabrera (95), Oswald Peraza (91), Ron Marinaccio (97), and Estevan Florial (90).

But the nineties were in vogue: Gleyber Torres homered and Cabrera drilled a twelfth-inning walk-off single to end the first game of the twin bill, then Kiner-Falefa hit a grand slam in the nightcap. "It doesn't matter if our big guys are here or they're not," Judge said. "We walk out there, we've got the pinstripes, we're wearing the 'NY.' Every single guy that walks in this clubhouse is going to get the job done. These kids are ready. They're not scared. They're ready to go from the very first pitch."

The promise of history was drawing larger crowds to the corner of 161st Street and River Avenue, though the Yankees needed no attendance boost on a very special night. September 8 marked the long-awaited date to celebrate Derek Jeter's 2020 induction to the National Baseball Hall of Fame, delayed by the COVID-19 pandemic, which had pushed his Cooperstown ceremony back a year.

As an active player, Jeter had little appetite to watch baseball games that he wasn't involved with—A-Rod once visited Jeter's home in Tampa, Florida, and had been incredulous to find that Jeter's television package didn't have the YES Network activated. But as he stood in a conference room on the stadium's suite level, even the former captain acknowledged that he was paying attention to Judge's march against Maris.

"Fifty-five home runs. You know, I can't relate," Jeter said. "It's hard enough to get a hit. I'm no expert, but I would assume you can get into some issues if you're trying to hit home runs. It can backfire on you. But the thing that's impressive is that he still hits for average. That's something that's overlooked and undervalued in today's game. He's hitting for average, driving in runs, hitting home runs. He's doing it all. He's got a chance."

It was a pregame lovefest for Jeter, the fourteen-time All-Star who'd delivered five World Series championships to the Bronx. Jeter, his wife, Hannah, and their family waved as they rolled at slow speed across the outfield in a motorized cart. Jeter set foot on the infield grass, gripping a podium near home plate and delivering remarks to a nostalgia-drenched house, ready to roll the clock back to the dynasty years. As he did, Jeter heard the familiar echoing chants of his name. "DE-rek JE-ter (clap, clap, clap-clap-clap)." He sensed that he was exactly where he belonged.

"I did miss the place. This is home for me," Jeter said. "I was here for twenty years, across the street and in this building. It's twenty years where I played pretty much every day. This is where I feel most comfortable."

CC Sabathia, Tino Martinez, Andy Pettitte, Jorge Posada, Mariano Rivera, and Joe Torre were all in attendance, grinning and backslapping ahead of Jeter's parents, Charles and Dorothy; sister, Sharlee; and nephew, Jalen.

But the ceremony turned sour when Hal Steinbrenner emerged from the home dugout, clutching an oversized check to represent a

$222,222.22 donation in the name of Jeter's Turn 2 Foundation. There were loud boos, and Jeter wasn't having it.

Grabbing the microphone, Jeter admonished the crowd sternly: "Let me tell you something, you'd better cheer. Trust me." Jeter thanked general manager Brian Cashman, which prompted more jeers. To that, Jeter quipped: "I see you guys are ready for the playoff push."

Jeter said that he was surprised Steinbrenner and Cashman would receive such harsh treatment from the fans, especially during a season in which Judge was challenging a beloved record and the team was still in first place, despite their second-half swoon. Then he sighed.

"But they boo everybody here. I got in trouble once for not telling them to stop booing," Jeter said, referring to the 2005 season, when Jeter was criticized for not defending teammate Alex Rodriguez against public outcry. All A-Rod did that year, by the way, was play in all 162 games while leading the American League in runs, homers, slugging percentage, and on-base plus slugging, winning his second MVP award.

Jeter occasionally wondered if his dynasty-era teams had set the bar too high by winning so frequently in the late 1990s; he joked about that later, saying that he'd "screwed it up" by insisting that any season the Yankees didn't win the World Series was a failure. But that mindset had been established by George Steinbrenner, not Jeter. The Boss refused to accept that baseball isn't football, and even a dominant team can lose one out of every three games. Organizational old-timers delight in telling stories about how Steinbrenner would threaten firings if the Yankees lost spring training games televised on the old Channel 11.

Even Jeter's admonishment couldn't quiet the crowd that night, jeering a dud of a contest in which Minnesota's Carlos Correa hit a late go-ahead homer. Forever stained by his involvement in the 2017 Astros scandal, Correa said he found "extra motivation when you play on such a big stage like Yankee Stadium and you're the villain." Jeter never experienced that; instead, Jeter appreciated the pulse of a rabid fan base that had spent the better part of two decades adoring his every action.

"Yankees fans expect excellence. They're never satisfied, which is a good thing," Jeter said. "Yankees fans boo because they want to win."

Jeter wasn't the only retired superstar tracking Judge's pace closely.

It had been twenty-four summers since Mark McGwire and Sammy Sosa toured the country on their home run chase. Members of the Maris family had been in attendance at St. Louis's Busch Stadium on the evening of September 8, 1998, when McGwire hit No. 62, a low line drive off the Cubs' Steve Trachsel that cleared the left-field wall by inches. Play stopped for eleven minutes that night as McGwire and 49,987 fans celebrated the moment, with the Cardinals offering their Paul Bunyan–esque slugger a vintage 1962 Corvette in recognition of setting the new single-season home run record. He'd go on to hit 70 homers that season, the first of six times that Maris's mark would be surpassed.

It had also been twelve years since McGwire admitted to using performance-enhancing drugs during his playing career, including the '98 season that had seemed so magical. McGwire had called Maris's widow, Pat, to apologize. Mrs. Maris was said to be disappointed.

"She didn't want to believe it," McGwire said. "I told her that I had to be honest. I told her I was so sorry for her, her family and Roger."

McGwire's admission, plus clouds of performance-enhancing drug suspicion regarding the home run totals of Sosa and Barry Bonds, prompted members of the Maris family to call for the restoration of 61 as the true major league record. McGwire belted 583 home runs in a sixteen-year career with the Oakland Athletics and St. Louis Cardinals, retiring after the 2001 season. In ten years of eligibility for the Hall of Fame, McGwire never received more than 23.7 percent of the necessary 75 percent of votes from members of the Baseball Writers' Association of America.

The Hall's Veterans Committee had also passed on McGwire, who had coaching stints with the Los Angeles Dodgers and San Diego Padres. He now spent his days watching his sons play high school ball near his home in San Juan Capistrano, California. When Judge had hit his 50th home run of 2017, breaking a rookie record set by McGwire in 1987, "Big Mac" had pinged Matt Holliday to acquire Judge's phone number.

McGwire left a voicemail message congratulating Judge, telling reporters at the time: "The future for him as a bona fide home run hitter is bright. Who knows what the number is going to be? Watch out, 73. Seriously."

As Judge clobbered opposing pitching late in 2022, McGwire doubled down, predicting that Judge was "definitely" going to eclipse Maris's Yankees record.

"I truly believe he'll break Barry's record, too," McGwire said. Not in 2022, mind you—McGwire hypothesized that Judge was only getting warmed up. The retired slugger envisioned Judge finishing with about 65 home runs in '22, then positioning himself to "get to 73 to 74 in the next five to eight years."

"I really believe he'll have that opportunity," McGwire said. "He's going to get close to it, and say, 'Where can I bunch in nine more homers?' God willing that he stays healthy, he's going to do that, too."

As for the debate concerning the steroids era, McGwire flatly indicated that he considered Bonds's 73 home runs in 2001 to represent the all-time home run record, as Major League Baseball also did.

"Seventy-three is the record," McGwire said. "Judge will have the record once he passes Barry."

Like McGwire, Sosa, Bonds, and now Albert Pujols, the resurgent St. Louis Cardinals star who was unexpectedly taking aim at joining the 700 home run club, Judge's at-bats were attractions. The sight of No. 99 on deck eased traffic at Yankee Stadium's concession stands and lavatories, prompting fans to delay their concourse wandering for just a few moments.

It was a phenomenon that reminded Brian Cashman of Darryl Strawberry's late-1990s tenure in the Bronx, across the street at the old stadium. "People stopped," Cashman said. "If you were in the stands going to get a beer or popcorn, and Strawberry was being announced, they stopped because this was something different. People would completely focus on it. Aaron's like that."

That kicked into high gear now as Judge's thudding footsteps grew louder behind Maris, though there would be no more long balls for the remainder of the homestand. The Yankees took two of three games from the Rays, recovering from a brutal opener in which the embattled Aaron Hicks was benched for missing two consecutive fly balls to left field that fell for run-scoring doubles.

Judge singled twice in a six-run first inning as the Yanks torched old friend Corey Kluber in a 10–3 rout, with Judge's three-hit effort raising his batting average to .307. Boone could sense that opponents were pitching around Judge more now, and the manager advised him to "take what the game gives you," a phrase that Boone said he'd lifted from Hall of Famer Mike Schmidt during his days as a Philadelphia Phillies clubhouse rugrat.

"Aaron does a great job of that," Boone said. "You can't go start chasing for it. You'll get yourself in trouble, and he knows that. His job is to go up and have a plan and try to execute, and control the strike zone, which he's done at such a special level with all of this going around."

The next day was September 11, and Judge wore customized size seventeen spikes for the moment—his left shoe read "9/11 Patriot Day" on the back and the right "9-11-01." Judge had toured the World Trade Center site during his first September as a big leaguer, gazing upon the reflecting pools where the massive towers once stood. He remembered solemnly reading the names of the fallen, trying to make sense of the events that took place there. Years later, Judge said he would get chills on the back of his neck just thinking about the visit. "You feel something different about that spot," he said. "You can feel the pain; there's something there. When I went through the tower, learning more about the history of what happened, it was something I'll never forget."

Judge was nine years old on the morning of September 11, 2001. He learned of the horrific events in New York, Washington, and Shanksville, Pennsylvania, while eating breakfast. Patty Judge was already awake, watching coverage in the kitchen of their Linden, California, home. Upon arriving at his elementary school, Judge found many of his fellow students gathered around a television in the cafeteria, where footage of the smoldering ruins of the World Trade Center and the Pentagon seemed to be on a constant loop.

"Our teachers broke down what happened, what was going on and how big of a situation it was," Judge said. "Being that age, the severity didn't really hit me. I remember how affected everybody was. Anything you turned on was talking about it; the news, sports channels, anything."

In the days that followed the attacks, U.S. flags began appearing on vehicles throughout the country, including across Judge's hometown. That enduring message of patriotism was one that Judge saw represented when he toured the National September 11 Memorial & Museum late in 2016, along with fellow rookies Tyler Austin and Rob Refsnyder.

"The coolest thing was, I remember seeing how we bounced back as a country," Judge said. "It didn't matter who you were, where you were from. Seeing how the whole country united arms and said, 'This isn't going to tear us down,' I remember seeing that as a kid. It brought people together, and it didn't matter your race, color or anything. We're all Americans, and we had each others' backs."

Domingo Germán paid tribute in a different way. The pitcher vividly recalled watching on television from the Dominican Republic as Sosa carried a miniature U.S. flag across Wrigley Field's outfield, holding the Stars and Stripes high to mark the Cubs' first home game following the attacks. Tabbed as the starting pitcher on that date twenty-one years later, Germán burst out of the dugout toward Yankee Stadium's right-field bullpen following a rain delay of nearly two hours, drawing cheers as he re-created Sosa's red, white, and blue dash. "It was a way to show support to the country, to the people, to the victims," Germán said.

That night, Boone placed Judge and Stanton in the No. 1 and 2 spots in the lineup, calling the tandem his "two wrecking balls to start it off." Judge had walked seven times in the previous four games, and Boone explained that he wanted to "try and get Judge in the best position to have a little bit of protection." With DJ LeMahieu and Andrew Benintendi injured, Boone considered Judge the team's best remaining option in the top spot. Judge lifted a bases-loaded sacrifice fly and Stanton went deep again, powering a 10–3 win over Tampa Bay that made the upcoming Delta flight to Boston a bit more pleasant.

"There was a lot of attention on him, but it still felt like it was all about the team somehow," said Clay Holmes. "I think it just shows how he's able to lead guys. There was a sense of, 'This is us going out there.' It was fun for everybody. I felt like we were all a part of it, and I think that speaks to how he goes about his business and treats people."

HOMER #56: September 13 vs. Boston Red Sox's Nick Pivetta (6th inning, solo)
Exit velocity: 109.7 mph. Distance: 383 feet. Launch angle: 24 degrees. HR in 14 of 30 MLB parks.
HOMER #57: September 13 vs. Boston Red Sox's Garrett Whitlock (8th inning, solo)
Exit velocity: 100.5 mph. Distance: 389 feet. Launch angle: 35 degrees. HR in 29 of 30 MLB parks.

Judge's game mantra was to keep it simple, locking in on what he needed to do to prepare for each day. Once a performance was over, good or bad, he liked to flush the results and move to the next one. This was the point of the schedule, on a temperate Tuesday evening at Boston's Fenway Park, where Judge finally allowed himself to consider the possibility that he would break Maris's record.

"It really didn't start to hit me until we started creeping up into the high 50s later in the season, that this is something that we'll be able to do," Judge said.

As the Yankees and Red Sox battled in Boston, Judge connected for solo shots in the sixth and eighth innings, tying the game both times. No. 56 came on a hanging curveball from Nick Pivetta that landed in Boston's bullpen. "Those pitches, they're pretty slow," Judge said. "You've got to try to see it pop above the zone and lay off the nasty one that looks like a heater."

Then in the eighth, Judge was at it again, sending a Garrett Whitlock slider over the Green Monster in left field for No. 57. Whitlock slumped his shoulders immediately, recognizing the baseball was probably not coming back. Though Judge said that a selection of Red Sox fans had been "wearing me out on deck," incredibly, even a few in Boston paraphernalia appeared to applaud as Judge rounded the bases, again inching ahead of Maris's pace with his tenth multi-homer game of the season.

As Judge returned to the dugout, he high-fived one of the fans seated near the dugout, Brown University student Cecilia Jacobs. In a viral-worthy clip, Jacobs celebrated wildly after having her right palm slapped, capturing the whole sequence on her camera phone.

"Once he hit the home run, I immediately started filming," Jacobs said. "We were all just screaming and so happy. We tried for the high-five the first time (Judge homered) and it didn't come through, but then the second time he came through, and I just freaked out."

In the clubhouse after the game, someone asked Judge if he was enjoying the frenzy surrounding his home run chase.

"Well, we're winning and we're in first place," he replied. "That's always fun."

Miguel Cabrera won the majors' last Triple Crown in 2012, when the Detroit Tigers star paced the American League in average (.330), homers (44), and RBIs (139). Before then, no one had achieved the feat since Carl Yastrzemski of the 1967 Red Sox, and no Yankee had done it since Mickey Mantle in 1956.

Judge was beginning to entertain thoughts of a batting title, closing within nine points of the Minnesota Twins' Luis Arraez, while owning healthy leads in the home run and runs batted in categories. Yet he reminded himself frequently: "If you're checking the numbers, you're going to get caught. The numbers will take care of themselves. If I have a good plan, a good approach, do what I need to do in the box—all that other stuff will show up."

That Cabrera season had been notable for Judge; it was the dawn of his junior season at Fresno State, and he'd found a seat alongside his Bulldogs teammates, having been issued a surprising classroom assignment. The required viewing on that date was a YouTube supercut, showing each and every hit Miguel Cabrera collected during his 2012 season.

The lesson that head coach Mike Batesole wanted Judge and others to absorb was to recognize the ease with which Cabrera appeared to handle the strike zone. "It was a long video, but it was well worth the watch," Judge said. "I think he really hammered home just how simple he makes everything. He doesn't try to overswing; he doesn't try to do too much, especially with guys on base. You'd see him poke a single to right field and score two runs. He just did the little things in the game, and if you do that over 162, you're going to have a pretty good year."

On a nightly basis, the Yankees were witnessing "one of the most historic offensive seasons of all time," as Gerrit Cole said, adding, "It's historical. I mean, it's wonderful. I'm riding it, dude. It's amazing."

Gleyber Torres's three-run, tenth-inning double off Jeurys Familia stood as the deciding blow that night, with Wandy Peralta withstanding a shaky home half to squeak out a save. The next night, Torres legged out a Little League homer that produced three runs in the Yanks' 5–3 win; Torres stroked a run-scoring single that drew a throw home from right fielder Alex Verdugo, then made a wide turn to draw a throw from catcher Connor Wong that sailed down the right-field line. The madcap dash was thrilling, but it hadn't been what the sellout crowd came to see.

"I think the casual person," Boone said, "just comes tonight and thinks, 'I'm going to see Judge hit a homer.' The reality is, he's getting off the right swings. He's making good swing decisions. It's going to come. But it is a peek behind at just how great a player he is, that when he doesn't hit the ball out of the ballpark, he's still impacting us in a big way by getting on base or his outfield play. With all the noise and excitement around this, he's still going out there and putting together good at-bat after good at-bat."

The Judge show was heading to Milwaukee, a city that the Yankees hadn't visited since 2014. Wisconsin's most populous city was once an American League hub, the gold-and-blue franchise of Paul Molitor and Robin Yount, having been shifted to the National League in 1998 so the leagues could balance with fifteen clubs apiece. There would likely be no complaint from the Yankees if baseball's honchos put the Brewers back in the AL and restored the Houston Astros to the NL, where they'd played their first fifty-one seasons, but that doesn't seem likely anytime soon.

The club stayed at the regal Pfister Hotel, constructed in 1893 and said to be the league's most haunted lodging. For decades, players throughout the circuit had swapped ghost stories about their stays at the Pfister; unexplained footsteps or knocking noises, relocated laundry, opening doors and flickering lights. As Giancarlo Stanton once said: "It's freaky as shit, with the head-shot paintings on the walls and the old curtains everywhere. It reminds me of the Disneyland Haunted House. The less time I'm there, the better."

Indeed, too many players over the years had claimed to have seen a spook, spectre, or ghost in those hallways. With an off day on a Thursday evening, it was a perfect time to get out and see the sights. Fortunately for Stanton and the rest of the Yankees, Judge had a plan.

Post Malone's Twelve Carat Tour was in town, with the rapper taking the stage at the Fiserv Forum, less than a mile from the hotel. There was no excuse to stay inside, so Judge invited his teammates out to the home of the NBA's Milwaukee Bucks for a night on the town, enjoying the ninety-five-minute hit-packed set.

"It's something that you don't expect," said Kyle Higashioka. "The fact that he's going far above and beyond to bring us all together off the field, it just struck me as something a captain would do. We would have team outings on occasion, but I felt like [in 2022], there was just more. Judge took it upon himself."

"I think it's really good whenever you can get your team together— eating, drinking and doing all these things, it's all good for camaraderie," Aaron Hicks said. "Especially when the whole team commits to something and we all go, it's fun."

As they sang along to recognizable chart-toppers like "Circles" and "Sunflower," Judge was pleased to have one of his closest friends on the trip. Tyler Wade had returned to the Yankees on a minor-league deal after beginning his season with the Los Angeles Angels of Anaheim. Wade traveled with the club that week as a taxi squad player in the event of injury, providing his buddy with a taste of the Judge experience.

"It felt almost like a playoff atmosphere, every time he came up," Wade said. "We went out to dinner a couple of times and talked about approach, just catching up on stuff. Obviously, I asked him about his season. He was like, 'Man, I just feel good. I'm healthy.' His work ethic, if you guys saw what he was doing every day, everything he does is so detailed. Even coming up through the minors, you could tell he was bound to do something special."

Judge stroked two hits in the opener, a 7–6 loss decided when rookie Garrett Mitchell stroked a run-scoring hit in the ninth inning off Clay Holmes. He doubled in three trips the next day, but right-hander Brandon Woodruff handcuffed the Yanks in a 4–1 defeat. That week, a few of the Yanks' coaches had been invited to receive a tour of the Bucks' performance facility, where they viewed a presentation. The NBA team's number one key to winning, they said, was player availability. Judge had shown up all year, and he wasn't about to stop now.

HOMER #58: September 18 vs. Milwaukee Brewers' Jason Alexander (3rd inning, solo)
Exit velocity: 111.6 mph. Distance: 414 feet. Launch angle: 35 degrees. HR in 30 of 30 MLB parks.
HOMER #59: September 18 vs. Milwaukee Brewers' Luis Perdomo (7th inning, solo)
Exit velocity: 110.3 mph. Distance: 443 feet. Launch angle: 30 degrees. HR in 30 of 30 MLB parks.

The roof was open as a crowd of more than thirty-five thousand continued to filter into Milwaukee's American Family Field on an overcast Sunday afternoon, a slight breeze whipping the flags from right to left. Again serving as the leadoff hitter, Judge saw the ball well; something about the lighting and colors felt right, almost from the first pitch tossed by Jason Alexander, Milwaukee's twenty-nine-year-old rookie starter.

Yes, as he heard hundreds of times from fans, he shared a name with the actor who played George Costanza on *Seinfeld*. There was no relation. This Alexander was a grinder who survived a lengthy injury history to beat the odds, despite having been twenty-four years old in rookie ball, one of the lowest rungs of the pro ladder. In his first at-bat, Judge smoked a line drive to center field that sent Milwaukee's Tyrone Taylor racing back toward the wall, where a stumbling grab robbed Judge of an extra-base hit.

It seemed to be a good sign for what was to come. Judge trotted out of the dugout toward his position in center field for the bottom of the second inning, accompanied by some of the relievers, who were making their way toward the bullpen. Judge nodded in their direction and said: "Hey, boys. I've got you. I'm going to hit one your way."

Facing Alexander in the third inning, Judge looked at a sinker and a changeup; both tailed inside near the batter's feet for balls. Alexander had to come back in the strike zone, dotting a sinker low and outside. Judge clipped it to the second deck in right-center field, an absolute no-doubter.

"He hit it right over the bullpen," said Lou Trivino. "We were just like, 'Man, he called it!' It was pretty awesome."

"You have to come with your best stuff against him," Alexander said. "I felt like I made some good pitches. It's tough when you can paint one on the outside and he still puts it 110 [mph] into the stands. It's a really thin margin of error."

Anthony Rizzo followed with a homer of his own, going deep after a brief stint on the injured list. The Yanks went back to back again in the seventh inning, with Aaron Hicks homering before Judge stepped to the plate. Luis Perdomo, a twenty-nine-year-old righty, was on the mound. Perdomo worked Judge carefully, missing with a slider inside before enticing Judge to swing and miss at the same pitch low.

Judge fouled off another slider, and Perdomo pressed his luck one pitch too many. The next slider hung and Judge blasted it; as the ball rocketed off the bat, Perdomo tossed his hands high above his head in exasperation, one of the most effusive reactions Judge would generate from a pitcher all year. The drive smacked off a concrete walkway beyond the left-field wall and rattled underneath Bernie Brewer's slide in Section 236, sending fans scurrying in pursuit.

"This is his moment right now," Perdomo said with a sigh. "When you make a mistake against him, he's going to take advantage of it."

Since Yankees director of security Eddie Fastook had approached Judge with the suggestion of obtaining Judge's home run balls after No. 52, the club had successfully made swaps for each. No. 59 would be the exception. A fan named Peter Sierra caught the ball on a bounce, and Sierra initially fielded a trade offer of autographed baseballs and caps. Another fan, Bryant Junco, offered Sierra a $1,500 Venmo payment on the spot. Sierra accepted, but when the funds moved digitally between their cell phones, Junco said Major League Baseball declined to offer authentication. Everyone wanted a piece of the Judge experience.

"Every day was like being in a clinching situation," said Pete Caldera of the *Bergen Record*. "The coverage was pretty intense from the time we made that Boston-Milwaukee trip. He hit 58 and you're like, 'Wow, that's pretty cool.' Then he comes up again and launches No. 59, and you're thinking, 'OK, this is a reality.'"

Judge came to bat once more in the game, the first time that specially marked baseballs were brought to home plate for his at-bat. Home plate umpire Gabe Morales fumbled with the balls, each individually coded with a secret letter-number combination that would prove its authenticity once submitted to examination under a black light. He tossed one to the pitcher, Trevor Kelley, who looked it over curiously.

"I remember someone mentioning to me, 'The balls are here,'" said Kristie Ackert of the *New York Daily News*. "They showed me the balls that were marked for him, and then he hit the home run in Milwaukee. Next at-bat, the balls were changed, and I was thinking: 'Wow, this is really going to happen. This is big.'"

Judge gave the Milwaukee crowd one last thrill, drilling his fourth hit of the afternoon, a run-scoring double to the wall in left-center field.

"He'd already hit two in that game, and then he barely missed another one," said Clay Holmes. "Everybody was just like, 'Man, this is getting way out of hand.' I think it was that moment when everybody was like, 'Wow, this is going to happen.' We were all talking about how close he was, and then he just went off for that series. That was so special."

As the Yankees packed their bags for the flight home to New York, Anthony Rizzo marveled at what his teammate and pal had already accomplished, voicing the belief that Judge's season would—and should—be viewed as a separate entity from the McGwire/Sosa/Bonds chases of the recent past.

"This hasn't been done in this era," Rizzo said. "Someone chasing 61 clean like this, with really no question marks about what's going on in the game. It's Judge's season. You watch his at-bats and you'd never even know he's one homer away from 60. It's a credit to his preparation and his demeanor, on the field, off the field, on the plane. He's just the total package."

◆

I'VE GOT YOU, BABE

Standing on the interlocking "NY" logo on the sidewalk at the intersection of East 161st Street and the Macombs Dam Bridge, you can imagine Babe Ruth showing up for an afternoon at the ballpark, tugging on a Gatsby cap and exiting a Model T to begin his workday. That is no accident. In granite and limestone, the new Yankee Stadium's exterior re-creates selections of its majestic 1923 predecessor, with the decorative eagle medallions alongside gold-leaf-embossed letters reading YANKEE STADIUM.

Sure, the ballpark was on the other side of the street now, but it was a building that the Babe would probably recognize. So would Mickey Mantle and Roger Maris; when Maris and his family had returned to see his uniform No. 9 retired and a Monument Park plaque belatedly dedicated in his honor on Old-Timers' Day in 1984, the retired slugger was deeply appreciative, but the post-disco renovation stadium bore little resemblance to where he'd hit 61 in '61.

So as banks of lights burned high above the Bronx's largest building and the Yankees made their final sprints across the outfield grass before that evening's game, Roger Maris Jr. felt mixed emotions. When Aaron Judge belted homers Nos. 58 and 59 two days prior in Milwaukee, the Steinbrenner family had invited the Maris family to be in the building as the Yankees opened their homestand against the Pittsburgh Pirates and Boston Red Sox.

The Marises had attended games at the new stadium previously, having been invited for ceremonies in 2011 and again in 2016, when the club honored anniversaries of the 1961 season. Wearing pinstriped jerseys with their father's No. 9 on the back, Maris's four sons had watched the familiar sequence on the large center-field video screen—the drive into the right-field seats off Tracy Stallard, the clamor for the ball in the seats, then Phil Rizzuto narrating the trip around the bases before Maris was pushed out of the dugout by his teammates for a curtain call.

And just as they did in 1961, the fans stood and cheered. "I think that day, to him, it was just a numb feeling," Maris said. "Even when he hit it, I remember him rounding the bases. You're just numb. You know you just did it, but you're just running. You don't even remember running, you're just shaking hands and all that stuff. Then as time goes on, you think back and you go, 'Wow, what did I do? What just happened?'"

This journey to New York from the family's home in Gainesville, Florida, felt different from previous trips for on-field ceremonies or bobblehead days. As he boarded the plane with siblings Kevin, Richard, and Sandra, Maris fully expected his father's record to fall in a few days; he was just happy that it would be by a Yankee, believing it would be good for baseball and the city of New York if it happened at Yankee Stadium.

"He had been hitting them in bunches, so we weren't sure what was going to happen," Maris said.

Maris hoped that there were a few people still around the ballpark who would have firsthand memories of the 1961 season. Suzyn Waldman, one of the Yankees' radio voices, remembered hearing Maris's home run live on Boston's WHDH 850 AM. Even in New England, fans had taken sides that summer, arguing if they preferred Maris or Mickey Mantle to break Babe Ruth's record.

"My mom used to let me take my little brother down to Fenway Park, where we'd watch the Yankees get off the bus," Waldman said. "Remember, 1961 was a very good year for the Yankees, and the Red Sox weren't so good. My brother was ten, and we took the streetcar down. Mickey and Roger came in; Mickey had a convertible. They were signing autographs for the kids, and Roger got to my brother. He froze; couldn't say anything. So Roger Maris tousled his hair and chucked him under the chin."

As Waldman recounted the tale for Maris, she said: "I'm so glad I got to tell you this story, because autographs get forgotten and they get lost. But my seventy-two-year-old brother, a retired lawyer and teacher, still talks about the day that Roger Maris tousled his hair."

Maris was touched. It was impossible to root against Judge, and he could find a few similarities with his father. They both came to the ballpark prepared to play, and did not appear to be "rah-rah guys," always putting the team's fortunes and winning championships ahead of individual statistics or success. Most of all, Maris loved how Judge reacted every time he slugged a homer.

"He drops his bat and runs the bases," Maris said. "He puts his head down and comes across home plate, just like Dad did. Aaron's not looking for fanfare. He's just looking out there to get the job done, just like Dad did."

HOMER #60: September 20 vs. Pittsburgh Pirates' Wil Crowe (9th inning, solo) *Exit velocity: 111.6 mph. Distance: 430 feet. Launch angle: 24 degrees. HR in 30 of 30 MLB parks.*

The Maris family watched from a suite high above the stadium, part of a crowd of 40,157 that welcomed the Yankees back for their penultimate homestand of the regular season. Judge had grounded out twice, walked, and struck out in his first four plate appearances, and the Yankees came to bat trailing by four runs in the ninth inning. Judge had leapt in vain at the right field wall in the top of the eighth, unable to snare a three-run homer by infielder Rodolfo Castro, and that had seemed to deflate the crowd like a week-old balloon.

But Judge's spot in the order was due to come up again, which prompted many to hang around, despite the unlikely odds of a comeback. According to FanGraphs, the Yankees' win expectancy hovered at 1.6 percent as Judge limbered in the on-deck circle, a number derived by calculating the current game situation (score, inning, number of outs, men on base, and run environment) to similar historical situations. On the mound was Wil Crowe, a twenty-eight-year-old righty from Pigeon Forge, Tennessee, who already owned a slice of Yankees history—in his family tree.

As Crowe explained to Brian Richards, the director of the museum, he counted Red Ruffing as his great uncle. The bloodline connection was convoluted, but Crowe could confidently trace his lineage. A Hall of Fame right-hander who spent twenty-two seasons in the majors from 1924 through 1947, including fifteen years with the Yankees, Ruffing and Ruth had shared a clubhouse from 1930 to 1934. Ruffing had been on hand for Ruth's famous "Called Shot" in the 1932 World Series at Wrigley Field; he died at age eighty in 1986, and in 2004, the Yankees had posthumously dedicated a plaque in his honor.

This was Crowe's first visit to the Bronx, and the Pirates had set up an opportunity to bring his wife, Hilary, and young son, Koa, on a guided tour of Monument Park. Richards escorted the young family through the wall of plaques early in the afternoon, sharing stories about Ruffing's playing career and military service.

Ruffing, Crowe was told, had not only been a terrific pitcher—he'd been the Yankees' best pinch hitter in the 1930s. Ruffing lost four toes on his left foot in a mining accident, which nixed his hopes of playing out-field, but Ruffing's strong arm and dangerous bat allowed him to enjoy a lengthy career. As they walked and talked, Crowe revealed that his son's middle name was Ruffing.

"We talked for maybe ten minutes total," Richards said. "It was a quick meeting, but it was a very nice meeting. He explained what his family relation was to Ruffing, and it was something he was very proud of."

The Yankees trailed by four runs as a wide-view camera from beyond third base showed teammates hugging the dugout railing, almost every soul standing in the field-level seats. As Judge cocked his bat near his right shoulder, many observers pointed their camera phones toward home plate, terabytes of data being captured from every vantage point of the stadium.

Crowe grooved a sinker that Judge took for a called strike, then missed low with a couple of sliders. He overthrew a fastball that sailed up and in, prompting Judge to lean away from the pitch as the fans jeered. Now Judge was firmly in the driver's seat on a 3-1 count, wiggling his fingers on the bat as he awaited the next offering. Crowe wasn't about to walk the leadoff hitter with a four-run lead.

"He's the best hitter in baseball right now, but for me, I can't put him on," Crowe said. "I have to go after him."

Signaling for a sinker, catcher Jason Delay dropped his right knee to the ground, gesturing for Crowe to keep it low. Crowe hit the target, but Judge was ready, belting a drive that cleared the fence and set off an epic scramble in the left-field bleachers.

"Slide over, Babe, you've got some company," Michael Kay announced on the YES Network broadcast. "Aaron James Judge has tied George Herman 'Babe' Ruth with 60 home runs!"

Kay felt that he had nailed the call, capturing the moment, but he later revealed that there had been an inordinate amount of stress and anxiety in waiting for Judge to hit his next homer.

"Once he got to 59, everybody became the cook in the kitchen, suggesting calls and stuff like that," Kay said. "This was like the first big milestone home run, I think, since the advent of all the keyboard warriors on social media. Everybody was going to have an opinion on this call. The biggest thing for me, and I told this to Derek Jeter when he was going for 3,000, was that I'm putting a frame around the picture that he's drawing. The last thing I wanted to do was mess it up."

Judge had hit his 60th in the Yanks' 147th game, which would have been notable in Maris's day, when Commissioner Ford C. Frick ruled that anything hit after game No. 154 would represent a separate achievement from Ruth's 1927 total. On the WFAN radio call, John Sterling used his trademark "It is high, it is far, it is gone," adding, "He's tied the Babe! It's a Judgian blast. His 60th home run of the year. Wow! All rise! Here comes the Judge!"

"I thought to myself, 'I never thought, in my lifetime of broadcasting, I'd broadcast a guy hitting his 60th home run,'" Sterling said.

Judge rounded the bases and performed his usual skyward point as he approached home plate. While there was celebration on the bench, it seemed muted because of the game situation: the Yankees were still behind by three runs. Judge seemed reluctant to accept a curtain call, though he eventually acquiesced at Boone's urging, in part so as not to distract the next batter.

"I kind of joked around, saying, 'Man, I've been here for six years and I've only got one curtain call,'" Judge said, referring to his 50th homer in 2017, which had broken Mark McGwire's rookie record. "I guess it takes 60 to get another one."

Richards, the museum director who'd escorted Crowe through Monument Park that afternoon, said he had mixed emotions about the blast.

"My first thought was, 'Oh no, I jinxed that poor guy,'" Richards said. "I just thought about how friendly and happy and appreciative he was to be in Monument Park. Just a couple of hours later, the guy gets stained by being on the bad side of history. His name will be remembered in the wrong way forever. But somebody had to give it up."

FanGraphs' calculations could not sense emotion or narrative. With New York still trailing, 8–5, the cold numbers behind Judge's homer only swelled the chances of a comeback from 1.6 percent to 3.7 percent. But on this night, the math was in the Yanks' favor. Anthony Rizzo sliced a double that rolled to the wall in left-center field, drawing pitching coach Oscar Marin to the mound. Marin patted Crowe's shoulder, in hopes of settling the hurler.

Gleyber Torres worked a five-pitch walk that brought Josh Donaldson to the plate representing the potential tying run. Donaldson lifted a soft fly ball that fell in front of right fielder Jack Suwinski for a single. The bases were loaded for Giancarlo Stanton, who hadn't done much since his memorable homecoming at the Dodger Stadium All-Star Game in July. Sidelined by a sore left Achilles for most of August, Stanton struggled to find his timing, batting just .125 with two homers since returning from the injured list. He'd been a strikeout machine, fanning in twenty-seven of sixty-nine at-bats, including three times earlier in the game against Pittsburgh hurlers.

During a dismal series against the Rays at Tropicana Field weeks earlier, Stanton had said that he had come back and "had basically zero production, so I'm disappointed in that. I need to find it. I need to be a boost here, not a blank spot in the lineup."

But, as Reggie Jackson liked to remind people, holding a bat in your hands offers an opportunity to rewrite the story. In the dugout, Judge leaned toward pitcher Jameson Taillon, dissecting the at-bat. Judge told Taillon: "If he hangs anything in the zone right here, [Stanton is] going to do some damage." The count stood at 2-2 as Stanton battled, most of the crowd on its feet again. Crowe tried a changeup, low and inside; it never reached its intended target.

Stanton drilled the ball deep to left field, sending Crowe into a crouch on the mound; the pitcher momentarily wondered if the ball had the necessary height to clear the eight-foot wall. It did and then some, clearing the bases for a walk-off grand slam, a signature Stanton missile. Flipping the bat aside, Stanton spread his arms wide and looked toward his teammates, who were excitedly spilling out of the dugout.

"I lost my mind," Judge said. "That's a signature Giancarlo Stanton ten-foot laser to the outfield. I had a good front-row seat for that one. I think our whole team lost their mind there when the stadium erupted. That was a pretty special moment right there. It was an all-around great team game. I look back on those last four at-bats leading up to Giancarlo. I'll remember those at-bats and Giancarlo's grand slam walk-off."

As Stanton raised his right hand to greet first base coach Travis Chapman, Stanton said he thought: "It's about damn time." Judge savored the moment as much as anyone, sporting a broad grin as he hopped near home plate, showing all the enthusiasm of a Little Leaguer as the Yankees gleefully pummeled the top of Stanton's batting helmet.

Unlike Judge's 50th home run in Anaheim, when he'd glumly lamented about the round-numbered clout coming in a loss, the comeback freed Judge to speak freely about the meaning of equaling Ruth's 1927 tally. Boone said that he felt "some kind of magical spark" was provided by Judge's homer, and Stanton said that Judge seemed "zoned in." With plenty of at-bats still to go, 61 seemed well within reach, as did 62 and more.

"It was an amazing night," Stanton said. "There were a lot of emotions, a lot of excitement. A lot of cool things happened that night, and ultimately the coolest was that we got a win on his historic 60th night. It was big to not put a damper on 60."

Troy Benjamin, calling the shots as a producer that night in the YES Network truck beyond the left-field wall, said that he considered the Stanton grand slam game "probably the best inning of baseball I've ever done."

"For eight innings, that game was a slog," Benjamin said. "But it was at home, we had all the cameras, and it was just magic. Judge with the booster and Stanton with a missile; the way the Yankees just came back. That stadium was electric."

So now only three Yankees had ever hit 60 or more home runs in a single season, all right fielders: Ruth in 1927, Maris in 1961, Judge in 2022. Of course, Judge needed no recitation of that fact, but hearing it spoken out loud still seemed to stagger him.

"When you talk about Ruth and Maris and Mantle and all these Yankees greats, you never imagine as a kid getting mentioned with them," Judge said. "It's an incredible honor and something I don't take lightly at all. We're not done."

Michael Kessler and three of his friends had made a last-minute decision to board the subway that night, hoping to witness Judge's 60th homer in person. It was the best MetroCard swipe of their lives.

A twenty-year-old student at the City College of New York who played on the school's baseball team, Kessler pounced on the ball and clutched it tightly to his chest. Approached by Yankees security, Kessler swiftly agreed to swap the ball for a bounty that included a clubhouse meet and greet with Judge, four autographed baseballs, and a signed game bat (though not the one Judge used to hit the homer).

In between photos, one of Kessler's friends took the opportunity to implore Judge: "Please re-sign." Judge laughed but did not reply, readying for the next camera flash.

Though it was suggested that Judge's 60th might be worth tens of thousands of dollars on the memorabilia market, Kessler said he did not regret his snap decision. The Yankees later contacted him to offer tickets through the remainder of the regular season, including any potential postseason home games. Jersey Mike's, a popular sandwich chain for whom Judge had shot a pandemic-era commercial, also offered $1,000 in gift cards.

"Judge means so much to the organization, especially this year," Kessler said. "He's just unbelievable. Just the way he is, he deserved to have the ball back. I have no second thoughts."

Judge had reached 60 homers in a season when the league's average home run production was far below that level. On the night Judge hit No. 60, the Philadelphia Phillies' Kyle Schwarber cracked his 40th, a tally that ranked second in the majors. Before Judge in '22, no player had completed a calendar day with a lead of 20 or more homers over his closest competition since 1928, when Ruth led Jim Bottomley and Hack Wilson by 23 homers on the last day of the season.

"The thing is, you would never know," Rizzo said. "You would not know he's walking around with 60 home runs under his belt. He just comes in and does his work, goes about his business. That's the beauty of him."

'61 FLASHBACK: 10/1/61

Roger Maris spent the evening before the Yankees' 163rd game stuffing envelopes with World Series tickets, gifts for the army of waitresses, busboys, and cooks who had taken care of him all season long. Quiet and nervous, he enjoyed a leisurely room service breakfast with his wife, Pat, in Room 324 of the Loews Midtown Hotel, then attended mass at St. Patrick's Cathedral before heading north toward the Bronx. The Babe was on his mind.

The last few games had not been Maris's best. Even casual observers could tell that Maris had altered his swing, chasing too many bad pitches, generating a sequence of grounders and pop-ups. Maris had expected the pressure to lift after game No. 154, but he had been wrong. As he remarked: "It's worse than ever now."

"Once Mickey got hurt, he was looking to break the record," Tony Kubek said. "He knew it was not going to be easy, and yet he still managed to do it. He really was pretty much at peace when he was on the field. It was all the stuff that went into it on the outside."

No. 60 came on September 26 off the Baltimore Orioles' Jack Fisher, a 2-2 pitch lashed into Yankee Stadium's third deck, about six feet inside the foul pole. Maris had stood and watched the ball to ensure it stayed fair, calling his equaling of Ruth's home run total "easily the greatest thrill of my life." Mrs. Claire Ruth shed tears as the ball bounced back onto the playing field, where outfielder Earl Robinson retrieved it.

The nationwide reaction to Ruth's record being tied, albeit in a longer schedule, was underwhelming. The Associated Press's wire story began: "Roger Maris blasted his 60th homer of the season Tuesday night, but it came four official games too late to officially tie Babe Ruth's 34-year-old record in 154 games." The next morning, Maris proceeded directly to Ralph Houk's office. "I'm beat. I need a day off," Maris said.

Houk disregarded him, saying, "You can't take a day off. You're going for the record." Maris said he wasn't playing, and if the press asked where he was, Houk could "tell them I went fishing." Houk didn't quite break out the rod-and-reel excuse; instead, he said that Maris had been "living in a madhouse" and needed a day for rest. The resulting fallout left Maris incredulous. Many of the same writers who chastised him for daring to chase Ruth's record now gave him grief for taking a day off. The fiasco steeled Maris's resolve to hit No. 61.

Maris was back in the lineup on October 1 at Yankee Stadium, where attendance was counted at a paltry 23,154. Most of those bodies were occupying the right-field seats. There was talk that Maris's 61st homer would fetch $5,000 (the 2023 equivalent of $50,000), and everyone wanted a chance at instant riches. Whitey Ford said that every Yankees pitcher except for that day's starter, Bill Stafford, had trotted down to the bullpen for Maris's at-bats, wearing their fielding gloves.

"As indicated by the sparse crowd on that day, Frick's ruling had taken the wind out of the sails," said Marty Appel, then a thirteen-year-old diehard in Spring Valley, New York. "After Game 154, it was anticlimactic. It grieves me to realize this now, but on that Sunday afternoon, my brother and I went out to the driveway to play catch while the game was on TV. I had my transistor radio to listen to the game, but it wasn't so compelling that I felt I needed to be there for history."

No. 61 happened in the fourth inning as Maris faced rookie Tracy Stallard of the Boston Red Sox. He whipped his thirty-five-inch, thirty-three-ounce Louisville Slugger to meet a fastball around his knees, belting a drive toward the right-field seats. Maris trotted briskly around the bases, his head down as he moved from the shadows of the grandstand into the sunlight bathing second base. Instead of slapping Maris on the back, as he usually did, third-base coach Frank Crosetti shook Maris's hand. The only other time Crosetti could recall shaking a player's hand would come years later, when Mickey Mantle hit his 500th career homer.

Yogi Berra, the on-deck hitter, waited at home plate with three bats on his shoulder, alongside Frank Prudenti, the team's batboy. Both greeted Maris. A fan had spilled out of the stands; Maris shook his hand, too, then descended the dugout steps. The fans were screaming and stomping their feet, demanding more. Three teammates, Héctor López, Moose Skowron, and Joe DeMaestri, pushed Maris back up the dugout steps. Maris didn't know what to do; his teammates yelled, "Tip your cap!"

Almost sheepishly, Maris acknowledged the fans; Ruth had turned some of his homers into a show, waving his cap as he gleefully rounded the bases, but grand gestures were not Maris's style. Maris received more handshakes and pats on the back, finding a place on the bench. He leaned back and sighed. There was quiet in the dugout as Maris's teammates inspected his sunken eyes, recognizing just how much the chase had taken out of him.

"No one knows how tired I am," Maris said that day. "I'm happy I got past 60, but I'm so tired."

Maris's homer was the only run of the game, as Stafford combined with Hal Reniff and Luis Arroyo on a shutout. In Stallard's estimation, that 1-0 loss had been probably his best game. He'd limited the Yanks to five hits over seven innings, striking out five, yet that single pitch to Maris would mainly define Stallard's professional career. "I'm not going to lose any sleep over this," he said. "I'd rather have given up the homer than walked him." There were two more Maris at-bats that day, a strike-out and a pop-out. There would be no 62nd homer.

The lucky individual to catch No. 61 was Sal Durante, a nineteen-year-old truck driver from Coney Island, New York, who delivered auto parts and played sandlot baseball. Durante was on a double date with his future wife, Rosemarie Calabrese, who had lent him $10 to buy four tickets. In the fourth inning, Durante watched intently as Stallard threw his first pitch high, the next one in the dirt, then grooved one into Maris's hitting zone.

"I watched the pitching motion, the release of the ball, and I had my eye on the ball all the way to Roger's bat," Durante said. "I didn't take my eye off that ball for a second."

Durante jumped on his seat and stretched as high as he could, saying that the ball slammed into the palm of his bare hand. Invited into the clubhouse later, Durante offered the ball to Maris, happy to receive nothing but a thank you. Maris told Durante: "Keep it, kid. Put it up for auction. Somebody will pay you a lot of money for the ball. He'll keep it for a couple of days and then give it to me."

Maris was right. Sam Gordon, a restaurateur from Sacramento, California, did just that. Durante received a check from Gordon, who then had the honor of returning the ball to Maris. The ball (which featured Durante's initials on it, a prehistoric method of authentication) remained in Maris's possession until 1973, when he donated it to the Hall of Fame. Durante retained other souvenirs from his memorable day, including a ticket stub signed by Maris, the Zippo lighter he and Maris used to light cigarettes together, and a baseball autographed by Maris and Stallard.

"Now, what do you think of this kid?" Maris said. "He's got bills. He's going to get married and he wants to give me the ball. That goes to show you there are still some good people left in this world."

Durante, who died in December 2022 at eighty-one, suffered from dementia and was unaware of Judge's pursuit. But during a 2011 event at Yankee Stadium, Durante was asked if he believed Maris's mark should be considered the record, considering the performance-enhancing drug clouds that hovered over Mark McGwire, Sammy Sosa, and Barry Bonds.

"How about if I just say, Roger deserved it," Durante said. "He did it on his own skill."

Maris celebrated that night at the Spindletop restaurant at 254 West 47th Street, in the heart of the theater district. His dining companions were his wife, Pat; their two closest friends in New York, Julie and Selma Isaacson; and Milton Gross, a sports columnist for the *New York Post*.

As Gross chronicled, Maris ordered a shrimp cocktail, a steak medium, a mixed salad with French dressing, a baked potato, two glasses of wine, a sliver of cheesecake, two cups of coffee, and three cigarettes. It was a well-deserved feast for Maris, who would later claim that his life would have been much easier if he had never hit 61 home runs.

Maris called for the check; he'd wanted to hustle to Lenox Hill Hospital's Room 411 to see Mantle and Bob Cerv before visiting hours ended. As he did, a teenage girl approached the table, asking for Maris's autograph on a menu.

"Would you put the date on the top, too, please?" she said.

"What's the date?" Maris asked.

He would remember 10/1/1961 for the rest of his life.

12

61

The strangest part was the silence.

As Aaron Judge closed in on Roger Maris's storied record, each at-bat down the stretch carrying the weight of long-gone legends, Yankee Stadium borrowed from the tranquil ambiance of a putting green at the Masters. The grandstands were packed, tens of thousands on their feet, hoping to capture a slice of history with their smartphones. Yet there was nary a sound.

If it looked and felt strange at home, imagine how it was for the man at bat, all reactions within the tristate area hinging upon the next pitch. Should Judge look at a pitch outside the strike zone, there were boos and jeers, daring the opposing pitcher to challenge the game's most fearsome long-ball threat. If Judge swung and missed, groans of disappointment were heard. That even happened a few times when Judge connected for base hits, collecting only one or two bases instead of the desired four.

These audiences had come to see one thing, and one thing only.

"It was definitely pretty wild and a little surreal," Judge said. "Being at Yankee Stadium, you've got the whole stadium on their feet as the pitch is thrown—man, that silence was a little different for me."

All eyes were on Judge as he jogged from the first-base dugout, performing his stretching and sprinting routine in shallow right field, then dropping to a knee in prayer. The Yankees drew more than forty-six thousand fans on a Wednesday night, their series continuing against a woeful Pittsburgh Pirates club that would finish the season with one hundred losses, thirty-one games behind the St. Louis Cardinals in the National League Central. Placed in the leadoff spot, Judge ripped the fifth pitch he saw down the left-field line for a double; there was an audible reaction of disappointment from the crowd as Judge left the batter's box, digging hard for first base.

"I really think everything he did after [No.] 55 was so impressive, because of how much pressure there was," said Aaron Hicks. "People were flying all over the place; there was a packed house all the time. It's tough to hit homers. He would get a base hit and people would be like, 'Aww,' you know what I mean? [Nos.] 55 through 62 are probably the most impressive homers I've ever seen, because of how much pressure it took to do that."

Oswaldo Cabrera hit his first career grand slam later in the inning, providing cushion for the Judge watch to continue. The crowd grew quiet; on the bench, Gerrit Cole gestured with his arms waving wildly, shouting: "We don't need to be quiet here! It's just a normal game!" Judge roped a drive to left again in his next at-bat, this one bouncing into the left-field seats for a ground rule double; again, sighs were heard from the crowd. Judge stood at second base, fidgeted with his helmet, and looked toward the dugout as if to say: "Can you believe this?"

"He'll deny it, but I thought there was a fatigue there, particularly when the whole thing started with the silence at the stadium," said Suzyn Waldman. "When you see someone every single day, I just saw a little difference on his face. The pressure was just different. That gave me the creeps, with 50,000 people being quiet and taking pictures. I remember going on a tirade at one point, saying, 'Watch the game!' You're looking in your camera. You're not seeing it with your heart, you're not seeing it with your own eyes."

Added Brendan Kuty of *NJ Advance Media*: "It was unlike anything any of us had ever seen in sports. No one sees Patrick Mahomes drop out for a pass and the crowd goes silent. No one sees LeBron James get the ball at the top of the key and no one says a word. Now Aaron Judge gets to the plate, and at-bats are long. It was strange and eerie."

The Red Sox were coming to town next, and how appropriate might it be if Judge's 61st came against Boston? They had been the visitors at Yankee Stadium on October 1, 1961, when Maris had cleared the right-field wall with his blast off Tracy Stallard. Judge had seen the black-and-white footage of Maris's 61st plenty of times; he and Samantha had also watched the *61** movie late in the season, a film that Judge recalled first seeing on HBO shortly after its 2001 release. Both in reality and in Barry Pepper's Hollywood performance, Judge had been impressed by Maris's reluctance to showboat in the most significant moment of his career.

"I know exactly the moment you're talking about, the team pushing him out of the dugout," Judge said. "It shows you what a leader, what type of player he was. Just hit his 61st, broke the big record at Yankee Stadium. It just shows you he was about the team and always focused on that. From what I've seen, old videos, he was a great teammate, never made it about himself."

Neither the baseball gods nor the Red Sox had interest in wrapping the Maris-to-Judge saga with a tidy bow.

In the series opener, a 5–4 Yankees win decided in ten innings by a Josh Donaldson walk-off single, Judge walked three times and struck out once before finally getting good wood on a pitch. The crowd roared as Judge lifted a ninth-inning fly ball off reliever Matt Barnes, but the ball hung up too long, secured by center fielder Kiké Hernández about four feet in front of the wall.

"When the numbers got to 60, it was like, 'Oh, this is real now,'" said Dillon Lawson, the Yanks' hitting coach. "One through 59 felt pretty casual, but 60 was like—all right, this is going to happen, so buckle up. You're just on the edge of your seat, waiting, waiting and waiting. For me personally, I was feeling the anticipation, but it didn't change anything he was doing."

Judge's best play of the night came on defense, firing a bullet to second base that cut down Boston's Tommy Pham attempting to stretch a ninth-inning single. "There's not many guys who can make that play," Pham said. "Judge is one of the few who can. That's an area of his game. Judge is one of the most complete players in the game."

Every pitch of that game had been televised nationally on FOX, and there was local uproar that the next contest could be seen only on Apple TV+, a streaming outfit in its infancy of televising Major League Baseball games. The tech giant had paid a reported $85 million for exclusive rights to stream a weekly showcase. Even though Apple offered the content to viewers free of charge (they would, however, have to submit a valid email account to obtain an Apple ID), numerous fans cluttered talk radio with gripes that they either could not understand the process or had no interest in signing up.

Numerous bars across the tristate area also would go dark, as many were not equipped with smart televisions to utilize the internet. After a season of wild swings between celebration and deep anxiety, it seemed immensely anticlimactic and unfair that the most important parts of Judge's home run chase could conclude with a relatively minuscule television audience. Had Judge hit No. 61 in that game, the call would not have belonged to the YES Network's Michael Kay, but Apple's team of Stephen Nelson, Hunter Pence, and Katie Nolan. Fans lobbied for YES to take the game, contract be damned, or at least for Apple to bring Kay into the booth. That prompted Kay to call John Filippelli, YES's president of production and programming, with an adamant message.

"I completely shut it down," Kay said. "I called Flip and said, 'Whoever's trying to do this, stop it. I'm not doing the game.' Stephen Nelson was on the call. If he hit it on that day, it's his call. It's not mine. I won't big-foot anybody, because I wouldn't want them to do it to me. A good number of people probably would have taken that chance, but I just couldn't. I thought it would have been the ultimate big-shot, big-timing thing."

The game ended with the same 5–4 score, with Judge again kept in the ballpark—a single, a flyout, and two strikeouts in four at-bats. All things considered, it was a win-win: Apple TV+ got to deliver a Yankees win, and Kay didn't miss a historic call. New York also topped Boston the next two nights, rattling off a four-game sweep, though Judge was finding that pitches to hit had grown scarce.

"I hated the fact that people were pitching around him, just because they didn't want to give up the records," said catcher Kyle Higashioka.

"It was a little chickenshit. If you're a major-league player and you're pitching around somebody because you're afraid of giving up a homer—I mean, in the right situation, fine. But nobody on, nobody out? Like, come on."

With the game back on the YES Network for a Saturday afternoon, ESPN opted to slice into its college football coverage, utilizing a split screen for Auburn-Missouri and Clemson–Wake Forest each time Judge came to the plate. Neither audience witnessed history, as Judge struck out twice and walked in a 7–5 win, but plenty of eyeballs were fixed on screens. Nine of the ten most-watched games in YES's history were aired between September 20 and the end of the season, with ten of the Yanks' twelve games in that span averaging five hundred thousand total viewers in the New York–designated market area. ESPN's nationally televised Yankees–Red Sox game on September 25 drew 2.2 million viewers.

"People were really engaged. You could break down to the minute, what it would get to when he was coming up to bat," Kay said. "There were times when it would get to 900,000, a million people. You knew that you had to be on your toes and couldn't have an off night. You knew the Yankees were going to make the playoffs, and this gave you a reason to really stay engaged."

The pressure was on now, with only one home game remaining before the Yankees hit the road for a three-game series against the Toronto Blue Jays.

"There was more weight for me," Judge said. "I wanted to knock this out for my teammates, my family. I had everybody showing up. I had family flying in, I had friends flying in for it. I really wasn't worried about trying to do it for myself. I was like, 'Man, I've got a lot of people that came here to watch this. I'd better get this done.'"

It seemed that Major League Baseball was leaning that way, too. However, an awful forecast was not. The Yankees and Red Sox reported to the stadium for a Sunday-night game that would be televised on ESPN—eventually. The outfield was soaked and fans roamed the concourses, seeking shelter as they swigged $16 beers and munched toward the bottoms of their chicken buckets. Only the prospect of history on the line seemed to ensure the game would begin. A ninety-eight-minute

delay preceded Nestor Cortes's first pitch, time that Judge had utilized
to hit in the underground batting cages.

He came ready; smoking a ground ball double to left in his first at-
bat, then working a walk and flying out in his next trips. It was pouring
by the sixth inning, when Marwin González lifted a routine fly ball
that right fielder Rob Refsnyder flubbed for a run-scoring error. The
umpires seemed to be enduring the deluge in hopes of giving Judge one
more chance to bat, but when No. 9 hitter Oswald Peraza struck out to
end the sixth inning, play was halted. The game would be called soon
after, the Yankees credited with a 2–0 victory and Cortes with a one-hit
shutout. Forty thousand fans grumbled in unison as they trudged toward
the exits.

"As we got to the final steps, it was the first time where you started
to see a little bit of pressure set in amongst the whole group," said Matt
Blake, the team's pitching coach. "Everybody was standing up for every
at-bat. I know he's hit a lot of home runs, but it felt like he had to hit a
home run in every at-bat or it would be a failure in the collective mind
of the group. I think it was a challenge, just to see how he battled that on
a daily basis and still got to 62."

There were red eyes and extra espresso shots on deck as phone alarms
sounded in the early afternoon on September 26, the Yankees arrived in
Toronto shortly after 4:00 a.m. Eastern time following the twice-delayed
Sunday-night extravaganza. The quick turnaround was tough, and Judge
opted for comfort as he dressed in his hotel room, eyeing a gray sweatshirt with small blue type across the front: "New York or Nowhere." The
garb seemed to be more than a well-placed advertisement for a SoHo
boutique by the same name.

"Aaron is nothing if not thoughtful," said Kuty. "He didn't put that
hoodie on because he thought it was cool. It was a real message."

Perhaps, though Judge remained coy when asked about the sweatshirt. Whatever his intentions, he was ready to go under the lights at
Rogers Centre, lining Kevin Gausman's fourth pitch for a leadoff single
before coming around to score the game's first run. The Blue Jays were
challenging Judge, but they were being more cautious. As Gausman said,

"I just don't want to be an answer to a trivia question. Obviously, he's a great player. He's had an unbelievable season, so you pitch him smart. I'll take my chances facing some of the other guys."

Judge walked and struck out twice as the contest proceeded into extra innings, not exactly what the Yankees hoped for after a fatiguing travel day. Judge's spot came up in the tenth inning with two men on, but Blue Jays manager John Schneider signaled for an intentional walk, loading the bases to bring up Anthony Rizzo instead.

Schneider even told home plate umpire Laz Diaz not to ask for a batch of specially marked baseballs: "You don't have to change them out. We're just going to walk him." Diaz still followed protocol, requesting the balls. The gamble worked; Rizzo chopped a grounder that first baseman Vladimir Guerrero Jr. smothered, ending the inning.

"Game on the line; that's where you want to hit," Judge said. "That's why I'm doing all the work, to put myself in a position to go out there and help the team out and help us get a win right there. But I trust every single guy in our lineup and every single guy on our bench."

A few minutes later, Clarke Schmidt surrendered a walk-off hit to Guerrero, sealing a 3–2 Jays win. Boone had permitted Schmidt to face Guerrero with first base open instead of issuing an intentional walk to catcher Alejandro Kirk, which the manager called a "pick your poison" situation. Later, Boone would offer a glimpse inside the Yankees' machinations. Undoubtedly, Vlad Jr. was more well known than the squat Kirk, but Boone pointed to Kirk's better batting average, better numbers with runners in scoring position, and better stats in September. The outcome hadn't been optimal, but there was logic behind the choice.

"It overwhelmingly stacked up to say, I think we'll take our chances [with Guerrero]," Boone said.

One day after the "New York or Nowhere" sweatshirt sparked attention, Judge's attire again contained a significant development—this time, after the game.

With his dripping ball cap turned backward, Judge beamed and popped the cork of another bubbly bottle in Rogers Centre's visiting clubhouse, dousing his teammates with delight. Appearing as though he'd gone for a fully clothed swim, Judge sported a soaked T-shirt that declared in bold white letters: "The East Is Ours."

When the Yankees first gathered as a complete squad six months prior, savoring a sunny spring afternoon that ended their winter of lock-out-related uncertainty, Boone had outlined the expectations. The first objective was to secure the American League East title, and with a 5–2 win over Toronto, they had done so. Though Judge tied a career high with four walks, kept in the ballpark for a seventh straight game, he said that the moment felt big—"especially for a lot of guys in that room that haven't had a chance to clinch a division."

The Yankees splashed the night away with a loud and lively party, packed shoulder to shoulder in a dressing area that bore a passing re-semblance to a Manhattan railroad apartment. Plastic sheeting covered each locker and hip-hop music blared as players donned ski goggles and double-fisted from Budweiser cans, providing icy-cold baths for anyone nearby. Gleyber Torres strutted about the room wearing a New York City firefighter's helmet, and rookie Oswaldo Cabrera shouted: "I'm living the dream!"

"We can say we're the best team in the best division this year, and it wasn't easy," Boone said. "Everyone in that room knows that. We took everyone's punches; we had some low moments. But tonight is to be celebrated. It's not easy going through the American League East and to survive. . . . This is step one, and we want to win a championship. That's our goal."

Someone called for the players to hurry to the diamond, where play-ers and coaches gathered between the mound and home plate, capturing the moment with a photograph. Amid the hollers, Boone sidled up to Judge, holstering a direct question. Judge had now played four dozen consecutive games; there had been a few team off days mixed in and Judge wasn't exactly threatening Cal Ripken Jr.'s record, but it seemed notable in the load-management era of baseball, especially near the end of a long season and with the added drama of a home run chase.

"You want a day tomorrow?" Boone asked his star.

Judge did not hesitate.

"Nah," he replied. "I'm in there."

Fair enough. As promised, Judge's name appeared in the lineup for the second game of three in Toronto, though it hadn't completely been Boone's call. During Boone's lone season with the Yankees as a player in 2003, he'd been amused by Joe Torre's tradition of having a veteran serve as a guest manager near the end of each season.

In '03, Roger Clemens took the reins for the Yanks' 162nd game. Clemens even trudged out of the dugout to execute a pitching change that day; David Wells, handing over the baseball as he remained in line for his two hundredth career win, told Clemens that he should have walked more slowly to make it seem authentic. "Now I know why the skipper gets ulcers," Clemens had said that day, leaning back in the leather office chair behind Torre's desk. "I can't see myself doing this, but it was fun."

With the acrid smell of stale champagne still baked into the carpet of Rogers Centre's visiting clubhouse, Boone tapped Anthony Rizzo as his guest manager for the evening, inviting Rizzo into the manager's office to go over the lineup behind Gerrit Cole. They agreed on Judge first as the designated hitter, then continued with Oswaldo Cabrera batting second and Josh Donaldson third.

Rizzo had a suggestion at shortstop, one that would serve as a prelude for events to come. When the Yankees promoted Oswald Peraza from Triple-A in early September, there had been no set plan to work the prospect into action; the thinking was that he might pinch-hit or pinch-run late in blowouts, but mostly the move was to provide the twenty-two-year-old Peraza with an opportunity to take in the big-league experience.

"If nothing else," Boone said, "we wanted him to be in our environment and be around the team, and hopefully along the way he'd get some playing time."

Many fans didn't want to hear it, but a conservative front office had no appetite to throw an untested rookie into the heat of a pennant race. As Hal Steinbrenner would remark the following spring, while discussing Anthony Volpe's prospects for cracking the roster: "Look, we're always concerned about our minor league players; are they truly ready? Because this is not New York, and this is not the regular season." Isiah Kiner-Falefa would remain the starting shortstop through September, with Boone having spent a good portion of the summer attempting to shield Kiner-Falefa from criticism, stating that the team's internal metrics painted him as a "top five to seven defensive shortstop" in the league.

But now that the division had been clinched, Rizzo lobbied for Peraza to start, deciding to bat him in the cleanup spot. Rizzo was taking his task seriously; once the lineup card was complete, he paced through the clubhouse, communicating with each relief pitcher. Nestor Cortes and Gleyber Torres showed up wearing wristwatches, part of their assigned role as Rizzo's "coaches," and Boone was delighted when Rizzo asked a clubhouse worker to shred the sleeves off a hooded sweatshirt, replicating Boone's game-day attire.

The new-look lineup pounced on Toronto starter Mitch White for three first-inning runs, including a run-scoring single by Peraza; Rizzo cheered and swiped his left index finger through the air after Peraza's hit cleared the infield, slapping hands with Cortes to celebrate. The Blue Jays, still fighting for position with Wild Card spots up for grabs, would punch back. Toronto scored three sixth-inning runs off of Cole to tie the game, prompting Blue Jays manager John Schneider to call to the bullpen in the seventh inning.

His choice was lefty Tim Mayza, who'd been credited with the win in the extra-inning series opener, having issued an intentional walk to Judge before inducing Rizzo to ground out. This time, he would have a chance to face Judge.

HOMER #61: September 28 vs. Toronto Blue Jays' Tim Mayza (7th inning, two-run)
Exit velocity: 117.4 mph. Distance: 394 feet. Launch angle: 22 degrees. HR in 29 of 30 MLB parks.

As Mayza completed his warm-up tosses, Judge stood near the steps of the first-base dugout, chomping on gum as he eyed the lefty with intent. The thirty-year-old Mayza hailed from the Philadelphia suburb of Red Hill, a twelfth-round pick in the 2013 draft who featured a sinker and slider combination.

His career path had also included several notable run-ins with the Yankees. In September 2019, Mayza had been facing New York when he threw a pitch that sailed behind shortstop Didi Gregorius. Mayza crumpled to the ground in pain; his left ulnar collateral ligament had ruptured, requiring reconstructive surgery. Mayza rehabbed through the COVID-19 pandemic and made it back to the big leagues in 2021, pitching a scoreless inning at Yankee Stadium in his return.

Aaron Hicks was batting ahead of Judge, and the switch-hitter stood in the right-handed batter's box, his more productive side. Mayza got ahead with a couple of strikes, and Hicks lined the third pitch into center field for a clean single. The crowd buzzed as Judge walked toward home plate; many did not stand for the at-bat, as they had in the Bronx, but they recorded with their phones nevertheless.

Mayza wanted to keep the ball down; he'd throw nothing but sinkers in this at-bat. Months later, Mayza would focus his off-season work on honing his slider; he didn't have enough confidence in the pitch to try it with Judge at the plate. "I wanted to challenge him and try getting the ball on the ground, especially with a guy on first," Mayza said.

Judge looked at the first sinker, then waved at another for a strike. The third sailed outside, and Judge fouled the fourth back with a healthy cut, denting an advertisement behind the plate for Valvoline motor oil. Mayza's 2-2 offering came close to the bottom of the zone; Mayza desperately wanted it called a strike, as did catcher Danny Jansen, who framed it nicely.

Judge had been rung up on more than his share of similar pitches over the years, as Boone's ejection tally could attest. This time, home plate umpire Brian O'Nora did not flinch. Judge fouled off the next two pitches as the battle reached eight.

Mayza came set at the belt again, raising his right leg to begin his delivery. The pitch came in down the middle and Judge walloped it to left field; Mayza flung his arms out, knowing he'd just surrendered a historic drive.

"He put together a pretty good at-bat," Mayza said. "I made one mistake and he took advantage. Congratulations to him."

On the YES Network, Michael Kay announced: "Drilled deep to left field! *This could be it!* See ya! He's done it! No. 61! He's been chasing history and now he makes it! He and Roger Maris are tied with

61 home runs, the most anybody has ever hit in a single season in American League history!"

There was a tribute in Kay's call, an homage to Phil Rizzuto, who'd stamped his voice onto Maris's 61st. "When he got to 59, I was sitting at the stadium and I called up Rizzuto's call of Maris's 61st on YouTube," Kay said. "I listened to it a couple of times. The exact line was 'This could be it, way back there.' I wanted to include that parenthetical statement as an homage to Rizzuto and Maris, but the ball that Judge hit out for 61 was a line drive. People think you can script things, but you can't. It just got out too quick, so all I could say was, 'This could be it!'"

At age eighty-four, travel had become more challenging for John Sterling, and the broadcasting ironman who called every pitch of Derek Jeter's career had reluctantly trimmed his schedule. His deep baritone remained strong, and though he was initially scheduled to miss the Toronto series, Sterling refused to miss an opportunity to call history.

At the crack of the bat, Sterling delivered: "It is high! It is far! It is gone! No. 61! He ties Roger Maris for the American League single-season record with 61 home runs! It's a two-run Judge-ian blast! Here comes the Judge! A two-run blast and the Yankees take a 5–3 lead on No. 61 for Judge!"

"I couldn't miss any games where this guy may set the record," Sterling said. "You can go weeks without hitting a home run. Sometimes the coverage is so ridiculous. It's not that easy to hit a home run. When he hit it, I have to admit, it's maybe one of the most thrilling things I've broadcast, and I've done four sports for now more than fifty years."

Seated next to Sterling, Suzyn Waldman watched the action and felt "almost as if the whole building let out a collective sigh. At least he was going to be there—he had tied Roger. It really got to me. You don't see history every day, and we were watching history for a whole year."

As Judge trotted toward first base, television cameras captured Patty Judge and Roger Maris Jr., side by side in the front row. Mom raised her hands high, sporting an expression that seemed to be one of delight and relief. Almost instantly, Maris hugged her.

"Without a doubt, she became the absolute star of that whole moment," said Troy Benjamin, the YES Network producer. "I mean, the kisses, a baseball mom—everybody loves a mother. She became the story of the season for us. Sixty-one, where she was sitting right above the dugout, it made for great TV." While that was happening in the seats, Judge's teammates spilled out of the dugout, applauding as he completed a tour around the bases. Boone said that he hung back from the celebration, trying to "take little pictures in my head of people's reactions." He'd later recount Judge's 2022 season as "an all-time great season," akin to performances by Babe Ruth, Jim Brown, Michael Jordan, or Wayne Gretzky. The players each hugged Judge, laughing and sharing a few personal congratulations.

Finally, Boone saw an opening to embrace his star, telling him, "I'm so happy for you." Judge did not miss a beat.

"We're not done yet," he replied. "We've got a lot left to do."

The coveted No. 61 ball was said to be worth as much as $2 million, by one estimate, and it was nearly caught by two fans seated in the front row of Section 137. Judge's drive smacked a concrete barrier a few feet below the fans' outstretched gloves, coming to rest in the Blue Jays bullpen. One of the fans, who identified himself as Frankie Lasagna, said: "The disbelief comes over you, and just the shock and amazement. I was like, 'Oh my God, I almost had it.'"

The other fan, dressed in a Bo Bichette jersey, threw his glove to the ground and was visibly distraught. He declined to speak to the media, folding his arms and staring vacantly at the playing field for several innings. Over the next several days, Lasagna (yes, that is his real name) fielded numerous interview requests, revealing the delicious twist that he owned and operated an Italian restaurant, Terrazza, in downtown Toronto.

"It's the most messages and people and texting and calling me, more than I've ever gotten," Lasagna said. "More than my wedding day, the birth of my kids. It's been wild for me."

As No. 61 came to rest in the Blue Jays bullpen, the ball was first touched by Matt Buschmann, Toronto's bullpen coach. It was marked with the letter-number combination "T 9," in large black text near the MLB logo. The thirty-eight-year-old Buschmann, a former pitcher who had made three appearances for the 2016 Arizona Diamondbacks, flipped it to David Howell, the Jays' pitching strategist. It was the most valuable game of hot potato imaginable. Howell panicked, telling Buschmann that he didn't want to hold it.

"We all just stood and stared at each other, thinking, 'What are we going to do?'" Buschmann said. "I didn't want to throw it back up in the stands. That's one thing I didn't want to do."

The ball was shoveled to Jordan Romano, the Toronto closer who had given up one of Judge's most memorable home runs of the season back on May 10. Romano safeguarded it for a few minutes as play resumed. Mark Kafalas, the Yankees' security guard, found a spot behind a row of chairs in the bullpen and kept his eyes peeled on Romano—the muscle memory of stakeouts from his previous life as an NYPD narcotics detective kicking in immediately.

Zack Britton, the Yankees' relief pitcher, grew curious about what was taking so long. Britton exited the visiting bullpen and ventured into enemy territory, taking it upon himself to help broker the deal. "By the time I got over there, Romano saw me coming and he was just like, 'Hey, here you go,'" Britton said. "He was good. It was great, he made it easy."

Britton told Romano that if there was anything the Blue Jays wanted from Judge, he would make it happen.

"We just didn't want to give it to the wrong person," Romano said. "I'm sure it would have gotten in the right hands. But when it came in, there were probably fifteen people back there and they wanted the ball. So when Britton came over, we made sure to give it to him."

"It was cool. You're holding history," Britton said. "Some of the bullpen guys, we were joking about our negotiations with Judge, what that was going to be like."

Buschmann later joked that they should have asked Judge not to re-sign anywhere in the American League East, unless it was with Toronto.

Judge knew exactly what to do with the ball once it arrived at his locker, delivered by Rob Cucuzza, one of the Yanks' longtime clubhouse managers. Cradling the ball in his right hand, Judge brought it to a service hallway underneath the first-base grandstand and presented it to his mother, Patty, just as he had done with his first major-league home run in 2016.

"She's been with me through it all," Judge said. "From the Little League days, getting me ready for school, taking me to my first couple of practices and games, being there for my first professional game. My debut, and now getting a chance to be here for this—this is something special, and we're not done yet."

As Patty held the ball for photographers, Roger Maris Jr. waited nearby. Patty and Roger had established a friendship in the previous days, sharing stories about their lives in the baseball universe. For Maris, it had been fun getting to know a bit about Judge's family, saying, "You can see why Aaron carries himself the way he does. You can see the apple doesn't fall far from the tree. The family seems very grounded. You can tell when you meet somebody, why the kid is the way he is. So kudos to the parents." The Marises had decided not to speak with Judge until No. 61; too many people were clawing for Judge's attention, and the team was still in a fight for postseason position. But now that the milestone homer had landed and the division was clinched, it was finally time for Maris to meet the second Yankee to hit 61 home runs in a single season.

It had been nine days since Maris traveled north from Gainesville, Florida, inching toward the edge of his seat each time Judge came to bat. Maris took note of the numerology—nine days, Dad wore No. 9, Judge wore No. 99. Thirty-five plate appearances had separated Judge's 60th and 61st, and as Maris shook Judge's hand, he joked: "Why did you wait so long?"

Judge thanked Maris for attending the games at Yankee Stadium and crossing the border to Toronto, telling him that it was an "incredible honor" to be associated with his father. Maris told Judge that his father would be proud of Judge because of the way he carried himself, pouring his physical and mental preparation into the goal of bringing a championship to New York.

"That's one thing that's so special about the Yankees organization, is all the guys that came before us and kind of paved the way and played the game the right way; did things the right way, did a lot of great things in this game," Judge said. "Getting the chance to be mentioned with those guys, I can't even describe it."

Soon after, Maris reiterated that he believed Judge should be considered the single-season home run champion, should he hit a 62nd home run.

"He's clean, he's a Yankee, he plays the game the right way," Maris said. "It gives people a chance to look at somebody who should be revered for hitting 62 home runs, not just as a guy who did it in the American League. He should be revered for being the actual single-season home run champ. That's really who he is."

Though Maris no longer held the Yankee record alone, Judge's season had helped to finalize the transition of Maris's legacy. For all the stress Maris endured during the summer of '61, a losing battle in the court of public opinion against both Babe Ruth and Mickey Mantle, his accomplishments were bathed in only positive light sixty-one years later.

Because of Judge's chase, a new generation had been introduced to Maris's achievement, coming to admire his steely determination and reputation as a winning teammate.

"It's wonderful to see how Roger Maris's legacy has transformed," said Brian Richards, the curator of the Yankees museum. "People like to break down history into 'good guy' and 'bad guy' boxes. If you watch the movie 42, Jackie Robinson is the good guy and [Phillies manager] Ben Chapman is the bad guy. Once somebody is in those two boxes, it's really tough to climb out of one and go to the other. Well, Roger Maris has climbed out of the bad guy box and into the good guy box."

Long after his final turn at bat, Maris remained scarred by his New York experience; in the spring of 1978, Maris was invited to join Mantle in raising the Bombers' 1977 championship flag at the club's home opener. Maris initially declined the invitation, telling a club official, "Why do I have to go and get booed?" It had taken a personal intervention from George M. Steinbrenner to convince Maris that his presence would be positively received, even detailing the exact script that public address announcer Bob Sheppard would use.

The cheers were indeed there for that April afternoon, as Maris stood in center field wearing a tan suit and burgundy tie, his hair still trimmed in a familiar crewcut. With Mantle by his side, Maris lifted his right hand to wave, and he grinned with relief. That was the beginning of the Maris–Yankees renaissance; Judge's home run chase simply authored the conclusion. With Judge and Maris in the headlines together, there was no loser. They were both winners, and baseball was better for it.

As they concluded their chat, Maris made one final request of Judge: "Get to New York, hit 62 and knock the top off Yankee Stadium. It's going to be fun."

13

◆

CHASE CLOSED!

Something felt a tick or two off with Aaron Judge's swing, and he was running out of time to correct it.

It had been six days since Judge had equaled Roger Maris's American League record with home run No. 61. The dream scenario had been for Judge to launch a 62nd home run at Yankee Stadium, the brightness of his white pinstripes eclipsed only by the flashes from thousands of digital devices, all held high in hopes of recording history.

Alas, if that moment were to occur, it would happen some 1,500 miles southwest in Arlington, Texas. Judge's chances of surpassing Maris in front of a Bronx crowd fell short on the afternoon of October 2, when he struck out three times with a walk against the Baltimore Orioles in the Yankees' final regular season home game.

From New York's perspective, Judge's at-bats were the most compelling reason to observe that series, with the American League East clinched and the rest of the roster in tune-up mode for the playoffs. If not for the home run chase, a forecast of inclement weather might have tempted cancellation; instead, the clubs played through light to steady precipitation, remnants from Hurricane Ian, which had pounded Florida's west coast earlier in the week.

Now they were off to Arlington, and as Judge dressed in a comfortable team-issued Nike tracksuit for the flight, he expressed regret that No. 62 had not been slugged in front of his most adoring audience.

"It'd be nice to hit it at home and do something special like that for the home fans, but at the end of the day, I've got a job to do," Judge said. "I've got to get ready for the postseason. It didn't happen [at Yankee Stadium], but the season's not over yet."

Indeed it was not. Against the Orioles, he'd singled with two walks and a strikeout in the first game. October 1 marked the sixty-first anniversary of Maris's 61st, but there was no symmetry to be had. Judge went hitless with a pair of strikeouts and walks that day, a Saturday contest for which ABC and ESPN interrupted a second consecutive week of college football telecasts, offering live cut-ins to Judge's at-bats.

The gridiron audience had fatigued of the interruptions; calling a game between Ole Miss and Kentucky, announcer Sean McDonough was told that the tarp had been placed on the field at Yankee Stadium. "Oh, what a shame," McDonough said, his tone dripping with sarcasm. McDonough had not been thrilled the previous week, either, when Judge's at-bat stomped over his call of Clemson's game at Wake Forest.

Of course, Judge had nothing to do with network programming decisions, though he was trying like heck to provide some good TV. After days of Judge tossing his bat aside at an unappetizing buffet of sliders and fastballs outside the strike zone, the Orioles gave Judge a few pitches to hit. None were put in play; facing Baltimore starter Kyle Bradish, Judge struck out looking in the first inning, whiffed in the third, then worked a five-pitch walk in the fifth. An opportunity to witness Judge trot to first base with a free pass was not what drew 44,322 fans to the corner of 161st Street and River Avenue on a gray, chilly afternoon. The crowd jeered Bradish for each pitch not grooved down Broadway, then sighed when Judge struck out against reliever Bryan Baker in the seventh inning.

Judge insisted that the scrutiny of the chase had not gotten to him, but he knew his swing and worried that something had gone awry within the last few weeks. It was probably imperceptible to the naked eye, but significant enough that it could throw him out of whack, a significant concern with the postseason just days away. The building blocks of Judge's

swing came with trying to stroke hits, not belt homers, and he was getting away from that.

As Judge's batting average ticked downward, Luis Arraez's numbers remained the same. Though the Minnesota Twins infielder dealt with left
hamstring tightness that kept him out of the lineup for a few games,
Judge still considered a Triple Crown within reach. He couldn't force the
Twins to play Arraez (whom, to his credit, said that he wanted to "win
the batting title fighting"), but he could attempt to focus on hits instead
of the long ball.

"If I have a good approach, the home runs are going to come," Judge
said. "It was about trying to get on base, drive guys in and get hits. That
Triple Crown was kind of at the forefront for me. I felt like, if I could get
four or five hits a game, it's going to help our team win. It was a challenge, but I had fun throughout the whole thing. We had clinched our
division, so the last couple of games were just about getting ourselves in
the right position for the postseason."

The Yankees had four regular season games remaining, against the
Rangers at Globe Life Field in Arlington, Texas. The trip included a
split-admission doubleheader, and Judge told Aaron Boone that he'd like
to play every day, but maybe not both ends of the twin bill. Noting that
there were several days off between the end of the regular season and
the beginning of the American League Division Series, Judge told the
manager, "That's when I'll rest."

For weeks, each of Judge's at-bats had carried the weight of history,
and he was pleased to cede that spotlight in the first game at Texas.
That was Luis Severino's turn to flirt with immortality, the right-hander
proclaiming his "1,000 percent" certainty that he would've completed a
no-hitter if given the chance.

Making his final tune-up before the playoffs, Severino had his arsenal
crackling over seven hitless innings, facing the minimum before a rising
pitch count forced the Yankees to turn the game over to the bullpen in a
3–1 victory. Severino struck out seven, the last of which was a swinging
punch-out of Nathaniel Lowe, prompting Boone to intercept the right-
hander at the dugout stairs.

Boone placed his hands on Severino's shoulders, asking, "What do you think?" When Severino replied, "I would die out there," Boone shook his head and was firm, saying, "I can't let you do it." Severino refused to make eye contact, the emotions of the moment overwhelming him.

It was only Severino's third big-league game since returning from the strained right lat that had removed him from the rotation in July, and Severino had been briefed about his pitch count limitations. Though Boone said that having to remove Severino put "a little damper on the night," he also believed that, if Severino were to have a realistic chance of completing a no-hitter, he might have to throw 120 to 130 pitches. These opportunities were rare; no one could promise Severino he'd ever have another opportunity for immortality.

Yet once the fog of battle had cleared, Severino stood at the center of the visiting clubhouse and admitted that he thought it "was a good decision," noting, "I don't want to go out there and hurt myself and not be good for the postseason."

As Severino and his teammates lamented what might have been, Judge set out to investigate what was holding him back from history. Held to a checked-swing infield single in four at-bats that night, Judge pulled out his iPhone and tapped a message to his swing guru, Richard Schenck, who had been watching the game from his home in St. Peters, Missouri. Judge provided Schenck with a link to a video of his most recent batting practice session.

"I think my direction has been off, and it looks better here," Judge wrote.

Schenck watched the video, then offered: "Yeah, I agree with you." Judge thanked Schenck, tucking away a note for the next day.

HOMER #62: October 4 vs. Texas Rangers' Jesús Tinoco (1st inning, solo)
Exit velocity: 100.2 mph. Distance: 391 feet. Launch angle: 35 degrees. HR in 29 of 30 MLB parks.

October 4 dawned sunny and temperate in Arlington, Texas, with forecasted temperatures in the mid-eighties. That prompted the Rangers to announce that the roof at Globe Life Field—the largest single-panel

operable roof in the world, weighing a whopping 24 million pounds—
would remain closed for the first game of the doubleheader. A major
factor in the reason why the Rangers had built their $1.1 billion colossus
was to escape the broiling heat at their former venue across East Randol
Mill Road, where there had been no roof and spotty air-conditioning.

The Yankees and Rangers were scheduled for a day-night doubleheader, and if not for the Judge chase, there would have been almost no
reason to watch. No one in uniform seemed excited about adding a long
day to the end of a long season, slapped on as part of the fallout from
an ugly and contentious spring lockout. The Yankees had originally been
booked to begin their 162-game schedule in Arlington; instead, they
would finish it there. The first game of the day saw Judge notch a single
and a run scored in New York's 5–4 win, a contest in which the normally
stoic Judge had shown a few flickers of frustration. He'd bashed his batting helmet after popping up a hittable pitch from Rangers right-hander
Jon Gray; true to form, though, Judge apologetically picked the helmet
up from the dugout floor and placed it in its appropriate slot. Judge usually saved those outbursts for the runway between the clubhouse and the
dugout, where television cameras couldn't capture it. This time, he didn't
hold back.

"It was the first time I'd seen it wearing on him, just a little bit," Cole
said. "We just wanted it to happen so bad."

Judge's late-night text message to Schenck had not come out of nowhere. He was in a mini-slump, batting .231 (9-for-39) with a homer,
eighteen walks, and fifteen strikeouts since hitting No. 60 off the Pittsburgh Pirates' Wil Crowe. Some of the opponents had shied away from
Judge, but not Texas. As Tony Beasley, the Rangers' interim manager,
said: "We were pitching to him. We had no intention of trying to walk
him. We were trying to execute pitches and get him out. The guys behind
him can hurt you, so we attacked him with our game plan."

Still, Judge's focus seemed sharp; one violent swing could make those
statistics irrelevant. As the first 30,553 fans of the day filed out of Globe
Life Field, many remaining close by to seek refreshments at the adjacent
Texas Live! bar before returning for the nightcap, Boone stopped by
Judge's locker for a status check. Their conversation was brief, as Boone

expected. Judge promised the manager that he was ready to go. Boone nodded, then returned to his office, finalizing the lineup card that he'd already decided on. In the top spot, Boone wrote: "Judge, RF."

The temperature had dipped to eighty-one degrees, and the Rangers announced that the roof would be open for the evening game, which locals swore helped the ball travel better. Boone said he hoped that was true. The clock ticked to 7:05 p.m. Central time—"It's baseball time in Arlington," longtime public address announcer Chuck Morgan bellowed, with echoing vibrato. Judge was the final player in the underground batting cage, completing his pregame routine before striding to home plate. He blinked twice and took his familiar stance, feet spread and bat cocked stiffly behind his right shoulder.

Standing six foot four and weighing 258 pounds, Jesús Tinoco had followed his big-league dreams from the dusty streets of San Antonio de Maturín, Venezuela. The hard-throwing right-hander had already participated in forty-seven previous big-league games, wearing the uniforms of the Colorado Rockies, Miami Marlins, and now the Rangers. Assigned to serve as an "opener" in the second game of this doubleheader, game No. 48 would be by far the most watched appearance of his twenty-seven years.

Tinoco had a few pitches at his disposal; he favored his sinker and slider, occasionally mixing in a curveball or four-seam fastball. He threw a ball, then a strike, setting up a 1-1 offering. Catcher Sam Huff set a target and Tinoco reared back to fire a slider, leaving it over the plate. Judge barreled the ball; it rocketed off his bat and soared deep to left field, where outfielder Bubba Thompson trotted back toward the 372-foot marker on the wall, little more than a curious witness to history.

"I had a good feeling off the bat," Judge said. "I just didn't know where it was going to land or what it was going to hit."

"High fly ball! Deep left! There it goes!" Michael Kay announced on the YES Network broadcast. "Soaring into history! He's done it! He has done it! 62! Aaron Judge is the American League single-season home-run leader!"

On the radio broadcast, John Sterling gave his trademark, "It is high, it is far, it is gone!" then added: "Number 62 to set the new American

League record! Aaron Judge hits his 62nd. All the Yankees out of the dugout to greet him. Just think of it: three Yankee right fielders—the Babe, hitting 60 in '27, the Jolly Roger, hitting 61 in '61, and now Aaron Judge hits his 62nd home run—the most home runs any American Leaguer has hit in a single season. And the American League has been alive for 120 years. This is Judgment day. Case closed!"

Former Yankees pitcher Jeff Nelson was by Sterling's side that day, filling in as a color commentator while Suzyn Waldman observed Yom Kippur. "I was so blessed to be there," he said. "I just laid back and listened to John make the call. Our broadcast booth was so high up in Texas that even John said, 'I didn't know if it was going to go out.' I said, 'Good thing you kept rolling with it.'"

Judge watched it all the way, tracking its flight as it cleared the wall and reached the seats. He felt an overwhelming sense of relief, the pressure of the past several weeks immediately lifting from his heavy shoulders.

A crowd of 38,832 roared inside the gleaming, glassy structure on Texas's north side; Judge's parents, Patty and Wayne, were in attendance, as was his wife, Samantha, who wore a vintage Mitchell & Ness T-shirt honoring the 1996 World Series championship. The Yankees hurdled the dugout railing and flooded onto the field, screaming and high-fiving each other while Judge rounded the bases. Judge grinned widely, stamping his left foot on home plate and embracing each teammate with the deep hugs usually exchanged between loved ones at airport terminals or train stations. Josh Donaldson said that the moment "felt like the college days," an opportunity to show the team's respect for Judge and his accomplishments.

"We were all anticipating it, and the season was running out," Stanton said. "So obviously, each at-bat was getting bigger and bigger. We all kind of downplayed it and suppressed it as teammates; it was our job to make it as comfortable as possible, and not make a big deal about things. We just tried to be normal. Everyone else was changing and acting differently, but we had the behind-the-scenes view of it, and we knew all the ins and outs. It was great to be a part of and to be able to see every day."

None of the Yankees' hitting coaches saw the homer in real time. They were still picking up baseballs in the cage, where Judge had just completed taking his practice swings. Dillon Lawson saw Tinoco on the mound and Judge at the plate on the in-house television feed. "We looked at each other, like, 'Did the game just start?'" he said. "We took off running. The double doors were open from the clubhouse to the dugout. We got there just in time to hear the crowd gasp. We got to see the ball land, but we didn't see it hit."

Neither did Kyle Higashioka, one of the few players still in the clubhouse. "To be honest, the chase had dragged on for a bit. I was searching for whatever I could do to make it happen, superstitionwise. Everybody wanted to be out there, so I was like, 'I'm going to stay inside.' Sure enough, he hit it, and I was like, 'I'll sacrifice that for him to get 62.'"

Hanging back to let the celebration breathe a bit, Boone said that he was thrilled, not only for Judge, but for Judge's family and teammates. The manager declared that Judge's 2022 would be remembered as "a historically great season, and one we'll talk about when we're long gone," the way feats accomplished by Ruth and Maris have endured. The American League (and Yankees) record for home runs finally belonged to Judge, who had clubbed the seventh-most home runs in a single season, behind Barry Bonds (73 in 2001), Mark McGwire (70 in 1998; 65 in 1999), and Sammy Sosa (66 in 1998; 64 in 2001; 63 in 1999).

"It's a big relief," Judge said. "I think everybody can finally sit down in their seats and watch the ballgame. It's been a fun ride so far."

Homer No. 62 soared for 5.7 seconds from bat to seats, clearing the fence between painted advertisements for Estrella Jalisco beer and State Farm insurance. In Section 31, Row 1, Seat 3, Cory Youmans heard Judge's blast before he saw it, the thirty-five-year-old Dallas native beginning to track the ball as it soared over shortstop Corey Seager. A friend had offered Youmans a ticket, and he'd accepted, mostly interested in a chance to see Judge in person.

Having changed in the parking lot from his workday suit and tie into a black T-shirt and a blue Rangers cap with the club's "T" logo on the front, Youmans was about to become the luckiest of the 38,832 souls to pass through the turnstiles that night, the largest crowd in the stadium's brief history. Youmans had hesitated to bring a glove into the ballpark, but he said that a friend told him, "If you were ever going to, this is the one you do it."

Youmans tucked the glove under his armpit with a hint of embarrassment, then relaxed once he reached the left-field seats. "When I got to the outfield, everyone was on the same page," he said. "Whether you were a kid or an adult, these people were ready to rock. There was a buzz; everyone was talking about what they were going to do if they caught it."

Scanning his surroundings, Youmans watched the first two pitches. Three seats were still open to his left; perhaps those fans had been held up at the beer lines, or by the lengthy waits at security screening. He squinted into the LCD lights, noting how bright they were, and tried to calculate the distance between himself and home plate. It was far. Then Tinoco wound and delivered. The sound of ball against bat echoed throughout the yard.

"Once I heard the crack, I'm like, 'Oh, this thing's gone,'" Youmans said. "I didn't know where it was going, but I knew it was a home run. Then I saw Seager look up, look over his shoulder, and I was like, 'Oh man, this thing's probably coming in our direction.' I was so nervous because it was coming straight at me. I knew I was either going to have to catch it, or I was going to drop it and something embarrassing was going to happen."

He'd been more of a basketball player in his youth, though he played some outfield and first base in middle school. Youmans put his old moves to the test, shuffling a few feet to present his glove. The ball thudded into the pocket with a loud pop. A different fan, one section over toward the left-field foul line, leapt from the grandstands and tumbled to a service walkway below—his plan, apparently, had been to secure the ball if it bounced out of the seats. Meanwhile, Section 31 became an instant party, fans slapping Youmans on the back and exchanging high fives.

"That's a feeling I'll never forget," he said. "I'd never caught a ball at a game before, let alone a home run ball. That was awesome. I didn't know how to react; it was just pure joy, pure excitement. It felt like the whole stadium was looking at me. I'm an introvert. I don't like public speaking, I don't even like my birthday. But I think I did some fist-pumps, and that's something I've never done in my life before."

Security swiftly hustled Youmans through the concourse to a private area, past a television camera operator who asked what he planned to do with the ball. Youmans replied that he hadn't thought about it yet. "Which was the exact truth," he said. "In retrospect, I didn't realize that those cameras were on and that would be the footage on the news. I feel like I was walking silly and just blowing by people."

Accompanied by a couple of Arlington police officers, Youmans found himself behind a curtained-off area in the center-field concourse, sparsely decorated by picnic tables and empty folding chairs. Youmans paced for a few minutes. His phone wouldn't stop ringing. There were too many text messages to count. "That's when the joy of the catch started to transition to like, 'Oh man, this is going to be a big deal,'" Youmans said.

An authenticator checked the markings on the ball, which had "C 13" written in black ink, surrounding a blue logo commemorating the Texas Rangers' fiftieth anniversary. It was also examined under a black light for secret markings, confirming that it was indeed the pitch that Tinoco had thrown. The ball was marked with a holographic sticker that read "YP 188527."

Eddie Fastook, the Yankees' executive director of security, entered the room and shook Youmans's hand. In a chat that spanned about five minutes, the broad-shouldered, mustachioed Fastook told Youmans that the team would be happy to offer memorabilia, photograph opportunities, or tickets for the ball. "If you want to sell the ball," Fastook said, "that's not going to be us." Youmans described their conversation as pleasant, but Fastook sensed that no deal would be brokered. No. 62 would probably not wind up in Judge's trophy case.

Youmans asked if he could leave; he was free to do so. He was steered through the stadium's interior in a golf cart, a journey that included a brief encounter with Ray Davis, the Rangers' owner. Behind the wheel of his vehicle in the Globe Life Field parking lot, he received a disturbing telephone call from his wife, Bri Amaranthus, a sports reporter who covers the Dallas Cowboys and Dallas Mavericks.

"Hey, are you close to home?" she said. "Our address is floating around online, and there's some people outside our apartment. I can't tell if they're supposed to be there."

As Youmans soon learned, social media had jumped to conclusions about his identity, including his net worth. Bob Nightengale, a *USA Today* columnist, tweeted that Youmans "doesn't exactly need the money," citing his position as a vice president at Fisher Investments, "which manages $197 billion worldwide." But Nightengale's Google search only told a portion of the story; Youmans was a vice president of sales; he did not own the firm or manage personnel. His status symbol was a Costco card.

"I started to get worried," Youmans said. "People think you're worth $25 million, and you have a $2 million baseball in your pocket, but really, you live in an apartment. I don't own a gun. I've got a kitchen knife and there's strangers all over my building. It got complicated."

Youmans walked through the door and hugged his wife, who had already packed an overnight bag and had their dog ready to go. They arranged to stay with friends a few miles away. As they traveled, Youmans's phone continued to buzz and ring. ABC's *Good Morning America* wanted to arrange an interview.

"I was like, 'I'm trying to figure out where my family is going to sleep,'" he said.

He began fielding numerous offers for the baseball. There was a legitimate offer for $3 million, buried within a stack of sketchy proposals, some sent by Instagram direct message. One person claimed to own a car dealership, promising Youmans he could select any four vehicles on the lot. Another boasted of an old cattle rancher with $2 million waiting in a safe on a South Dakota ranch; that sounded like the plot of a bad movie.

Youmans needed help, and he signed on with Dave Baron, a Palm Springs, California–based attorney who knew Amaranthus's parents from college. The ball was parked in a bank's safe-deposit box as Baron investigated the private offers.

Ultimately, the couple opted to send the ball to the Goldin auction house, preferring a transparent process. Coincidentally, news of the rejected $3 million offer broke on the same evening that Judge was crowned the American League's Most Valuable Player.

"It's a lot of money," Judge said. "I guess he's got a better plan or thinks he can get some more, but he caught the ball. He was the one that made the play out there in left field, so it's his right to do what he wants with it. Hopefully he's making the right decision for him and his family."

Judge said that he wouldn't bid on the ball, joking that it would be "out of his price range" until his next contract was secured. The most expensive baseball ever sold at auction was Mark McGwire's 70th home run in 1998, which went for $3.05 million to Todd McFarlane, the comic book artist best known for creating the *Spawn* series.

Eight days before Christmas, Judge's 62nd sold for $1.5 million, to a collector identified only as "Joe from Wisconsin." Youmans said that he planned to use the proceeds to purchase his first home, for some international travel, and to build an automotive workshop for his father in Oregon.

Looking back on the episode, he is grateful and appreciative, but also stung by how his identity and reputation were portrayed by some members of the media. He would never be another Sal Durante, the teenager on a date who'd puffed on a couple of Camel cigarettes with Roger Maris in the Yankees' clubhouse.

"You look at Sal, and that's a very romantic story. I totally get the appeal of that," Youmans said. "I had hoped to be involved and participate in as much of the story as I could. I wanted to be a good sport, and I feel like I had a respect and appreciation for the moment. But there was just something about me that was different than Sal. I don't regret catching the ball; I'm very thankful for the money.

"But I'm just a little bit disappointed in, it was distilled down to 'catching baseball equals money.' I had hoped there would be something else."

After witnessing a dozen games in New York and Toronto, including Judge's 60th and 61st home runs, Roger Maris Jr. had peeled off the home run chase. Watching the game from his Gainesville, Florida, home, Maris used his Twitter account to announce that he considered Judge the "clean" single-season home run champion, adding that Judge is "all class and someone who should be revered." Though Judge continued to state that he considered Bonds's record valid, he thanked the Maris family for their support.

"I know it's a tough situation; it's your dad's legacy and you want to uphold that," Judge said. "Getting a chance to meet their family, they're wonderful people. Having my name next to someone who's as great as Roger Maris, Babe Ruth, and those guys, it's incredible."

When Maris had hit his 60th and 61st home runs in 1961, telegrams from fans and celebrities alike had been delivered to the home clubhouse at Yankee Stadium. The 2022 equivalent was a tweet. Celebratory words were sent across the country, prompting congratulatory messages from movie stars, Hall of Fame ballplayers, and President Joe Biden, who said: "History made, more history to make." President Bill Clinton thanked Judge "for giving baseball fans everywhere a thrilling season," and long-time Yankees fan Billy Crystal said that watching Judge's 62nd "made me feel like I was 13 all over again.

"I was such a Mantle fan, but I was thrilled that [Maris] did it," Crystal said. "I loved the fact that Roger finally did do it and became a big fan of his, and learned to appreciate his overall ability. What's missing from this [2022] chase is that there's no Mantle. There's no co-conspirator. It's interesting that this guy we're watching play is so good, and so polished. This is a finished product of so much hard work, and to make it look so easy and graceful, it's an extraordinary athlete that we're seeing."

Watching from afar, Hal Steinbrenner applauded his team's best player. "I wasn't alive in '61, but I know enough about it," he said. "Anytime you're talking about a Yankee record of that magnitude, with somebody like Roger Maris involved, it was incredible."

Even the Empire State Building lit up in Yankees pinstripes to celebrate the blast, with blue and white lights sparkling at the top of the 102-story skyscraper for sixty-two seconds. The public nods from Judge's contemporaries seemed to mean the most.

"There's no higher honor in my book," Judge said. "That's what it's always been about for me; my teammates and my peers."

Chants of "M-V-P!" greeted Judge as he took his position in right field during the next half-inning, and Judge tipped his cap, acknowledging the many fans wearing Yankees paraphernalia. Judge expressed regret that he could not achieve the milestone at home; more than 137,000 fans attended the Yanks' final three regular-season home games, hoping to witness history.

"They were booing pitchers for throwing balls, which I've never seen before," Judge said, chuckling.

The Rangers defeated the Yankees, 3–2, but the final score hardly mattered. As players returned to the visiting clubhouse, there was a long table with a black cloth in the center of the room, and dozens of small plastic cups awaiting the popping of bottles. None of the bubbly was sprayed on this occasion; this was a day for pouring and toasting, honoring Judge and Cole together. Rizzo produced an impressive Rolex watch for which the Yankees had pooled funds; an appreciative Judge immediately strapped it on his wrist.

"It was an amazing thing that I'll tell my kids about for years," said Jose Trevino. "I'm going to be able to tell that story forever. I might even get to pick an actor who's going to play me in a movie, you know what I mean? I'm sure Billy Crystal is out there right now, scheming it up. It was incredible. He deserves it, man. He works so hard, day in and day out. He just deserves it."

A bit overshadowed by Judge's 62nd, Cole had struck out nine batters over six innings, establishing a new single-season franchise record. Ron Guidry had set the previous mark of 248 during his Cy Young Award–winning season of 1978. Anthony Rizzo took command of the celebration, announcing that "Louisiana Lightning" was on the phone.

In words broadcast to the entire team over the clubhouse's Bluetooth speakers, Guidry told Cole, "I've been waiting ever since you put the Yankees uniform on for this moment, because I knew you were going to do it at some point in time. You've earned it."

"When you think about the Yankees, often times we're reminded of the legends that live in Monument Park and the accomplishments they've had," Cole said later that evening. "Even just to tie the record, let alone break it, it's a bit surreal. Obviously, on a night like tonight, it's like, 'Whoa.' That's a lot of history going on."

Judge posed for photographs on the field with friends and family, joined at times by Cole, who was basking in the afterglow of his accomplishment. Micah Parsons, a linebacker for the Dallas Cowboys, also found his way to the Judge party in shallow left field. Parsons was a professional athlete who had played his sport at the highest level, but he was a fan in this moment. Parsons produced his ticket stubs from the club level along the first base line, and Judge graciously swirled his signature with a black Sharpie marker.

"I'm just a fan of greatness," Parsons said. "He's just great at what he does. He did something in his game that took him to the next level. I just wanted to talk to him. The thing I was really excited about was, he knew who I was."

Five plastic cups still rested on the large table about an hour later, as Judge finally unbuttoned the gray jersey with NEW YORK embroidered across the front. He was only beginning to absorb the accomplishment, planning to share the moment with his family and wondering aloud about what might come next.

Judge didn't think he would be able to fully appreciate No. 62 until after the postseason, saying, "That's really our main goal and our main focus." But his teammates wanted him to soak it in: Stanton said that the team rented out a private space at their hotel, the Four Seasons Resort and Club Dallas at Las Colinas, keeping the party going for just a little bit longer.

"We all hung out," Stanton said. "We just told him, 'You got it done. Don't worry about tomorrow. You can finally take a day off, and now go get ready for the playoffs.'"

There was one game remaining on the schedule, and it felt a lot like the last day of school before summer vacation, the clubs speed-walking through nine prescribed innings. Boone toyed with the idea of having Judge serve as the designated hitter, considering his fading hopes of chasing Arraez for the batting title, but ultimately decided to let his star rest. The record would show that it was Arraez over "All Rise," .316 to .311.

Judge could live with that. He did lead the majors in runs (133), homers (62), runs batted in (131), on-base percentage (.425), slugging percentage (.686), OPS (1.111), OPS+ (211), and total bases (391), while pacing the AL with 111 walks. A television screen displaying MLB Network hung in the visiting clubhouse at Globe Life Field, and a couple of the talking heads were discussing Judge's numbers that morning, within earshot of the player himself. You didn't need an expert to tell you that these were video game statistics, produced in a season of deflated league-wide offense.

"You can look on the back of anybody's baseball card and see the stats, see the numbers, see the records and everything they break," Judge said. "Ultimately, for me, it's about those relationships you build with your teammates and the fans. I want to be remembered not only as a great teammate, but a great competitor and a friend that they can count on."

As he accepted a few more congratulations during the morning of the final regular season game, Judge made a point to seek out Kay, complimenting the announcer on his call for No. 62. Truth be told, Kay preferred his calls for Nos. 60 and 61, believing that he had rushed through No. 62 because it left the ballpark so quickly. But he was thrilled that Judge liked it.

"That meant the world to me. That was the only criticism that I cared about," Kay said. "He said, 'That was a really good call. You did a great job.' That made me happy, because he's the one who had to like it. His family has to live with it, will be connected to it for all time. The fact that he said it made me proud, and I felt that I'd done my job."

The Yankees were looking toward the playoffs, eyeing an upcoming Wild Card Game between the Cleveland Guardians and Tampa Bay Rays that would determine their next opponent, while also warily looking forward to a potential showdown with the Astros. Judge spent most of the game relaxing in the clubhouse and said that he hadn't heard the fans chanting "We want Judge!" in the ninth inning, clamoring for one more at-bat.

Judge had already closed the book on his regular season statistics. At that point, the only number he cared about was No. 28.

14

UNFINISHED BUSINESS

There were several adjectives to describe Brian Cashman's demeanor after the club's workout at Yankee Stadium, four days before the scheduled start of the American League Division Series against the Cleveland Guardians. As he paced in manager Aaron Boone's office, just outside the Yankees' clubhouse, the longtime general manager could accurately be described as furious, irate, disappointed, or distressed. He was not, however, surprised.

Cashman and Boone had just spoken via telephone with Aroldis Chapman, seeking an explanation for why the left-hander had missed a mandatory team workout in the Bronx. They gave him the benefit of the doubt; perhaps Chapman had a family emergency or some other development the club was unaware of. They reached the pitcher at his home near Miami, Florida, where the thirty-four-year-old had traveled after the regular season finale on October 5 in Arlington, Texas. That was fine; all players had the green light to skip the charter flight back to New York if desired, as long as they would be back in the Bronx for the workout.

When attendance was taken, Chapman was the team's only no-show, the only such occurrence Cashman could recall in his twenty-four years as a general manager. Chapman's confidence had been irreparably shaken, dented by the injuries and ineffectiveness that allowed Clay Holmes to take over as the club's closer. He would only travel to New York, he said, if Boone and Cashman promised to include him on the twenty-six-man ALDS roster.

"I was like, 'Are you shitting me? What did he say?'" Cashman said. "He didn't want to come back unless he was guaranteed to be on the postseason roster. We hadn't even had our meetings yet; we weren't playing for another five days. We told him we were going to go through the week and then make our decisions. As it turned out, he probably would have been on the roster."

It seemed an ignominious end to Chapman's Yankees tenure, which yielded three All-Star appearances and 153 saves. The Cuban fireballer had arrived in a trade with the Cincinnati Reds during the 2015–16 off-season, then returned after helping the Chicago Cubs win the 2016 World Series. Yet Chapman's time in New York would be remembered most for high-profile failures, particularly his stunned expression after surrendering a José Altuve home run that ended the 2017 American League Championship Series. The infected leg that had sent him to the injured list in August, after Chapman had received an ill-advised in-season tattoo, ranked a close second. "The thing of it is, we probably would have carried him," Cashman said, noting that relievers Scott Effross and Ron Marinaccio missed the playoffs due to injuries. Instead, Chapman was off the team. Months later, after signing with the Kansas City Royals, Chapman would explain the situation as a "miscommunication" and admit that he had been wrong. "When you add everything up, it's not surprising," Cashman said. "There's some questions about whether he's been all in or not for a little while. He's maintained verbally that he's in, but his actions don't match those words."

As the Yankees prepared for their most important games of the season, Aaron Judge organized one last team event, booking a private room at TAO, an upscale Asian fusion restaurant in New York City. Judge clinked a glass and made a brief speech to a packed house of teammates and staffers, attempting to pump up the battles to come.

There was thumping music as the guys munched on sushi and finger food, refusing to let him out of the building without toasting his special season once more. They would never forget the year that Judge hit 62, and they appreciated being a part of history.

"It was really, really good," said Clarke Schmidt. "It was a lot of fun, kind of like a little surprise type thing. I would say almost every guy was there. It was great to have one more team event, just being able to celebrate him. I'm sure it was an emotional time for him, so it was good to have Sam there and a lot of people who have been with him since Day 1."

The AL Division Series opened in New York on October 11, with Terry Francona's Cleveland Guardians having swept the Tampa Bay Rays in a two-game series to advance past the Wild Card round. The deciding contest between Cleveland and Tampa Bay had been an incredible fifteen-inning battle, with Cleveland's Oscar Gonzalez homering for the game's only run.

That alone put the Guardians at a disadvantage when they arrived in New York, a team that hardly homered now matched against a club that went deep more than anyone. The Yankees had pounded Cleveland during the regular season, outscoring the Guardians, 38–14, while winning five of six games.

The series seemed to be a mismatch on paper—Cleveland really was just happy to be there. Francona said that if anyone back in spring training could have guaranteed him that the Guardians would be playing in the ALDS: "Shoot, I might have jogged to New York."

The lights darkened before the first pitch of Game 1 at Yankee Stadium, leaving only shadows as a solitary figure raced across the outfield grass. The White Stripes' "Seven Nation Army" rattled the sound system as the lights came up, revealing Nick Swisher, who draped Judge's No. 99 across his back while waving a large blue flag with the interlocking "NY" logo.

Swisher was synonymous with the Yankees' 2009 World Series championship, then a switch-hitting outfielder who seemed to treat every day with the excitement of his tenth birthday party. Sure, having him essentially serve as a team mascot was a little silly, but it also felt fresh and fun, a radical departure from the traditional pomp and circumstance usually trotted out for postseason games in the Bronx.

"That was one of the coolest things I've ever done," Swisher said. "I'm out there high-fiving the West Point cadets, and they're like, 'You've got to go, bro!' Then I'm out there waving the flag, running as fast as I can on these knees now. I've still got that [moment] as one of my screen savers. How many people can say they've done that?"

In Game 1, Harrison Bader and Anthony Rizzo homered as Gerrit Cole rose to the occasion, marking his first Yankee Stadium postseason start in pinstripes. On the winter morning he set pen to paper in December 2019, agreeing to the largest contract ever issued to a free-agent pitcher, Cole would never have anticipated it might take that long to experience the thrill of a Bronx postseason crowd. The pandemic-shortened 2020 season and an all-too-brief '21 playoff run kept Cole from living his boyhood dream, but as the ovation came in loud and strong, rolling in waves from the ballpark's faraway decks, Cole reached for the bill of his cap and doffed it ever so slightly. He had done his job, and done it well.

"It was very special for me," Cole said. "The game's not over, so it's not the most comfortable time to acknowledge the crowd, but I certainly felt it and appreciated it. I thought they were in every pitch. What a wonderful experience to have them behind us."

Major League Baseball built in a scheduled off day, so the teams sat idle on a crisp and clear Thursday afternoon, awaiting their Friday-evening date. When game time arrived, no one with access to a weather forecast was surprised by the outcome: steady rain and fog arrived in the Bronx around 4:00 p.m., prompting a postponement. Given a night's rest in their New York hotel, the Guardians responded with a 4–2, ten-inning win in Game 2. The Yankees had not expected to fast-forward through the ALDS; they held too much respect for the level of competition in what Boone called "the highest level in the land." An early Giancarlo Stanton home run off Shane Bieber suggested they might blast their way to a healthy series advantage, but the Bombers' bats went quiet and a couple of costly tenth-inning bloops off the bats of José Ramírez and Oscar Gonzalez found grass. Judge did not panic, remarking, "We've had adversity throughout this whole long season on our way to winning the division. This isn't anything new to us."

Having made his postseason debut with five solid innings, Nestor

Cortes promised that the Yankees would soon "punch back." Still, it already seemed notable that Judge's historic regular season had not carried over into the playoffs. He struck out four times in Game 2 and was 0-for-8 with seven strikeouts and a walk through the first two games, hearing boos from a crowd of 47,535 at Yankee Stadium, a scene that would've been unthinkable a week prior. "Just a little late," Judge said. "When you're a little late, you're missing pitches that you usually do damage on. You're swinging at stuff that you usually don't."

Alex Rodriguez, serving as an analyst for FOX, was among those clamoring for Boone and the analytics department to remove Judge from the leadoff spot. On the air, the three-time AL MVP referred to the Yanks' lineup construction as "gimmicky baseball," saying no serious team should go into a playoff game with its best hitter hitting first.

"Babe Ruth didn't do it. Barry Bonds didn't do it," Rodriguez said. "It doesn't exist. The reason why is you want to protect [Judge]. You play chess; it's like the queen on the chessboard. You want to put the best two hitters in front, and the best two hitters behind, and protect. The Yankees are putting the worst two hitters, the eighth and ninth hitter, and it puts an enormous amount of pressure [on Judge]."

Boone seemed miserable as the series moved to Cleveland for Game 3, and it had nothing to do with A-Rod trying to fill out his lineup card. Dating to the mid-September series in Milwaukee, the manager had been carrying a dry, hacking cough; in fact, much of the traveling party seemed to be ping-ponging it around, and a few of the reporters stopped complaining about the mask mandate for media members that would remain in place through the end of the 2022 postseason. As he sat in the visiting clubhouse at Progressive Field, Boone gestured toward half-consumed bottles of DayQuil and NyQuil, promising guests to his work space that the situation was improving. It didn't seem to be, and one kindhearted writer made a habit of offering cough drops ahead of Boone's pregame availability.

"My God, he was sick forever," said Kristie Ackert of the *New York Daily News*. "I remember we were on the field in Texas and he was coming out to do a TV interview, just hacking away. I had those cough drops in my pocket and I was like, 'Please, just try this.' We get special cough drops from Ireland—they're called Jakemans, and you can get them here, but they're not as strong. The next time I saw him, he's like, 'You got any of that good stuff?'"

As he sucked on a cooling menthol lozenge, Boone claimed not to have heard whatever Rodriguez had said on the air, but Judge was out of the top spot. Judge had hit leadoff for twenty-five straight games, beginning on September 9, and now Gleyber Torres was getting a turn as the table setter. It showed how different the Yankees' lineup looked without DJ LeMahieu and Andrew Benintendi healthy, removing a pair of reliable, contact-oriented bats. Boone claimed that he "just kind of woke up on it," believing hitting second might allow Judge to settle into the game's flow. He added that, even without LeMahieu and Benintendi, the roster felt "a little more whole" than ten days prior, a factor in his decision to change the order.

Judge responded with his 63rd home run of the year, a game-tying two-run shot off right-hander Triston McKenzie in the third inning. It was Judge's 12th career postseason homer, tying him for fifth place on the franchise list with Yogi Berra and Reggie Jackson, and one of three long balls the Yankees hit that night. Yet the outcome was a 6–5 loss, which Boone described as "a gut-wrenching ending."

New York held a two-run lead in the ninth inning, but a fatiguing Wandy Peralta appeared to be on the ropes. The phone rang in the visitors' bullpen and pitching coach Matt Blake's voice crackled through the earpiece, identifying Clarke Schmidt as the choice to warm up. No one was more surprised than Clay Holmes. Boone had bypassed his All-Star closer in favor of Schmidt, handing the twenty-six-year-old rookie the most challenging assignment of his young career.

It did not go well. With runners at the corners and one out, Amed Rosario stroked a run-scoring single to left field that cut New York's lead to a run. José Ramírez reached on a bloop single that loaded the bases for Oscar Gonzalez, an affable rookie and local fan favorite who used the *SpongeBob SquarePants* theme song as his walk-up music. Still the Yankees stayed with Schmidt, who watched Gonzalez rip a two-out, two-strike single into center field, past Schmidt's last-ditch effort to swipe his glove through space.

Schmidt walked off the field, stunned; his teammates followed closely behind. Cleveland had rallied for an unlikely victory and stood nine innings from ending the Yankees' season. The choice of Schmidt spurred waves of second-guessing inside the visiting clubhouse. Sure, the injury-marred bullpen lacked the automatic, dominant options of years past; Metallica's "Enter Sandman" no longer accompanied Mariano Rivera across the outfield grass, nor could Boone call upon Chapman or Zack Britton, the saves leaders during his managerial tenure.

The club leader in games finished during the regular season was Holmes, who sustained a right shoulder strain during the series in Toronto, two days before Judge hit No. 61. The Yanks guarded him carefully, and because Holmes had thrown sixteen pitches in Game 2, Boone refused to use him on two consecutive days. That had not been communicated to Holmes, who watched from the bullpen as Schmidt tried to extinguish the flames.

"I felt like I was available to pitch," Holmes said. "Whenever my name is called, I'm ready to go out there and give it everything I've got. They asked and I said I was good to go if needed. That's how the conversation was. Those decisions aren't mine."

The situation reminded of a communication issue within the clubhouse earlier in the season, when Luis Severino had been blindsided by his assignment to the sixty-day injured list. Severino argued vehemently, insisting he'd be ready to pitch long before that date. When Cashman attempted to explain the move, pointing to a calendar, Severino had looked away. Asked about Holmes's absence, Severino said: "There shouldn't be people down in the playoffs. That's something that you guys need to ask Boone or [pitching coach Matt] Blake to see what was going on."

Boone said that he considered Holmes only for "an emergency situation," but they had no more intention of using him than the batboy. If Holmes truly was unavailable, why did the Yanks use Jonathan Loáisiga for two outs (fifteen pitches) in the seventh? Why Schmidt over more experienced choices like Miguel Castro or Domingo Germán? There were more questions than answers, and now they needed to win twice to avoid hearing them all off-season.

"I certainly believe in Aaron Boone," Cashman said. "He's paid to make difficult decisions on the run. I know a lot goes into them. Every one he makes, am I going to agree with? The answer's obviously not going to be yes. But I'm certainly not capable of managing a major-league team. There's very few people that are, and I think he's really good at it. It comes with the territory, being able to take the criticism and talking about why you make decisions."

Isiah Kiner-Falefa's defense at shortstop had developed into another concern. Boone's repeated verbal bouquets about the advanced metrics that painted Kiner-Falefa as one of the league's best glovemen felt hollow, and the eye test never quite supported what analytics like Total Runs Saved and Range Runs claimed, even before the postseason. An AL scout explained that those metrics give more weight based on the perceived difficulty of the play, and it was true that Kiner-Falefa's athletic ability allowed him to range deep into the hole and make highlight reel plays. His issue stemmed more from balls hit directly at him; the routine double-play grounder that could end an inning, and frustrated pitchers when they did not.

Kiner-Falefa agreed with the scout's take. "I make some plays that other people can't make—and I finish them," he said. "The routine ones, it was like I was telling myself, 'Don't mess it up.' It was like, 'Don't mess it up' instead of, 'Let's win the game.'"

Now, Kiner-Falefa appeared to be struggling even more under the brightest lights. He'd dove over a first-inning Josh Naylor grounder that allowed the game's first run to cross home plate, threw errantly on an Andrés Giménez grounder that could have ended the sixth inning, and lobbed a ninth-inning throw from shallow left field that allowed Myles Straw to take second base on his bloop single. Boone said he sensed Kiner-Falefa was playing tentatively, consciously trying "not to make that mistake."

Kiner-Falefa received a text message from Boone the morning of Game 4, informing him that he would not be in the starting lineup. Instead, Oswaldo Cabrera would start at shortstop, with Aaron Hicks in left field.

It was win or winter. By the seventh inning of Game 4, as waves of fatigue began to crash in his prized right arm and legs, Cole had already achieved his objective of cutting through noise and finding his postseason focus. Still, Cole dug for more, vowing to leave no ounce of adrenaline unused. Cole pumped his 110th and final pitch of the night through the strike zone, celebrating his eighth strikeout with a fist pump and a primal roar. With his team's backs against the wall, the $324 million man had delivered, leading the Yankees to a 4–2 victory.

"When they told me I was going Game 4, you know there's an opportunity to clinch or go home," Cole said. "I didn't approach the game any different. I just went out there and did my job."

Harrison Bader hit his third homer of the ALDS, a two-run shot off Cal Quantrill, while Holmes and Wandy Peralta split the final six outs. Josh Naylor homered in the fourth off Cole, an at-bat punctuated by Naylor's enthusiastic "Rock the Baby" celebration around the bases. Cole said he didn't see Naylor's antics during the game, but someone alerted Cole later, and the hurler was unimpressed.

"Yeah. Whatever. It's cute," Cole said.

The clubs jetted to New York, where fans endured an infuriating delay of 2½ hours before a worsening forecast of inclement weather prompted Major League Baseball to push Game 5 back a day. The beer and chicken buckets did brisk business on the concourses, and the players wondered if they were playing; Boone had looked up from one of his six weather-related Zoom calls to see Judge darkening the hallway of his office door, uniform jersey buttoned and eye black applied, asking: "What's going on?"

The green blob hovering over New Jersey on the radar screen looked threatening, but the conditions in the Bronx seemed playable. At one point during the delay, Cleveland outfielder Myles Straw—the same one who'd called the Yankees' faithful the "worst fan base on the planet" during their heated April series—emerged with a football, playing catch with a few hardy patrons behind the third base dugout. When the stadium fun police put a stop to that, at least something was raining down—boos.

Many of those same customers returned for Game 5, and it proved worth the wait. Stanton and Judge both homered to support Nestor Cortes's gritty effort as the Yankees sent Cleveland home with a 5–1 victory, confirming that for the third time in six years, they would travel to Houston with a trip to the World Series on the line. Stanton flipped his bat emphatically after a three-run homer off starter Aaron Civale, who recorded only one out.

"We threw the first punch, and had them chasing us the whole game," Stanton said.

When Judge clubbed a solo shot in the second inning off Sam Hentges (homer no. 64), he marched toward a television camera stationed near the first-base side of the Yankees' dugout, grabbing the interlocking "NY" on his jersey and kissing it—an uncharacteristic gesture that sparked thoughts of his pending free agency. Judge claimed that it had been for the fans, saying that he had "been watching a lot of Premier League soccer games, and I think that got the best of me."

Asked about that moment months later, Judge confirmed that he was thinking about more than the English football league system: "I think I said from day one, I wanted to end my career here and finish in pinstripes. . . . Your emotions kind of get the best of you in moments like that. I don't know if I was dropping too many bread crumbs. I think I was just giving you guys the whole loaf throughout the whole year, of where I wanted to be."

It was no surprise that the path to success would have to run through the Astros, who dominated the AL West with a 106-win campaign. Yet, already in October, the favored Cardinals, Blue Jays, Mets, Dodgers, and Braves had been dispatched by teams with fewer regular-season victories. These Yankees hoped to be the next to upset. A crowd of 48,178 deliriously filed out of Yankee Stadium, filling Babe Ruth Plaza and marching toward the elevated subway along 161st Street.

Over and over, they chanted: "We want Houston!" They would get their wish.

Roger Clemens wore denim jeans, a tight-fitting black polo shirt, and a camouflage ballcap with the Texas Longhorns' logo as he stood in the rear of the press box at Minute Maid Park, having just tossed a ceremonial first pitch across home plate. It was the top of the first inning, and the seven-time Cy Young Award winner was formulating a game plan for how the younger version of himself might have handled the Yankees' best hitter.

"Very carefully," Clemens said, with a chuckle. "Here, you could pitch him away a little bit easier than in. I'll be curious to see how both of those guys, him and Stanton, go at it with the short left field. At Yankee Stadium—even though I pitched at the old Yankee Stadium—it's still a chip shot there. The famous line from a movie I was in, *Cobb*, was: 'My sister Florence can hit the ball out of right field at Yankee Stadium.' Those guys are strong enough to hit it out anywhere. I'd be careful with him. Solo home runs are good. You want to stay away from the three-run homer."

Clemens and the Astros' pitching staff shared that opinion. Long balls with men on base seemed to be the Yankees' best chance of pulling off an upset in the American League Championship Series. As Cashman watched batting practice on the field at Minute Maid Park on the afternoon of October 19, exchanging pleasantries with Houston manager Dusty Baker and general manager James Click, he came to the unsettling realization that his team would have to play a near-perfect series to advance.

The Yankees weren't accustomed to being the underdogs, but this matchup saw them firmly ensconced in that role. Andrew Benintendi's right wrist still hadn't healed, and though DJ LeMahieu gamely insisted he could play on the fractured sesamoid bone in his right big toe, the medical staff still said he was too compromised to help. Cashman resolved that they would do their best with the personnel they had remaining.

Justin Verlander outpitched Jameson Taillon in Game 1, a 4–2 Astros win. Taking the mound in a ballpark that once played host to his childhood heroes, Taillon bobbed and weaved into the fifth inning, but nothing ever felt comfortable against the high-octane Houston lineup. He'd tried not to be fazed when he spotted Jeff Bagwell and Craig Biggio watching from the seats; in Verlander, there was a different Hall of Fame–level talent to be concerned with.

"It's a really good lineup with a ton of playoff experience," Taillon said. "It's their sixth ALCS in a row. They've played in big moments, they've played under pressure and they've seen us a good amount. You have to have everything going."

When a one-out double chased Taillon in the fifth inning, Boone chose Schmidt to extinguish the flames. It had been four days since Schmidt landed on the wrong side of a blown save in the Yanks' deflating Game 3 loss in the ALDS, and he now savored a moment of redemption, dotting a sinker that induced Kyle Tucker to hit into an inning-ending double play.

Schmidt whirled and pumped his fist, a display that tempted Boone to keep the good vibes rolling. Despite swelling his roster to thirteen pitchers for this round, the manager couldn't find the right buttons to push. Houston took control in the sixth, as Schmidt surrendered homers to Yuli Gurriel and Chas McCormick before exiting. Boone said that the Yanks "knew it was going to be a slog getting through those middle innings," and it had been.

Verlander was excellent, striking out eleven, though he wobbled early. After Judge contributed a tremendous diving catch in the first inning that robbed Alex Bregman of an extra-base hit, potentially saving two runs, Bader belted his fourth homer of the postseason. The daring deadline trade with the Cardinals, in which Cashman had shed a serviceable starter in Jordan Montgomery to bring in an outfielder who spent weeks limping around their clubhouse in a walking boot, was suddenly looking like a stroke of genius. Somewhat improbably after their grueling ALDS battle and early-morning arrival in Houston, the Yankees had a lead on Verlander.

Martín Maldonado touched Taillon for a game-tying double, but New York was set up in the third when Anthony Rizzo walked and Giancarlo Stanton smoked a double. A fly ball would have restored the advantage; instead, Josh Donaldson struck out and Matt Carpenter was caught looking—the second of four strikeouts for Carpenter, whom despite his best efforts was not ready for prime time; he was essentially trying to rehab from his foot injury against elite postseason pitching. That began a string of six consecutive strikeouts for Verlander, who held New York to just three hits.

In Game 2, the Yankees' last best chance to depart with an ALCS split rocketed off Judge's bat in the eighth inning. Judge's opposite-field drive drew a gasp from the sellout crowd at Minute Maid Park, soaring like many of the 62 home runs the slugger launched during his regular-season chase for history. Judge's teammates leapt toward the dugout's top steps; this one was destined to land in the seats, they seemed certain. But Judge felt the wind would keep it in, and soon after Kyle Tucker's spikes crunched into the warning track, the rest of the world knew for sure. The Yankees' hopes were dashed four outs later, absorbing a 3–2 loss.

It was a cruel dagger for the visitors that, according to Statcast, Judge's 345-foot fly ball would have been a home run in precisely one ballpark: Yankee Stadium. Kyle Higashioka asked for the exit velocity; told that it had been 106.3 mph, the catcher nodded and said, "I was kind of amazed it didn't go out." Giancarlo Stanton said he thought Judge's ball might have left the park if the roof had been closed; with first-pitch temperatures at an enjoyable seventy-eight degrees on a clear evening, however, there was no need for controlled conditions. "Who would have thought," Boone said. "I think the roof [being] open kind of killed us."

Yet that decision was made by Major League Baseball, not the Astros, who typically prefer the louder atmosphere of a closed roof. But the Yanks' shortcomings were not just one lifted fly ball into swirling crosswinds—rather, the greater issue was the thirty whiffs that had come from New York's lineup through eighteen innings. After striking out seventeen times in Game 1, the Yanks added thirteen in Game 2, with Houston starter Framber Valdez fanning nine.

"The idea ain't just to touch it. We've got to score," Boone said. "They're about as tough as there is to score against, but we've got to figure out a way."

The series shifted back to Yankee Stadium, where the Yankees posted an MLB-best 57-24 home record (.704) during the regular season. But these Astros were too much to contain. Boone's Game 3 walk toward the mound seemed to transpire in slow motion, each step measured across the infield grass as he approached the gaggle of Yankees clustered around Cole. The bases were loaded with none out, and seemingly with some hesitation, the manager extended his right finger to summon a fresh arm. All three runs came around to score against reliever Lou Trivino, and no return punch would come in a 5–0 loss.

Later, Boone would second-guess his decision not to stick with Cole, explaining that he'd hoped Trivino would generate weak contact to induce a double play, rather than asking Cole to try for a strikeout.

"That's one," Boone said, "where I feel like I should have stayed with Gerrit."

Ultimately, it wouldn't have mattered much, since the Yankees didn't score. Stoking memories of the combined no-hitter in June (and a preview of what the Astros would do in the World Series against the Phillies eleven days later), the Yankees were held to just one hit through the first eight innings by Cristian Javier and four relievers.

Judge went hitless in four at-bats, striking out twice, and again heard boos. It was tame compared to what Josh Donaldson was hearing in the series. Yet in Houston's bullpen, the Astros' relievers couldn't believe what they had witnessed.

"I don't understand why you would boo a guy that has given you nothing but joy, especially this year," closer Ryan Pressly said. Though the narrative of fans jeering Judge after his historic season was gaining traction, Boone said that he believed it was overblown.

"Look, he's beloved here. He knows that," Boone said. "He loves it here. I think he loves the fan base. He's one of those guys that truly isn't affected by that. He understands there's going to be moments in time that literally everyone probably experiences at some point if you wear this uniform long enough, even if you're great."

Judge reminded his teammates that their backs had been against the wall all year, "even in this postseason, especially when we went down [two games to one] to Cleveland." Bader said the Yankees faced "a mountain," but needing to win four straight against Houston felt like Everest.

In MLB history, there had been thirty-nine previous teams to fall into an 0-3 hole during a best-of-seven series. Only one emerged on the winning side: the 2004 Boston Red Sox.

Eighteen Octobers had passed since Kevin Millar prowled the Fenway Park infield during batting practice for a seemingly decided American League Championship Series, the camera-friendly Boston first baseman warning anyone who would listen: "Don't let us win tonight."

Within the Yankees' clubhouse walls, it could have easily happened on the morning of October 23, hours before Game 4 of the ALCS—because it did.

A video recapping Millar's speech, Dave Roberts's stolen base, and Boston's comeback from a staggering deficit to topple, yes, the Yankees, was distributed electronically among New York players and coaches. The video was sent by Chad Bohling, the Yankees' director of mental conditioning. It was not uncommon for Bohling to send similar clips, from different sports or walks of life; earlier in the season, players and coaches had viewed motivational wisdom from players like the late Kobe Bryant. The point was that an 0-3 hole was difficult to climb out of, but not impossible.

But the '04 Red Sox? Yuck. If only there had been a different comeback to highlight.

"I think [the message was] just the belief that they had," Boone said. "They had confidence; you see Millar, 'Don't let us win one.'"

With talk of that curse-reversing squad of "idiots" thick in the air, ESPN broadcaster Eduardo Pérez happened to be a guest in Boone's office when David Ortiz popped up on the television screen. Ortiz was wearing a Philadelphia Eagles jersey as part of an NFL pregame show, and Pérez noticed Boone—a diehard Eagles fan since childhood—had a green-and-white Brian Dawkins throwback jersey hanging near his private restroom. On a lark, Pérez placed a FaceTime call, and Big Papi answered.

"He was like, 'Dude! You guys have got to do what we did back then,'" Pérez said. "He said, 'Just keep the energy, one game at a time. That's what [Ortiz] told [Boone], but with his passion, which I definitely cannot replicate. But he just said, 'Hey man, just go play and have fun.' So what, basically.'" So what? David Cone had retired by 2004, but he played with key members of that club, like Derek Jeter, Jorge Posada, Bernie Williams, and Mariano Rivera. As he stood on the field at Yankee Stadium, preparing for a YES Network hit, Cone said that drawing upon the '04 Red Sox for inspiration probably wouldn't have gone over well with his pals.

"I know there's some people in Red Sox Nation laughing right now,"

Cone said. "I understand rallying the troops and the intent. There's not a lot of examples down 3-0. I think there's some irony there that's not to be missed."

Of the motivational tactic, Jeter said: "I still don't like to talk about [the 2004 ALCS] myself. It makes me sick just thinking about it."

Added Posada: "Different times, different attitudes, and definitely different type players."

Ultimately, the Yankees could not "slay the dragon," as Boone had quipped earlier in the season about their likely Houston–New York ALCS matchup—unlike in '17 and '19, they were not even able to win a single game. Houston defeated the Yanks for the ninth time in eleven games, including the 6–5 loss in Game 4. For the third time in six years, the Astros were toasting the final out of the Yanks' season.

"I said we needed to slay that dragon. We haven't done it yet, and that hurts," Boone said. "It's also a motivating factor to try to continue to get better. I looked at that Astros team, and whether it was their four starters they were rolling out there, or the depth and health of their bullpen—I felt they were at their best."

Cashman said the abrupt ending "sucked for us all, and for our fans and ownership the worst of all." Judge also did not mince words in the aftermath, sticking to an all-too-familiar script. "If we're not the last team standing, it doesn't matter what you do or what happened. It's a failure," Judge said. "We came up short. We didn't finish our goal."

On a brisk evening that started about ninety minutes late due to rain, the Yankees built an early three-run lead against Lance McCullers Jr., snapping a fourteen-inning scoreless streak that dated to the fourth inning of Game 2. But Nestor Cortes exited in the third inning with a groin injury and, though Harrison Bader continued his tremendous October with a fifth postseason home run, Gleyber Torres committed an error on a critical seventh-inning double-play ball that opened the door for two runs.

Torres said the Yanks "missed too many opportunities," and though Hal Steinbrenner concurred, he wondered how the series might have looked if Benintendi or LeMahieu could have helped against the dominant Astros pitching staff. They might have scored more runs, but no one could definitively state that Benintendi and LeMahieu alone would have changed the outcome.

"It's difficult, in any sport, to roll into the playoffs not healthy," Steinbrenner said. "We just were a different team in the second half of the season than the first. I don't say it every year because injuries are part of the game, but this year, they had a significant impact. And you can't deny that if you're going to try to figure out what the heck happened."

In a year when so much of the Yankees' world revolved around Judge, from his chase to shatter Roger Maris's single-season AL home run record to his candidacy for AL MVP to his unsettled contract situation (heck, even the team's regular-season win total was ninety-nine), the final at-bat of the autumn fittingly belonged to Judge. Assuming his familiar, imposing stance, the game's most recognizable slugger was the team's last hope of staving off winter. But the clock had already struck midnight in New York, and soon it would, too, for the 2022 Yankees.

Judge's mighty cut produced only a routine tapper back to Pressly, who jogged the ball toward first base and completed the play with an underhand flip. Judge planted his right foot on first base, then glanced over his left shoulder as the Astros began celebrating on the field—his field.

Though, technically, it wasn't anymore: for the first time in his professional career, Judge was untethered, about to test free agency. In the home clubhouse, Judge referred to his Yankees tenure several times in the past tense, a jarring departure for the ultimate team-first player.

"Getting a chance to wear the pinstripes and play right field at Yankee Stadium, that's an incredible honor," Judge said that night. "I definitely didn't take it for granted at any point. I always checked myself pregame when I'd say a little prayer, I'd kind of look around the stadium and pinch myself. There's very few individuals who get a chance to run on that field and play in front of the fans."

The postseason had gone poorly for Judge, and he had perhaps been gassed by the grueling chase for the record, though he'd never admit it. Boone later said that the chase could have fatigued Judge more than he had let on. Over nine postseason games, Judge batted .139 (5-for-36) with two homers and three RBIs, going hitless with a walk in the ALCS finale.

"It's possible, sure," Boone said. "It's impossible to say that. There was talk, did he wear down at the end? I think he was in a good place physically. It's fair to at least ask the question. The standard Aaron set, obviously we'd have all loved for him to have a dominant postseason."

He was 1-for-16 against Houston pitching; Cashman used that performance as a reference point when discussing his later statements concerning the organization valuing "process over results," explaining why wholesale changes to the coaching staff and analytics department would not be made in the wake of the Astros sweep.

"Is Aaron Judge a bad player because his postseason wasn't good? No," Cashman said. "Ultimately, I don't think people recognize the slippery slopes of the postseason. Our process led to the second-best team in the American League, one of the best teams in baseball. We're proud of that. It's nothing to be ashamed of. People want to call it an excuse that injuries prevented us from reaching the highest level. I'm not saying if we were fully capable that we would have gotten by the Astros, but we would have had a better shot."

During Cashman's first decade with the Yankees organization, he had watched George Steinbrenner impetuously fire talented personnel as punishment for the failure to win a championship; Bobby Cox and Pat Gillick had each collected paychecks with the red, white, and blue top hat logo, for example, and both were in the Hall of Fame because they'd helped other teams to the top of the mountain. Cox and Gillick, Cashman said, "had great processes that didn't play out in the time frame, and we didn't pay attention to what was real."

"New York is a tough grading system," Cashman said. "The only A you get is if you finish with that trophy in hand. Otherwise, you get an F. There's nothing in between."

Steinbrenner said there was no debate about Boone, who would return for a sixth year as manager. As he eyed the coaching staff for 2023, Cashman similarly refused to give in to the bloodlust of the fan base. He recalled watching a Buffalo Bills football game on television in the weeks after he'd made his "process over results" comment, thinking: "If you took eight prominent guys off this Bills team right now, are they still going to be flying as high as they could fly?" The answer was obviously no. "So I don't know why people are like, 'Oh, you can't say that!' It's a fact. We had a great team that significantly improved on the previous year's team, as part of our process. We had a shot, and I'm proud of that."

That came as little consolation to Judge, who fumed that his team had come to the World Series' doorstep for a third time, only to be turned away. He hated the idea that his narrative, thus far, was comprised of great regular season numbers but no championship rings. When Ruth hit 60 homers, the 1927 Yankees had won a championship. When Maris hit 61 homers, the 1961 Yankees did the same. Judge's 62 homers deserved a better ending.

He paused when asked if he still wanted to be a Yankee for life, as he'd stated during the spring. Judge was now in negotiating mode, and his measured response hardly inspired confidence.

"Yeah, I've been clear about that since I first wore the pinstripes," Judge said, annoyance evident in his tone. "But we couldn't get something done before spring training. I'm a free agent. We'll see what happens."

Judge stood near his locker and shook hands with club staffers and numerous reporters; Kristie Ackert of the *New York Daily News* said it felt "almost like a wedding, or a funeral with a reception."

"That silence in a clubhouse after a loss is probably the worst feeling a ballplayer can have," Judge said. "You don't know what to say, you don't know what to do. All of a sudden, you're going from preparing for the most important game of your life to now you're done and your offseason begins. You try to reflect on the game and what you could have done differently, and could this have changed the outcome? But then it's straight to work."

On his way out the door, Judge stopped in Boone's office. Boone relayed his appreciation for Judge and how their relationship had grown. Judge nodded.

Unprompted, Boone asked Judge about the Opening Day press conference, when Cashman had revealed the financial figures of the rejected contract extension. Judge made it clear that he was still upset about how it all went down; Boone understood. Boone told Judge he hoped to manage him again in 2023, saying he couldn't think of a better guy to lead the team. Judge appreciated that; they shook hands and hugged.

With that, Judge exited, following the maze of hallways that led to the players' parking lot deep under the right-field grandstand. He passed the club's twenty-two retired uniform numbers, pinstriped circles affixed to bricks on a white wall. There was Yogi Berra's No. 8, Whitey Ford's No. 16, Thurman Munson's No. 15, and—yes—Roger Maris's No. 9.

Eyes fixed straight ahead, Judge wondered if he was traversing those halls for the final time.

"It weighed on me, for sure," Judge said. "You never know what the future holds."

15

NEW YORK OR NOWHERE

Ripping through blue skies at approximately five hundred miles per hour, Aaron Judge peered out the oval-shaped passenger window of a private jet, pointed toward California upon takeoff from Tampa International Airport. They were somewhere west of San Antonio, Texas, and baseball's most coveted free agent was trying to relax, taking in the scenery from the cream-and-mahogany cabin of a chartered Cessna Citation X. It was proving to be a futile exercise; this flight, and the decisions stemming from it, would have a seismic effect on his future.

It had been more than six weeks since Judge tapped the slow grounder on the Yankee Stadium turf that ended the American League Championship Series, beginning what figured to be the most tumultuous off-season of his career. The Houston Astros had been crowned World Series champions yet again, dispatching the Philadelphia Phillies in an entertaining six-game Fall Classic, and one day later Judge had become an unrestricted free agent.

As expected, Judge had been named the AL's Most Valuable Player, an announcement made on November 18. Judge received twenty-eight of thirty possible first-place votes from members of the Baseball Writers' Association of America, with Shohei Ohtani of the Los Angeles Angels of Anaheim receiving the other first-place votes (both came from the

Los Angeles chapter). It was a vote that had not been nearly as close as expected, despite Ohtani finishing with 34 home runs and a 2.33 ERA in 28 starts. Joel Sherman of the *New York Post*, one of two MVP voters from the New York chapter, put it like this: "Imagine having the year Ohtani had and yet, when asked what you remember about 2022, his name will not be the first evoked. This was Judge's year."

Yordan Alvarez of the Houston Astros placed third as Judge became the first Yankee to be crowned an MVP since Alex Rodriguez in 2007, and the first Yanks outfielder to win one since Mickey Mantle in 1962. On the night the MVP was announced, Judge had been in New York City, finalizing details for his ALL RISE Foundation's charity gala, held underneath the marble columns and soaring ceilings of Cipriani 42nd Street. He received the news while seated in a private movie theater, holding Samantha's hand as Patty and Wayne looked on with pride.

(That the video call would transpire from a venue usually utilized for popcorn-munching summer blockbusters was an amusing coincidence, considering Vladimir Guerrero Jr.'s spring training boast about how the rest of the division "would see the movie.")

"I was extremely nervous," Judge said. "You're going up against Yordan Alvarez, one of the top premier hitters in this game, and Shohei Ohtani is by far one of the best players on this planet. You never want to assume anything. Both of those guys had incredible years, and it's been fun competing with them over the years."

Judge was promised his hardware, which he would claim from the New York chapter of the BBWAA at their annual dinner in January. Now he needed to secure his next contract. The Yankees had been more than transparent, identifying retaining Judge as their top priority. One day after the conclusion of the ALCS, Hal Steinbrenner and Brian Cashman had spoken directly with Judge, with Steinbrenner telling Judge how important it was that he remain with the club. Judge and his agent, Page Odle, received an eight-year, $304 million proposal from the Yankees, one year longer and with a higher average annual value than the extension rejected in the spring. That offer would soon swell to eight years and $320 million.

Told that Judge liked to spend most of his off-season in Tampa,

Steinbrenner invited the slugger for a one-on-one, face-to-face meeting at the owner's home. Within five minutes of Judge's entry, Steinbrenner laid it on thick, just in case there was any lack of clarity about the team's position.

"You're not a free agent, as far as I'm concerned," Steinbrenner told Judge. "You're going to be a Yankee for life. We're going to get this deal done."

Judge felt his heart leap, but he had kept his poker face, playing it cool.

"When he offered for me to come over and sit down with him, really start to build that relationship, that meant a lot to me," Judge said. "When I talk with our team, that's what I say. I want to come here and be part of your family. Hal, from the very beginning, wanted to do that and reached that olive branch out for us to build something here."

They talked for about sixty minutes that day, and Judge stated that if he returned, he wanted to be in contention for a championship every year: "Not only just getting into the playoffs. I want to be the driving force of a team to beat."

Steinbrenner promised Judge that the organization had the financial resources to satisfy him and "make other things happen," with the front office already eyeing flame-throwing lefty Carlos Rodón. Judge also suggested that the Yankees re-sign outfielder Andrew Benintendi, whose pinstriped cameo had been cut short by injury. Judge called that meeting with Steinbrenner "a great sign," but he had not been ready to press pen to paper.

After coming this far through the process and exceeding all reasonable expectations for a contractual walk year, Judge did not want to leave unchecked boxes in the free-agent period. Besides, the wining and dining was the most fun part. The Yankees did not sit on their hands, making their first off-season move by re-signing Anthony Rizzo to a two-year, $34 million deal. Rizzo was one of Judge's closest friends on the team; he and his wife, Emily, had grown close to the Judges.

"I wasn't recruiting as hard as you would think," Rizzo said. "It was really, 'What's going to make you happy?' It was just kind of being more of a friend throughout the process instead of a teammate. I was a little bit worried just like everyone else, but you've got to do what makes you happy and what's going to be ultimately best for you. I did send him a couple of pictures of our dogs together, because we both have Dachshunds, saying, 'We can't break them up.'"

Technically speaking, Cashman was a free agent, too, his contract as general manager having expired on Halloween. As they had five years prior, he and Steinbrenner operated on a handshake agreement. Now an at-will employee, Cashman checked his bank statement on November 15 and was pleased to see a direct deposit, as usual. Cashman and Steinbrenner would delay hammering out a new contract for the GM until the team's more pressing business was settled; specifically, Judge.

Cashman acknowledged that Judge was exactly what the franchise needed in the present and future, calling him "our best player." They had just been gleeful passengers on Judge's "magic carpet ride" of a 62-homer campaign, and desperately wanted to catch the next flight. But Cashman stopped short of predicting an outcome, recalling his summer days carrying buckets of ammonia and oversize brushes to muck out stalls on his family's farm.

"I grew up in Kentucky. I wouldn't handicap anything," Cashman said. "The only one who really knows or can predict how it will play out is Aaron Judge."

And Judge was keeping everyone guessing. Like a certain record-setting right fielder, NBC's *The Tonight Show* owned ties to both coasts. The Johnny Carson, Jay Leno, and all-too-brief Conan O'Brien iterations were rooted in California, but when Jimmy Fallon took the reins, the venerable late-night program moved its studios back to New York City and Rockefeller Center's Studio 6B, where it had resided through Judge's entire career in pinstripes.

The program counted numerous Yankees fans on staff, including Fallon, who frequently joined *Saturday Night Live* maven Lorne Michaels to attend games in the front row behind home plate at Yankee Stadium. It was more difficult to blend in than it had been for his Bryant Park appearance in May 2017, but Judge gave it a try, surprising shoppers at the MLB Store on Sixth Avenue as part of a "Celebrity Photobomb" segment.

Dressed as an umpire, Judge worked home plate behind Fallon, who wore Yankees pinstripes and a catcher's mask. Shoppers were invited to have pictures taken against a backdrop that appeared to be Yankee Stadium's batter's box, only to have their shock captured when Judge—sporting a comically oversized chest protector from the 1970s—removed his umpire's mask.

Judge and Fallon argued over imaginary balls and strikes as a woman covered her mouth in disbelief, gushing: "No way! I'm shaking right now!" A man gawked at Judge, offering: "Are you kidding me right now?" Two young boys, each wearing No. 99 shirts, faced off in the batter's box as Judge looked on. Fallon called a "strike," prompting Judge to bark: "That's clearly a ball." The younger boy, stunned, pointed to Judge wordlessly. Another couple didn't even need Judge to remove the mask; the sound of his voice calling "Ball four" prompted a young lady to drop the bat and shriek. Two other young ladies were distracted as the catcher and plate umpire took selfies; one offered Judge a hug, remarking: "Thank you for everything you've done for New York City."

Was the *Tonight Show* appearance an indication that Judge remained in an Empire State of mind, or was it a last hurrah? Fans were left to wonder.

The Giants were also curious; Farhan Zaidi would not speak in specifics, but he didn't need to. Judge remained the talk of baseball as the general managers' meetings opened on the Las Vegas Strip in early November, with decision-makers for all thirty teams pacing the hallways of the massive Conrad Las Vegas at the Resorts World complex. While tourists fed their hard-earned dollars into pinging slot machines on the casino floor, hoping against long odds for life-changing riches, the San Francisco GM was gauging opportunities to spend an allocated fortune. There had been a published report that the Giants were prepared to outbid any club for Judge's services, and Zaidi hardly dampened that.

"I think, from a financial standpoint," Zaidi said, "there's nobody that would be out of our capability to meet what we expect the contract demands will be."

That had been catnip for Judge's camp, who would schedule a two-day, cross-country journey to meet with the Giants. Three days before Thanksgiving, the Judges enjoyed a group private-chef dinner at the posh Gotham Club, where they were introduced to a sommelier from Napa, then took a tour of Oracle Park. Judge asked detailed questions during the visit; he could envision splashing a few opposite-field drives into McCovey Cove, and the Giants produced studies that showed their ballpark—once a pitcher's paradise—now seemed to play neutral. The Giants just needed the right guy; San Francisco's leading home run hitter in 2022 was Joc Pederson, who had hit 23 long balls. No Giant had hit 30 homers in a season since Barry Bonds in 2004.

As the visit concluded, Judge opted to walk through the front doors of the St. Regis Hotel, where a woman recorded a thirteen-second, TMZ-style video clip. Judge told her that he was in town to visit family and friends, then winked, footage that MLB Network soon aired. The Giants weren't sure what it meant, and neither were the Yankees.

"I felt, for a long time, we were flying blind," Cashman said. "I could not get a feel for where things were at."

Judge had never shied away from his roots and maintained many ties to his hometown of Linden, California. Though he spent most of his time on the East Coast, Judge's parents, Patty and Wayne, still preferred the Golden State. Mom and Dad insisted that they did not want to sway Judge's decision, but Judge could sense that they were interested in having their son, Samantha, and any future grandchildren within the same time zone.

"I would tell them, 'Well, what do you guys think?'" Judge revealed later. "They said: 'Well, we don't want to tell you.' They've met a lot of great people with the Yankees; workers on the concession stands, front-office people, families. They voiced their opinion about that, and they also said it would be nice to have you a little closer to home."

The Giants attempted to tug on those heartstrings, setting up a meet and greet with former infielder Rich Aurilia, who had been Judge's favorite player as a ten-year-old. The team connected Judge's camp with Golden State Warriors point guard Steph Curry, though a plan to have the stars meet fizzled when the Warriors' charter flight from New Orleans was delayed. Instead, Curry and Judge settled for swapping text messages, which Curry later said was his way of "doing my part as a loyal Red Sox fan"—Curry, who grew up in North Carolina but rooted for David Ortiz and the 2004 Red Sox, even had his bachelor party at Fenway Park in 2011.

Barry Bonds was also scheduled for a surprise visit, but Bonds tested positive for COVID-19 and had to cancel. "Would I bet on him? Hell yes," Bonds said. "It's going to be a very interesting negotiation. I just hope we win." Once the ballpark visit had concluded, San Francisco executives showed Judge and Samantha some of the nicer neighborhoods in the area, hoping to breathe life into Judge's long-shelved dreams. As he'd recount, Judge had been a student at Linden High School when he'd once predicted that within a decade, he'd be married to Samantha and playing for the Giants. One had already come true, and now the second was being offered. The Giants' nine-year proposal rang in at $360 million, and Judge was presented with a difficult decision.

"I want to win," Judge said. "I want to be in a winning culture and be on a team that's committed to winning, not only for the remainder of my playing career, but I wanted a legacy to live on with any organization."

The Yankees could fulfill both; though they hadn't been to a World Series since 2009, Judge had participated in the postseason during each of his six full seasons in the majors, and New York's rich tradition was second to none. He'd just spent an entire year chasing the ghosts of Babe Ruth and Roger Maris; clearly, he needed no introduction to Monument Park. There was also the ever-rarer appeal of spending his entire career with one franchise. Jeter had done it, as had Jorge Posada, Mariano Rivera, and Bernie Williams. But Andy Pettitte had briefly been a Houston Astro, and Judge recalled other oddities that didn't look quite right, like Jimmy Rollins playing with the Los Angeles Dodgers and Wade Boggs kissing home plate at Tropicana Field after that three thousandth hit with the Tampa Bay Devil Rays.

The Giants loomed large for other reasons. Zaidi laid out a scenario where Judge would be a building block of a perennial contender. San Francisco was one year removed from a 107-win season, having fallen to the Los Angeles Dodgers in a five-game National League Division Series. Gabe Kapler's third year at the helm had gotten off to a promising start, with the Giants winning 37 of their first 64 games, but a second-half slide left them with an 81-81 record—good only for third place in the NL West, and on the outside looking in for postseason play despite the expanded playoff picture. The Giants could celebrate rich history of their own, the franchise of Willie Mays, Willie McCovey, Orlando Cepeda, and Bonds. They'd won three World Series since the Yankees' last, celebrating titles in 2010, 2012, and 2014—teams that had triumphed during Judge's formative years.

"It was tough, because you're hearing from so many different teams," Judge said. "You've got media talking about this and that, and you've got friends telling you what they want you to do, especially back home in California."

Major League Baseball's Winter Meetings opened at San Diego's Manchester Grand Hyatt on the afternoon of December 4, and some big names were beginning to come off the free-agent board. Star pitcher Jacob deGrom had agreed to leave the New York Mets in favor of a five-year, $185 million deal with the Texas Rangers, who were shaping up to have a much better staff in 2023 than the Yankees faced in their final series of the regular season.

The Mets, steered by no-holds-barred billionaire Steve Cohen, would respond by signing American League Cy Young Award winner Justin Verlander away from the Houston Astros with a two-year, $86.7 million contract. There was big money for the taking, and Judge was positioned perfectly to grab a huge chunk. Cashman had said that the 62-homer season had put Judge in line for "a pot of gold." He was about to find out just how large the prize at the end of the rainbow could be.

As the sport's movers and shakers navigated the four-star lodgings overlooking north San Diego Bay, Judge and his wife appeared on the sidelines at Raymond James Stadium in Tampa, Florida, taking in the Tampa Bay Buccaneers' Monday-night game against the New Orleans Saints. Judge wore the red, black, and white No. 13 jersey of Bucs wide receiver Mike Evans, returning a favor after Evans had been photographed sporting Judge's No. 99 after the 62nd homer.

In the end zone tunnel, Judge exchanged handshakes and a hug with quarterback Tom Brady, who asked, "Do you want to play tight end for us tonight?" Judge laughed, then enjoyed watching Brady steer the Bucs to a 17–16, come-from-behind win.

Unbeknownst to anyone in the building, Brady only had six games remaining in his storied NFL career; Judge still had plenty of tomorrows to ready for. Joined by a group of current and former teammates that included Nestor Cortes, Michael King, Corey Kluber, and Mike Tauchman, Judge revealed little regarding his free agency.

"It was super unplanned," Cortes said. "I had come into Tampa for an [autograph] signing and I shot him a text, like, 'Hey A.J., I'm in Tampa, I don't know if you're here.' He goes: 'Yeah, I'm coming to the Bucs game tomorrow, if you want to come.' He sent me the tickets that night. I didn't ask him about [the free agency]; I wanted to respect his decision and space. I wanted him to make the right decision for him and his family."

"I didn't want to bother him about it," King said. "I feel like, at that time, the only conversations he was having were about that. It would be nice to go to a football game and not even think about free agency. There was no chance I was going to bring it up, because I didn't want to put him in an even more awkward situation where he'd have to lie to me or beat around the bush."

The group had no idea that one of the long-shot clubs hoping to obtain Judge's services played their home games just a few miles away, across the Howard Frankland Bridge in St. Petersburg. The Rays—yes, *those* Rays—offered a proposal for Judge, projecting him as the missing piece to help generate attendance at Tropicana Field. He already lived in the area, and if Judge played for the Rays, they could draw enough fans to help save baseball in St. Pete.

Judge appreciated the offer, but ultimately passed; playing eighty-one games on artificial turf held little appeal.

So Judge wasn't going to play for Tampa Bay, but the Yankees' confidence in re-signing their superstar was shaken by the publication of a *Time* article, celebrating Judge as the publication's 2022 Athlete of the Year. The piece contained Judge's sharpest quotes yet regarding the rejected $213.5 million offer in the spring, where he said that he felt the negotiation tactic had been intended to "turn the fans against me, turn the media on me." Judge later acknowledged that he "was upset because there is a difference of memory, I think, in when things were said about when they'd release things."

As the *Time* quotes made the rounds, Judge was thinking about Hawaii, where he and Samantha had planned an anniversary vacation for that week. Their packing was interrupted by a phone call from his agents, who told him about a new offer he should check out in person. The Padres were willing to foot the bill for a private jet, and Judge agreed to change his plans. Aware of a report that Judge was flying toward San Diego, Boone sat on a couch in the Yankees' suite at the Grand Hyatt, an observer as Cashman and his lieutenants worked the phones and tapped on laptops.

The Yankees had no meeting set with Judge, so if he was coming to town, it was for someone else. The manager sensed a knot forming in his stomach.

"I just didn't have this great feeling. It was like, 'Where is this going?'" Boone said.

It was 2:20 p.m. on the West Coast when Jon Heyman, a *New York Post* columnist and MLB Network insider, tapped out a tweet that rattled the sports universe: "Arson Judge appears headed to Giants."

The Yankees' command center flashed into crisis mode. Boone had returned to his room for a quick shower, preparing to put on a crisp blue shirt and houndstooth sport coat for a previously scheduled meeting with the media. He scanned his messages and hurriedly dialed Cashman, asking with panic if the report was true.

"I've got no idea," Cashman replied. Cashman asked Boone if it had come from a verified account. Boone noted that Heyman had misspelled Judge's first name as "Arson," in what was likely an iPhone autocorrection, but it otherwise appeared to be legitimate.

Cashman pondered dialing managing general partner Hal Steinbrenner, in what would have amounted to a "911" call. Instead, Cashman spoke with Judge's agent, Odle, who wasted no words: "It's bullshit. It's not true." Cashman breathed a sigh of relief, calling Boone and telling him they were still in play. The mood in the war room dipped from code-red panic back to its usual level of general anxiety.

Seven minutes passed before Heyman retracted the tweet, announcing: "Giants say they have not heard on Aaron Judge. My apologies for jumping the gun."

"I heard that he was going to the Giants from a couple of people, so I thought it was good enough," Heyman said. "It was an error to go that quickly with it."

Hopes of retaining Judge were still alive, but the Yanks' spirits were glum. "Did we lose him?" one longtime staffer concernedly asked in the Grand Hyatt lobby. That prompted a shrug, though the wind seemed to be blowing in that direction. Cashman also sensed that time was short, especially when word of San Francisco's nine-year offer came in. Where there was smoke, there was usually fire—and, sometimes, arson.

"I was nervous," said Gerrit Cole, whose brother-in-law is the Giants' Brandon Crawford. "Obviously, he charmed the Giants; shocker, he charms everybody. Brandon said that the meeting went well. I tried to tune out the noise, but that was quite loud. Yeah, I was sweating with the rest of us a little bit."

Said Anthony Rizzo: "I was texting with one of the guys, and they were like, 'I think he's gone.' I was like, 'What?' It had been a few days since we'd exchanged texts or calls, and I was just off the Internet that day. I didn't see any of those reports, so I just called Aaron. Then I saw the reports, so I kind of felt like an idiot."

New York's offer still stood at eight years when Judge's jet touched down in San Diego, with passengers disembarking around 4:15 p.m. local time. Judge was hungry; he asked his agents if they had time to swing by In-N-Out Burger. There had been no Wi-Fi service on the flight; Judge clicked his phone out of airplane mode and discovered it had filled with voicemails and text messages.

"People were saying, 'We're going to miss you, have fun,'" Judge said. "I was like, 'Have fun? I just took a flight. What are they talking about? I'll be back.' It was a weird couple of hours."

Reporters eyed the front doors at the Grand Hyatt warily, believing that Judge and his agents might enter at any moment. Two decades earlier, Alex Rodriguez might have shaken things up with a grand entrance, but those photo opportunities weren't Judge's style.

Instead, the American League's Most Valuable Player was hustled to a clandestine three-hour meeting at Petco Park with the Padres, who surprised Judge and Odle by loosely discussing the framework of a deal that would best the offers on the table from the Yankees and Giants—a $414 million package spread over fourteen years, the extra seasons tacked on as a spurious attempt to reduce the immediate luxury tax hit.

The Padres were pivoting after missing their top target in shortstop Trea Turner, who went to the Philadelphia Phillies. San Diego had the most years and dollars on the table, figures that Judge said left his head "spinning."

Some speculated that Judge only met with the Padres to build leverage, but San Diego GM A. J. Preller refuted that, saying, "We wouldn't have taken the meeting if we thought there was no chance. We went into that meeting just open-minded, kind of seeing what was going to happen. From both sides, we talked about our situation, what we were looking to do, and hear what may be important to him. It really didn't progress much past that."

There were surely worse fates than spending the next decade in Southern California. Still, as Judge toured the Padres' clubhouse, weight room and batting cages, he felt that accepting the San Diego offer would tarnish his legacy in the name of cold hard cash.

"In my heart, I knew where I wanted to be," Judge said. "Going through this process was a valuable lesson. It was a valuable tool to go through and see what other organizations are about. I feel like maybe I might have kicked myself if I didn't go through the process. Going through it eventually helped me come to a better answer and a clearer answer, which was that I belong in New York."

While the Padres executed their sneak attack, the Yankees still fumbled around in the dark. They had no idea that Judge was at Petco Park (if they had, club brass could have walked the nine blocks to intercept him) and were trusting media reports for details on San Francisco's offer. Boone recalled trudging out for what he described as a "somber" dinner that evening with Matt Daley, Jay Darnell, Jim Hendry, and Tim Naehring, all valued members of the club's front office. Boone's mind went to an ugly place; he'd noted during the meal that the Yankees were scheduled to open the 2023 season against the Giants. The baseball veterans shuddered at the thought of Judge standing on Yankee Stadium's third-base line for pregame introductions, clad in orange and black.

"I'm pretty optimistic by nature, but I was worried," Boone said.

The bill was about to arrive at their table, and Boone asked: "Should I call him?" The others nodded and replied: "Yes!"

Boone dialed Judge's number, and was pleased when Judge answered: "Hey, Skip." As he'd done after Game 4 of the ALCS, Boone reiterated how much he felt Judge meant to the organization and him personally. Judge valued the respect that Boone showed, saying that it "really spoke volumes" and would weigh into his final decision. As they concluded the call, Boone asked Judge not to agree to any deal without circling back to give Steinbrenner a chance to match an offer. Judge promised that he would.

"I wasn't going to wake up in the morning and see him with another team, having not touched base with him one more time," Boone said.

The iconic image of a baseball closer is Mariano Rivera jogging through the bullpen gates at Yankee Stadium, No. 42 stitched across the hurler's back as some fifty thousand fans go wild. There is no video of Hal Steinbrenner parking a rented vehicle in a highway rest area somewhere in the mountainous region between Milan and the French border, but it was no less of a save situation.

Nine hours ahead in Italy, Steinbrenner was vacationing with his wife, Christina. It had been a memorable trip, including an audience with Pope Francis. Yet Cashman had encouraged Steinbrenner to take an active role in this particular negotiation, and Steinbrenner's thoughts were an ocean away. Sensing that negotiations were trending in the wrong direction, Steinbrenner began sending text messages directly to Judge.

"What's the holdup? What's it going to take to get this to the finish line?" Steinbrenner wrote in one.

Steinbrenner sent more, telling Judge, "It doesn't matter the time. Give me a call." Back and forth they went for about three hours, when Steinbrenner pulled off the road, taking in the gorgeous snowcapped vistas of Mont Blanc while scanning for cell service.

"I don't know why, but I just felt like something wasn't going right," Steinbrenner said.

It was around 3:00 a.m. on the West Coast; Judge had arrived in Linden about a half hour earlier, having flown from San Diego to Stockton, California. He took the call in a quiet nook of his parents' home. For about twenty minutes, he and Steinbrenner spoke without interference, just as they had weeks prior in Tampa.

Steinbrenner asked Judge, point-blank: "Do you want to be a Yankee?"

Judge affirmed that he did, as he had maintained since spring training. Steinbrenner continued: "You've just got to talk to me. I want to know, what's important to your parents, your wife and you? What is the most important thing?"

Judge and Samantha had gone down that road many times over the previous weeks; Judge felt in his heart that he belonged in New York, where he said that he had "unfinished business," but he didn't volunteer that. In his conversation with Steinbrenner, Judge mentioned the ninth year, stating his belief that he would be a productive player through the 2031 season.

"I've gotten a chance to know some athletes that are playing in their forties; I feel like I could play through my 40s," Judge said. "But for me, I want to be at the top of my game for my whole career. I don't want to come here and be a liability at the end of my career, where it's, 'Where are we going to put this guy? How can we move him around to hide him?' I want to continue to make an impact, so I thought nine years was the right amount of time." Steinbrenner said: "We want you here. If nine years is what it takes, then it's nine years. Let's get it done."

That was it: there would still need to be physicals taken and reams of paperwork sifted through, but Judge would be a Yankee for life. "It came down to me and Hal getting on the phone and talking about some things," Judge said. "I think I could have probably finished free agency in two days if I would have just talked to him twice."

Steinbrenner said that he sensed Judge was "very grateful and emotional" as they finally found common ground. As Judge and Steinbrenner concluded the call, Steinbrenner had one more important thought to share.

"Thurman Munson was my favorite player growing up, and I want to make you a captain, just like he was," Steinbrenner said.

Judge said that he was "lost for words," his mind racing through the annals of the Yankees' rich tradition. As someone drafted and developed within the franchise, he'd learned early on about the lineage that he was about to join.

"I don't think I said anything; it felt like five minutes, but it was probably only a couple of seconds," Judge said. "I was just pretty taken aback."

Judge hugged and kissed Samantha, then found his parents. "I woke them up; I said, 'I've got something you'll want to hear,'" Judge said.

There was one more phone call to make as Steinbrenner tested the limits of his international calling plan. Steinbrenner reached Cashman at 3:37 a.m. Pacific time, telling his general manager, "We got it done."

Steinbrenner's vacation had one day remaining; he intended to enjoy it. Now it was Cashman's turn to take the ball, staying up through the night hammering out contractual details with Odle and his team.

"If I'm acting a little off," Cashman said the next morning, "it's because I am off."

Farhan Zaidi, the Giants general manager, had also experienced a sleepless night. Tossing and turning in his hotel room, Zaidi heard his phone buzz at around 5:00 a.m. with a text message. He feared bad news, and for the Giants, it was: Judge's representatives were thanking teams for their offers, providing a heads-up that he had decided to return to the Yankees.

Zaidi said he was happy for Judge and his family, and disputed a suggestion that Judge's camp had used the Giants to drive up the price.

"People in the Yankees organization all talk about his character, and part of that is loyalty," Zaidi said. "It's loyalty to an organization that he's been with, the fans, teammates, and so part of what we really liked and valued about him was something that was probably going to create this draw to stay with the people he's been with over the years."

Logan Webb, a Giants pitcher who participated in the club's recruiting pitch for Judge, had a different take: "I think all of us in that meeting were butt-hurt a little bit, because we all thought we did a pretty good job."

The news broke at 5:20 a.m. Pacific time. MLB.com's Jon Paul Morosi had the scoop, calling dibs by sending the following tweet: "Sources: Aaron Judge is in agreement with the #Yankees." There were more details to come; Morosi's edge came from setting his alarm so he could wish his wife, Alexis, a happy birthday back home in Michigan.

"By waking up very early, I got the right text at the right very early hour," Morosi said. "All the credit, really and truly, goes to my wife."

Judge also had set his alarm early that morning, departing Linden for the airport before sunrise. There was still the matter of taking and passing a physical examination, but unlike the situations to follow with Carlos Correa and the Giants or Mets, that was largely a formality. Judge had been in the Yankees' system since 2013; they knew what they had.

Finally, he and Samantha could enjoy their long-awaited anniversary vacation in Hawaii.

"We sat on the beach and did nothing," Judge said. "We relaxed a little bit and just enjoyed it. It was a whirlwind of a year. Everything moved fast, and then you had the free agency process on top of that. It added another little firestorm. It was just good to get away from things for a little bit, knowing that we got the deal done."

16

◆

CAPTAIN

It was billed as a press conference, but as Aaron Judge walked through the halls of Yankee Stadium on the morning of December 14, the occasion felt more like a celebration and a coronation. This was the date that Judge would acquire his pinstripes for life, with Hal Steinbrenner making good on his promise to name Judge the sixteenth captain in franchise history.

Days prior, Derek Jeter had answered his phone at his Miami home, where he was briefed by director of media relations Jason Zillo on a budding plan within the team's hierarchy. As Jeter's wife, Hannah, looked after the couple's three children, Jeter listened intently. Steinbrenner wanted to present Judge with the captaincy at his reintroduction, and Zillo told Jeter that he should be there as a symbolic passing of the torch.

The negotiation was simple, spanning about ten minutes. Jeter said he would be happy to attend, especially if the Yankees would pick up his travel. Steinbrenner soon called the former shortstop to personally brief Jeter on specifics, offering to fly him on a private aircraft. Jeter had his jet, and he was on his way back to the Bronx.

The Judges were also bound for the Big Apple, tanned and rested from their week in Hawaii. Judge flashed fresh bling on his left wrist, sporting a stunning gold "Eye of the Tiger" Rolex that featured thirty-six diamonds around the bezel and 243 more on the dial, creating a tiger-stripe pattern. (Retail value: if you have to ask, you can't afford it.)

Shoppers and tourists hustled through streets and avenues in Manhattan, where a lavishly decorated eighty-two-foot-tall Norway spruce loomed over the Rockefeller Center ice-skating rink, but it was baseball season once again in the Bronx. The dais was set in the press conference room on Yankee Stadium's basement level, adjacent to the home clubhouse.

From right to left at the podium, cardboard nameplates were set for chief operating officer Lonn Trost, manager Aaron Boone, general manager Brian Cashman, team president Randy Levine, Judge, Samantha, and agent Page Odle. There was an empty chair between Odle and Samantha, which observers speculated could be for a surprise guest.

"Somebody whispered to me, 'I think that's Jeter. Jeter's probably here,'" Michael Kay said. "I thought it was a fait accompli if he came back, because he'd earned it. He'd been the de-facto captain anyway. The fact that they did it there, I guess it was a little bit of a surprise, but certainly no shock."

"I kept saying on the air, 'They've applied a tag for a mystery guest,'" Suzyn Waldman said.

The topic of naming Judge as the Yankees' next captain had been raised on that very stage two months prior, when Nestor Cortes used the bully pulpit of a starting pitcher ahead of an American League Championship Series game to declare that "if he's back here next year, he's our captain."

"We follow everything he does. He leads by example," Cortes said. "He's not really a guy that comes out and screams at anybody. But if he has to, that's his job. I think he's earned that right. He's a great baseball player, but he's a better human. He treats everybody the same. He follows up on everybody every day. He's the last one to leave from the clubhouse on the road, and we don't leave until he leaves. I think he's a perfect example for the game of baseball."

Cortes didn't have the power to unilaterally make that decision, nor did Anthony Rizzo, who voiced similar thoughts. "The fitting thing would be for him to do a press conference receiving not only the money he deserves, but also the captain title," Rizzo had said.

Apparently, the Steinbrenner family had been listening, because Rizzo's suggestion was exactly what would happen.

"You don't give the captainship to just anybody," Steinbrenner said. "He definitely checked all the boxes. Aaron's leadership this year was greater than ever, in the tough times and the good times. He's just incredibly well respected, and then with what he does on the field—it's going to be a good nine years."

About thirty minutes before the event began, Judge was ushered to Steinbrenner's office on the stadium's suite level to formally sign his nine-year, $360 million contract. Judge was shown to a chair behind a large mahogany desk, informed that the furniture had previously belonged to George M. Steinbrenner. This was where some of the most significant deals in franchise history had been agreed on, and Judge's deal was a Boss-sized move—at $40 million per year, he was now the game's highest-paid position player.

Cashman said Steinbrenner's actions "reminded me a lot of how his dad went about business." There was no better place for Judge to press pen to paper. "There's no doubt," Steinbrenner said of his father, "he would have done it."

As photographers jockeyed for position to capture the moment, Judge fidgeted with the pen in his right hand as he quickly scanned the sheets of legalese. The room fell into an awkward silence. Judge noticed, remarking, "Wow, it's really quiet." Seated to Judge's right, Cashman replied, "Yeah, it's like one of your at-bats," referring to Judge's chase to break Roger Maris's single-season American League home run record. That broke the tension, and in the time it took for one of Judge's 62 blasts to leave the ballpark, the paperwork was complete.

"I've already started writing a list with my wife about things I want to do in my hometown, Fresno State, here in New York," Judge said. "There's so many different people that you can help and things you can build. Youth is so important to me, so getting a chance to use that money to build some special things, we're truly blessed."

The group moved back downstairs, with the YES Network and MLB Network warming up, set to carry the press conference live. It was a busy news day in New York; across town, the Mets had agreed to terms on a twelve-year deal with infielder Carlos Correa, although—like Correa's previous agreement with the San Francisco Giants—the pact would be scuttled over medical evaluations of Correa's right ankle, eventually sending Correa back to the Minnesota Twins.

Judge had already passed his inspection with flying colors, and there was a hint of what might be to come as Willie Randolph found a seat in the front row; a rock-solid infielder on the Yankees clubs of the 1970s and '80s, Randolph had served as a co-captain alongside Ron Guidry from 1986 through 1988. Guidry and Randolph had been followed in the captaincy by Don Mattingly (1991–95) and Jeter (2003–14). Within minutes, Judge would officially join their ranks.

"A perfect choice," Randolph said. "There was no other choice to be made. Watching this kid over the years, he's become that captain. You can see the way he handles himself on and off the field, the way he goes about his business. I'm proud to be a part of him and the way he's grown. He's going to be an outstanding captain, and the players already know that."

It was an interesting morning for Jeter, who felt a bit like a guest in his own home that day, watching club officials frantically coordinate details of the Judge press conference. He attempted to recall his first time crossing paths with Judge, deciding that it had probably been in 2015, less than six months after sealing his pinstriped career with a walk-off single in his final Yankee Stadium at-bat. Judge placed their first meeting two years earlier, when Jeter had been rehabbing an ankle injury at the team's minor-league complex in Tampa, Florida.

Regardless, they both remembered Jeter's participation in the club's appropriately named "Captain's Camp," a weeklong workshop that had been the brainchild of player development head Gary Denbo, whom Jeter would eventually hire away to fill a similar role during his Miami Marlins tenure. Denbo had brought Jeter in as a surprise guest speaker, sharing dinner with a group of promising Yankees prospects, and Judge seemed to hang on Jeter's every word.

"His size was the first thing that stands out, because you don't see too many baseball players that size," Jeter said. "Everyone at that camp was kind of quiet; they didn't say too much. But you could tell he was respectful. You can tell if people are paying attention; sometimes you see people just going through the motions. You could tell that he was listening."

Jeter flashed his Madison Avenue smile and joked that he would like to "take all responsibility" for Judge's ascent to the captaincy. Jeter had been named captain on June 3, 2003, during an interleague series against the Cincinnati Reds at Great American Ball Park in Cincinnati. The Boss's marching instructions to Jeter, delivered by telephone, had been: "Don't change anything."

"I was happy I wasn't in trouble," Jeter said, recalling that Steinbrenner had been critical of Jeter's off-the-field lifestyle that spring, a delicious back-page saga that resulted in an iconic Visa commercial (they had shot only one take of Steinbrenner shaking his rear end at the back end of a conga line, at the Boss's insistence). Jeter said that he believed Judge had done "a great job" of handling himself in the spotlight, identifying the same winning-first mindset that fueled Jeter during his two decades as the club's shortstop.

"You talk to his teammates, his coaches, his manager—that tells you all you need to know," Jeter said of Judge. "Look, I'm a Yankees historian, so this is historic. People will be talking about it twenty, thirty, forty years from now. There's only a short list of Yankees captains. It's not a title that's thrown around too lightly."

They entered quickly to a cacophony of camera shutter clicks, Judge dressed in a sharp silver suit, white shirt, Yankee-blue tie, and a white pocket square. Samantha wore a gray blazer and a black turtleneck; Boone, also dressed in a black turtleneck, joked that they had coordinated their outfits. There were a few gasps and excited whispers as Jeter entered the room behind Samantha and sat next to Odle, sporting a well-manicured beard that would not have passed muster during his playing days. The connection was obvious: Jeter had no reason to be there unless Judge was about to be named captain.

Zillo spoke first, welcoming a media contingent of about one hundred reporters and the many fans watching at home. Zillo noted that after his new contract, Judge would have been part of the franchise from 2013 through 2031, prompting Judge to nod and grin. In his prepared remarks, Cashman called it a "rare occurrence" to draft, develop, and retain a player throughout his entire career, citing Mattingly, Jeter, Jorge Posada, Bernie Williams, and Mariano Rivera. He also mentioned Andy Pettitte, overlooking the three years Pettitte spent in Houston. Judge was now part of that legacy.

Boone took his turn; the manager asked how long he was permitted to speak, noting, "I can talk about Aaron for a good while." Boone's timeline drifted back eight days, when the "Arson Judge" tweet prompted queasiness and uncertainty.

"People have asked me over and over, what it was like, that day before we were able to reach an agreement," Boone said. "So I'm going to put it in layman's terms for you. It's that feeling if you lost your cell phone, your keys, your wallet, and your iPad. Gone. And then the next morning, someone knocks on the door and says, 'Were you looking for this?' That's a little bit akin to what this was like."

Flowers were presented to Samantha and Patty Judge, with Boone making the handoff to Samantha and Jeter offering to Patty. Boone ceded the microphone to Steinbrenner, who said: "It is my great pleasure, thankfully, despite a brief absence, technically speaking, to welcome Aaron not only back to the Bronx, but to welcome Aaron back to the Bronx as the 16th captain of this great organization, the New York Yankees—an honor and a position which he greatly deserves."

There was applause as Judge removed his blazer; Steinbrenner offered a handshake and a pinstriped jersey with No. 99 on the back, remarking: "This, you've worn before."

It took Judge twenty seconds to unbutton the jersey, slip it over his dress shirt and tie, then re-button it. "It still fits," Judge said, drawing smiles and laughter from those on the dais. There was no "C" on the jersey; Jeter had never worn one, nor had any of the team's other captains. As Judge later said: "We don't do that here." Pulling on a ball cap and creasing the brim as though he intended to play nine innings in the field, Judge cradled his hands on a wooden podium and leaned in for his first words as the team's captain.

"Wow," Judge said. "First off, I want to thank Mr. Steinbrenner, the Steinbrenner family and the whole Yankees organization for believing in me the past six years and all the way back to 2013. Believing in my ability, a little kid out of Fresno State, and bringing me to the Big Apple. It was a blessing and an honor, and getting a chance to continue something the Yankees are so big on, which is legacy. Getting a chance to continue my legacy here in pinstripes, in the best city in the world, the best baseball city and in front of the best fans, this is an incredible honor."

Judge paused, and now his thoughts moved to the captaincy. At the turn of the twentieth century, baseball teams had been required to name an active, uniformed player as captain, performing many duties of a modern-day manager, such as changing pitchers, positioning fielders, and arguing with umpires. Nonplaying managers at the time were limited to directing players from within the confines of the dugout; it was not until the mid-1910s that the designation of a captain became largely ceremonial.

Through 2022, 1,759 players had appeared in at least one game for the Yankees. Only fifteen had been named captain: Clark Griffith (1903–05), Norman "Kid" Elberfeld (1906–08), "Wee Willie" Keeler (1909), Hal Chase (1910–11), Frank Chance (1913), Rollie Zeider (1913), Roger Peckinpaugh (1914–21), Babe Ruth (1922), Lou Gehrig (1935–39), Thurman Munson (1976–79), Graig Nettles (1982–84), Willie Randolph (1986–88), Ron Guidry (1986–88), Don Mattingly (1991–95), and Derek Jeter (2003–14).

"I looked back at the list—that's a pretty good list right there," Judge said. "Not only of great baseball players, but great ambassadors of the game and great ambassadors of the New York Yankees, how they pride themselves on the field day in and day out, how they take pride in what they do off the field to represent this organization and represent these pinstripes."

Before leaving Yankee Stadium that day, Judge posed with a pinstriped Yankees jersey with No. 62 on the back—a callback to the photograph Maris had taken in the clubhouse on the final day of the 1961 season, when he and Sal Durante had held up a No. 61 uniform top. Judge also ventured to Monument Park, where he inspected the plaque dedicated with "belated recognition" in Maris's honor on July 21, 1984. With that, ninety-nine days remained before Judge would slip his pinstripes back on for a sprint from the first-base dugout, leading the Yankees—*his* Yan-kees—onto the field for Opening Day.

"One thing that always pops into my head is, literally, I picture us winning it at home," Judge said. "Packed stadium, Game 6, Yankees. I can just picture myself in right field. It's the last inning, the ninth inning. Out No. 1, you kind of feel the crowd stir a little bit more. All of a sudden, it's a ground ball to short, out No. 2.

"I just have that vision in my head for some reason. Just running in and storming the field, dog-piling, the city going crazy. Hopefully some fans run on the field, like in the 1970s. You hear about those things, you dream about those things. Those are the things that get me going."

62 was history. It was time to get to work.

◆

Home Run Statistics
Player Statistics
62 Scorecard

Aaron Judge's 2022 Home Runs, Nos. 1-62

Date	Pitch	MPH	Pitcher	Opponent	EV (MPH)	LA
4/13/2022	Sinker	92	Berríos, José (R)	vs. TOR	108.4	27°
4/22/2022	Four-Seam FB	91.0	Morgan, Eli (R)	vs. CLE	112.0	34°
4/22/2022	Four-Seam FB	92	Tully, Tanner (L)	vs. CLE	112.0	19°
4/26/2022	Curveball	72	Wells, Alex (L)	vs. BAL	98.5	34°
4/28/2022	Slider	84	Fry, Paul (L)	vs. BAL	113.6	23°
4/29/2022	Four-Seam FB	98	Coleman, Dylan (R)	at KC	105.4	34°
5/1/2022	Four-Seam FB	94	Lynch, Daniel (L)	at KC	113.5	27°
5/1/2022	Sinker	98.0	Staumont, Josh (R)	at KC	106.8	35°
5/3/2022	Four-Seam FB	96.0	Manoah, Alek (R)	at TOR	114.9	25°
5/10/2022	Slider	84	Romano, Jordan (R)	vs. TOR	112.5	31°
5/12/2022	Four-Seam FB	95	Burr, Ryan (R)	at CHW	114.0	25°
5/13/2022	Four-Seam FB	93	Velasquez, Vince (R)	at CHW	103.8	31°
5/17/2022	Four-Seam FB	92	Watkins, Spenser (R)	at BAL	105.5	29°
5/17/2022	Slider	79.0	Krehbiel, Joey (R)	at BAL	112.2	25°
5/22/2022	Sinker	97	Graveman, Kendall (R)	vs. CHW	111.1	28°
5/23/2022	Sinker	90	Lyles, Jordan (R)	vs. BAL	112.0	22°
5/23/2022	Slider	80	Lyles, Jordan (R)	vs. BAL	103.1	32°
5/29/2022	Four-Seam FB	91	Poche, Colin (L)	at TB	107.4	31°
6/2/2022	Slider	86	Ohtani, Shohei (R)	vs. LAA	109.9	21°
6/3/2022	Four-Seam FB	94	Rodriguez, Elvin (R)	vs. DET	104.2	34°
6/4/2022	Four-Seam FB	95	Brieske, Beau (R)	vs. DET	106.4	31°
6/7/2022	Four-Seam FB	93.0	Sands, Cole (R)	at MIN	107.7	31°
6/11/2022	Four-Seam FB	90	Swarmer, Matt (R)	vs. CHC	107.3	41°
6/11/2022	Four-Seam FB	91	Swarmer, Matt (R)	vs. CHC	115.5	18°
6/15/2022	Curveball	84.0	McClanahan, Shane (L)	vs. TB	104.1	24°
6/22/2022	Slider	86	Baz, Shane (R)	at TB	99.9	34°
6/22/2022	Curveball	75	Poche, Colin (L)	at TB	109	41°
6/26/2022	Slider	80	Martinez, Seth (R)	vs. HOU	112	20°

Dist (ft)	Count	Inning	PA Result
413	0-0	Bot 5	Aaron Judge homers (1) on a fly ball to left center field.
397	3-1	Bot 3	Aaron Judge homers (2) on a fly ball to center field. DJ LeMahieu scores.
364	3-2	Bot 5	Aaron Judge homers (3) on a line drive to right field.
392	0-1	Bot 8	Aaron Judge homers (4) on a fly ball to left field.
415	3-1	Bot 8	Aaron Judge homers (5) on a fly ball to left center field. Kyle Higashioka scores. DJ LeMahieu scores.
389	0-1	Top 7	Aaron Judge homers (6) on a fly ball to right center field. Kyle Higashioka scores. DJ LeMahieu scores.
453	1-0	Top 1	Aaron Judge homers (7) on a fly ball to center field.
395	2-0	Top 9	Aaron Judge homers (8) on a fly ball to right center field.
427	3-2	Top 6	Aaron Judge homers (9) on a fly ball to left field.
414	1-2	Bot 9	Aaron Judge homers (10) on a fly ball to left center field. Jose Trevino scores. DJ LeMahieu scores.
456	3-2	Top 7	Aaron Judge homers (11) on a fly ball to left center field.
355	0-2	Top 4	Aaron Judge homers (12) on a fly ball to right field.
410	2-2	Top 3	Aaron Judge homers (13) on a fly ball to center field.
422	1-0	Top 5	Aaron Judge homers (14) on a fly ball to center field.
431	0-2	Bot 8	Aaron Judge homers (15) on a fly ball to left field.
418	1-1	Bot 1	Aaron Judge homers (16) on a fly ball to center field.
405	2-2	Bot 5	Aaron Judge homers (17) on a fly ball to left field. Anthony Rizzo scores.
420	1-0	Top 8	Aaron Judge homers (18) on a fly ball to center field.
405	1-2	Bot 3	Aaron Judge homers (19) on a line drive to left center field.
378	2-1	Bot 3	Aaron Judge homers (20) on a fly ball to right field.
378	0-0	Bot 1	Aaron Judge homers (21) on a fly ball to right center field.
431	2-2	Top 1	Aaron Judge homers (22) on a fly ball to center field. DJ LeMahieu scores.
383	1-0	Bot 1	Aaron Judge homers (23) on a fly ball to left field.
431	1-0	Bot 5	Aaron Judge homers (24) on a line drive to left center field.
364	3-2	Bot 1	Aaron Judge homers (25) on a fly ball to right center field.
396	0-0	Top 4	Aaron Judge homers (26) on a fly ball to left field.
406	1-2	Top 7	Aaron Judge homers (27) on a fly ball to left field.
417	0-1	Bot 10	Aaron Judge homers (28) on a line drive to left center field. Aaron Hicks scores. Matt Carpenter scores.

con't

Aaron Judge's 2022 Home Runs, Nos. 1-62 (continued)

Date	Pitch	MPH	Pitcher	Opponent	EV (MPH)	LA
6/29/2022	Sinker	91	Irvin, Cole (L)	at OAK	111.3	26°
7/6/2022	Sinker	94	Bañuelos, Manny (L)	at PIT	114.7	24°
7/14/2022	Four-Seam FB	95	Hoffman, Jeff (R)	vs. CIN	112	23°
7/16/2022	Slider	86	Pivetta, Nick (R)	vs. BOS	102.6	26°
7/16/2022	Slider	86	Ort, Kaleb (R)	vs. BOS	108.5	26°
7/21/2022	Sinker	94	Bielak, Brandon (R)	at HOU	111	33°
7/22/2022	Four-Seam FB	94	Wells, Tyler (R)	at BAL	108.6	26°
7/22/2022	Changeup	87	Wells, Tyler (R)	at BAL	113.5	25°
7/24/2022	Curveball	76	Kremer, Dean (R)	at BAL	111.1	31°
7/26/2022	Four-Seam FB	97	Walker, Taijuan (R)	at NYM	112.1	29°
7/28/2022	Four-Seam FB	95	Barlow, Scott (R)	vs. KC	109.6	35°
7/29/2022	Changeup	81	Bubic, Kris (L)	vs. KC	110.2	29°
7/29/2022	Changeup	86	Kowar, Jackson (R)	vs. KC	105.1	29°
7/30/2022	Four-Seam FB	95.0	Heasley, Jonathan (R)	vs. KC	105.2	22°
8/1/2022	Cutter	87	Gonzales, Marco (L)	vs. SEA	105.5	29°
8/8/2022	Slider	89	Borucki, Ryan (L)	at SEA	107.7	23°
8/10/2022	Slider	80	Murfee, Penn (R)	at SEA	105.2	32°
8/12/2022	Four-Seam FB	93.0	Eovaldi, Nathan (R)	at BOS	113.8	31°
8/22/2022	Four-Seam FB	96	Scherzer, Max (R)	vs. NYM	109.6	26°
8/23/2022	Sinker	95	Walker, Taijuan (R)	vs. NYM	115.9	26°
8/26/2022	Slider	79	Sears, JP (L)	at OAK	109	31°
8/29/2022	Slider	81	Tepera, Ryan (R)	at LAA	111.1	34°
8/30/2022	Four-Seam FB	95	Mayers, Mike (R)	at LAA	107.5	36°

Dist (ft)	Count	Inning	PA Result
429	3-2	Bot 1	Aaron Judge homers (29) on a fly ball to left field. DJ LeMahieu scores.
419	0-1	Top 8	Aaron Judge hits a grand slam (30) to left field. Isiah Kiner-Falefa scores. Kyle Higashioka scores. DJ LeMahieu scores.
435	2-1	Bot 8	Aaron Judge homers (31) on a fly ball to center field.
401	3-2	Bot 5	Aaron Judge homers (32) on a fly ball to left center field.
444	0-0	Bot 6	Aaron Judge homers (33) on a fly ball to center field. DJ LeMahieu scores.
410	2-1	Top 9	Aaron Judge homers (34) on a fly ball to left field. Isiah Kiner-Falefa scores. DJ LeMahieu scores.
436	2-1	Top 3	Aaron Judge homers (35) on a fly ball to center field. Joey Gallo scores. DJ LeMahieu scores.
465	2-1	Top 5	Aaron Judge homers (36) on a fly ball to center field.
456	1-1	Top 3	Aaron Judge homers (37) on a fly ball to left field. DJ LeMahieu scores.
423	3-2	Top 1	Aaron Judge homers (38) on a fly ball to right center field.
431	0-0	Bot 9	Aaron Judge homers (39) on a fly ball to center field.
449	2-0	Bot 3	Aaron Judge homers (40) on a fly ball to left center field. DJ LeMahieu scores.
370	0-0	Bot 8	Aaron Judge hits a grand slam (41) to right center field. Aaron Hicks scores. Isiah Kiner-Falefa scores. DJ LeMahieu scores.
364	2-2	Bot 2	Aaron Judge homers (42) on a line drive to right center field. Jose Trevino scores.
420	0-0	Bot 2	Aaron Judge homers (43) on a fly ball to center field. DJ LeMahieu scores.
423	2-2	Top 9	Aaron Judge homers (44) on a fly ball to center field.
412	0-0	Top 7	Aaron Judge homers (45) on a fly ball to left field.
429	1-0	Top 3	Aaron Judge homers (46) on a fly ball to left center field.
383	1-1	Bot 3	Aaron Judge homers (47) on a fly ball to right field.
453	3-2	Bot 4	Aaron Judge homers (48) on a fly ball to left field.
427	0-0	Top 5	Aaron Judge homers (49) on a fly ball to center field. Oswaldo Cabrera scores. DJ LeMahieu scores.
434	1-1	Top 8	Aaron Judge homers (50) on a fly ball to center field.
378	1-2	Top 4	Aaron Judge homers (51) on a fly ball to right center field. DJ LeMahieu scores. Andrew Benintendi scores.

con't

Aaron Judge's 2022 Home Runs, Nos. 1-62 (continued)

Date	Pitch	MPH	Pitcher	Opponent	EV (MPH)	LA (
9/3/2022	Changeup	90	Adam, Jason (R)	at TB	103.5	26°
9/4/2022	Sinker	94	Armstrong, Shawn (R)	at TB	115.3	30°
9/5/2022	Slider	88	Megill, Trevor (R)	vs. MIN	109.6	34°
9/7/2022	Changeup	85	Varland, Louie (R)	vs. MIN	102.1	28°
9/13/2022	Knuckle Curve	76	Pivetta, Nick (R)	at BOS	109.7	24°
9/13/2022	Slider	87	Whitlock, Garrett (R)	at BOS	100.5	35°
9/18/2022	Sinker	92	Alexander, Jason (R)	at MIL	111.6	35°
9/18/2022	Slider	87.0	Perdomo, Luis (R)	at MIL	110.3	30°
9/20/2022	Sinker	95	Crowe, Wil (R)	vs. PIT	111.6	24°
9/28/2022	Sinker	95	Mayza, Tim (L)	at TOR	117.4	22°
10/4/2022	Slider	88	Tinoco, Jesús (R)	at TEX	100.2	35°

Dist (ft)	Count	Inning	PA Result
392	1-0	Top 9	Aaron Judge homers (52) on a fly ball to right center field.
450	1-0	Top 1	Aaron Judge homers (53) on a fly ball to left field.
404	3-1	Bot 6	Aaron Judge homers (54) on a fly ball to left field. Gleyber Torres scores.
374	2-1	Bot 4	Aaron Judge homers (55) on a fly ball to left field.
383	0-0	Top 6	Aaron Judge homers (56) on a fly ball to right center field.
389	1-1	Top 8	Aaron Judge homers (57) on a fly ball to left field.
414	2-0	Top 3	Aaron Judge homers (58) on a fly ball to right center field.
443	1-2	Top 7	Aaron Judge homers (59) on a fly ball to left center field.
430	3-1	Bot 9	Aaron Judge homers (60) on a fly ball to left center field.
394	3-2	Top 7	Aaron Judge homers (61) on a fly ball to left field. Aaron Hicks scores.
391	1-1	Top 1	Aaron Judge homers (62) on a fly ball to left field.

Player Statistics

Aaron Judge

Full name: Aaron James Judge	Bats: Right
Position: Outfielder	Throws: Right
6'7", 282 lbs.	Born: April 26, 1992, Linden, Calif.

Drafted: By the Oakland Athletics in the 31st round of the 2010 MLB June Amateur Draft from Linden HS (Linden, CA) and the New York Yankees in the 1st round (32nd) of the 2013 MLB June Amateur Draft from California State University, Fresno (Fresno, CA).

Year	Team	G	AB	R	H	TB	2B	3B	HR	RBI	BB	IBB	SO	SB	CS	AVG	OBP	SLG	OPS
2016	NYY	27	84	10	15	29	2	0	4	10	9	0	42	0	1	.179	.263	.345	.608
2017	NYY	155	542	128	154	340	24	3	52	114	127	11	208	9	4	.284	.422	.627	1.049
2018	NYY	112	413	77	115	218	22	0	27	67	76	3	152	6	3	.278	.392	.528	.920
2019	NYY	102	378	75	103	204	18	1	27	55	64	4	141	3	2	.272	.381	.540	.921
2020	NYY	28	101	23	26	56	3	0	9	22	10	0	32	0	1	.257	.336	.554	.890
2021	NYY	148	550	89	158	299	24	0	39	98	75	2	158	6	1	.287	.373	.544	.917
2022	NYY	157	570	133	177	391	28	0	62	131	111	19	175	16	3	.311	.425	.686	1.111
MLB Career	-	729	2638	535	748	1537	121	4	220	497	472	39	908	40	15	.284	.394	.583	.977

CAREER HIGHLIGHTS

Yankees Captain (16th player in history)
AL Most Valuable Player: 2022.
AL All-Star Team: 2017, 2018, 2021, 2022
AL Hank Aaron Award Winner: 2022
AL Rookie of the Year: 2017
AL Silver Slugger: 2017, 2021, 2022
AL Single-Season Home Run Record: 62 HRs in 2022
The Associated Press Male Athlete of the Year: 2022
Wilson Defensive Player of the Year in RF: 2019
Baseball America "Player of the Year": 2022
Baseball America: "Rookie of the Year": 2017
Sporting News "Player of the Year": 2022
Sporting News AL "Rookie of the Year": 2017
All-MLB First Team: 2021, 2022

62 Scorecard

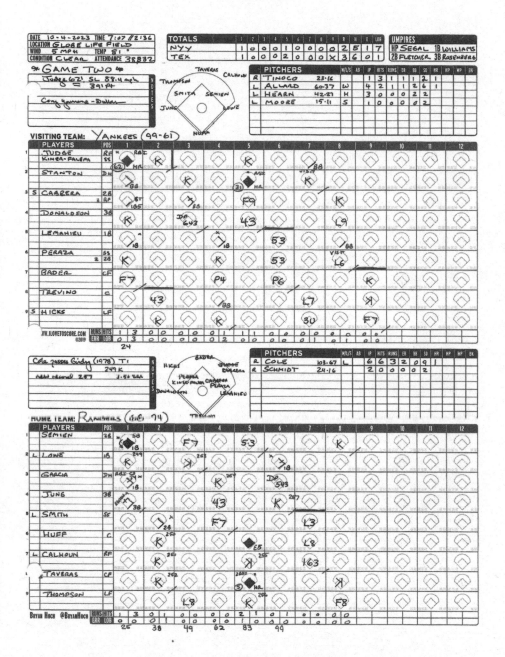

ACKNOWLEDGMENTS

---◆---

Aaron Judge couldn't help but smile.

On the day I approached Judge in front of his Yankee Stadium locker, relaying the news that I was considering writing a book about his historic 62-home-run season, his expression hardly moved. There have been other books previously written about Judge, as you'd expect for an immensely popular star who played his home games in the world's media capital.

Then I began to explain the concept—this would not be a paint-by-numbers biography, nor a day-by-day recounting of Judge's performance in an already well-chronicled campaign. It would tell the story of the entire Yankees team—his team—as they navigated the highs and lows of a memorable year in the pinstriped pressure cooker.

It would trace a straight line between three power-hitting Yankees right fielders of vastly different eras—Babe Ruth, Roger Maris, and Aaron Judge—while bringing those long-gone legends' lives and accomplishments back into modern-day focus.

And to that, Judge flashed that wide, aw-shucks grin; the one I first saw that day at the Oakland Coliseum in 2013, and that fans have come to know and love.

As part of the research for this book, I surveyed most of Judge's teammates about their favorite moment of the 2022 season, other than No. 62;

it was an easy conversation starter, and I was genuinely curious about what would stand out for them, months after the fact. Most pointed to Judge's walk-off against the Blue Jays on May 10. We had a difference of opinion there.

The snapshot that comes to mind immediately for me isn't that homer, nor No. 61 in Toronto, or even No. 62 in Texas. No, it's that September series in Milwaukee.

My lovely wife, Connie, and our wonderful daughters, Penny and Maddie, had taken the family SUV up to Boston for a two-game series against the Red Sox that week. Our schedule was clear for the weekend, and we planned to vacation in New England, a rare break before the craziness of the playoffs. Then Judge hit Nos. 56 and 57 in the series opener at Fenway Park, and my editors at MLB.com wanted me on site in Milwaukee, just in case Judge hit 60, 61, or 62.

No problem; I didn't want to miss history, either. There was the matter of our car and our kids. Connie volunteered to drive back to New York, and I could have flown out of Boston. But one of the many things I love about this woman, and the family we have created, is that we are always down for a road trip adventure. So while Judge and his teammates were spending their off night seeing Post Malone, the four of us embarked on a casual sixteen-hour road trip across six states, pulling into downtown Milwaukee somewhere around 4:00 a.m.

It was a great trip. We posed for photos with the Bronze Fonz, had the girls reenact the theme song from *Laverne & Shirley*, and sampled copious amounts of Wisconsin cheddar. The real highlights came later in the weekend; while I worked in the press box, Connie and the kids explored American Family Field. Between innings, Judge tossed Penny (age six) a baseball, and they'd all later have an incredible view as he hit homers Nos. 58 and 59.

Talk about winning fans for life. Twenty years from now, when the residuals from this book are putting Penny and Maddie through college (hey, it could happen), my girls will probably still be talking about that weekend—just as fans in 1961 still recount where they were when Maris went deep off Tracy Stallard. Baseball is incredible at linking genera-tions, allowing fans from the Maris and Mickey Mantle era to celebrate memories and debate points about the Thurman Munson, Don Mattingly, Derek Jeter, and Judge years. I hope this book helps connect some of those dots.

Every baseball season presents new challenges, and we are fortunate to be part of a deep championship roster of All-Stars. To Mom, Dad, Ray, Eileen, Joan, Alex, Allison, Brian, Danna, Ernie, Francesca, Griffin, Harold, Jaclyn, Jacob, Jerri, Julia, Joanna, Joe, Linda, Luca, Raymond, Samantha, Seth, Shawn, Steve, and the rest of the 'Schwab Mob': your fingerprints are on these pages. We are thankful for your love and support.

It was a thrill to emcee the New York Baseball Writers' dinner in January, introducing Judge as the American League's Most Valuable Player. But my MVP, as always, is Connie. This book could not have been completed without your inspiration, patience, and understanding. I love and appreciate you more than words can express. No one in this world gets me like you. Thank you for reminding me to keep things light and fun as we raced against deadlines; as Bruce Springsteen would say, "Someday we'll look back on this, and it will all seem funny."

To Penny and Maddie, each a dazzling Rookie of the Year in your own way. Penny, your sparkling personality is a rare gift, and your zest for life brings us so much joy. Maddie, you possess a warm heart, sharp wit, and infectious laugh, a winning combination that is certain to take you far. Mommy and Daddy will always be proud of you both; we only wish that you were not growing up so fast. You are our moon and stars. We love you.

Thank you to Aaron Judge, Samantha Judge, Patty Judge, and Wayne Judge, for providing one of the most compelling stories in New York sports history.

I am deeply appreciative to to Roger Maris Jr. and Aaron Boone for your contributions of a foreword and preface, respectively.

There would be no book without the numerous New York Yankees players, coaches, and front-office personnel who were interviewed, spanning many hours in person, on the telephone, and Zoom. I hope we faithfully captured your valuable perspectives of a once-in-a-lifetime season. My thanks also to Jason Zillo and the Yankees' media relations department for your assistance over the years.

Thank you to the broadcasters, reporters, and writers who cover this sport, many of whom are cited in the back of this book. You helped to paint a complete picture of the baseball world in 2022. I would like to recognize my teammates and editors at MLB.com, who are the best in the business. Gregg Klayman, Jim Banks, and Arturo Pardavila were especially supportive.

My terrific colleagues in the Yankee Stadium press box continue to drive and motivate me to perform my best possible work, every day of the year. It is an honor to be challenged by so many excellent professionals, and I value each of our friendships.

Thank you to Stacey Glick and the team at Dystel, Goderich and Bourret, and to Nicholas Ciani and Ifeoma Anyoku at Atria, for your efforts in speeding this book from concept to shelves at an impressive clip. Laura Wise and Rob Sternitzky did an amazing job in the copyediting phase, taking this work to the next level.

Most of all, thank you to the scores of fans around this sport who shared in the drama and excitement of that unforgettable chase for 62. Sure, Judge was the one hitting the homers, but the scope of that experience was greater than any individual—it truly involved all of us, and we will never forget being a part of it.

NOTES

---◆---

Introduction

2 *"Sixty! Count 'em, sixty!"*: Robert W. Creamer, *Babe: The Legend Comes to Life* (New York: Simon & Schuster, 1992), 309.

3 *"While Ruth is undoubtedly the greatest"*: "Babe Ruth Accepts Terms of Yankees," *New York Times*, January 7, 1920.

3 *"Gee, I'm glad that guy's"*: Bill Francis, "One Hundred Years Later, Sale of Ruth to Yankees Remains Pivotal Point in History," National Baseball Hall of Fame, https://baseballhall.org/discover/sale-of-ruth-to-yankees-shook-baseball-world. Accessed: March 17, 2023.

6 *"there would have to be some distinctive mark"*: Shirley Povich, "Frick's 'Asterisk' Demeaned Maris," *Washington Post*, September 7, 1991.

7 *"When I hit 61"*: Anthony Rieber, "Roger Maris' Home Run Chase a Far Cry from Aaron Judge's Experience," *Newsday*, September 17, 2022.

7 *"I had a better year than he did"*: Dave Anderson, "Baseball Finance Sets a Gall Standard," *New York Times*, February 11, 1990.

11 *"No matter what people want to say"*: Tom Verducci, "Inside Aaron Judge's Season in the Shimmer," *Sports Illustrated*, September 13, 2022.

Chapter 1: "OK, Can I Go Out and Play?"

16 *"Remember, we are a star-vehicle town"*: John Cassidy, "Yankee Imperialist," *New Yorker*, June 30, 2002.

17 *"My greatest accomplishment and achievement"*: "Patty Jacob Judge: 'Life Is Full of Surprises!'" *HERLIFE Magazine*, April 27, 2022, https://www.herlifemagazine.com/centralvalley/inspirations/patty-jacob-judge-life-is-full-of-surprises/.

17 *"We kind of joked that he looked like"*: Kevin Kernan, "'Blessed' Yankees prospect elicits Stargell, Stanton comps," *New York Post*, March 11, 2015.

18 *"Aaron has a pretty good compass"*: Ibid.

18 *"At one practice, one of the guys said"*: Randy Miller, "'Aaron Judge's Path to Yankees Captain Traces to His Roots; Here Are His Favorite Stories," *NJ Advance Media*, March 18, 2015.

18 *"That's what it's all about"*: Ibid.

19 *"Here we are in the Mother Lode League"*: Mike Klocke, "A Linden Legend," *Stockton Record*, January 13, 2019.

20 *"Both of them are teachers"*: Bob Klapisch, "Yankees' Aaron Judge Never Forgot His Roots," *Bergen (NJ) Record*, June 23, 2017.

20 *"I just put him in the system"*: Ian O'Connor, "Former Yankees Scout Tim McIntosh on Aaron Judge: 'There Was Nothing There,'" *New York Post*, September 21, 2022.

21 *"My dad has always talked about him"*: Mike Mazzeo, "Aaron Judge Has a Big Fan in Yankees Great Dave Winfield," New York *Daily News*, April 23, 2017.

21 *"I'm like, 'Who is this six-foot-seven donkey?'"*: Jake Saldate and Chad Rothford, "Jordan Ribera," *Hit or Die* podcast, episode 172, September 13, 2022.

22 *"His freshman year, I'm out there"*: Jon Schwartz, "Aaron Everlasting," *Yankees Magazine*, March 23, 2020.

22 *"felt like I was swinging a toothpick"*: Bryant-Jon Anteola, "Yankees See Judge Fit for First Round," *Fresno Bee*, June 7, 2013.

23 *"a lot of guys were going max effort"*: Mark Feinsand. "Oral History of Yankees Drafting Aaron Judge," MLB.com, October 4, 2022, https://www.mlb.com/yankees/news/featured/oral-history-of-yankees-drafting-aaron-judge-c278026828.

25 *"If you listen to Judge talk"*: Jake Saldate and Chad Rothford, "Jordan Ribera," *Hit or Die* podcast, episode 172: "Jordan Ribera," September 13, 2022.

25 *"I love that. That comes from Mom and Dad"*: Anthony McCarron, "How Aaron Judge Became a Yankee: From Small-Town California Kid to Bombers Superstar," New York *Daily News*, October 5, 2022.

26 *"not sure if I could ever live here"*: Bryant-Jon Anteola, "Yankees See Judge Fit for First Round," *Fresno Bee*, June 7, 2013.

27 *"I've always remembered that"*: Dan Martin, "Did He Call His Shot? Great Stories of an Older Derek Jeter," *New York Post*, May 13, 2017.

28 *"Even when I was in Charleston"*: Nathan Maciborski, "Might at the Museum," *Yankees Magazine*, July 12, 2022.

31 *"[Judge] was like, 'Should I keep 99?'"*: Ryan Ruocco and CC Sabathia, "Aaron Judge on the 2022 Lockout Offseason & His Baseball Future," *R2C2* podcast, February 17, 2022.

Chapter 2: Launch Quickness

35 *"Aaron struggled so bad"*: Andy McCullough, "Before He Was Aaron Judge's Agent, David Matranga Was a Literal One-Hit Wonder," *The Athletic*, April 9, 2020, https://theathletic.com/1733815/2020/04/09/be fore-he-was-aaron-judges-agent-david-matranga-was-a-literal-one-hit -wonder/.

37 *"There was a lot of negative feedback"*: Marc Carig, "'If I'm going to fail, I'd rather fail my way.' The Untold Story Behind the Rise of Aaron Judge," *The Athletic*, May 29, 2018, https://theathletic.com/369532/2018/05/29 /if-im-going-to-fail-id-rather-fail-my-way-the-untold-story-behind-the -rise-of-yankees-superstar-aaron-judge/.

39 *"Adam Judge"*: "Aaron Judge Asks Yankees Fans About Aaron Judge," *The Tonight Show Starring Jimmy Fallon*, May 15, 2017.

39 *"I had the best time in the whole world"*: "Sotomayor Joins Yankees Booth," MLB.com, August 31, 2017, https://www.mlb.com/video/sotomayor-joins -yankees-booth-c1796548483.

Chapter 3: On the Clock

45 *"The sport that we're playing"*: Ryan Ruocco and CC Sabathia, "Josh Donaldson on Learning to Play Free," *R2C2* podcast, April 13, 2022.

54 *"I knew something was eventually going to be up"*: George A. King III, "Yankee Prank Catches Roger," *New York Post*, February 27, 1999.

54 *"I wanted to hear him out"*: Ryan Ruocco and CC Sabathia. "Josh Donaldson on Learning to Play Free," *R2C2*, April 13, 2022.

54 *"Last year was the trailer"*: Shi Davidi, "Guerrero Jr. Captures Blue Jays Outlook Perfectly with Trailer for Movie Quip," Sportsnet.ca, March 17, 2022, https://www.sportsnet.ca/mlb/article/guerrero-jr-captures-blue-jays -outlook-perfectly-with-trailer-for-movie-quip/.

58 *"We kind of said, 'Hey, let's keep this between us'"*: Sean Gregory, "Athlete of the Year: Aaron Judge," *Time*, December 6, 2022.

'61 Flashback: The MVP

60 *"A customer walks up to me"*: Associated Press, "Roger Surprised, Sorry to Leave KC," *Binghamton Press and Sun-Bulletin*, December 12, 1959.

61 *"Not all that happy"*: Maury Allen, *Roger Maris: A Man for All Seasons* (New York: Donald J. Fine, 1986), 104.

61 *"Listen, kid. Yankee players don't dress like you"*: Tony Kubek and Terry Pluto, *Sixty-One: The Team, the Record, the Men* (New York: Simon & Schuster, 1989), 9.

61 *"The hell with them"*: Ibid.

62 *"Nobody will touch it"*: Associated Press, "Despite 8 More Games in '61, Ruth Record Safe, Says Maris," *Buffalo News*, January 24, 1961.

63 *"I'll never make the mistake"*: George F. Will, "The Wonders of Being 70," *Washington Post*, May 6, 2011.

63 *"I was running as hard as I could"*: Ken Plutnicki, "Mantle's Knee Injury Was Just the Start," *New York Times*, May 4, 2012.

64 *"There are a lot of things"*: Tony Kubek and Terry Pluto, *Sixty-One: The Team, the Record, the Men*. (New York: Simon & Schuster), 1989, 241.

64 *"I hope he plays 162 games"*: Miles Coverdale Jr., *The 1960s in Sports* (Lanham, MD: Rowman & Littlefield, 2020), 65.

Chapter 4: Swinging Big

67 *"When you unwrap a Reggie! bar"*: Mike Downey, "Reflections on Reggie, Number 44," *Los Angeles Times*, August 2, 1993.

68 *"He looked on Google"*: Jeff Seidel, "Crazy Story of Why a Waterford Baseball Facility Shut Down for a Pair of New York Yankees," *Detroit Free Press*, April 21, 2022.

68 *"I swear to God"*: Ibid.

69 *"They'll come"*: Dan Martin, "Aaron Judge Reveals Early Regrets about Turning Down Yankees Offer," *New York Post*, November 10, 2022.

71 *"He's made for Yankee Stadium"*: Jake Saldate and Chad Rothford, "Mike Batesole," *Hit or Die* podcast, episode 35, January 6, 2020.

71 *"Some of the things that were said"*: Paul Hoynes, "Guardians' Oscar Mercado, Myles Straw Go Toe-to-Toe with Yankee Stadium's Bleacher Creatures." Cleveland.com, April 24, 2022, https://www.cleveland.com/guard ians/2022/04/guardians-oscar-mercado-myles-straw-go-toe-to-toe-with -yankee-stadiums-bleacher-creatures.html.

72 *"People say all kinds of stuff"*: Mark W. Sanchez, "Guardians' Myles Straw Got Death Threats after Ugly Yankees Fan Incident," *New York Post*, October 10, 2022.

74 *"One thing I picked up a lot"*: *Leadership in the Clubhouse*, Aaron Judge and Anthony Rizzo, All Rise Foundation, January 24, 2023.

75 *"There were so many times"*: Ibid.

75 *"He came as advertised"*: David Haugh and Bruce Levine, "Brian Cashman Shares What He Learned from Ryan Poles, Calls Jameson Taillon 'A Gamer,'" *Inside the Clubhouse*, 670 The Score, February 4, 2023.

80 *"taking more time to see the data"*: Paul Sullivan, "Anthony Rizzo draws backlash for opting not to get the COVID-19 vaccine," *Chicago Tribune*, June 11, 2021.

Chapter 5: Best View in the House

91 *"It's probably time for me to retire"*: Erik Boland, "Rob Thomson, Kevin Long remember Aaron Judge's noisy first impression," *Newsday*, October 29, 2022.

93 *"If you don't execute"*: Tim Stebbins, "Yankees Providing Tough Early Test for White Sox," NBC Sports Chicago, May 14, 2022, https://www.nbc sports.com/chicago/white-sox/yankees-rough-white-sox-vince-velasquez -providing-tough-test.

94 *"Leaned on him a little bit"*: Scott Merkin, "Velasquez Guts It out amid Tough Stretch for Sox," MLB.com, February 8, 2023, https://www.mlb.com/news /vince-velasquez-strong-against-yankees.

97 *"Hand's not sticky anymore"*: Steven Taranto. "Ozzie Guillén Unloads on Josh Donaldson for Accusing White Sox's Lucas Giolito of Cheating," CBSSports.com, July 1, 2021, https://www.cbssports.com/mlb/news/ozzie -guillen-unloads-on-josh-donaldson-for-accusing-white-soxs-lucas-gio lito-of-cheating

97 *"I kind of feel like today's Jackie Robinson"*: Stephanie Apstein, "Tim Anderson Is Going to Play the Game His Way," *Sports Illustrated*, April 30, 2019.

99 *"Usually you have inside jokes"*: LaMond Pope, "'Utter bull(bleep)': Chicago White Sox Closer Liam Hendriks Rejects Josh Donaldson's Explanation for His 'Jackie' Comment," *Chicago Tribune*, May 22, 2022.

100 *"At one point, the cops were looking for him"*: Susan Slusser, "A's Donaldson Takes Nothing for Granted," *San Francisco Chronicle*, May 23, 2013.

102 *"Making motherfuckers"*: Andy McCullough, "Tim Anderson Silences Yankee Stadium as White Sox Sweep Doubleheader," *The Athletic*, May 22, 2022, https://theathletic.com/3328174/2022/05/22/tim-anderson-si lences-yankee-stadium-as-white-sox-sweep-doubleheader/.

109 *"I whiffed"*: Maria Guardado, "Eppler 'Stunned' by Ohtani Choosing Angels," MLB.com, December 10, 2017, https://www.mlb.com/news/angels -billy-eppler-stunned-by-ohtani-news-c263195818.

'61 Flashback: Old-Timers' Day

114 *"wasn't hitting the size of his breakfast check"*: Phil Pepe, *1961: The Inside Story of the Maris–Mantle Home Run Chase.* (Chicago: Triumph, 2011), 67.

114 *"We want you to stop worrying"*: Maury Allen, *Roger Maris: A Man for All Seasons* (New York: Donald I. Fine, 1986), 130.

114 *"No matter what you say"*: Tony Kubek and Terry Pluto, *Sixty-One: The Team, the record, the Men* (New York: Simon & Schuster, 1989), 25.

Chapter 6: "Adversity Is Coming for You"

121 *"The offseason is where I build my base"*: Matthew Jussim, "Yankees Star Aaron Judge Is Already a Home Run–Hitting Goliath. Here's How He Trains to Get Even Better," *Muscle & Fitness*, May 16, 2018, https://www.muscle andfitness.com/athletes-celebrities/interviews/yankees-star-aaron-judge -already-home-run-hitting-goliath-heres-how/.

122 *"Dad always said records are meant to be broken"*: Dan Martin, "Roger Maris Jr. Would Be 'Very Happy' If Aaron Judge Breaks Dad's Record," *New York Post*, June 9, 2022.

124 *"I've learned to navigate through lineups"*: Ted Schwerlzer, "Cole Sands Finding Success through Consistency," Twins Daily, July 1, 2022, https:// twinsdaily.com/news-rumors/minnesota-twins/cole-sands-finding-success -through-consistency-r12588/.

124 *"[I] certainly don't miss some of the things over there"*: Maddie Lee, "Cubs' Clint Frazier: Hard to Understand 'Where It Went Wrong' with Yankees," *Chicago Sun-Times*, June 9, 2022.

125 *"I'm a very picky eater"*: Gordon Wittenmyer, "Cubs' Frazier Reveals Newly Discovered Weight-Loss Secret," NBC Sports Chicago, May 29, 2022, https:// www.nbcsports.com/chicago/cubs/cubs-clint-frazier-reveals-effective -new-iowa-weight-loss-plan.

129 *"To be honest, this is like an infield glove"*: Nathan Maciborski, "Might at the Museum," *Yankees Magazine*, July 12, 2022, https://www.mlb.com/news /yankees-magazine-might-at-the-museum.

131 *"Sometimes it's that guy next to you saying"*: *Leadership in the Clubhouse*, Aaron Judge and Anthony Rizzo, *All Rise Foundation*, January 24, 2023.

141 *"You see the pictures of him"*: Peter Botte, "Aaron Judge, Yankees Get Taste of Roberto Clemente's Legacy in Pittsburgh," *New York Post*, July 5, 2022.

141 *"To get back here and see"*: Kevin Gorman, "'It Gives Me a Thrill': 1960 World Series Hero Bill Mazeroski Returns for Pirates-Yankees Opener," *Pittsburgh Post-Gazette*, July 5, 2022.

Chapter 7: Hollywood Swinging

148 *"I threw a first pitch slider"*: Chris Kirschner, "Inside Aaron Judge's Astonishing March to MLB, and Yankees, History, One Home Run at a Time," *The Athletic*, October 4, 2022. https://theathletic.com/3615387/2022/10/04 /aaron-judge-hr-chase/.

151 *"The place that made me love baseball"*: Austin Laymance, "Stanton doubles down on #ASGWorthy case." MLB.com, May 21, 2017. https://www.mlb .com/news/marlins-giancarlo-stanton-hits-3-doubles-c231522656.

152 *"Where was I going to go"*: Mark Saxon, "Mike Bolsinger Laughs Off

Giancarlo Stanton's Blast," ESPN.com, May 13, 2015. https://www.espn
.com/blog/los-angeles/dodger-report/post/_/id/14302/mike-bolsinger
-laughs-off-stantons-blast.

154 *"I know he doesn't throw hard"*: Greg Joyce, "The Moments That Launched
the Underdog Yankees Legend of Nestor Cortes," *New York Post*, May 26,
2022.

155 *"Tell me what I did in the minor leagues"*: Adam Kilgore, "Nestor Cortes
Wasn't Sure He Had a Job. Now He's the Yankees' Best Pitcher," *Washington
Post*, May 20, 2022.

157 *"I grew up in Miami"*: Ibid.

'61 Flashback: Halfway to Ruthville

162 *"Listen, I don't give Babe Ruth a thought"*: Tony Kubek and Terry Pluto,
Sixty-One: The Team, the Record, the Men (New York: Simon & Schuster,
1989), 88.

162 *"Roger the red-necked Yankee"*: Joe Trimble, "Rog the Red Thriving on Bad-
Pitch Service," New York *Daily News*, June 20, 1961.

163 *"I used to tell him this wasn't North Dakota"*: Ibid.

164 *"I liked it in Queens"*: Ibid.

165 *"The built-in characteristics of the ball haven't changed"*: Howard M. Tuckner,
"'61 Ball May (Or May Not) Account for Homers," *New York Times*, August 14, 1961.

165 *"The conclusions of this research are wholly inaccurate,"* Bradford William Davis,
"Major League Baseball Used at Least Two Types of Balls Again This Year,
and Evidence Points to a Third," *Insider*, December 6, 2022. https://www
.insider.com/mlb-used-two-balls-again-this-year-and-evidence-points-to
-a-third-2022-12.

Chapter 8: Walk-Offs and Magic Wands

168 *"They're definitely our kryptonite"*: C. J. Nitkowski and Ryan Spilborghs, "Michael King," *Loud Outs*, MLB Network Radio on SiriusXM, February 3,
2023.

169 *"We've got the best record in baseball"*: Randy Miller, "Yankees Realize They
'May Have to Slay the Dragon' after Astros Win 2 More 'Practice Tests,'"
NJ Advance Media, July 22, 2022, https://www.nj.com/yankees/2022/07
/yankees-realize-they-may-have-to-slay-the-dragon-after-astros-win-2
-more-practice-tests.html

169 *"Ultimately, we may have to slay the dragon"*: Ibid.

170 *"It's actually really impressive to see"*: Chris Kirschner, "Inside Aaron
Judge's Astonishing March to MLB, and Yankees, History, One Home

Run at a Time," *The Athletic*, October 4, 2022, https://theathletic.com /3615387/2022/10/04/aaron-judge-hr-chase/.

171 *"It doesn't help whenever you throw it down the middle to him"*: Andy Kostka, "Orioles Can't Overcome Aaron Judge's Two Homers in 7-6 Loss to Yankees to Start Second Half of Season," *Baltimore Sun*, July 22, 2022.

171 *"After the conversation, I said"*: C. J. Nitkowski and Ryan Spilborghs, "Michael King," *Loud Outs*, MLB Network Radio on SiriusXM, February 3, 2023.

Chapter 9: Heroes and Ghosts

179 *"Of course sex is natural. So is eating"*: "Frank Talk on Youth and Sex," *Life*, August 18, 1961.

180 *"Ralph, what do you think about me bunting"*: "Math Muscles in on the Race against Ruth," *Life*, August 18, 1961.

181 *"This is star money"*: Buster Olney, "Baseball's Shyest Superstar; Highest-Paid Yankee Still Walks Alone," *New York Times*, July 15, 1999.

186 *"For me, the first thing is"*: Leadership in the Clubhouse. Aaron Judge and Anthony Rizzo, *All Rise Foundation*, January 24, 2023.

189 *"I was always worried about getting booed"*: Ryan Ruocco and CC Sabathia, "Jordan Montgomery on Being Traded to Cardinals and Finding His Stride in St. Louis," *R2C2* podcast, September 8, 2022.

192 *"It's not fair"*: Josh Horton, "Yank Aaron! Judge Hammers HR into Orbit," MLB.com, July 22, 2017. https://www.mlb.com/news/aaron-judge-s -homer-nearly-leaves-safeco-field-c243599652.

195 *"If they don't like me"*: Brendan Kuty, "Yankees Fans Push It Too Far, Attack Isiah Kiner-Falefa's Father on Twitter," *NJ Advance Media*, August 15, 2022. https://www.nj.com/yankees/2022/08/yankees-fans-push-it-too-far -attack-isiah-kiner-falefas-father-on-twitter.html.

198 *"I recognize how good of a hitter he is"*: Anthony DiComo, "Scherzer's Birthday Gift: 3 K's of Judge," MLB.com, July 28, 2022. https://www.mlb.com /news/starling-marte-hits-walk-off-single-for-mets-vs-yankees.

199 *"It does get tough day after day"*: Leadership in the Clubhouse. Aaron Judge and Anthony Rizzo, *All Rise Foundation*, January 24, 2023.

201 *"I hadn't seen the slider yet"*: Matt Kawahara, "A's, JP Sears fall 3-2 to Yankees on Aaron Judge's Blast," *San Francisco Chronicle*, August 26, 2022.

201 *"On the replay, you get the side angles"*: Leadership in the Clubhouse. Aaron Judge and Anthony Rizzo, *All Rise Foundation*, January 24, 2023.

201 *"The stadium in Oakland"*: Jake Saldate and Chad Rothford, "Jordan Ribera," *Hit or Die* podcast, episode 172, September 13, 2022.

'61 Flashback: The M&M Boys

204 *"I ran into Roger in the men's room"*: Tony Kubek and Terry Pluto, *Sixty-One: The Team, the Record, the Men* (New York: Simon & Schuster, 1989), 93.

204 *"I just hope both of my guys do it"*: Ibid., 96.

205 *"as though he'd stuck a red-hot poker into me"*: Jane Leavy, "The Last Boy," *Grantland*, October 10, 2011. https://grantland.com/features/the-last-boy/.

205 *"I thought I had a chance"*: Tony Kubek and Terry Pluto, *Sixty-One: The Team, The Record, The Men* (New York: Simon & Schuster, 1989), 229.

206 *"There were so many games"*: Ibid., 29.

206 *"I'll tell you, I felt bad about what some people said"*: Ibid., 25.

207 *"That's it. I'm through"*: Ibid., 116.

207 *"Well, this is your last shot"*: Ibid., 118.

208 *"I'd like to have it"*: Roger Kahn, "Pursuit of No. 60: The Ordeal of Roger Maris," *Sports Illustrated*, October 2, 1961.

Chapter 10: The Greatest Show on Dirt

211 *"They get paid to hit, just like we get paid to pitch"*: Jeff Fletcher, "Mike Mayers Allows 3 Homers in Rough Start, Ending Angels' Winning Streak," *Orange County Register*, August 30, 2022.

211 *"He's in a groove right now"*: Ibid.

218 *"Aaron Judge hit a home run against you"*: Starter Sports Training, Twitter Post, December 29, 2022, 11:03 AM. https://twitter.com/starters_sports/status/1608493879191281670.

220 *"extra motivation when you play"*: Scott Orgera, "Correa Answers Boos with Go-Ahead HR, Twins Top Yanks 4-3," *Associated Press*, September 9, 2022.

221 *"She didn't want to believe it"*: Mel Antonen, "McGwire Details Steroid Use," *USA Today*, January 11, 2011.

221 *"The future for him as a bona fide home run hitter"*: AJ Cassavell, "McGwire Congratulates Judge," MLB.com, September 25, 2017, https://www.mlb.com/news/mark-mcgwire-congratulates-aaron-judge-c256084264.

222 *"I truly believe he'll break Barry's record, too"*: Bob Nightengale, "Mark McGwire Thinks Aaron Judge Will Best Bonds and Pujols Is a Lock for 700," *USA Today*, September 11, 2022.

225 *"Once he hit the home run"*: Chad Jennings, "'I Was in Disbelief': Yankees' Aaron Judge High-Fives Fan with Front Row Seat to History," *The Athletic*, September 14, 2022, https://theathletic.com/3592732/2022/09/13/aaron-judge-yankees-high-five-fan/.

227 *"It's freaky as shit"*: Stacy Pressman, "The haunting of MLB's A-List," *ESPN The Magazine*, May 31, 2013. https://www.espn.com/mlb/story/_/id/9315544/justin-upton-more-mlb-players-spooked-milwaukee-haunted-hotel-espn-magazine.

230 *"You have to come with your best stuff against him"*: Adam McCalvy, "Brewers on the wrong side of Judge's HR tear," MLB.com, September 18, 2022. https://www.mlb.com/news/brewers-lose-series-finale-allow-two-homers-to-aaron-judge.

230 *"This is his moment right now"*: Ibid.

Chapter 11: I've Got You, Babe

'61 Flashback: 10/1/61

240 *"It's worse than ever now"*: Tony Kubek and Terry Pluto, *Sixty-One: The Team, the Record, the Men* (New York: Simon & Schuster, 1989), 123.

241 *"easily the greatest thrill of my life"*: Ibid.

241 *"I'm beat. I need a day off"*: Ibid., 124.

241 *"You can't take a day off"*: Ibid.

241 *"tell them I went fishing"*: Ibid.

242 *"No one knows how tired I am"*: Ibid., 129.

242 *"I'm not going to lose any sleep over this"*: Ibid.

243 *"I watched the pitching motion"*: Richard Sandomir, "Sal Durante, Who Caught a Bit of Baseball History, Dies at 81," *New York Times*, December 6, 2022.

243 *"Keep it, kid"*: Don Duncan, "Take 2: Sal Durante, Who Caught Roger Maris' 61st Homer, Remembers Trip to 1962 Seattle World's Fair," *Seattle Times*, October 11, 2016.

243 *"Now, what do you think of this kid?"*: Tony Kubek and Terry Pluto, *Sixty-One: The Team, The Record, The Men* (New York: Simon & Schuster, 1989), 129.

244 *"How about if I just say"*: Richard Sandomir, "Sal Durante, Who Caught a Bit of Baseball History, Dies at 81," *New York Times*, December 6, 2022.

244 *"Would you put the date on top"*: Mike Vaccaro, "Roger Maris Dished True Feelings to *The Post* after Breaking Home Run Record," *New York Post*, September 23, 2022.

Chapter 12: 61

247 *"There's not many guys who can make that play"*: Randy Miller, "Red Sox Admit It: They're Also in Awe of Yankees' Aaron Judge, Who Just Burned Them with His Arm," *NJ Advance Media*, September 23, 2022. https://www.nj.com/yankees/2022/09/red-sox-admit-it-theyre-also-in-awe-of-yankees-aaron-judge-who-just-burned-them-with-his-arm.html.

253 *"Now I know why the skipper gets ulcers"*: Associated Press, "With Rocket Subbing as Skipper, Yankees Top O's in Funny Finale," September 28, 2003.

255 *"I wanted to challenge him"*: Chris Kirschner, "Inside Aaron Judge's astonishing march to MLB, and Yankees, history, one home run at a time," *The
Athletic*, October 4, 2022. https://theathletic.com/3615387/2022/10/04
/aaron-judge-hr-chase/.

255 *"He put together a pretty good at-bat"*: Ibid.

257 *"The disbelief comes over you"*: Jordan Horrobin, "Fans Miss 61 HR Ball,
Jays Bullpen Coach Gets It to Judge," Associated Press, September 29,
2022, https://apnews.com/article/mlb-sports-baseball-toronto-canada
-3756f913e278b238e18cbe96e4bf5085.

257 *"It's the most messages"*: Gregory Strong, "Frankie Lasagna Back in the
Kitchen at Italian Restaurant after Viral Baseball Moment," *Canadian Press*,
September 29, 2022.

258 *"We all just stood and stared"*: Dan Patrick, "Matt Buschmann and Sara Walsh
Discuss Aaron Judge's 61st Home Run," *The Dan Patrick Show*, September
29, 2022.

Chapter 13: Chase Closed!

264 *"win the batting title fighting"*: Do-Hyoung Park, "With Batting Title in
Sight, Arraez Forced to Sit with Hamstring Pain," MLB.com, February
28, 2023. https://www.mlb.com/news/luis-arraez-left-hamstring-pain-bat
ting-title.

272 *"doesn't exactly need the money"*: Bob Nightengale, Twitter post, October 4, 2022, 9:38 PM, https://twitter.com/BNightengalc/status/157
7468154694889472.

274 *"History made, more history to make"*: Joe Biden, Twitter post, October 4,
2022, 8:56 PM, https://twitter.com/POTUS/status/15774626715821342
72?s=20.

274 *"for giving baseball fans everywhere"*: Bill Clinton, Twitter post, October 4,
2022, 9:09 PM, https://twitter.com/BillClinton/status/157746590287413
6577?s=20.

274 *"I was such a Mantle fan, but I was thrilled"*: Michael Kay, "Hour 3: Billy
Crystal on Aaron Judge's Chase for 61," *The Michael Kay Show*, ESPN
Radio, September 23, 2022.

Chapter 14: Unfinished Business

285 *"I make some plays that other people can't"*: Brendan Kuty. "Why Yankees' Isiah
Kiner-Falefa Believes That His Struggles Were a 'Blessing,'" *The Athletic*,
February 24, 2023. https://theathletic.com/4245601/2023/02/24/yankees
-isiah-kiner-falefa-benching/.

287 *"I think I said from day one"*: YES Network. "Aaron Judge Discusses Why

Returning to the Yankees Means So Much," YouTube video, 3:26, December 21, 2022. https://youtu.be/scpcv19G5To.

291 *"I don't understand why you would boo"*: Erik Boland, "Astros Players Surprised That Aaron Judge Got Booed at Yankee Stadium," *Newsday*, October 28, 2022.

295 *"New York is a tough grading system"*: David Haugh and Bruce Levine, "Brian Cashman Shares What He Learned from Ryan Poles, Calls Jameson Taillon 'A Gamer,'" *Inside the Clubhouse*, 670 The Score, February 4, 2023.

Chapter 15: New York or Nowhere

299 *"Imagine having the year Ohtani had"*: Joel Sherman, "Aaron Judge Edges Shohei Ohtani for AL MVP in *Post*'s Regular Season Awards," *New York Post*, October 1, 2022.

302 *"I think, from a financial standpoint"*: Evan Webeck, "SF Giants make their case to Yankees free agent slugger Aaron Judge," *The Mercury News*, November 22, 2022.

303 *"doing my part as a loyal Red Sox fan"*: Monte Poole, "How Steph's Pitch to Lure Judge to Giants Unfolded," *NBC Sports Bay Area*, November 24, 2022, https://www.nbcsports.com/bayarea/giants/how-steph-currys-pitch-lure-aaron-judge-giants-not-yankees-unfolded.

304 "Would I bet on him?' Barry M. Bloom, "Barry Bonds: Judge Should Break Record, Sign with Giants," *Sportico*, September 23, 2022, https://www.sportico.com/leagues/baseball/2022/barry-bonds-judge-should-break-record-sign-with-giants-1234689435/.

305 *"Do you want to play tight end for us"*: Tom Dierberger, "Brady makes free-agent pitch to Judge at Buccaneers game," *NBC Sports Bay Area*. December 6, 2022. https://www.nbcsports.com/bayarea/giants/aaron-judge-receives-tom-bradys-free-agent-pitch-buccaneers-game.

306 *"was upset because there is a difference of memory"*: Sean Gregory, "Athlete of the Year: Aaron Judge," *Time*, December 6, 2022.

308 *"I heard that he was going to the Giants"*: Damon Bruce and Ray Ratto, "Jon Heyman," *Damon and Ratto*, 95.7 The Game, December 6, 2022.

312 *"I think all of us in that meeting"*: Maria Guardado, "Webb Optimistic Despite Giants' 'Weird' Offseason," MLB.com, February 5, 2023, https://www.mlb.com/news/logan-webb-talks-giants-offseason-at-2023-fanfest.

BIBLIOGRAPHY

◆

BOOKS

Allen, Maury. *Roger Maris: A Man For All Seasons*. Boston: Dutton, 1986.

Appel, Marty. *Pinstripe Empire: The New York Yankees from Before the Babe to After the Boss*. New York: Bloomsbury USA, 2012.

Castro, Tony. *Maris and Mantle: Two Yankees, Baseball Immortality and the Age of Camelot*. Chicago: Triumph, 2021.

Clavin, Tom, and Danny Peary. *Roger Maris*. New York: Touchstone, 2010.

Hoch, Bryan. *The Baby Bombers: The Inside Story of the Next Yankees Dynasty*. New York: Diversion Books, 2019.

Kubek, Tony, and Terry Pluto. *Sixty-One: The Team, the Record, the Men*. New York: Macmillan, 1987.

Leavy, Jane. *The Last Boy: Mickey Mantle and the End of America's Childhood*. New York: Harper, 2011.

Pepe, Phil. *1961*: The Inside Story of the Maris-Mantle Home Run Chase*. Chicago: Triumph, 2011.

Richardson, Bobby. *Impact Player: Leaving a Lasting Legacy on and off the Field*. Carol Stream, IL: Tyndale House, 2014.

Stout, Glenn. *The Selling of the Babe: The Deal That Changed Baseball and Created a Legend*. New York: St. Martin's Press, 2016.

PERIODICALS

Chicago Sun-Times
Detroit Free Press
Forbes
GQ
Life magazine
New York Daily News
New York Post

Newsday
New York Times
Pittsburgh Post-Gazette
San Francisco Chronicle
Sports Illustrated
Time magazine
USA Today
Wall Street Journal
Washington Post

INTERNET

The Athletic
Baseball-Reference.com
BaseballSavant.MLB.com
MLB.com
NBC Sports Bay Area
NJ Advance Media
Outkick

ABOUT THE AUTHOR

Bryan Hoch has covered New York baseball for more than two decades, working the New York Yankees clubhouse as MLB.com's beat reporter since 2007. He is the author and coauthor of several books, including *The Baby Bombers*, *Mission 27*, and *The Bronx Zoom*. He lives with his wife, Connie, and their daughters, Penny and Maddie. Find out more at Bryan-Hoch.com and follow him on Twitter and Instagram @BryanHoch.